OP 52

30 —

20 —

PHILOSOPHY FOR MODERN MAN

PHILOSOPHY

FOR

HORIZON PRESS · NEW YORK

MODERN MAN

A Popular Survey

by L. H. Grunebaum

Preface by Ernest Nagel

IN MEMORY OF LEONARD NELSON (1882–1927)
inspiring teacher, clear thinker, fighter for justice

In this age of anxiety and skepticism philosophy can play a significant role in restoring intellectual confidence, clarifying our problems and helping us to define our goals. There is, however, a dearth of good non-technical philosophic books that appeal to the general reader.

Philosophy for Modern Man offers the lay reader and the beginning student a survey of modern philosophy. Its purpose is to answer, from a naturalistic and humanist point of view, his searching questions about the nature and content of philosophy; about the nature of truth, knowledge and science; about mind, freedom of will, morality and ideals; about our knowledge of God; about the significance of existentialism; and, finally, about the meaning of life and of man.

Because this book presupposes no previous knowledge of philosophy or its history, I have tried to write it in an easily understandable way. A few technical matters do require at least a brief discussion, but I have dealt far more fully with those problems that concern every thoughtful person than with those that are largely of interest only to other philosophers. In pursuit of this objective I have tried to search out the clearest statements of the best thinkers in the vast literature of contemporary philosophy. Because there are many philosophic problems which philosophers still debate vigorously, I have pointed out several of these controversies.

The book is an outgrowth of a course titled "The Main Questions of Philosophy" which I have been teaching for some years at The New School for Social Research, New York. I am grateful to Dr. Hans Simons, the then President of The New School who invited me to give the course. Subsequent presidents and other academic officers of The New School have lent me their constant support. The questions, criticisms and reactions of the numerous students who have attended my classes have been an unfailing source of stimulation.

I am grateful to my son Henry for the role he played in the

creation of this book. It was he who first urged me to put my thoughts on paper. I hope he is satisfied with the final product.

This book would never have been started and could not have been finished without the encouragement and constructive advice of two friends, the philosophers Ernest Nagel and Sidney Morgenbesser, both of Columbia University. They gave unstintingly of their time in helping me to clarify many problems and criticizing the manuscript. It goes without saying that the views expressed here are not theirs, but those of the author. In fact they disagree with some of my ideas.

Several personal friends have read individual chapters and I am indebted to them for their favorable evaluation; I am grateful in particular to Carol Stix, whose confidence in the work gave me much needed assurance.

In the preparation of the manuscript I had the cooperation of three thoughtful and patient editors. Marion Kuhn worked closely and untiringly with me, chapter by chapter, in clarifying my language and frequently my thoughts. As she represented the educated reader, she played a creative role in asking questions, pointing out obscurities and helping in the difficult task of expressing complex ideas clearly. When the manuscript was finished, Patricia Rogow hunted down overlong passages and cooperated skillfully in the revision of several segments. And finally Horizon's Susan Waldron, who went over the manuscript with a fine-toothed comb.

L. H. GRUNEBAUM

Scarsdale, N. Y.
January 1970

William James was probably right when he remarked that all men have a philosophy, in the sense that every person has general views on the universe and strong commitments to certain inclusive values. Such convictions and attitudes explain much else a man believes and does, so that as James also declared they are perhaps the most interesting and important things about a human being. However, a man's philosophy so understood is commonly the product of blind custom and a narrowly limited experience. Most people are hardly aware that they do have a philosophy, or that their controlling conceptions of the world rest on assumptions whose validity may be dubious. It is not surprising that the philosophies men acquire in this way are frequently incoherent and are incompatible with one another as well as with the findings of ongoing factual inquiries.

But such inconsistencies can also be effective stimuli to critical thought. This has in fact happened throughout the centuries and in many societies. Men in all walks of life have made deliberate efforts to obtain a coherently integrated perspective on things, by making explicit, scrutinizing, and assessing cardinal assumptions underlying traditional beliefs. To engage in this critical activity is to *be* a philosopher, not merely to *have* a philosophy.

In any case, those who pursued this enterprise systematically have repeatedly raised certain fundamental questions whose formulation and exploration involved the introduction of numerous distinctions and the development of a technical vocabulary. Indeed, although this has not always been so, philosophy is now a professional discipline, often limited to the investigation of various highly specialized problems, sometimes with the aid of distinctive tools of intellectual analysis. To be sure, whether or not they are formal members of some established profession, philosophers continue to differ, as did their predecessors since ancient times, concerning the ultimate objectives, the proper methods, and the legitimate scope of philosophical inquiry. They are nevertheless in substantial agreement that whatever else may be included in the aims of the philosophical enterprise, it does have the task of explicating the major concepts men use in making their experience intelligible, analyzing the basis for warranted claims to knowledge, examining the grounds for validity of norms, and clarifying the conditions for responsible moral judgment.

These are comprehensive themes, each the matrix of recurrent but also specific questions. The questions thus generated are characteristically recurrent ones, for continuing advances in knowledge and the invention of new analytical tools typically cast doubt on the adequacy of previously proposed answers. Moreover, each comprehensive theme has ramifications that require the exploration of frequently subtle and technical issues. Many of these issues can be stated with suitable generality and discussed with precision only by abstracting them from the familiar contexts out of which they emerged. In consequence, much philosophical analysis is unavoidably esoteric, and often appears to deal with matters quite irrelevant to the normal concerns of men.

But this appearance of wholesale irrelevance is in the main deceptive, as Mr. Grunebaum's enlightening book demonstrates. In it he explores some of the persistent questions thoughtful men continue to ask when they try to find an integrated rationale for their lives—questions concerning the place of man in the scheme of things, the validity of knowledge, the reality of human freedom, and the authority of moral standards. These matters are discussed by Mr. Grunebaum in a manner suitable for readers who are not professional philosophers; but his discussions nonetheless embody ideas first elaborated with technical refinements in seemingly remote philosophical investigations. But however this may be, his analyses of issues are uniformly readable, and his critical evaluations of philosophical doctrines are cogently argued. Mr. Grunebaum's readers may not always agree with the answers he proposes to the issues presented, but they will undoubtedly be stimulated in any case to examine the grounds for their own convictions. His book offers a mature and reasoned perspective on man and nature, and is an engaging introduction to the perennially timely problems of philosophy. It is at the same time an invitation to participate in the philosophical enterprise.

ERNEST NAGEL

Columbia University
January 1970

CONTENTS

Foreword–*3*
Preface by Ernest Nagel–*5*
Prologue–*11*

I: What Is Philosophy? Its Role in Life–13

Man as Philosopher–*13;* Words as Tools–*14;* Several
Meanings of the Term "Philosophy"–*15;* Man's Concern
with Philosophy–*22*

II: Truth–28

Observation Statements–*29;* "Truth"–*30;* The Importance of Meaningfulness–*34;* Logic and Mathematics. The
Search for Certainty–*38*

III: Everyday Knowledge–44

The Tests of Empirical Knowledge–*44;* Dreams, Hallucinations and Irregularities–*47;* Subjective Appearances
and Objective Reality–*51;* The Doubter–*52;* The Reality
of the World. Idealism and Dualism–*54;* The Possibility
of Trustworthy Knowledge–*61;* Poetic Outlook–*62*

IV: Error and Skepticism–65

Obstacles to Knowledge–*65;* Roger Bacon's and Francis
Bacon's Lists of "Idols"–*70;* Sociology of Knowledge–
73; Mass Media and Propaganda–*74;* Divergent Religions–*77;* Cautious Approach to Truth–*79*

V: The Nature and Role of Science–82

Common Sense and Science: Basic and Applied–*82;* The
Meaning of "Science"–*85;* Causality and Induction; Ex-
planation and Prediction–*95;* Problems Presented by
Modern Physics–*102;* Scientific Discoveries and Scientific

Errors–*108;* The Aim of Pure Science–*111;* Science: Pro
and Con–*114;* Science and Religion–*115*

VI: "Man's Place in Nature"–120

The Biblical Version of Man's Nature and Its Over-
throw–*121;* The Universe–*123;* What Is Life?–*127;* Evolution–*131;* The Special Traits of *Homo Sapiens*–*135;*
Cultural Development–*138;* Man's Future–*141*

VII: Man's Mind and Freedom–147

Abilities of the Mind–*147;* On Knowing the Minds of
Others–*150;* Body and Mind–*153;* Monistic and Dualistic
Theories–*156;* The Identity Theory–*161;* The Evolution
of Mindedness–*165;* "Electronic Brains"–*166;* Man's Free-
dom to Choose–*167;* Determinism and Criminality–*172;*
Free Will in a Lawful Universe–*173*

VIII: Are There Ethical Norms?–182

Ideological Chaos–*182;* Murder: Cain and King David–
186; Changing Customs and Ethical Truth–*191;* The
Nature and Uses of Ethics–*192;* "Thou Shalt Not Kill"–
198; General Rules, Exceptions–*203;* Relativism in
Ethics–*206*

IX: Ethical Norms and Conduct–209

The Moral Point of View–*209;* Duty–*210;* Justice–*213;*
Utilitarianism–*217;* Moral Decisions–*221;* Ends and
Means–*228;* Subjective and Objective Rightness. The
Moral Person–*233;* The Wrongdoer. Punishment–*237*

X: Ideals to Live By–247

Happiness Through Pleasure, Through Peace of Mind–
247; Happiness Through Fulfillment–*254;* Flaws in the
Happiness Doctrine–*256;* Humanistic Excellence–*260;*
Love of Truth, of Good, of Beauty–*265;* Personal Harmony–*270;* The Ethics of Family Life and of Sex–*273*

XI: The Justification of Ethical Beliefs–284

Objectivity of Ethical Values–284; Can Ethical Judgments Be Proved?–288; Conscience and Religion as Basis of Ethics–291; Morality and Traditional Religion–295; Empirical Basis of Ethics–297; The Emotive Theory of Ethics–302; Rational Basis of Ethics–305; Why Be Moral?–310

XII: Religion and Truth–314

What is Religion?–315; God–321; Traditional Basis of Belief in God–322; Religious Experiences–327; "Proofs" of God's Existence–331; Faith–334; Verifiability–342; Contemporary Trends in Theology–345

XIII: Existentialism–357

What Is Existentialism?–357; Existentialism in the English-Speaking World–360; Origin of Existentialism–361; Existentialism, Naturalism and Psychology–363; Existentialist Ethics–367; Religious Existentialism–370; Difficulties of Existentialism–371

XIV: On Ultimate Questions and the Meaning of Life–376

The Meaningfulness of Nature as Such–376; Man as a Creature of Nature–382; The Meaning of Nature to Man–385; The Problem of the Meaning of Man's Life–388; The Tragic View and Other Aspects of Life–396; The Art of Living–402; The Life of Evildoers–404; Man's Attitude Toward Death–404

Recommendations–409
References–411
Index–429

Several years ago, a short time after I began teaching philosophy, I had two experiences which started me thinking about writing this book. The first was a hike I took in the White Mountains with a small group of young college students: my children and some of their friends. Several times in our conversations they touched on problems which I had been lecturing on in my philosophy classes. The relevance of philosophy to everyday life has long interested me, and I was intrigued with the number of philosophic ideas which came up in our talk during those days, even though the word "philosophy" was never mentioned.

At the beginning of the hike a young man teased the girl walking beside him by telling her that the mountains she thought so beautiful were merely empty space with trillions of particles chasing each other through the void, and that the shapes and colors she saw so vividly were merely "in her mind." Another young man carried the idea further, saying that the particles were all waves and probability functions. But the girl insisted stubbornly, "They're still mountains to me, whatever you think." This seemed to me to express very nicely in a nutshell the problem of "common sense" versus the "scientific view" of reality.

In the evening we built a campfire, and someone said that a circle of people seated around a campfire always symbolized for him the human need and search for community. Later that evening, a young girl, looking up at the brilliant sky, quietly said it made her feel that God was with us under the stars. Such a simple affirmation of religious belief, and what a complex subject for philosophers! Her remark reminded me of Kant's famous statement: "Two things fill the mind with ever new and increasing admiration and awe . . . the starry heavens above me and the moral law within me." I mention only a few of the many philosophic comments made on the hike, which impressed me with their variety.

Later that year I began to meet with friends to talk about

books, topical ideas and politics, but after several weeks one of them commented that our "bull sessions" seemed to raise more questions than they answered. Whether we were discussing foreign policy, or a book on sociology, or a novel, he said that there remained for him the basic questions which he thought we were refusing to confront. What did all the things we discussed add up to? Did the tragedies we saw around us and talked about have any meaning? Did any of the events and our critical comments about them make any sense ultimately?

"After all," he continued, "so much of what we're saying depends on ideas that are implicit but never talked about."

"Like what?" someone asked.

"Like truth, error, good, justice, freedom."

"But we aren't here to make what you call 'ultimate sense,'" another argued.

"Why not?" came the retort.

There was a good deal of talk about "why not," the general idea being that "ultimate questions" could be answered, if at all, only by philosophy or religion.

"Agreed," someone else said. "But will that get us anywhere? There's no sense in carrying on arguments that have gone unanswered for more than 2,000 years."

I raised the point that it really didn't matter that philosophers were still debating the "old questions"; after all, scientists were still working on questions raised by the oldest civilizations and were not certain about their answers. They were able to be more exact and factual now, but then so were philosophers.

The discussion then turned to the role of philosophy in this complex modern world, and someone asked me my opinion. I said I thought philosophy was very relevant and repeated some of the ideas that had been expressed on the hike in the White Mountains. "Surprisingly enough," I concluded, "I agree that topical discussions would make more sense if we answered some of the basic questions first. But I admit I'm biased."

Everyone laughingly concurred that my bias was not to be questioned. But they also agreed that a few evenings devoted to analysis of the "basic questions" might be useful. The outlines I provided for those evenings were the groundwork for this book, but its inspiration came from the discussions and from the excitement of seeing vehement anti-philosophers becoming ardent believers in the relevance of philosophy for today's world.

CHAPTER I

What Is Philosophy?
Its Role in Life

Man as Philosopher

Man has been variously described as the tool-using creature, the playing, the laughing, the talking and the symbol-making animal. *Homo sapiens,* wise man, is the rather arrogant scientific name given to our particular species of man which is about 70,000 years old. I think, however, it would be more meaningful to stress man's capacity to think instead of his potential wisdom.

We have no direct knowledge of early man's thoughts prior to the time when he began to write, about 5,500 years ago, but we can draw inferences from what we know of his activities and his art. When primitive man began making tools, over a million years ago, he must have had some sense of why he was trying to make a particular weapon or tool, and later, the development of his capacity to think is illustrated by the magnificent cave paintings, which have been found in Southern France and northern Spain, dating back 15–25,000 years. Early burial cults bear witness to man's concern about life and death, and temples were built in Mesopotamia more than 6,000 years ago. Evidently man must have given thought to invisible powers superior to himself, divinities who controlled the weather and the rivers, who could assist or interfere with his daily tasks, with his hunting and his farming.

We know more about man's thinking from about 3,500 B.C.
when he began to write. Some of the earliest written records
deal, in elaborately developed myths, with ideas about the origins
of the earth and man, and of how men ought to act. Thus philosophizing, in the broadest meaning of the word, began many
thousands of years ago. When we trace our religions, philosophy
and science back to the Jews and the Greeks, we are inclined to
forget that these people continued work done by much older
civilizations.

It was around 600 B.C. that Greek thinkers began to free
themselves from myths. They started what they and we call philosophy, a systematic, critical speculation about some of the very
questions that came up on the hike I described in the Prologue.
The first literary document in which the term "philosophy" actually appears is a fragment from the Greek philosopher Heracleites, who lived around 500 B.C., a hundred years before Plato.
Here Heracleites says: "Men who love wisdom must inquire into
a great many matters," and for the four English words, "Men
who love wisdom," the Greek text reads *philosophoi*. Indeed, it
goes without saying even today that only a well-informed person
can be a good philosopher.

The word "philosophy" is thus not a modern word based on
Greek or Latin roots, as microscope, television, telephone, automobile, and many others are. "Philosophy" has been in European
languages for 2,500 years. It consists of two roots: *philia*, love, or
philos, friend, lover, and *sophos*, wise. Both Greek roots appear
in other contemporary words: philharmonic (love of music),
philately (love of stamps), philanthropy (love of man); also
Sophie, sophomore, sophist.

Words as Tools

Words are of central importance in philosophy, because
they are the main instrument in forming and communicating
ideas; we cannot reason abstractly without them. Our arguments
would produce ambiguities and pseudo-solutions unless we employed the utmost care in their choice.

Words are a meaningful group of letters. A group of letters
may look like a word, even sound like a word, but if it holds no
meaning, it is a nonsense syllable or syllables, not a real word.
A classic example of such meaningless constructions is Lewis

Carroll's poem, "Jabberwocky": " 'Twas brillig, and the slithy toves / Did gyre, etc."

Words are a man-made tool, an instrument to convey meaning. But words are imperfect tools. For one thing, they frequently have several meanings. We speak of the neighborhood bar, a bar in front of a door, and the Bar examinations; of a wheat field, a field of concentration in a student's study program, and an electromagnetic field; of the grace of a woman or statue and the grace of God. The meanings of these words are obvious from the context in which they are used.

When we speak of love, however, it is not clear whether we mean romantic love or sexual love. What is "religion"? Is it one of the great historical organizations or is it the spiritual impulses that animate an individual? Is a liberal one who is interested in freedom of thought or in free enterprise, or both? One could go on indefinitely. These words not only have multiple meanings, but they are vague and, even in their contexts, often ambiguous. Unfortunately, this is characteristic of every one of the key terms in philosophy: truth, real and reality, nature, existence, mind, free, good, justice, liberty, happiness, God. The difficulty is compounded by a natural tendency to use words pictorially and metaphorically.

The problem of semantics (the precise meaning and definition of words) is one with which Socrates and Plato struggled valiantly, as has every serious philosopher after them, but it is the special merit of contemporary philosophy that it not only has stressed the importance of semantic tools but has sharpened them too. One cannot change the fact that the key terms in philosophy have multiple meanings, but one can exercise great care not to slip and slide from one meaning of a term into another. There is also the opposite danger of forcing words into a strait jacket, of deciding that they can or ought to have only one meaning, *the* meaning. Language is a cultural product, rich in nuance and complexity, and one cannot and should not ask for semantic precision when using the ordinary words of everyday life. But theoretical and philosophic discussions demand utmost clarity.

Several Meanings of the Term "Philosophy"

The term "philosophy" is used in several ways, some of which are closely related. As it is merely a name and rarely enters a theoretical argument, its vagueness is of little consequence. "Philosophy" still means wisdom to us as it did to the Greeks. But in this sense the word is used more as an adjective than as a noun. We praise someone's philosophic outlook or temperament; we say a certain person takes things philosophically. Such people show a largeness of spirit, a certain serenity, an inner detachment, an understanding of others and themselves. In American history, Abraham Lincoln symbolizes this wisdom. This philosophic attitude, this ripeness, can be acquired without much theoretical knowledge, without the study of academic philosophy or of science and history. Indeed, the intellectual, the very knowledgeable man or woman, may be overbearing or pedantic. He may lack this "wisdom beyond learning," a proper philosophy of life.

This peculiar paradox is contrary to the ideas of Socrates and Plato and most of the great thinkers of the past. The more man knows, they thought, the better he understands not merely the world around him, but himself, and will govern himself accordingly. Though the ancients knew the strength of man's passions—we have only to remember Achilles' anger and Medea's murderous jealousy—they thought that love of wisdom and knowledge could control emotions. Regrettably, philosophy, in the sense of knowledge, does not make us philosophic, that is, wise.

It is only in recent years, particularly since Freud, that we have become more fully aware of the limited influence that rational thinking, knowledge, and intellectual understanding have on the character and actions of man. The intellectual atmosphere today is saturated with the emphasis on the strength and influence of unconscious and conscious drives, so that it sounds old-fashioned to stress the importance of "the rational temper of intellect, character and understanding" (Brand Blanshard, *Reason and Goodness*).

Originally, philosophy embraced all of knowledge, but early in the Christian era theology became a separate discipline, at first hostile to philosophy. In the splendid centuries of the Middle Ages, however, the two disciplines worked together for the glory of God and the Church. St. Thomas Aquinas (ca. 1225–1274) represents the pinnacle of this development. In modern times the sciences, too, have been divorced from philosophy. Isaac Newton (1642–1727) called his great work on physics

Principles of Natural Philosophy. But today the word "philosophy" would not appear in the title of a book on physics, even though the book contained some fundamental philosophic analyses, as Newton's did. The biological and social sciences, psychology, psychiatry, mathematics and history are no longer a part of philosophy.

Human knowledge today is divided into a great number of specialties and the task of presenting a total view, of showing us the design of the whole, is entrusted to philosophy. Here is a second meaning generally regarded as *the* meaning of the word "philosophy." *Philosophy is world view*, a master perspective, a clear, unified vision of reality, a system of orientation; the "big picture." Most men it seems have a drive to find an integrated world view that will give them an understandable position in the universe, one that will also answer the spiritual questions, the ultimate questions, the "accursed questions" in contradistinction to the immediate problems that press upon us as we go about our daily tasks. As Reinhold Niebuhr, the distinguished contemporary theologian, says:

> The sense of the ultimate is a natural expression of the human spirit; for it is obvious that man has a unique freedom to stand outside and over even the most pressing tasks and preoccupations and to survey the total plan of life, to inquire after its total meaning, if any.

Metaphysics is that part of philosophy which is concerned with ultimate reality, with the most general causes and principles of things.

But what about the sciences? Can they not answer all our questions and give us a unified world view? If not now, may we not expect that they will in the further course of their development? Science, the metaphysician will answer, is piecemeal, blind to values. Science does not even tackle the problem of the meaning of existence, of our own destiny. "Ultimate questions," to use Niebuhr's expression again, are not within the domain of science. It is metaphysics that deals with what comes after physics, with that which goes beyond physics; it is metaphysics that tries to "comprehend the universe as a whole," as the English philosopher F. H. Bradley puts it.

It has been said that unless we understand why the world is as it is and what our relationship is to the world and to each other, we will become lost in "chaotic creedlessness." And in-

deed we have been scolded time and again for our lack of ultimate faith. Everyone today is puzzled, and perhaps it is true that
we have lost the way, as Gertrude Stein remarked, and that
therefore we ought to study philosophy.

There has always been a deep split in the ranks of the philosophers regarding the feasibility of the metaphysical enterprise
and the possibility of answering the ultimate questions. Plato was
opposed by the Sophists, who doubted the possibility of knowledge of ultimate reality. The power of the early Christian
Church drove metaphysical skepticism underground, but it made
a dynamic reappearance in the eighteenth century and has remained vigorous ever since. In fact, the dominant philosophic
schools in the Anglo-American world today have pushed aside
the task of answering the "accursed questions" and have concentrated too exclusively on other problems that hold little interest
for non-philosophers.

There is a good reason why modern philosophers do not
deal with the traditional problems of so-called metaphysics.
They are convinced that the knowledge to which the great
system-builders of the past lay claim is illusory, "a bewitchment
of our intelligence by means of language" (Wittgenstein).* A
new spirit of intellectual sobriety has entered philosophy, which
restrains it from asking "improper questions," from "adventur-
ing beyond space and time." As C. I. Lewis, the American philosopher, has well put it, it is impossible "by sheer force of rational
reflection [and irrational vision, I add] to transcend experience
altogether." He says further: "Philosophic truth, like knowledge
in general, is about experience, and not about something
strangely beyond the ken of man, open only to the seer and the
prophet." The age of vast systems and of complicated fustian
speculations has ended for philosophy; instead, we find exactness,
realism, and common sense.

What, then, remains of philosophy if the search after the
"ultimate" is discarded? The philosopher's function is to analyze
such fundamental concepts as real, matter, mind, self, truth and
good. In addition it is his job to uncover the presuppositions of
common experience, of science and of moral conduct. The philosopher also tries to interpret the historical process, the story of

* Ludwig Wittgenstein (1889-1951) was one of the most influential philosophers of the twentieth century. He taught at Cambridge for several years.

man's doings through the ages. Is it progress or retrogression? Can we learn anything from it? And, finally, of the religions and the ideologies of the past and of the present and of the answers to the ultimate questions he asks: What do they mean? Is there any sense to them or not?

There are enough questions left for an Age of Analysis. For the naturalistic philosopher philosophy is, to use the words of Ernest Nagel, "at its best a *critical* commentary upon existence and upon our claims to have knowledge of it; and its mission is to help illuminate what is obscure in experience and its objects rather than to profess creeds." (My italics)[1]* For the modern professional philosopher a comprehensive world view goes beyond philosophy in the technical sense of the word, and to achieve it one must also use science, history and imagination.

Philosophy has been an academic subject since before Plato. *Akademia* was the name of the institution where Plato taught philosophy. It was Plato, his teacher Socrates and Aristotle who laid the foundations of Western philosophy and it was they who have exerted the most profound influence on the course of philosophy for over two thousand years. Socrates (470–399 B.C.), one of the most interesting characters in man's spiritual pilgrimage, left nothing in writing. We know about him through Plato (427–347 B.C.), through other pupils and through a comedy of Aristophanes. Plato's *Crito*—for all its brevity one of the masterpieces of world literature—his *Apology* and the first and last few pages of his *Phaedo* deal eloquently with Socrates' death. It was after the shock of that death that Plato began his important philosophic activity, and he wrote masterpieces in all fields of philosophy. Besides those already mentioned, the best known is *The Republic*, on the nature of justice.† In this work he recommends that states ought to be ruled by philosophers. Through the Neo-Platonic School (ca. 250–550 A.D.) Plato's metaphysical and mystical tendencies exerted a great influence on early Christian theology. Aristotle (384–322 B.C.), in turn, was a pupil of Plato

* Numbers refer to references at the end of the book.
† By one of the miracles of history, we have the text of every book Plato wrote, that is, every book mentioned by his disciples and by later philosophers. Even a few of his letters have come down to our day. However, the manuscripts through which we know Plato's works are codices written around 900 A.D., 1250 years after his death; of the Greek period itself we have only a few pages of papyri fragments.

and became the tutor of Alexander the Great. He, too, was interested in all phases of philosophy but on a more commonsense and
realistic basis. He was a student of government and the sciences
of his day. Despite advances that were being made in logic, his
treatise remained the basic one until the middle of the nineteenth
century. His influence is most noticeable on Catholic, Thomistic
philosophy.

Plato's *akademia* lasted for almost a thousand years, from
400 B.C. until the Byzantine emperor Justinian, as a measure in
Christianity's fight against heresy and paganism, closed it in 529
A.D. Then, gradually, the Dark Ages descended on Europe and
its institutions of learning. But when town life revived in the
twelfth and thirteenth centuries, universities were established all
over Europe, and philosophy became one of their disciplines.
Since then philosophy has always appeared in the curricula of
institutions of higher learning, and some men have called
themselves "philosophers." Practically speaking one may say:
Philosophy is what philosophers do. Philosophers treat logic, the
theory of knowledge, of truth and of science, ethics, metaphysics, esthetics; and, furthermore, philosophers deal with philosophy of religion, of history, of law.

A great many philosophers specialize in the history of philosophy. As philosophy obviously has not progressed, or perhaps
cannot progress, to a state as certain and definite as the exact
sciences, the history of philosophy and the presentation of the
various philosophic systems becomes more interesting and more
important. In fact, the study of the history of philosophy is often
substituted for the development of a system of philosophy, particularly at a time when there is doubt about the possibility of a
unified philosophic view.

This concentration on past philosophies is a unique phenomenon. If one studies physics or medicine he expects to be taught
contemporary physics or medicine. The same holds true in the
social sciences. The study of the history of science is a special
occupation. Science is a self-critical and cumulative undertaking,
but art, music and literature are not cumulative. One is not limited to the contemporary in these endeavors, nor does modern
art supersede the old masters, the art of earlier centuries or other
cultures.

The history of philosophy is a journey to the old masters of
philosophy, which many find fascinating. Philosophy, however,

is not an imaginative artistic creation of the mind; it attempts to contribute to knowledge and to find truth. Belief in the possibility of philosophic truth is not a naive hope of an uninformed general public; it is a belief shared by all great philosophers from Plato to our contemporaries, all of whom have regarded philosophy as a serious, self-critical enterprise. Consequently, we must go beyond the great visions of the past and work out a modern philosophy, even if in so doing, we find important elements of Plato's or Spinoza's or Kant's philosophy to be erroneous. The philosophic specialist studies the philosophies of the past critically. The layman, who wants to find a single modern philosophy, is too often presented instead with a series of odd and antiquated theories. Little wonder, then, that today's intellectual community has fallen into skepticism. This, however, is a peculiarity of the contemporary scene and is not true of other centuries.

But there is one important difference between the self-critical nature of science and that of philosophy. In science the errors of the past have no place; a practical consensus on new discoveries and theories is eventually achieved. No such unanimity ever exists in philosophy. There are fundamental splits that have never been bridged: for example, between modern realistic naturalism, Thomistic (Catholic) philosophy and existentialist philosophy. Theories regarded as false by most philosophers find continuous support in some minority schools. One may almost say that philosophic errors never die.

There is, finally, a bastard use of the word "philosophy." At a trade convention a speaker may orate on "the philosophy of retailing." I have read of "a general philosophy of economic aid," or of "a school board's philosophy not in accord with community demands." Frequently in these expressions "philosophy" merely means "generalizations," "theories," or "principles."

Two remarks on what philosophy is *not* are pertinent. Philosophy is not psychology. Both deal with man's mind, but with different aspects of it. Psychology is a natural science that examines the operations of the mind: thinking, sensing, feeling, learning, acting, dreaming, adjusting and so forth. Philosophy deals with the meaning and the truth or lack of truth of thoughts on abstract subjects. Of course, there are areas where philosophy and psychology touch each other closely.

Philosophy is also not a superscience. Philosophy does not

give us a simple world formula. It does not integrate everything into everything. Rather, it presents us with a certain order and deepens our understanding of what the sciences mean to us. *Philosophy presupposes the sciences.* Without science no true world view is possible, and when science changes the picture of the world, philosophy itself has to change. A philosophy based on a view of nature that holds man to be the center of nature and a special creation thereof or of God will be quite different from a philosophy that accepts the fact that man is only an infinitesimal speck in a tremendous universe.

Man's Concern with Philosophy

Who really is or ought to be concerned with philosophy? Everybody, I think; not merely those who study philosophy, but those also who may not care or who even laugh at the notion. The latter are in good company. Even Plato has one of his debaters make fun of the study of philosophy. In *Gorgias* he has the sarcastic Callicles say: "Any adult who still philosophizes ought to get a good beating. Philosophy is only something for young lads." Immanuel Kant (1724–1804), a German philosopher, who, as Richard Brandt says, "had perhaps the most powerful original mind in modern philosophy," might have been rebuking him in a stately manner when he wrote: "It is in vain to assume an artificial indifference in respect to inquiries the object of which cannot be indifferent to human nature."

One can be indifferent to such questions as, What does meaning mean? Does absolute space exist? But no one can be indifferent to some of the questions that were raised on the White Mountains hike. The butcher, the baker and the candle-stick maker do not go through life without thinking about what they are doing and what they ought to do. Everyone is concerned with the problems of education and the rearing of his children; with the ethics of his occupation, whatever it may be and with the morality of filling out an income tax form. No one can be oblivious to the race problem. Many political questions are basically philosophic. And then there are the religious and metaphysical problems. These may not occupy one a great deal of the time, but who has not asked, as Kant did, "What may I hope?" This search is a continuous process that begins at some point in the life of a young child and ends only with death.

Socrates, the first philosopher about whom we know a good deal and who is the main speaker in Plato's Dialogues, used to go around the market place, accosting friends and even total strangers and asking: What does justice consist in, and what is a good life? Socrates was convinced that everyone has some thoughts about philosophic problems, though not everyone is a specialist in philosophy. We are not our own lawyers, physicians, architects, but we are our own philosophers, and it makes no difference that our philosophy may be unsystematic, fragmentary, often contradictory, that one of our theories may disagree with another, that we may not be clear about the total body of our opinions and beliefs.

The conviction that everyone, to a greater or lesser degree, has a philosophic faculty is one of the foundation stones of our democratic system, for that system is viable only if men, as Jefferson wrote, are "habituated to think for themselves, and to follow reason as their guide." Opposed to this is the aristocratic view that some people are made to govern, and the masses are made to be governed. Plato was of this opinion; in his ideal state especially trained philosophers were to be the kings. This and other aristocratic ideas and concepts, such as the divine right of kings, the hierarchy of the Church, the dictatorship of a party or of a leader, have played a role throughout history.

However, one must also recognize the existence of abnormal and criminal people in our society. There are those who live only to satisfy their hunger and thirst and sexual desires by whatever means, who have no moral values, who hold no love, who feel no remorse, no regard for others; who admire only that which gratifies their cravings. There are also the amoral and nihilistic, some of them criminals, possibly psychopaths, but they are warped people.

People generally have some philosophic viewpoint, composed of a mishmash of ideas acquired in adolescence or early adult life. But they do not give much thought to it, unless something philosophically disturbing happens in their lives which makes them uncertain about their prejudices. Furthermore, I believe it can be truthfully said that Americans are not a particularly philosophically inclined people. We are a practical, active, tool-making people. For us philosophy is essentially a university enterprise, which is not good for philosophy, nor for public life. Philosophy's place is taken by science, psychiatry, sociology and great schemes of history; by literature, criticism and religion.

Nor is this age in which we live conducive to philosophizing. There is no time for it. We are too busy handling complicated machines and gadgets, reading enormous newspapers and
numberless periodicals, attending committee meetings and
watching entertainment. The starry sky that might fill us with
admiration and awe has disappeared from our cities and suburbs.
Even farming, which once fostered contemplation, is now an industrialized enterprise. It is good that we can still hike in the
White Mountains and see nature's greatness and think philosophic thoughts.

There are two reasons to study philosophy. It is pleasurable
and it is also useful; we who are all by nature philosophers will
become better philosophers. Fortunately, the educated man derives deep satisfaction and enjoyment from acquiring knowledge. "Life has meaning, to find its meaning is my meat and
drink" (Robert Browning). "The unexamined life is not worth
living for a human being," said Socrates, and Plato wrote of philosophy, "no greater good ever was given or will be given by the
gods to mortal man." Equally beautiful, though extravagant and
unrealistic praise was expressed by Aristotle in these remarks:

> Now the activity of philosophical reflection or wisdom is ad-
> mittedly the most pleasant of excellent activities; at all events
> it is held that philosophy or the pursuit of wisdom provides
> pleasures of marvelous purity and permanence. . . . If accord-
> ingly the attributes of this activity are found to be self-
> sufficiency, leisureliness, such freedom from fatigue as is pos-
> sible for man, and all the other attributes of blessedness, it fol-
> lows that it is activity of reason that constitutes complete
> human happiness—provided it be allowed a complete span of
> life. If reason is something divine in comparison with the rest
> of human nature, so also is the love of reason in comparison
> with human life as a whole. . . . We ought so far as possible to
> achieve immortality, and do all that man may do to live in ac-
> cord with the best that is in him, for though this is insignificant
> in size, in power and worth it far surpasses all the rest.[2]

Less exalted but more practical was the attitude taken by
the seventeenth century English philosopher John Locke, who
admonished us with homespun words "to be employed as an
under-laborer in clearing the ground a little, and removing some
of the rubbish that lies in our way of knowledge." Self-

knowledge, knowledge of principles, of philosophy, all take one
closer to inner freedom. Philosophy is for those who resent in-
doctrination, who do not surrender to fashionable ideologies or
accept without question the often facile rhetoric of politicians.
People who wish to be autonomous and free, who wish to lead
their lives according to their own thinking and planning, are
those who feel the need to acquire a philosophic view. John
Dewey was quite correct when he said: "Theory is, in the end,
the most practical of all things," but personal usefulness of philosophy was perhaps summed up best by Spinoza (1637–1677):

> The more the mind knows, the better it understands its forces
> and the order of nature; the more it understands its forces or
> strength, the better it will be able to direct itself and lay down
> rules for itself; and the more it understands the order of nature,
> the more easily it will be able to liberate itself from useless
> things.

Spinoza was perhaps the most thorough believer in the power of
human reason. He concludes the above statement with the claim:
"This is the *whole* method." Obviously, this goes too far. Philosophy is a rational, intellectual enterprise, and it pre-supposes a
healthy and reasonable mature mind. Philosophic analysis cannot
take the place of psychoanalysis, although the techniques of psychotherapy too are designed to give man greater self-knowledge.
Freud himself was a firm believer in rationality:

> The voice of the intellect is a soft one, but it does not rest until
> it has gained a hearing. Ultimately, after endlessly repeated re-
> buffs, it succeeds. This is one of the few points on which one
> may be optimistic about the future of mankind, but in itself
> it signifies not a little. (*The Future of an Illusion*)

A mere accumulation of knowledge is not sufficient, however. Every real collector, whether of stamps, books, records, or
pictures, has a certain system and order in his collection. It
should be no different with the acquisition of knowledge. The
mere knowing of innumerable facts, the reading of great numbers of books, furnish us only with the materials of real knowledge. We must understand what we know; we must impose
order on our intellectual collection. Spinoza, of course, took this
for granted; but it is important in this age of specialization to
stress the fact that scholarship alone is not true intelligence. As
Milton wrote:

> Who reads / Incessantly, and in his reading bring not / A
> spirit and judgment equal or superior / Unsettled and uncertain
> still remains, / Deep versed in books but shallow in himself.

And T. S. Eliot asked, "Where is the wisdom we have lost in
knowledge? / Where is the knowledge we have lost in information?"

I have mentioned the influence, during the formative years of
Christianity, of the doctrines of Plato and Aristotle, but I have
not commented on the important role of philosophy in politics
and government. No nation owes as much to philosophy as the
United States. Our Founding Fathers had absorbed the ideas of
the English and French philosophers of the seventeenth and
eighteenth centuries, the Age of Enlightenment, and especially
of John Locke. His liberal ideas, and those of Montesquieu regarding the separation of governmental powers, were embodied
in the Declaration of Independence, the Constitution and the Bill
of Rights, and have become part and parcel of our social and
political life. Rousseau was one of the spiritual fathers not only
of the American Revolution but of the French Revolution as
well. We are not merely the oldest great democracy; with all our
faults we are as egalitarian as any and more so than most. For this
all of us owe a debt to philosophy.

Both Communism and Fascism can be traced to the German
philosopher Hegel. As Eric Hoffer well says in *The True Believer*,[3] an excellent analysis of the fanatic: "A movement is pio-
neered by men of words, materialized by fanatics and consoli-
dated by men of action." Karl Marx, sitting quietly in the British
Museum, laid the groundwork for all Socialist and Communist
parties in the world and Nietzsche's glorification of the superman influenced the Fascists and Nazis.

W. Macneile Dixon says, in *The Human Situation*: "If
anyone pictures ideas as shadowy, innocent, harmless things . . .
let him look around. It is thought which has turned the world
upside down, shy, retiring, invisible, unobtrusive thought." It
follows that good philosophy is not merely the private affair of
each individual but a matter of great public importance, although Marxists would not agree with this emphasis on the
power of ideas. If we consider the influence of Marx and of
Lenin, we must agree with Herbert J. Muller when he writes:
"Marxism, for all its theoretical determinism, is the clearest

illustration of how history is made by man's beliefs about what
has happened, what is happening, and what should happen." [4]
One would not have to search far for other illustrations of the
relevance of philosophy.

Philosophy's role in life is suggested in the broadest terms
by four Kantian questions: "What can I know? What shall I do?
What may I hope? What is man?" Kant's questions are guide-
lines for what I have to say about the vast landscape of philosophy—philosophy understood as world view—which I hope to
clarify and illuminate. The only philosophic subject I will not
touch upon is the problem of beauty, but for the other major
philosophic questions, as one can see from the table of contents, I
want to provide a context, a point of view. One cannot teach
philosophy without teaching a philosophy. I have been guided
by the belief that if one encounters a clear and strong philosophic opinion, it is easier to hammer out one's own views by
accepting or rejecting what one has read or heard. Each of the
problems dealt with deserves, of course, far more intensive treatment than is possible in one volume.

In conclusion, I want to indicate my own philosophic position. I can describe it as critical humanistic naturalism. It is the
philosophy held by most philosophers in the English-speaking
countries, though with considerable variations. But classifying
terms ending in ism have numerous meanings and are therefore
not too helpful. The meaning of the terms "humanistic" and
"naturalism" will become clear in the course of my exposition. In
regard to the word "critical," I refer again to the description of
philosophy by Ernest Nagel, according to which philosophy is a
"critical commentary upon existence and upon our claims to
have knowledge of it." I also use "critical" because it has come to
be regarded as a description of Kantian philosophy as set forth in
his three main works: Critique of Pure Reason, Critique of Practical Reason, and Critique of Judgment. Because of my esteem
for Kant and because some of my philosophic ideas have been
influenced by him, I like to use the term "critical humanism."

CHAPTER II

Truth

"Truth is truth to the end of reckoning."
—SHAKESPEARE

"Nothing can be tested, nothing verified.
Truth—what do they mean by it?"
—BARBUSSE

These two quotations express two opposing attitudes towards the nature of truth. Shakespeare's provocative assertion is jarring. Is it possible for anything to be true to the end of reckoning, for eternity? Is not truth something personal, something that changes with time, nationality, religion, culture? The French novelist, Henri Barbusse wrote the remark quoted fifty years ago in his book, *L'Enfer* (Hell); I saw it again in a more recent book, Colin Wilson's *The Outsider*, in both instances it reflects the skepticism of European and American intellectuals after the first and second World Wars. Both quotations point to the question, what is the basis for our belief that we can know the truth? Despite Barbusse's declaration of total skepticism, the conviction that truthful statements can be made is taken for granted in our daily lives and in civil and business conduct. The possibility of making truthful statements is equally important in philosophy and science.

Observation Statements

In order to gain clarity about the nature of truth I suggest that the reader imagine himself engaged in a philosophic discussion with a group of friends during which one of them makes the observation: "There are people here now." Under the given circumstances no one can sensibly doubt this factual statement which will be understood by every reader. It is sometimes suggested that in philosophy all terms ought to be defined, but that is impossible. The meaning of words can be explained only in two ways. Certain words, those referring to sensual impressions, words, like red, soft, hot and bitter can only be explained by exhibiting or pointing to the object to which the word refers. We might do this also with the word "people," which can be explained through sign language. The usual way of explaining words, is, of course, as the dictionary does, defining one word through other words already known. Most words can be defined only in this way. It is correct, in a philosophic discussion, to demand full explanations for everything that is unclear, ambiguous, or unknown to hearer or reader. But this is not the case with the sentence, "There are people here now."

This sentence is true. Before comparing this trivial statement with the two quotations, I want to mention four problems pertaining to it which I shall discuss in later chapters.

1. How does one learn the truth of such a sentence? What is the basis of truth for a factual statement like the one under discussion?

2. How did the discussants know that there were people there? Perhaps this was a dream or a vision. Obviously, there are distinctions. How do we make them? But, if this whole business were a dream or vision, it would be a vision or a dream of "people here now."

3. How do we deal with someone who doubted the statement and claimed, "There is no one here"?

4. What is the real or ultimate reality of objects? (This question may seem mystifying. I shall discuss it briefly in a later chapter.)

Is the assertion, "There are people here now" true only for those who were in the room? Of course not. It is true for everybody that there were people in the room during the discussion. If

one had invited the President of Liberia or the Secretary of the
Russian Communist Party, he would have to agree with our observation. The observation is also true for all succeeding generations. If Plato and Aristotle were visiting from their philosophic
heaven and heard a translation of our sentence, they also would
agree with it. In other words, this statement is true not just for
those present but for all people and all ages; it is true "to the end
of reckoning," and Barbusse's skepticism, at least here, is unjustified. We know also that the assertion can be tested. Each participant could see the people in the room and could hear them.

My claim that there is something like objective truth per-
tains, up to now, to one simple observational statement. However, if one agrees that this type of statement can be true, then
one must also accept a great many other similar observations,
such as, "There is a yellow sweater here; there is a red tie there;
windows, chairs and walls here." One can even generalize and
say, "Everyone has a head," and so forth. Or one can say,
"Everyone has a heart and a brain." Under ordinary
circumstances one cannot see a heart or a brain, but their reality,
if necessary, could be made obvious. There are, of course, countless numbers of other true statements which we can make about
observed reality: houses, gardens, cities, clouds.

It must be apparent to the reader that I was calling on his
common sense to tell him that those simple, unphilosophical,
observational statements were obviously true. And what is true
for common sense must also be true for the philosopher.

A skeptical intellectual might protest that he is being
trapped into accepting the existence of eternal truth, though his
world view does not permit such truth. But to assert that "truth
is eternal," does not assert anything about eternal objects. My
statements were about physical objects.

"Truth"

Up to now I have not discussed what we mean by the word
"truth." "What is truth?" The question appears in the Gospel of
St. John, a rather philosophic book, written around 120 A.D., experts believe. Jesus is before Pilate, then Roman governor of Palestine, who asks:

> "Art Thou a king then?" Jesus answered, "Thou sayest that
> I am a king. To this end was I born, and for this cause came I

into the world, that I should bear witness unto the truth. Everyone that is of the truth heareth my voice."

Pilate saith unto him, "*What is truth?*" And when he said this, he went out again unto the Jews, and saith unto them, "I find in him no fault at all." (John 18:37–38)

Is it true that Jesus was kind of the Jews? Protestants and Catholics would accept this, but Jews would deny it vehemently. Hindus, pagan tribes or modern agnostics might comment that the whole Christ story doesn't make sense to them. Some might even call it a fairy tale. Communists might say that the Bible was propaganda and religion an opiate given by exploiters to the oppressed. Clearly, there would be quite an argument. And this would be the case with the holy books of all religions. It might also be true of a great many—who knows, perhaps all—moral questions. In the fields of religion and ethics, then, a case could perhaps be made for Barbusse. A general state of uncertainty seems to prevail there. But should the position of skepticism embrace *all knowledge:* Nothing can be verified; truth is meaningless?

Before finally coming to the question—What do we mean by truth?—I want to ask first of what objects, entities in the world, can it be said that they are true, false, or erroneous. We apply these adjectives to statements, to declarative sentences, to propositions and to beliefs. It is a technical and debatable question, whether we attribute truth to the words themselves—the signs we hear or see in print—or to the meaning of these signs. The latter seems more natural.

People often think that *facts* are true. Actually, it is not the facts that are true but what we say or write about them. The tree in my garden is tall and full of fruit, but it is not true or false. If I state, "It is an apple tree," that is true if it really is an apple tree, but it is untrue if it happens to be a pear tree. The facts, the given, are not what we can call true. The adjectives "true" and "false" can properly be applied only to what we say about the objects, the facts, the events. True judgments are not the same things as existing facts, or states-of-affairs, an expression much used by philosophers. Judgments, of course, are related to and pertain to the facts in that they describe them either truthfully or not. The question is often not an easy one to resolve.

What are the characteristics of a true proposition? Here are some simple definitions: "The truth of a proposition consists in

its stating what is the case." (Ernest Nagel) "A proposition is
true when the state-of-affairs expressed by the sentence asserting
it is actual, and false when it is not actual." (John Hospers)[1] Let
me end with an intriguing definition by Aristotle, which still
holds good, though it takes a moment to digest:

> To say of what is that it is not, or of what is not that it is, is
> false, while to say of what is that it is, or of what is not that it
> is not, is true.

These definitions make quite clear that truth is a quality of a
statement quite independent of all personal elements. Factual
statements and ethical rules either are true or they are not true;
they cannot be true for me and untrue for you. Perhaps I don't
know that a statement is false and you do. But then that is my
mistake and does not affect the statement. I may believe a statement to be true which is not true. This often happens to all of us.
However, the beliefs we hold are one thing; the truth of these
beliefs is something else, which depends entirely on whether the
statements assert or do not assert what is the case.

It is important to emphasize that the frequently used locution, that something "is *true for* me," is unclear and dangerous.
We must distinguish between the intent to express a personal
opinion about A and the intent to state the truth about A. When
I say, "The maxims of traditional ethics are true for me," I may
be making a correct personal observation about my opinions. I
might even make the further observation that the maxims of ascetic ethics are true for my friend. As long as these expressions
are meant as descriptions of personal ideals, they can pass; they
acknowledge the obvious fact that people have different opinions. There is no contradiction in my believing X and you non-
X. However, my meaning would be much clearer if I said, "I
believe in traditional morality; I hold it to be true." But frequently people have something quite different in mind when
they say that a thing "is true for me." They mean by their statement that different maxims if held by different people can be
equally true for the various people who hold them; but this is
contrary to the meaning of the term "true." "True for" is an
incongruous and ambiguous expression. The misunderstanding
can be avoided if we use the locution: something is true according to my opinion.

Consider now the following statement: The earth is flat. Although it was believed to be true by most of the ancient Greeks,

while we hold it to be false, it would be a mistake to say that it was true for the Greeks but is false for us. The statement was *always* false. If it should be established at some later time that the earth is not ellipsoid, almost spherical in shape, as we take it to be, then we have always been wrong, even though we have been convinced of the correctness of our opinion. Opinion does not make truth.

Some people think that Einstein's theory of relativity demonstrates that truth is relative. However, they are misled by the name "theory of relativity" and misunderstand the theory. It is a physical theory and deals with the behavior of physical systems that are in relative motion to each other. "It is a theory of space and time." (Einstein) Although this theory modifies certain previously accepted laws, physicists believe that like other laws of science it is "true" in the sense I have been discussing. Einstein's theory of relativity is not concerned with the nature of truth.

"True," and "truth" are applied in ordinary and in philosophic language to statements and beliefs of various kinds—factual, scientific, mathematical, philosophic—be they theoretical or valuational (ethical), and to religious statements and beliefs. Whether it is possible to discover the "truth" in all these fields is a problem I want to take up in later chapters. At the outset I want to discuss only philosophic problems of factual knowledge pertaining to everyday activities and to science.

The philosopher's use of the word "true" is no different from the layman's, as the dictionary will bear out. If we say, "Johnny, is it true that the teacher said this?", we presuppose a state-of-affairs about which we would like to become clear; we want to find out "what is the case." *

The word "truths" is often used for important beliefs, dogmas and opinions: "We hold these truths to be self-evident"; "The truths of the Catholic religion are not acceptable to Jews"; "I can live only in accordance with my own truths." Such expressions do not indicate whether the truths (beliefs) we are talking about are really true in the sense that they state something which is the case. When we affirm certain truths that are dear to us, we are usually quite aware of the fact that we are dealing with beliefs basic for us but not necessarily for others

---

* The word "true," also has other, related meanings, with which we are not concerned here. When we talk about a true friend, true love, true followers, "true" stands for faithful. The true king is a legitimate king.

and whose real truth status is doubted by many though not by us.

One acts in accordance with his own beliefs and opinions, or in accordance with the opinions of others to the extent that he has made them his own, either because they have become his convictions, or because he obeys the commands of others, as a soldier or a party or church member. To call my personal principles and views, important as they are to me, my subjective truth, is to court philosophic disaster. Our language has many words to indicate the personal element; let us reserve the word "truth" or "true" for statements that are true, that assert what is the case independent of our feelings and convictions.

The Importance of Meaningfulness

If we accept this proposal, we have arrived at an important divide between rational and irrational philosophy. Let me briefly analyze the use of the term "truth" by two irrational thinkers.

> What is truth? . . . Is truth in reason, or above reason, or beneath reason, or outside of reason? . . . Is only the rational true? May there not be a reality, by its very nature, unattainable by reason, or perhaps, by its very nature, opposed to reason? And how can we know this reality if reason alone holds the key to knowledge?

This was written by the Spanish writer and philosopher Miguel de Unamuno in his important and peculiarly fascinating book *Tragic Sense of Life*,[2] which first appeared in 1912. Unamuno was a precursor of existentialism. His book is devoted mainly to proving the absolute necessity of a belief in immortality. His point of view, implicit in his questions, is characteristic of a large group of religious thinkers who are convinced that "reason is the enemy of life" (Unamuno)—a statement that could have been made also by Martin Luther—who believe in higher truth "unattainable by reason" but given to us by faith, by our heart and imagination. For many religious thinkers this higher truth does not stand in contradiction to reason; Unamuno and others, however, have gone further and believe, to use Unamuno's words, that we must affirm contradiction and strife between what our heart and our head say. "It is precisely this inner contradiction that unifies my life and gives it its practical purpose."

Intentional paradox like this seems to most serious philosophers unworthy of human intelligence, whether it endeavors to understand the world of everyday life or to encompass philosophy and religion.

Now to a quotation on truth from a contemporary American philosopher, William Barrett, which I chose because it, too, is typical of a modern intellectual trend. It is from his book *Irrational Man. A Study in Existential Philosophy.*[3]

> Truth itself—the truth for man—is just this standing face to face with life.* Such truth can not come from the intellect, for the intellect may in fact veil it, placing us . . . in that impersonal zone where we know only "the reflection of life" through concepts, precepts, all the abstract formulae of social routine; rather, truth is of the whole man. . . .
>
> Theirs is not an intellectual, but an existential truth. It consists in nothing more nor less than that they now stand more directly "face to face with life itself."

Frankly, to me this is a pretentious hodgepodge about questions of great importance. It is evident that Barrett is here not talking about observational statements; neither is he dealing with important scientific theories or political facts. He has in mind the decisive choices and postures of life. This is, indeed, a favorite subject of all existentialists. "What and where should I study?" "Should I join the army?" "Whom should I marry?" "Can I trust my wife?" "What, if any, religion should I profess?" We base such decisions on knowledge, inclinations, life goals, personality traits and conscious and subconscious drives. Many writers and thinkers have dealt with the dynamics of human behavior. The importance of these elusive elements of our decision-making does not entitle or compel us to confuse truth and decision-making or truth and individual personality and character.

One of the necessary preconditions for deciding on the truth or falsity of a statement is that it must assert something, it must have meaning. Modern philosophy has devoted a great deal of attention to an examination of meaning. For a while modern philosophy was dominated by a radical school which, aside from logic and mathematics, accepted only factual meaning based on perceptual knowledge. This procedure made ethics and religion

---

* The phrase "standing face to face with life" Barrett has taken from Tolstoy's *Anna Karenina*. In the episode he is commenting on, Tolstoy is discussing Karenin's doubts of his wife's faithfulness.

meaningless, for they are not based on perceptions. Most philosophers, however, have realized, in the meantime, that this was
going too far.

Strong emphasis on meaningfulness has had two effects.
One is that philosophic sentences are now tested much more
carefully in regard to their meaningfulness. The quotations from
Unamuno and Barrett may serve as examples. What does it mean
to ask: "Is truth in reason, or above reason, or beneath reason, or
outside of reason?" This is not poetry. And if it is to be used as a
philosophic argument, we must protest that neither reason nor
truth are in space and thus truth is neither in, above, beneath, nor
outside of reason or of anything else. Now to Barrett: "Truth
itself is just this standing face to face with life." I wonder what
this "standing face to face with life" means. Perhaps it means
merely facing life. A young person leaves the security of his
home and faces life alone in college; a young couple faces life
together; or their only child dies, and they face this tragedy.
Why should this be called truth instead of experience? I wonder
how "truth" can be identified with "facing life." High-sounding
phrases, when analyzed, often reveal their banality.

Much philosophizing has always consisted of unclear thinking and unclear writing, and still does even today. Arthur Pap
has collected a typical group of interesting examples: "Time is
the moving image of eternity"; "Matter is the principle of indi-
viduation"; "Contradiction is the principle of all movement";
"Every being is a potential for becoming." Although these are
grammatically correct sentences, their meaning is so indefinite or
confused that it would be difficult if not impossible to investigate
or verify or disprove them. Such oracular assertions may give
admirers a certain elation, but those who do not like riddles
must turn away.

Close scrutiny for meaning has had a very wholesome effect
on philosophy. While the establishment of a general atmosphere
of clarity in philosophy is something new, criticism of turgid,
unintelligible, and vague but high-sounding writing itself is not
new. (See John Locke's remarks, p. 24, above.) There have always been great philosophers who would have applauded Bertrand Russell's preferences:

I LIKE PRECISION. I LIKE SHARP OUTLINES.
I HATE VAGUENESS.

The other consequence of the study of meaning has been the discovery that sentences which seem to be assertions, that is, not commands and questions, may have meanings and purposes that are not cognitive. When a young man addresses his love with the words, "Darling, how wonderful to be with you!", his assertion serves the purpose of an emotive and persuasive appeal. In all political campaigns statements are made that are exaggerated and even untrue. Their purpose is not to give information but to arouse sympathy or a fighting mood.

Finally, poetry has its own goals and meaning. If we examine a poem for its cognitive content, it may appear to be nonsense, but this does not detract from its expressive and evocative poetic value. Let me cite an old-fashioned poem by Robert Browning because it uses the word "truth" and because its assertions, if examined for their factual content, are incomprehensible. But the poetic meaning of the verses is quite unmistakable.

Summum Bonum
All the breath and the bloom of the year
  in the bag of one bee;
All the wonder and wealth of the mine
  in the heart of one gem;
In the core of one pearl all the shade and
  the shine of the sea;
Breath and bloom, shade and shine,—
  wonder, wealth, and—how far above them—
Truth, that's brighter than gem,
Truth, that's purer than pearl—
Brightest truth, purest trust in the universe—
  all were for me
In the kiss of one girl.

At this point, I shall not discuss the vexing problem of obscure religious statements: "All the paths of the Lord are mercy and truth." (Psalm 25:10) Or, "In the beginning was the word, and the word was with God, and the word was God." (John 1:11) What do these sentences mean? Are they true? I will say more about this in the chapter on religion.

Logic and Mathematics. The Search
for Certainty

A discussion of truth must include logic and mathematics, the paramount examples of truth "to the end of reckoning." These are *necessary truths*, whereas "there are people here now" is a *contingent truth*. A contingent truth states something that could be different; its denial is not logically impossible. It is conceivable that the discussion mentioned in the beginning of this chapter did not take place. All happenings of everyday life could be different; consequently, all statements about them are contingent, and their truth depends on the facts of each particular case. This is equally true of science. Blood does not have to be red; the earth could have two moons; the structure of atoms could be different. We have to study how things are before we know what is true and what is false. All factual truth and all laws of science are contingent.

No observation is necessary, however, to evaluate the assertion: "Many bachelors are married to beautiful women." We do not need a Kinsey study of bachelors to know that it is false, because the word "bachelors" is defined as men who are not married. Therefore, the meaning of the word is sufficient to establish the falsity of the statement. A necessary truth states something that cannot logically be thought differently. The contrary of a necessary truth leads to a contradiction. It is a contradiction to say of bachelors that they are married. Let me mention a few other statements that are necessarily either true or false: thunder is a sound; all brothers are male; thoughts have no weight. We have only to "unpack the meaning" of the terms used to discover the truth or falsity of these sentences.

We also know that 3 plus 5 necessarily equals 8. However, ⅓ plus ⅕ does not equal ⅛ but ⁸⁄₁₅. Those of you who have studied Euclidean geometry know that the sum of the three interior angles in *every* Euclidean plane triangle equals 180 degrees. We know this by the laws of geometry through thinking alone.

Having described what is meant by necessary truth, which is rational truth—that is, truth derived through reason alone—I shall outline what logic and mathematics are. Both disciplines, important as they are, are not within the scope of this book. For all practical purposes they have little influence on our personal world view. But I hardly need to remind you that our philosophic ideas should not run counter to the laws of logic, nor should one part of our philosophy contradict another part. Some philosophies have glorified paradoxes, but these seem to me graveyards of truth and philosophy. In this early stage of our study we can only *hope* not to run into the road blocks of contradiction.

Logic states the correct way of inferring conclusions from propositions; it gives us the "conditions of valid thinking." It states rules for deciding whether or not given conclusions are validly drawn from given premises. It also tells us when proofs are false. According to Frege's concise description, logic deals with the "laws of truth." An example:

Climbing the White Mountains is strenuous.

Jean climbed the White Mountains.

Therefore, Jean did something strenuous.

Or let's take an invalid argument:

Some men are stupid.

All our Presidents have been men.

Therefore, all our Presidents have been stupid.

Logic tells us why the first deduction is right and the second is wrong.

"We all distinguish, at a common sense level, between good and bad inferences, though we may not find it easy . . . to codify the rules which distinguish good inferences from bad." Proof, deduction, inference, implication, premise, conclusion, contradiction, negation, all are terms of the logic of everyday usage.

We try to think and argue logically, but we rarely pay any attention to the unspoken inferences upon which our arguments and actions are based. Scientists use applied logic in devising experiments to prove or disprove their hypotheses and in drawing conclusions and establishing laws from the facts they have established. In the judicial process logic is used in applying the laws of the land, in establishing proof, and in weighing evidence.

Mathematics is of tremendous practical importance today. Statistics and nearly all fields of science use it extensively. Our modern technology and weaponry could not get along without it. It is difficult to give a concise definition of mathematics that is meaningful to a layman. The American philosopher Charles Peirce, quoting his father, Benjamin Peirce, defined mathematics as "the science which draws necessary conclusions." We may find more satisfactory, however, the practical description: Mathematics is what mathematicians do. All of us study arithmetic, algebra, and geometry in school. Many students go much further. In 1941, the great mathematician, Richard Courant could still complain that "some educational administrators are trying to demote mathematics from its traditional place." * Today the pendulum has swung the other way, an interesting example of how quickly and completely intellectual and educational tendencies can change.

The philosophic nature of mathematics is surrounded with controversy. Some mathematicians and philosophers regard it as an extension of logic, others hold that mathematics has its own basic entities, irreducible to logic. Some base it on intuition, others do not. There is no controversy, however, about the method; it is the same in all mathematical fields, which are logically developed from sets of simple mathematical assumptions or postulates, often called axioms, that must be internally consistent. From these postulates all theorems of mathematics can be deduced by strict logical procedures. All mathematical theorems are, therefore, objectively true and certain, but only within the framework of a particular axiomatic system. This limitation was unknown to philosophers and mathematicians until so-called non-Euclidean geometries were developed in the second quarter of the nineteenth century.

These brief remarks about the logical and systematic structure of mathematics may give an erroneous impression of the actual historical development of mathematics. Progress in mathematics came first, partly through the ingenuity and intuition of mathematicians, partly as the result of the "practical" needs of astronomy, physics, cartography, business, statistics and technology. It is interesting to note that the determination of the underlying axioms occurred after a group of theorems had already been established.

The fact that mathematics, and in particular geometry, is the oldest fully developed field of human knowledge has had a

---

* From the preface of Richard Courant's and Herbert Robbins' book, *What Is Mathematics?* (New York: Oxford University Press, 1941). His title notwithstanding, Courant does not attempt a definition of mathematics. Instead, he states: "It is not philosophy but active experience in mathematics itself that alone can answer the question: What is mathematics?" He then proceeds to deal with many fields of mathematics.

profound influence on philosophy. Plato and Aristotle and all
their successors until the seventeenth century lived in an intellectual atmosphere in which geometry was the only exact and systematically ordered discipline. Its axioms seem evident and true
beyond any possible doubt. Who can dispute that a straight line
is the shortest distance between two points on a plane or that of
three points on a straight line one is located between the other
two?

The clarity and certainty of mathematics could not help but
exert a magnetic pull on philosophy, so prone to vagueness and
uncertainty. It was only natural to ask why all knowledge could
not be constructed in the same rational, logical manner as geometry, starting with incontrovertible axioms, establishing theology,
logic, metaphysics and ethics—and even science—on a secure
basis. That logic is sufficient to prove the existence of God had
seemingly been demonstrated by the theologians of the early
Middle Ages; it remained the conviction of most thinkers until
the eighteenth century and is still accepted by Thomistic philosophers. The culmination of the rationalistic development in philosophy coincided, interestingly enough, with the beginnings of
modern experimental and exact science, science based on factual
observations and experiments. Rational philosophy, however,
began with self-evident philosophic axioms and by pure reason
attempted to "develop an absolutely true and certain science of
reality by demonstrating successively the various theorems implied." [4] The rationalistic method is well described by Descartes:

> In our search for the direct road towards truth we should busy
> ourselves with no object about which we cannot attain a
> certainty equal to that of the demonstrations of arithmetic and
> geometry.

Descartes (1596–1650) and Spinoza (1637–1677) are the
two foremost rationalists. Descartes is generally regarded as the
initiator of modern philosophy, breaking away from scholasticism, the philosophy of the Middle Ages. Descartes' famous
statement, "Cogito ergo sum" (I think, therefore I am), is often
quoted but it is not as philosophically useful as Descartes believed
it to be in validating his own and the world's existence, assuming
that special philosophic proof should be required at all.

Spinoza, whom I quoted earlier, was a deeply religious, admirable person, whose life was entirely devoted to philosophy.

His *Ethics*, written *modo geometrico*, started with definitions and axioms, through which he proved the propositions. We can admire its stoic nobility without accepting its method. During his lifetime and for the next hundred years Spinoza exerted little influence. But from the end of the eighteenth century on, German, English and French writers and poets were deeply inspired by his "obsession with God," by his propensity for seeing Him in every manifestation of nature, indeed for identifying nature with God, a religious view known as pantheism (*pan* meaning all, everything).

To "attain a certainty equal to that of the demonstrations of arithmetic and geometry" is a common goal, but it is a veritable passion with those who seem unable to live with uncertainties and perplexities. Yet a great many of the problems of philosophy, science, politics and daily life do not permit simple and certain solutions; we have to learn to live with uncertainties and probabilities. To become reconciled to the precariousness of our knowledge and its many puzzles is one of the accomplishments of a philosophic attitude.

There are many, of course, who are driven to find substitute certainties in religious dogmas, superstitions, prejudices, hearsay, propaganda and so on. "The true believer"—I refer again to Eric Hoffer's small book—is one of these. His refuge is a blind faith in what he accepts as infallible doctrine, the one and only truth. He entertains no misgivings; he knows *the* truth. This is a comfortable state of mind, yet nothing is more dangerous to intellectual progress than the narcotic of certainty, which puts all doubt to sleep. Unfortunately, certitude and truth do not necessarily go together. You may believe with absolute conviction, but what you believe may be wrong. A questioning, skeptical attitude, therefore, is healthy, even though total skepticism is self-defeating. "Know the truth, and the truth shall make you free," as the Gospel of St. John (8:32) encourages us.

Let me return to the beginning. Even though the confidence of the Rationalists in the capacity of reason to solve all human problems was extravagant, and we are therefore left with doubts about many of our beliefs and the realization that there are large areas in which certain knowledge is lacking or impossible, it is nevertheless true that truth is truth to the end of reckoning, and it is incorrect to say that *nothing* can be tested or verified. However, we must grant Barbusse that there have been many "truths" which men thought had been tested or verified but which were later proved to be wrong. The methods of testing non-rational (contingent) truth is one of the central subjects of philosophy which will be explored in the next chapter.

CHAPTER III

Everyday Knowledge

The Tests of Empirical Knowledge

It is easy to establish the truth of the observational statement, "There are people here now," if one is in a group of people because one can see and hear and touch the other people present. But not all observations are of the same degree of certainty. Suppose I am walking on an unfamiliar country road on a foggy afternoon, and notice something low and darkish some distance away. Is it a bush, or a cow, or a car that has stopped? Or I may wonder whether the lovely ivy climbing to the ceiling of a hotel dining room is a live vine—"real"—or a clever plastic imitation. An anxious young mother may think she hears her child crying when actually it is a cat meowing in the garden. My perceptions, therefore, do not lead necessarily, obviously, and automatically to correct conclusions about the world.

If all observational statements were invariably true, free from error and doubt, a theory of knowledge might seem superfluous. Theory of knowledge, also called epistemology, from the Greek word *episteme* meaning knowledge, is as old as philosophy. Plato deals with it in his dialogue *Theaetetus*. To this day not all its more esoteric problems have been entirely clarified; its main ideas, however, are quite simple.

The source of our knowledge of the external world as well as of our own inner experiences is our senses—sight, hearing, smell, taste, feeling—and an introspective awareness of our mental processes. The term "feeling" as commonly used covers several different capacities. We can experience pleasurable sensations or feel discomfort or pain in various parts of our body. We distinguish a tactual sense (hard, soft, hairy); a temperature sense; a kinesthetic, or muscle, sense, so that without looking we can know that an object is thick or thin, square or round.

What actually happens before we can truthfully say, "This is a banana"? (I choose a banana as an example instead of a person because bananas are easier to describe.) I see something yellowish, which seems rounded in one direction, long and thin in another direction, about as long as my hand, somewhat pointed at one end, broken off at the other end. These impressions do not occur one after another; they are simultaneous. And quite automatically I realize that often before I have received similar impressions, which were identified as constituting "banana," and therefore that which appears to me now must also be "banana." There is no doubt in my mind. A small toddler cannot pronounce the word, but he recognizes "nanas" and will reach out for one. But more is involved here than the correct recognition of various things; we also see that a baby learns early to differentiate between an at first chaotic background of impressions and the objects it is interested in: mother, father, rattle, finger, "nanas," etc.

I must qualify my description of the correct recognition in one respect. I may be in the house of a joker. What looks like a banana, or perhaps even feels like one, may be a plastic imitation intended to fool me. My sensual experiences may thus far not be sufficiently complete for me to make a positive identification. Closer examination and perhaps even biting into the "banana" may be necessary before I can say that this is a real banana or merely an imitation, a non-banana. The principle, however, is the same. A number of visual and tactual impressions plus the memory of previous similar sets of experiences plus the knowledge of a name attached to the set of experiences are the basis of the truthful propositions: This is a banana; or, this is an imitation of a banana.

The immediate data of our sensual impressions, the "given," are the ultimate basis of our perception of objects and of our statements about them. "Direct experience is neither certain nor uncertain, because it affirms nothing—it just *is*. It involves no

error, because it testifies to nothing but its own appearance. For
the same reason, it affords no certainty." (Charles S. Peirce)[1]
This ineffable experience is neither true nor false as long as we
merely experience and do not name, describe and think.

What happens when we see something that looks like a tomato is graphically described by H. H. Price.[2]

> When I see a tomato there is much that I can doubt. I can
> doubt whether it is a tomato that I am seeing, and not a
> cleverly painted piece of wax. I can doubt whether there is
> any material thing there at all. Perhaps what I took for a tomato
> was really a reflection; perhaps I am even the victim of some
> hallucination. One thing, however, I cannot doubt: that there
> exists a red patch of a round and somewhat bulgy shape, stand-
> ing out from a background of other color-patches, and having
> a certain visual depth, and that this whole field of color is
> directly present to my consciousness. What the red patch is,
> whether a substance, or a state of a substance, or an event,
> whether it is physical or psychical or neither, are questions
> that we may doubt about. But that something is red and round
> then and there I cannot doubt. Whether the something persists
> even for a moment before and after it is present to my con-
> sciousness, whether other minds can be conscious of it as well
> as I, may be doubted. But that it now *exists*, and that *I* am
> conscious of it—by me at least who am conscious of it this
> cannot possibly be doubted. And when I say that it is "directly"
> present to my consciousness, I mean that my consciousness of
> it is not reached by inference, nor by any other intellectual
> process.

In ordinary circumstances we do not hesitate to say: "This
is a tomato, this is a banana, there are people here now." It is our
common experience that in most cases these statements are true;
they *correspond* with what we experience. The phrase "correspondence theory of truth" has gone out of fashion, but in its
loose, metaphorical sense the word "correspond" indicates the
relationship I have been describing between immediate apprehen-
sion and what is said about it.

Observational statements should correspond with impressions. They can be true only under two conditions: first, we
must know the language correctly, and second, our sensual
impressions must give us sufficient basis for the statement. We
may have spoken too quickly; perhaps we should have felt the
banana- or tomato-like objects first in order to determine with
certainty whether they are the real thing or imitations. (Please

note the way the word "real" is used here. The imitations are real in the sense that they exist as objects; they are not real in the sense that they are artificial, fakes made to look like the "real thing.")

We appreciate these testing processes better if we are uncertain about an object we see, say, at dusk, or on a foggy day, or in an unfamiliar room. Our immediate visual impressions are not sufficient. We draw closer to the object, walk around it, or touch it, before we make any statement, and even then we say cautiously, "I believe this is an armchair," or "This seems to be an abandoned plow," "Or in the night, imagining some fear, how easy is a bush supposed a bear." (*A Midsummer Night's Dream*)

Dreams, Hallucinations and Irregularities

But perhaps what we saw was unreal in another sense: It may have appeared in a dream or hallucination. Suppose you are attending a fancy dinner party. People are seated around a table eating. Bowls of fruit, including tomatoes and bananas, are on the table. Suddenly there is a terrible commotion; in some unaccountable way the dinner party disappears, and all the guests chase you through dark woods. You become more and more terrified; you stumble and scream—and awake to find yourself in bed in a dark room. Gradually you collect yourself, and, applying, again quite automatically, another test to the apparent visual and emotional impressions you have lived through, decide that while the dream as dream was real, that is, it took place as a private event, none of the objects exist nor did the events actually occur. You distinguish the fictitious dream-world from the thing-world, *appearance* from *reality*.*

The judgment that you have been chased through dark woods conflicts with the fact that you are lying quietly, if somewhat upset, in bed at 3 A.M. This fact, however, fits in, or, to use a technical term, *coheres* with your previous experiences, with your knowledge of having gone to bed and of not having gotten out of it, and with your subsequent experiences of getting up and going about your daily activities. You have learned through ex-

* In ordinary language "real" has three opposites. We distinguish between that which is real and that which is fake, between a real event and an event of a private nature (dream, vision), and between that which is real and that which is merely imagined.

perience that you—and others—normally dream, though a particular dream may surprise you.

Children are easily upset by dreams; they live in a more uncertain world in which they are not yet accustomed to using tests of coherence which adults apply quite automatically. Adults too sometimes become confused: it has happened on occasion that I am not quite sure whether I spoke with certain friends or only dreamed that I did so.

Similar tests help us distinguish illusions, mirages, visions and hallucinations from events in the natural world. Let us examine a common yet strange experience. As I drive on a sunny day over a blacktop country road, the road looks wet to me though it has not rained there for days. I get out of the car and find that the road is dry. Then I recall that in bright sunlight certain roads appear to motorists to be wet though they are really dry. The experience and my recollection cohere when I realize that what I see is an illusion created by peculiar reflections.

While young children and people with certain mental diseases find it difficult to distinguish reality from mere appearance and facts from fairy tales, the normal adult knows about dreams, mirages, illusions, created by nature or by magicians, and about hallucinations following the use of alcohol or drugs, or caused by mental disorders. The walking ghost of Hamlet's father, witches riding through the night, may be correctly described subjective events, but they do not report actual facts of the real world. Visions of saints and the Devil, which appeared to Martin Luther and other pious people, may be explained by intense religious fervor. In the culture of both primitive and literate people myths have always played an important role. Some are merely fairy tales, but others are based on actual events, natural and historical, which they recount, explain and elaborate (thunderstorms, earthquakes, floods, meteors; the Trojan War, the flight of the Jews from Egypt). Throughout history and up to the present, myths have found acceptance as an integral part of a world picture regarded as true; for instance, the story of the Flood and Noah's Ark, the Greek god Helius driving his chariot across the heavens from east to west, the impregnability of the Maginot Line. Unlike people in the Middle Ages and in other more romantic periods and cultures, hardly anyone today believes that he experiences fairies, ghosts, saints, the Devil, or the Virgin Mary. We are less excitable and credulous. Our world is one of hard facts, except for borderline phenomenon such as flying saucers.

In a mocking mood, or in despair, or in a bull session someone may say, "Maybe everything *is* an illusion," or "We are always dreaming," or "Aren't we all crazy?" These expressions have their genesis in states of mind, with which we are not concerned here. But they also manifest a semantic error. Whatever terms we use to describe our life, we cannot argue away the fact that there exists a distinction between dreaming in the usual sense and not dreaming, between illusions in the usual sense and veridical observations, and, finally, between psychotics in the usual sense and the rest of humanity. These distinctions are not abolished by emotional and meaningless generalizations.

A number of other problems connected with the proper description of reality need to be clarified.[3] In *Theaetetus* Plato raises the following question:

> Things are to you such as they appear to you, and to me such as they appear to me. . . . A wind is blowing, and one of us may be cold and the other not. . . . Now is the wind, regarded not in relation to us but absolutely, cold or not; or are we to say that the wind is cold to him who is cold, and not to him who is not?

There is nothing wrong with the first two sentences or with the end of the third sentence. It is no contradiction for one person to feel warm and another cold in the same wind or the same room. Many families carry on a running argument over whether the house is too warm or too cold. Where Plato gets into deep water is in asking whether the wind itself is cold or not, for the Greeks had no way of measuring the cold or warmth of the wind and had to rely on subjective impressions. For us this is an easy matter to settle. With a thermometer we may find that the temperature of the wind is 58° and that I feel warm while my wife feels cold. There is no contradiction among these three observations.

We are so constituted that the very same temperature may create different impressions on different parts of our body. If I put one hand into very cold water and the other hand into hot water and then put both into tepid water, the one hand will feel that it is in warmish water, while to the other hand the water will feel cool. If I want to know what the temperature of the water really is I must use a thermometer.

Somewhat more puzzling are the following observations. Someone remarks, "The grass is the same gray color as the roadway." But to me the grass is green and the roadway grayish. I must conclude that the speaker is color-blind, unable to distinguish between certain color values. Unless we gave special thought to the problem, it would not occur to us to say that the grass *looks* green to us. We are convinced that the grass *really is* green because an overwhelming majority of people can distinguish between this color and gray. To only a small group of people does green appear as gray. Just as there is no contradiction between the statement of a totally blind person, "I don't see anything," and my visual observation of an endless number of things, so there is no contradiction between the statement of the color-blind person that grass looks gray and my statement that it appears green.

The question may now be raised as to what color the grass itself really is, independent of our impressions. This is a meaningless question. Color is something we sense when light of a certain wave length stimulates our eyes. Color impressions are responses to certain physical phenomena. Grass absorbs light of most of the wave lengths of the visual spectrum and reflects only light of that wave length which registers as green. This reflected light appears green to most people, but to my friend it is gray. The statement that the grass is green does not describe a subjective quality of the human beholder; it states a quality of the grass itself, that it reflects light of that wave length which makes people with normal vision see green—normal because part of the vast majority.

Another minor problem is illustrated by the dress that is dark blue in sunlight and practically black in artificial light. Conventionally, it is called dark blue because that is its color in most kinds of light. Anyone who is buying clothes or decorating a room is aware of changing color effects under various light conditions.

A coin may look round, elliptical, or flat depending on how we hold it. What is its *real* shape? Its periphery is circular, and its upper and lower surfaces are parallel planes. We say it is round because that is its most significant and characteristic shape. The laws of perspective explain its elliptical appearance; its round and flat appearances are the result of its given shape.

A straight stick looks bent when part of it is immersed in

water. Is it really bent at the point where it enters the water? When you first notice this phenomenon, you may think, naively, that the water has bent or broken the stick. But then you observe that when you pull the stick out of the water, it is still straight, and that you can repeat the same experiment as often as you wish with the same result. You may also establish that when you slide your hand along the stick, it does not feel bent even at the point where it looks bent. You therefore decide that the stick has not been bent by the water, that its bent appearance is a regularly occurring illusion for which a special explanation should be found. This the physicist has done in the laws of refraction.

Subjective Appearances and Objective Reality

The truth of observational statements rests, then, on the innumerable sensual impressions—colors, sounds, smells, tastes and feelings—that we experience. In the typical situation our mind, without taking thought, sorts these experiences into separate definite things and happenings, while our memory reminds us of similar experiences in the past, which, because we know a language, we can then name. Our senses merely give us impressions; they do not give us knowledge. Knowledge comes to us through other mental processes, which transform the flood of sensations into the world of distinguishable things. The title of C. I. Lewis' book, *Mind and the World Order*,[4] succinctly indicates what I have just described. Lewis writes:

> The world of experience is not given in experience; it is constructed by thought from the data of sense. This reality which everybody knows reflects the structure of human intelligence as much as it does the nature of the independently given sensory content. It is a whole in which mind and what is given to mind already meet and are interwoven.

Our mind "works on stuff," to use Francis Bacon's expression. When we decide that this is a banana or a tomato, when we say, "There are people here now," our statements correspond with the "given." They cohere also with other experiences, past and present. Human experiences fit into an orderly structure.

There are some seeming anomalies, however, which brings me to the second question I asked previously: "Are there *really* people here now, or is this perhaps a dream or a vision?" Dreams and visions also have their proper place in the world-order if we distinguish the world of reality from the world of subjective impressions, a freewheeling world not bound by "stuff." If we attend a meeting and watch people arriving and seating themselves in the room, we can truthfully observe, "There are people here now." This kind of observation refers to *public* states-of-affair and true statements about them contain *objective* knowledge. But I know nothing of your dreams, and you cannot know mine unless I talk or write about them. What happens in a dream is fleeting, largely incredible, and in contradiction to lying in bed. Awakening, we realize that we have been sleeping. Dreams are merely *subjective* states-of-affair.

Thus we find that we live in an experiential world in which our statements can be brought into a coherent scheme embracing objective reality and subjective appearances, one which includes not only our own observations and knowledge but also the statements of others concerning their observations and conclusions.

(It must be apparent that I have had to skip lightly over a great deal of difficult and controversial territory. But this situation is not peculiar to philosophy. One who explains complicated theories of genetics or nuclear physics to laymen has to do the same.)

The Doubter

We now turn to the third question mentioned in the last chapter: How do we deal with someone who doubts our statement that there are people here now? Let us assume that a stranger enters a room in which I am watching television with friends. He walks over to the television set, turns it on loud, and behaves as though he were alone in the room. I ask him what he is doing. At first he completely disregards me; but finally he concedes that I am in the room but no one else. What am I to make of this peculiar behavior? Is he lying or joking, or is he just being disagreeable? Is he suffering from a strange form of insanity with respect to people? He challenges me to prove that there are other people present, and I invite him to look, to listen, and to go over to someone else. But he refuses to do any of these things and persists in his denial. Now I am stymied, for there is no way I can prove to him by means of logic that there are people in the room with me.

Logic tells us how we can derive one truth from other truths. If someone learns that there are people with me, then he also knows, because of the meaning of the word "people," that they are warm-blooded, thinking beings, who cannot fly and who do not lay eggs. But that there are people with me can be proved (in an extended, loose, but customary sense of that term) only through observational testing. There is no logical proof that the world is as it is; only experience can tell us the nature of the world. If there are people with me and someone denies that fact, he is definitely wrong, but he cannot be made to concede this if he chooses to disagree. Everyone is at liberty to remain silent or to speak falsehoods and nonsense, but the fact that people are with me is so obvious that it does not permit of any real doubt, whatever my guest may say or think.

Let us consider another situation. Suppose that a friend and I go walking in Harriman State Park, forty miles from New York City. Suddenly my friend exclaims, pointing, "Look! Over there! There's a lion!" Laughing, I look, but don't see the lion. My friend then tells me quite seriously that my laugh frightened the animal away. At that point the chances of convincing me that a lion had really been there are very slight. But then, a few minutes later we both hear a loud roar and growling, and my skepticism begins to fade. And when, the next day, I read in the newspaper that a lion escaped from the circus and was shot in the Park, I am ready to believe that my friend actually did see a real lion. The statements that, my friend sees a lion in the Park, I do not see a lion, we both hear something that sounds like a lion's roar, and a lion has been shot in the Park, can easily be brought into coherence if we regard it as a fact that there was a lion in the Park which I heard but did not see.

Knowledge of the existence or nonexistence of tomatoes, people, or lions in certain places depends on our seeing, hearing, and/or touching them. This is equally true of our knowledge of all other existing or nonexisting things. We know that stars, oceans, plants, houses, exist because our senses tell us so. We know that centaurs, nymphs, Pegasus and dragons do not exist because no one has ever seen, heard, or felt them.

What I have described and analyzed so far is known to every reader. It is everyday knowlege. The contribution philosophy makes is the clarification of that which is taken for granted in ordinary experience.

The Reality of the World. Idealism and Dualism

But are we not on uncertain ground if we rely on our seeing, hearing, and feeling plus our memories as a basis for making the definite statements that there are bananas, tomatoes, people out there, objects which supposedly do not merely appear to us, like dreams, but have an objective existence in an external world, independent of our subjective mental processes? How can we jump to the conclusion that things exist or that we have substantial and enduring bodies when all we have to go on are certain processes in our minds?

Are we spectators observing a real world, or is the world a play that we are constantly writing? In other words, what is the relation of subjective experience to the real world? This is a question that we do not usually ask in the course of our daily activities. It is, nevertheless, one of the basic problems of the theory of knowledge. We take it for granted that we are living in a real world, a world that does not originate in our heads and is not merely "such stuff as dreams are made on." But how can we be so sure that the world and everything in it is real when all we know about it is the result of our individual mental processes? I can feel a table, but this feeling of the table is merely an "idea" of mine. You tell me that you see the table, but my hearing you is just another "idea."

Could our common sense conviction be wrong? Can a case be made for the theory that "existence consists in being perceived"? In the history of philosophy this viewpoint found a brilliant spokesman in the English philosopher George Berkeley (1685–1753).

> I see this *cherry*, I feel it, I taste it: and I am sure *nothing* cannot be seen, or felt, or tasted: it is therefore *real*. Take away the sensations of softness, moisture, redness, tartness, and you take away the cherry. Since it is not a being distinct from sensations; a *cherry*, I say, is nothing but a congeries of sensible impressions, or ideas perceived by various senses; which ideas are united into one thing (or have one name given to them) by the mind. . . . Hence, when I see, and feel, and taste, in sundry certain manners, I am sure the *cherry* exists, or is real; its reality being in my opinion nothing abstracted from these sensations. But if by the word *cherry* you mean an unknown

nature distinct from all these sensible qualities, and by its existence something distinct from its being perceived; then indeed
I own, neither you, nor I, nor anyone else can be sure it exists.[5]

The Berkeleyan idealism presents us with two basic
difficulties: *

(1) In any discussion about the statement, "there are people
here now," we assume that our sensations are similar; that is to
say, every member of the group has a sensation of other people.
But if there are no corporeal people present, nothing "distinct
from its being perceived," how does this common agreement of
sensations arise? According to Berkeley, this agreement of the
perceptions of different people is due to the workings of God.
However, to the believer and the unbeliever alike, such a device
must seem artificial and miraculous.

(2) There is an even more basic difficulty. "Take away the
sensations of softness, moisture, redness, tartness, and you take
away the cherry. It is not a being distinct from sensations." But
why not? If I "take away the sensation," then of course this
mental process will end, but not necessarily the cherry, the object of the experience. A cherry in a dream ends when the experience of the dream ends, but ordinary cherries do not end when
the sensation ends, unless we assume dogmatically that when I
close my eyes cherries become nonexistent except as the cherries
remain in being through the intervention of God's mind.

Berkeley confuses the sensation of the cherry with the
cherry itself; the mental process, the experience, with the object
or the content of the experience. There is as little identity between the cherry and the seeing of it as there is between the
cherry and the eating of it.

In a Berkeleyan vein Schopenhauer wrote that "the world is
my idea." But the world is the world, perhaps an object of my
idea, but it is as little an idea of mine as another person is an idea
of mine.

The refutation of this epistemological idealism is only a pre-
liminary step in the task of establishing the reality of things, people, the world, as entities independent of our mental processes.
There is a psychological point which should be made here. Even
a very young child is aware that objects are real apart from what

* The term "idealism" has two distinct meanings in philosophy: first, it
has the usual meaning, that of striving for ideals; second, it has been used as a
name for many different metaphysical theories and systems, for which Ideas,
Mind, Spirit, are the main structural elements of the universe.

he can see and do himself. When a mother goes into another
room, thereby becoming invisible, she is followed by her child. If
a child's toy rolls under a sofa while he is playing, he doesn't
conclude that it has vanished; rather, he looks everywhere for it.
From countless experiences the child learns of the reality of a
great big world, reality that is independent of his senses and his
wishes, that contains liquid and solid objects, pleasant and unpleasant objects, objects that constantly surround him and objects that come to him or to which he goes. Later, through the
experience of dreams, he begins to understand that, in contradistinction to real things, there are unreal "things," whose existence
depends entirely on his fleeting mental processes.

Are we able to prove the existence of things in the real
world? In the strictly logical meaning of the term "proof," of
course not. Basic knowledge, on which everything else logically
rests, cannot itself be proved. However, basic assumptions can be
made credible beyond any doubt. Our conviction about the reality of objects is not arbitrary. It is the only explanation of the
experiences we have of the things and persons that we encounter.

I would like to return once more to Mr. Price's tomato
(above, p. 46) and analyze the various possible doubts he lists.
The experience he describes is, "that there exists a red patch of a
round and somewhat bulgy shape, standing out from a background of other color-patches, and having a certain visual
depth." He wonders whether it is a tomato or a cleverly painted
piece of wax. We can resolve this question by touching the object we see, by feeling the whole fruit and perhaps biting into it.
Price then asks whether it is a material thing at all, or a reflection;
or a hallucination. We determine these matters by further
observation of the tomato, of its environment, and of ourselves.
Price makes us wonder whether it is "a substance or a state of a
substance or an event, whether it is physical or psychical or neither . . . whether [it] persists . . . whether other minds can
be conscious of it."

As philosophers we decide these uncertainties in the same
way that we resolve questions in our daily affairs, by logical clarification and further observation. We find that the tomato persists even when it is not seen, when it is in the refrigerator for
days. We also find that others can see it and, if they want to, can
feel it; if we bite into it or cut it, we discover that it is a compli-

cated, organized, substantial whole consisting of liquid and solid parts that may be soft or rather hard.

Not all the objects of which we can have knowledge and which are real in the sense that they are not merely the product of our minds (dreams, fantasies, etc.) are *things*. The tomato is a thing, a tangible, lasting object. When we say that something is a thing, we make a prediction that the particular object will persist for a time until it is destroyed by some cause. But the world also contains wind and rain, thunder and lightning, fires, waves, earthquakes, rainbows and reflections. These states-of-affairs are real and independent of us. Statements about them fit into the totality of corresponding and cohering propositions.

Thus, the validity of our conviction that there are objects out there rests, first, on a lengthy sequence of impressions deriving from one or more of our senses, which pertain to a particular object. We can study many objects from various angles and distances. The momentary impressions we receive are associated with similar remembered impressions from the past. In our mind all these impressions and memories intuitively coalesce to enable us to apprehend objects.

Second, we know that objects are independent of us because they persist whether or not we apprehend them. Houses and gardens do not disappear when we sleep; children come home from school; cities and landscapes remain although we may not see them for years.

Third, we can manipulate many of the objects out there and some objects can manipulate us. I may get the happy "idea" to kiss an attractive girl, but she may resist and become angry. Objects in the world do not necessarily accord with our wishes: roads are where they are; cities are ugly; climatic conditions are hard. If the world were merely my idea, a play that I write, why would I arrange things so that I suffer financial worries, sickness and death, see my sons go to war and my parents and friends die?

Finally, we must assume that the dictionary in which we look up the meaning of a word exists independent of our individual minds, which could not have put it together. The same is true of the mathematics book over which we struggle and the Japanese scroll that we cannot even read. There is no reason for assuming that we could have written the novel whose episodes we follow with great excitement. We could not have created the buildings and paintings we admire, or the symphonies we hear for the first time. How can scientific work and discoveries be explained unless we presuppose a world full of secrets, which we may gradually penetrate? Thus, the denial of an objective world leads to an infinity of impossibilities and absurdities, all of which find a simple solution in the acceptance of the existence of real things. Our customary naive realism proves to be in agreement with the philosopher's analysis. Experiencing is a mental process, but the objects we experience exist independently. Our senses are like windows through which we see and apprehend an objective reality.

A new philosophic puzzle arises immediately. Do we see the world as it *really* exists, or do the windows of man's mind force distortions on us? Must we not distinguish between an objective reality and our subjective view of it, which is conditioned by our senses and the categories of our mind? This plausible argument seems to demonstrate a distinction between appearance and underlying reality. I am not referring to the difference between the appearance of the stick, bent at the point it enters a water-filled vessel, and the real unbroken straight stick, nor to the difference between the apparently wet but really dry road. These are explainable physical and visual occurrences. Something much more radical is involved in the argument under discussion. Our *total* world picture is not a true picture of the external world but one conditioned by the special character of our senses and reason. Behind the empirical realm of phenomena is a reality not conditioned by our human limitations. It is the reality of things-in-themselves, as Kant called them, which we cannot know, but about which our moral and religious insight may give us some ideas. This *dualism* of phenomena and things-in-themselves is a cornerstone of Kant's influential system.

The main argument for Kant's dualism is that we cannot know objective reality; we can sense and know the world only within the limitations imposed by our human condition. This sounds plausible, but there is no sense in philosophizing about objective reality, about things-in-themselves, as there is no method at all that is independent of or that transcends ordinary thinking and disciplined philosophic and scientific endeavors. Whatever efforts we may make to learn about the higher realms of things-in-themselves, Absolute Reality or Being Itself, and about the factual world and ourselves, all we can acquire is human knowledge. There is no way of getting around the truism that whatever faculty of mind we ascribe to ourselves, it is always a human faculty. However long and intensely we study, think, and imagine, we are always engaged in human activities. Just as children must see the world from their own point of view, so we can experience, discuss and speculate on the world only from the human perspective. As C. I. Lewis has written:

> If the real object can be known at all, it can be known only in its *relation* [my italics] to a mind; and if the mind were different the nature of the object as known might well be different. Nevertheless a description of the object as known is a true description of an independent reality. (*Mind and the World Order*)

The view based on the distinction between phenomena and reality has been influential and enduring in the history of philosophy and human thought. Holders of this view differentiate between the ordinary natural world around us and some *higher* realm of being. Plato, for example, distinguished the immutable, eternal, perfect Ideas, or Forms, which we can apprehend in thought, and the transitory and confused shadowy world of things, of which our senses give us mere opinion. From then on, for more than two millennia, the mainstream of philosophy was dualistic in this sense. One of its strongest supports was the urge of Western thinkers to find a sphere for God, who had created man in His image, endowing him with a free and immortal soul. Kant was decisively affected by this current of thought.

The ideological climate of the nineteenth century and its scientific and technological accomplishments gradually undermined the strength of dualism. Philosophy lost its speculative and rationalistic character and became more factual, pragmatic, and analytic. Today dualism is practically dead, except among religious thinkers. The reason is simple and one which I have already mentioned—whatever higher or lower reality we try to grasp can be known only through human faculties. Admittedly, this argument may seem too simple to one who has come under the influence of a dualistic philosophy and who does not wish to relinquish an eternal realm supreme over the world of shadows, phenomena, illusions, the vale of tears.

The attitude of modern philosophy is epitomized in this

somewhat modified dictum of Ludwig Wittgenstein: Whereof one cannot know anything, thereof one must be silent. Philosophic treatises, therefore, no longer discuss the core concepts and visions of the great metaphysicians of the past. If philosophy has thus become emptier, it has also become more modest, realistic, truthful and less speculative, which may make it less interesting to those striving for "higher truths." Philosophers today are silent about the Absolute, Objective, Higher Realm. ("Behind the bare phenomenal facts . . . there is nothing." William James, *Pragmatism.*) The only reality we can know is the reality we *do* know—the one great universe. We belong to this universe, and our mental processes, our knowing, feeling, striving, acting, as well as our dreaming and our mental disturbances, are special, observable, real events of this universe. This philosophy has been called relational or perspective realism, or simply empiricism or naturalism, depending on where various philosophers have placed stress.* This is a monistic view that holds that there is only one kind of reality (from the Greek *monos*, single).

The disappearance of dualism is an interesting example of the historical fact that most philosophers do not interminably debate the same problems, as has been alleged. That certain philosophic problems are no longer discussed is more obvious in ethics than in other areas. Who today would seriously doubt that slavery is morally wrong, that women ought not be subordinate to men, that the community is responsible for its sick and poor?

Let me mention in passing that empiricism, like dualism, has roots in Greek philosophy. Until the last century, however, it constituted a minority view, mainly because of the great strength of religious dualism, which distinguished the realm of God *beyond* space and time from the universe of nature *in* space and time. (What naturalistic philosophy has to say about God and the *ultimate* nature of man and about the possibility of transcending our human-ness, creature-ness, through faith will be discussed in later chapters.)

* The opponents of contemporary philosophy also use the terms "materialism" and "positivism" to belittle it. These terms are unclear and should be avoided. Materialism is discussed in Chapter VII. Positivism is the name given to the doctrine of the French philosopher Auguste Comte (1798–1857). "Logical positivism" denotes a recent philosophic theory which, in its pure form, has few remaining adherents.

The Possibility of Trustworthy Knowledge

From our present vantage point we can now look back at the initial statement, "There are people here now." Contrary to Barbusse's challenge, we have found that truth is possible—we can state what is the case. And we can test it. If our statements stand up under the tests, then we have established that they are a segment of the totality of corresponding and cohering judgments.

We discover and test scientific and everyday knowledge by looking and listening, by comparing various observations with one another, and by reflecting on what we observe. We compare the view of the bent stick with the feel of the straight stick, and after further study understand what is happening. But is there no better way? We compare a portrait with the person who is the subject to see if it is a good likeness. We hold a reproduction of Van Gogh's *Sunflowers* next to the original painting to determine the quality of the reproduction. If we are so inclined, we can even establish the realism of the original picture by comparing it with sunflowers growing in the garden. Can we not get nearer the truth if we compare our view of the stick with the stick itself? But that is impossible. In fact, it is a truism that the stick-itself is not manifest to us independent of our knowledge. Some thinkers have been disturbed by this situation and have envisaged a realm of a higher knowledge of things-as-they-are, free of the limitations of the human mind. But knowledge beyond knowledge is impossible. The final one of the four questions posed in the last chapter is thus unanswerable.

Truth is gained by comparing innumerable bits of knowledge. While a particular particle of knowledge may be uncertain, every particle in the totality of our knowledge corrects or corroborates every other particle. It is a gradually learned, cooperative venture, in which everyone benefits through communicating and exchanging experiences with others. Thus, everyday knowledge and scientific observations are parts of a tremendous structure in which most elements are reasonably certain. Silent observations or spoken assertions rest on an infinity of impressions and judgments mutually modifying or supporting one another. On the basis of this spontaneous procedure we can proclaim what we know with some warranted degree of probability or certainty.

This is also true of the observations on which science is grounded—whether instruments are used or not. We should bear in mind, however, that evidence of the truth of our assertions is not equally strong for every statement we may make. What evidential basis would I have for saying to someone I had just met for the first time, "You are 22 years old and have an I.Q. of 160"? No sensible person would make such an assertion unless he had more justification. All I would be warranted in saying is, "I *believe* you are *about* 22 years old and have a pretty high I.Q." Regrettably, we are not always sufficiently careful. Scientists and laymen alike proclaim as truth opinions and theories that should be carefully qualified.

In principle, therefore, it is possible to gain trustworthy knowledge that withstands all tests and the onslaughts of skepticism. Philosophy upholds and clarifies, in this case at least, our everyday unthought-out attitudes. It does not *prove* knowledge; it analyzes how we achieve truth and helps us understand what knowledge means. It shows us pitfalls and limitations and accounts for them. But it also strengthens our "self-confidence of reason," an expression used by Leonard Nelson.

If the skeptic is still unconvinced and repeats his "Nothing can be tested," or T. S. Eliot's "All things are unreal," one may ask him what he means by "testing" and "unreal." What reasons can the skeptic put forward for doubting his reality or mine? What tests can he suggest other than those we normally use? The term "unreal" can have meaning only if there is something that is real. To make doubt possible there has to be something that is not doubtful. It is a disingenuous paradox to declare that there is only one truthful statement, namely, that nothing can be tested and that there is no truth. Total skepticism is meaningless.

Poetic Outlook

What meaning is conveyed to us by such expressions as "I feel as if I had wings"; "All things are unreal"; Shakespeare's previously quoted line, "We are such stuff as dreams are made on"; and Robert Browning's "Life is an empty dream"? From the mere fact that some experiences are dreams and illusions we cannot conclude that all things are unreal and everything is a dream. Expressions such as these ought not to be regarded as assertions at all but as poetic utterances. The Hindu assertion that, "The world as we know it is merely an illusion, a shadow play without even a plot" is the statement of a religious position. In poetry and religion words have metaphorical and symbolic meanings; they do not assert, they evoke.

However, we cannot make light of the real conflict that often prevails between what poets write, on the one hand, and common sense, science and philosophy on the other hand. It is a universal human urge to get away from confused, raw, cruel reality and try to look behind things and dream of their higher essence. There is a romantic, poetic, irrational streak in almost everyone. The following poems of three very different poets demonstrate this conflict between reality and the poetic outlook.

First, Wordsworth's well-known lines from "The Tables Turned":

> One impulse from a vernal wood
> May teach you more of man,
> Of moral evil and of good,
> Than all the sages can.
>
> Sweet is the lore which Nature brings;
> Our meddling intellect
> Misshapes the beauteous form of things—
> We murder to dissect.
>
> Enough of Science and of Art
> Close up those barren leaves;
> Come forth, and bring with you a heart
> That watches and receives.

The sixth song of "Song of Myself" by Walt Whitman begins as follows:

> A child said *What is the grass?* fetching it to
>   me with full hands,
> How could I answer the child? I do not know
>   what it is any more than he.

It is, of course, easy to explain what grass is and to talk about its economic importance or biological nature, but to know what ideas crossed the poet's mind, one must read the poem itself.

And, finally, e.e. cummings' lines:

> while you and i have lips and voices which
> are for kissing and to sing with
> who cares if some oneeyed son of a bitch
> invents an instrument to measure spring with?

The influence of such universal poetic feelings is a matter of considerable importance. The drive to extend knowledge into areas of the irrational has played a role in philosophy from Plato's Idealism to the treatment of Being by some existentialists. The truth of knowledge can be objectively tested; what feelings tell us must remain subjective. "Knowledge is knowledge, and cannot without confusion be identified with intuitive insight or with the vivid immediacy of profoundly moving experiences." [6] But the mind encompasses more than knowledge. There is no reason why knowledge and truth should destroy our emotional life or our sensitivity to the beautiful and ineffable.

CHAPTER IV

Error and Skepticism

"Is not the truth the truth?" Shakespeare asks. Naturally, this is so. Moreover, we have seen that truth can be achieved; we can state what is the case about the world—truth—if our statements are in conformity with our experience and cohere with one another. No one seriously doubts that there are people in a certain place when he sees and hears them; that there are mountains, plants and clouds when he hikes in the White Mountains. It is possible to describe a great many empirical situations with almost complete truthfulness.

But if this is all there is to the matter, how do we explain the pervasive feelings of doubt and disbelief? Why do we "suspect that everyone has an angle and that there is no such thing as truth anyway"?[1] Even if Barbusse may have overstated the case for skepticism and the impossibility of tests and truth, his scorn strikes a responsive note in us. We may indeed ask, "truth—what do they mean by it?" Where can we find it?

Obstacles to Knowledge

This skeptical attitude springs from the fact that the discovery of many important truths is considerably more difficult than it is in the factual examples I discussed, that errors and disputes are frequent, that many great questions are undecided, that opinions change, and, finally and most significantly, that in many spheres of life people hold very different convictions. Tom believes, say, that murderers should be hanged, that our national budget should be balanced, and that we are all immortal, while Dick holds that capital punishment should be abolished, that the budget need not be balanced, and that immortality is an idle dream. Dogmas that are true for a Catholic are not the same as those that are true for a Protestant, a Jew, or a Buddhist. Slavery was considered right by the Greeks, as was human sacrifice by many peoples; to us both seem wrong.

The belief that truth is impossible is called skepticism; the idea that it is relative to the character, education, situation, and idiosyncrasies of different people, nations and cultures is called relativism. Chapters II and III showed in a general and theoretical way that the idea of subjective truth (relativism) is self-contradictory, as is absolute skepticism. Since logic is the basis for all *correct* thinking, it ought to persuade every thinking person, but the amazing fact is that it does not. Frequently it is brushed aside with contempt. A deeply-ingrained conviction cannot easily be broken down by "mere logic." Relativism and skepticism represent very basic trends in current Western ideologies.

To study the intellectual forces influencing our world view we need to go beyond philosophy in today's technical sense of the word. Besides common sense and personal experience we need the findings of social and natural science to form our world view.

The contemporary anthropologist Ashley Montagu[2] has written that man "can confuse himself very much more efficiently than any other creature." Confusion begins with each one's ideas about himself. Ever since Dostoevsky, writers have persisted in tearing the mask from man's face, and Freud has bared our rationalizations. We are, therefore, much more conscious of the fact that in reality we are not what we seem to ourselves. This is excellently brought out in Dostoevsky's short story "The Gentle One," in which a man soliloquizes about his life as he stands beside the body of his wife who has committed suicide. He cannot understand why this tragedy has happened; in self-exculpation he recounts to himself all his good deeds. However, as we listen to his own story, we become aware that he was a foolish autocrat who crushed his gentle young wife.

It is surprising what difficulties stand in the way of arriving at the truth about something with which we are as intimately acquainted as our own person. Our defenses and suppressions hide from us the reality of our true self. It is well established that most of us nurse deceptive impressions about our growing-up process and later development and about the reasons and motives for our actions. Most of us look on our parents with distorted vision; our relations with them, their relations with and influence on us. But this is not the proper place for a detailed psychological analysis, nor would total self-knowledge, were it possible, solve all our personal difficulties.

Another field of uncertainty involves the decisions we have to make in our daily lives; for, much of the time, we have to rely on guesswork in planning our actions. Living in a free society instead of one bound by tradition, we face crucial decisions early: Shall I go to college, and where? What work shall I choose? Where shall I live? Whom shall I marry, and when? These vital decisions must be made when young people are often rather confused about themselves and when their experience and learning are limited. For many these early years are not merely the most intense but also the most articulate. Hence, the strong expressions of skepticism—even despair—of so many young people.

At the outset of our adult lives, then, we are concerned with truth-finding about ourselves, our environment and our future, when tests are difficult, often impossible, and when what is the case or will be the case cannot be established with any certainty. Decisions have to be made, however, and so we are forced to play a hazardous game with the directions of our lives. Because this precarious situation is universal and unavoidable, its influence on our psychical make-up, and thus on our thinking, tends to be overlooked.

Factual uncertainties do not end with adolescence, of course. All our lives we have to evaluate people and make decisions in practical matters. But to predict the effect of decisions is all the more difficult because every event is the result of a unique combination of many factors. As Samuel Butler has said so well: "Life is the art of drawing sufficient conclusions from insufficient premises."

If the determination of the future is hazardous, can we be certain at least about the present and the past? To a great extent, we can. We refer jocularly to 20/20 hindsight. But even here, in trying to find the truth about what is happening now or what has happened, there are remarkable uncertainties. What went wrong in the rearing of a child? Why did I enter into a stupid business transaction? Judges and jurors are sworn to establish the truth about past events. Do they and, indeed, can they?

There is constant disagreement about the current business picture, about the situation in Eastern Europe or in Southeast Asia. Who can know what is in the mind of statesmen and dictators? But how can we plan what to do unless we know what is going on? Our fears may be baseless, but they influence our decisions.

The past too is full of riddles and the subject of vigorous controversy. Do the history books give objective truth? Unfortunately, we are not sure what was the case—the truth—about some of the most significant historical events. What could be more important for relations between Christians and Jews than the Gospel story of the trial and crucifixion of Jesus? But are these reports unbiased, or, if only partly truthful, what is the real story? Can it still be established? What were the ideas of Socrates, who wrote nothing? In Plato's Dialogues Socrates is the main speaker, but we cannot distinguish between the opinions that are Socrates' and those Plato may have merely put in his mouth. There is controversy about the causes of World War I, about the depression of 1929–1932, about the necessity for dropping atom bombs on two Japanese cities to bring a quick end to the war and about President Kennedy's assassination. Resignedly we echo the old saying: "There are three sides to every question: yours, mine, and the facts."

There are also technical difficulties involved in discovering the truth. Science has made tremendous progress in the last two hundred years, but there are still a great many things we do not know. All too frequently doctors do not agree in their diagnoses, and indeed may not be able to arrive at any diagnosis at all. We do not know why everyone must die nor can we predict—fortunately—when we will die. The causes of cancer and of many other diseases are yet to be determined. Insanity is still very much of a mystery; in fact, mind itself is still a book with seven seals.

There are some things we cannot even experiment with:

stars, clouds, social and economic systems. Large-scale experimental projects in education are difficult, and educators hesitate to resort to them. Accordingly, the truth about the weather, inflation, depression, the consequences of economic planning, educational methods, juvenile delinquency, is hard to come by. These are matters of urgent importance to everyone, yet when experts disagree violently the layman can only stand helplessly by. In addition, even experts make mistakes. Discoveries and theories are often announced prematurely because investigators are careless or hungry for publicity.

The uncertainties of scientific forecasting are beautifully demonstrated in an experiment by Phillipp Frank, an outstanding physicist and philosopher of science. While standing before his class, he tossed up a small, irregularly shaped scrap of paper, which sailed slowly through the air, finally landing somewhere on the floor. Although nothing could be simpler than this straightforward event, and although we all know that the torn paper will eventually come to rest, we cannot determine exactly where or how quickly, as the effects of the many small air currents in the room cannot be measured. How much more difficult it is to forecast events that are subject to hidden psychological forces, economic interests, or political currents.

That which is new, just discovered, and vigorously discussed receives the most publicity. Because general attention is focused on uncertain hypotheses, new experiments and the most recent tentative findings, we get a lopsided idea of the uncertainties of science. We do not see the rows upon rows of volumes in the scientific libraries that contain solid truths.

What conclusions may be drawn from this catalogue of uncertainties? Is what I have said inconsistent with the earlier conviction that one can establish what is the truth with respect to certain things, situations and events? By no means!

The totality of data required to make truthful statements about many events of the past, of the present and certainly of the future is unavailable, but this is not to say that it is impossible to make any truthful statements at all about the future. We can predict the time of sunrise and sunset, the course of tides and of the planets. We can be quite definite about our aging processes and absolutely certain as to the inevitability of death. With a very high degree of probability we can state the date of future

presidential elections. We cannot forecast details of future
weather, but there is no doubt that in the Northern Hemisphere
it will be hotter on the Fourth of July than at Christmas and that
the reverse is true in the Southern Hemisphere.

There is a range of gradations from certainty to uncertainty. It is just as foolish to doubt a statement, the truth of
which can be tested, as it is to proclaim as truth something that
cannot be verified. No *general* criterion of truth exists, no simple
yardstick with which to measure the correctness of assertions;
every judgment must be verified by observations within its own
special realm.

An additional difficulty arises from the fact that the human
mind abhors a vacuum. When important questions cannot be
answered properly, when reliable information is unavailable, we
grasp at substitutes, eagerly embracing opinions, half-truths,
myths and stereotypes. As Freud wrote to his fiancée, "Reason is
frightfully serious and gloomy. A little superstition is rather
charming." Every people has invented a story about the origin of
the world and the creation of man. It is hard to bear the thought
that death is the irreversible end to our being, and many different
heavens and hells have been offered as consolations. Man has
tried by various means to get around the fact that the future is
precarious and unpredictable: he has resorted to oracles; the
reading of entrails and tea-leaves; stock market indices; and as-
trology. With prayers and sacrifices he has attempted to change
the weather, fix the outcome of battles, settle his own fate and
that of his family, his tribe and his country. The underlying
premises have never been tested nor could they have been. Even
today medical faddism in health and dietary remedies is rampant.
And what has been true of medicine is still true to some extent of
pedagogy, economics and political science, fields where it is difficult to disentangle passionately held opinions from proven theories.

Roger Bacon's and Francis Bacon's
Lists of "Idols"

All-too-human inclinations obscure our judgment. Attempts to catalogue these tendencies were made by two philosophers, with similar and thus confusing names, who are occasionally quoted today: Friar Roger Bacon (1212–1292) and Francis

Bacon, who lived more than three hundred years later (1561–1626).

Roger Bacon, living at the apogee of the Middle Ages and a contemporary of St. Thomas Aquinas, lists "four causes of ignorance: First, the example of frail and unsuited authority. Second, the influence of custom. Third, the opinion of the unlearned crowd. Fourth, the concealment of one's ignorance in a display of apparent wisdom." [3] These "four plagues," as Russell calls them, are as prevalent today as they were seven hundred years ago and the admonition not to take a display of apparent wisdom for the real thing is highly pertinent, particularly in philosophy.

Francis Bacon saw the chief sources of error in what he called "The Four Idols," an expression frequently referred to today. They are:

1. The Idols of Tribe, which "have their foundation in human nature itself, and in the tribe or race of men. . . ."

2. "The Idols of the Cave are the idols of the individual man for every one (besides the errors common to human nature in general) has a cave or den of his own, which refracts or discolors the light of nature. . . ."

3. The Idols of the Market Place "are formed by the intercourse and association of men with each other . . . on account of the commerce and consort of men there. . . . Words plainly force and overrule the understanding, and throw all into confusion, and lead men away into numberless empty controversies and idle fancies."

4. The Idols of the Theatre, "which have immigrated into men's minds from the various dogmas of philosophies, and also from wrong laws of demonstration. . . . In my judgment all the received systems are but so many stage-plays, representing worlds of their own creation after an unreal and scenic fashion." * [4]

Francis Bacon's detailed description of the Idols is a forceful reminder of similar contemporary criticism of the prevalence of untruths, the influence of mass media, the substitution of mere images for reality and the survival of old superstitions and prejudices.

* Francis Bacon's fame does not rest on his four Idols alone. He was the first philosopher of the Age of Discovery. His *Novum Organum* contains the beginnings of the modern philosophy of science. His slogan, "Knowledge is power," has a very contemporary ring.

Prejudice, not only between individuals, but between groups, is another source of error. "Human thinking is a social act and moves within a conceptual frame-work that belongs to a group." (Charles Frankel) Whites have preconceived ideas about Negroes, and Negroes about whites. It is unnecessary to detail the indignities and cruelties of slavery and all the evils of segregation that this prejudice has caused. After all the arguments on both sides are in, the ineluctable fact remains, which the white man must recognize, that he is a member of a minority group. Other such pairs of stereotypes are: Gentile and Jew, Protestant and Catholic, blond Anglo-Saxon and dark south Mediterranean, German and Slav. Thoughtlessly we talk about *all* Catholics, or *all* Germans, or *all* Southerners.

There are class and social prejudices between capital and labor, farmers and city people, the rich and the poor, but national prejudices are the most dangerous. The Germans hated the French and the Poles, and the French and the Poles hated the Germans. Such attitudes are the seed-beds from which wars spring. Today, the arch-enemy seems to be the atheistic communist, be he Chinese, Russian, or Cuban. As the political picture changes so do the stereotypes. The traitorous "Jap" becomes the industrial leader of Asia in a beautiful country. Our concept of the Germans has reverted to certain pre-World War II notions: hard-working, scientific leaders, *gemütlich*. And the Chinese, formerly looked upon with the greatest respect, what are we to think of them? "Truth—what do they mean by it?" It goes without saying that prejudices—political, social, racial, religious —are not confined to the West. They are universal. I remind you of the violence following the partition of India in 1947, in which Moslems and Hindus massacred each other, and more recently the intertribal violence in Africa.

It is unfortunately true, as Charles Frankel says so well, that "social passions have an epidemic character while social information moves sluggishly and distortedly through the social structure."

There are, finally, errors that belong to a particular historical period. (I am again stressing factual errors, not prejudices of a moral or religious nature.) As I have mentioned, every people has had its own mythical explanation of the origin of the world.

All are totally untrue. In Chapter VII I shall discuss, in greater detail, the Biblical creation story, which is the most significant for us. Until a few hundred years ago most people were convinced that the earth was flat. They overlooked certain simple indications that this belief was wrong, for example, that ships at a distance not merely became smaller but disappear under the horizon, the hull first, then the masts and sails. Circumnavigation of the globe was not effected until the sixteenth century.

It is sad to realize that superstitions, such as the belief in witches and their devilish influence, were held not merely by the uneducated, but by learned men as well, who wrote elaborate tomes on how to recognize the creatures—misguided or malevolent inventions!

To people in other periods the world looked quite different from the way it looks to us. The body of beliefs, that is, the body of what men *held* to be knowledge, has recurrently changed. But in the last four hundred years, following the introduction of experimental methods, the means of investigating the truth have become ever more numerous, varied and exact. The area of testable and tested knowledge has expanded enormously.

Sociology of Knowledge

The fact that our assumptions have changed throughout the ages has led some social scientists and philosophers to elaborate a "sociology of knowledge." In its extreme form this theory claims that objective knowledge is impossible, as all knowledge is a function of historic development. This is true, of course, in the obvious sense that everything known has to become known at a certain time. There was a period long ago when manlike beings discovered the use of fire and a much later period when early man domesticated cows. Thus, in a certain sense, the truths that fire burns and that cows produce nourishing milk "depended on" developments in man's earliest history. The truth of the statements, "fire burns," and "cows give nourishing milk," had to be learned.

The Greek historian Herodotus, a contemporary of Socrates, on visiting Egypt expressed great surprise that the Egyptians, whose economy was completely dependent upon the periodic Nile floods, had never investigated the reasons for these floods but ascribed them to all kinds of supernatural causes. It was not until the last century that the sources of the Nile and the causes of the floods were discovered. Would anyone assume that gods regulated the Nile before the nineteenth century, while natural forces now prevail? Would anyone doubt that the earth had and still has a globelike shape, though for millennia millions held that it was flat?

There are still, as I have pointed out before, a great many things we do *not* know; there are also subjects which are still being hotly debated—the size of the universe, for example, but we also have a vast body of facts that are known beyond reasonable doubt: the shape of the earth, the distances to the moon and the sun, the cause and treatment of many diseases, the physical laws governing jets and rockets, to list a few. And the list grows all the time.

We thus arrive at another meaning of the term "sociology of knowledge." This sociology of knowledge tries to investigate the peculiar concatenation of intellectual and social circumstances that brought about this modern age of science. Equally tantalizing questions are presented by other unique periods of greatness: the Renaissance; the flowering of Greek culture in the sixth and fifth centuries B.C.; the period between the eighth and fifth centuries B.C. when all around the civilized world, from China and India to the Mediterranean, prophets and moral teachers appeared. We can describe these sudden eruptions of creative energy and untangle their historical sequences, but we cannot determine the general laws that govern these events so as to predict future ones.

Mass Media and Propaganda

The organized attempt to mold our thinking in contemporary society is another factor in our skepticism. Our great-grandparents read few newspapers. Their interests were limited, more or less, to their immediate environment. But today nearly everybody reads newspapers and magazines, listens to the radio and looks at television. Advertising and propaganda through the mass media try to shape our opinions and direct our buying habits. Public relations experts work subtly to change our attitudes. Careful analysis and exact information are replaced by one-sided and manipulated "truth." Practically everyone in the Western countries can read and consequently is open to the printed lie, and we and our children are attacked by television.

A great deal of criticism has recently been leveled against the advertising fraternity of Madison Avenue. Some of it is probably unjust, as advertising has contributed to economic growth and thus to a rising standard of health and comfort. Though the amount of propaganda and its high-pressure quality are new, the phenomenon itself is old. Remember the story of the Pied Piper of Hamelin?

Our political attitudes too are constantly subjected to partisan influences which distort everything that is being done and planned. The electorate as well as its officials are swamped by propaganda disseminated by political, economic, educational, religious, and scientific organizations, their lobbyists and publications. The party out of power violently attacks the leaders in power, who in turn assail those who try to take power from them. The game of character assassination, which began with George Washington, has never stopped. Half-truths and untruths are bandied about when what we need is accurate information and analysis. This may be an aspect of the democratic process at work, but unfortunately it also makes for apathy or deep-seated skepticism. "Fifty per cent of what we say in the campaign is baloney," a politician once proudly admitted. It is astonishing that the body politic survives these antics and that our leadership frequently is good.

Today more people than ever before consume more political information and misinformation and do so at an earlier time in their lives. Thus we are haunted by the feeling that, at least as far as political problems are concerned, "nothing can be tested, nothing verified. Truth—what do they mean by it?" The claim of truth "to the end of reckoning" thus seems almost ludicrous. Yet even here careful, dispassionate study and observation will frequently yield judgment, the truth of which can be asserted with some degree of justification. As Abraham Lincoln supposedly said, "You can fool some of the people all of the time, and all of the people some of the time, but you can't fool all of the people all of the time."

If truth is difficult to find in political matters, it is so not solely because of contradictory claims. The issues are objectively complicated and the solutions uncertain. Economics, education and foreign policy are not exact sciences. Yet most of us try to have some kind of answers to the important questions of the day, answers which are usually based on official or newspaper over-simplifications. How can we eliminate domestic unemployment, poverty and segregation in housing and jobs? How can we stabilize prices? How can we best educate all our children and young people? What is to be done about the misery of underdeveloped nations, about the population explosion? And, finally, by what means can we bring about world peace? Theoretically, all these questions have answers, but, practically, they are as difficult or even as impossible to arrive at as the landing place of Phillipp Frank's piece of paper.

The electorate is all the more stymied because many questions have become so complicated that they are entrusted to experts who often do not agree with each other, or so important for our defense that they are "classified," i.e., secret, so that neither we nor reporters digging for truth, nor independent, non-governmental experts can examine and test official handouts. And, as I have mentioned previously, if we do not know the truth, we choose substitutes, so that conjecture and speculation take the place of correct information.

It has often been said that figures lie. Sometimes they do and sometimes they don't. Nothing is more exact and convincing than a set of figures, properly set up, with unequivocal explanations. But figures and curves can be ambiguously or deceptively arranged. An article in the Cleveland Trust Company Business Bulletin (July 16, 1956) stated:

> In 1955 the American public saved 8 billion, or 17 billion, or 61 billion, or some other amount, depending on what is meant by saving and which set of figures is being used. Several Government agencies publish statistics on 'saving' of one sort or another. At first glance, a comparison of these reports is likely to *induce a feeling of total confusion. After some study, this may be reduced to a state of only partial confusion.* (My italics)

And what about the clamor and disputes that accompanied the first publication of the Kinsey Reports? Were these statistics of sexual behavior true? What did they mean?

Slogans are another effective means of mass propaganda and befuddlement. I have referred to the fact that words as such are merely neutral conveyors of information, but they can be used to evoke positive or negative emotions. There are hmmm-words (good words) and brrr-words (bad words). Democracy, religion, God, salvation, freedom and happiness are words that give us a good feeling; "free enterprise system" and "the wave of the future" have the magic quality of giving us security. But dictatorship, communism, deficit, socialized medicine, "You want your daughter to marry a 'nigger'? " are expressions designed to frighten us. Judge Benjamin Cardozo has said, "Catch words hold analysis in fetters."

The most extreme form of opinion-molding is, of course, brainwashing. This is a systematically worked out and surprisingly successful technique, much used in totalitarian countries, to expunge certain ideas and attitudes from the mind of an individual and to substitute other, opposite ideologies. Milder forms of thought manipulation have frequently been resorted to by nationalist groups to stir up animosity between people.

Distorting war propaganda is an especially deplorable practice, fostering hatred of the enemy. Fortunately, peace usually restores a more balanced view.

An interesting development in the area of attitude formation is psychological warfare, which uses mass media behind enemy lines to sow dissension among the people and thus to weaken the enemy's will to fight. Warring nations in the name of high ideals spread untruths, each glorifying its own cause and people and denigrating its adversaries.

Divergent Religions

Although for the time being I will refrain from discussing religion, I want to touch here on one phase of it. Organized religion is powerful and wealthy, engaging in the education of the young and propagating certain beliefs. The stories and dogmas of the several communions are different and often quite fantastic. They frequently contradict each other. Either the Flood and the building of the Ark took place or the story about them is a myth; either the mother of Jesus was a virgin or she was not; either God exists or He does not; and if there is a God, He is either Triune (Father, Son, Holy Ghost) or He is not. Notwithstanding the special difficulties of deciding religious claims to knowledge, groups of people cling to the conviction that *they* know the truth. But if one set of religious judgments is true then all the others must be wrong.

We scarcely realize how strange it is that we are not
shocked by the fact that large groups of people hold very different beliefs, some or all of which must be erroneous. If millions of
Protestants, Catholics, Jews, Mohammedans and atheists can
convince themselves of the truth of contradictory tenets, then it
would seem that truth is something rather uncertain. It is in the
nature of young people to be especially concerned with metaphysical and religious problems. How can they feel optimistic
regarding the possibility of discovering truth when they and the
people around them live in a farrago of conflicting religious
claims to truth, as if such a state of divergence was the most natural thing? I see in this unavoidable tolerance a major source of
our feeling of general intellectual insecurity. "Truth—what do
they mean by it?" Of course the fact that one religion has more
adherents than another does not make its dogmas more true.
Numbers do not count in truth; tests do.

We have heard people, in despair over the uncertainties involved in moral and religious questions say: "Everyone has to
live by his own truth." But the term "own truth" is senseless.
Something is true or it is not true. Yeats said somewhere: "I
make the truth." He was wrong. We only find truth, we do not
make it. Truth as such is independent of people; there is no such
thing as "my own truth" or "your own truth." If, however, the
statement intends to say that everyone has to live by his own
opinions or convictions, then it is a truism. We can live only in
accordance with what we think to be so, whether it actually is so
or not. If we follow someone else's suggestions or teachings, by
adopting them we make them our own. The only exception to
this is a person who is forced to obey commands: a soldier, a
prisoner, or someone who has been hypnotized. In all other situations each person can think and act only within the framework
of the knowledge and values he has acquired, be they right or
wrong. But that does not make truth individual.

It is not, however, the truth as such that influences our thinking and our actions, but what we hold to be the truth. Our opinions are the operative factor. If we hold night air to be un-
healthy, we keep our windows closed. If we believe that prayers
can cure disease or that poverty is due to laziness or that spanking strengthens a child's character, we behave and legislate in accordance with these ideas.

Nature goes on undisturbed by what we think. But individual behavior and cultural and political developments are determined by our thoughts, ideas, attitudes. "In the dynamic field of human interaction mistakes become part of that reality which is continuously affected by how we think and act, how others, and how the one influences the other." (Hans Simons)

Cautious Approach to Truth

This discussion of the difficulties inherent in arriving at truth may make us feel like one of the holy men painted by fifteenth-century artists: surrounded and frightened by fierce animals, witches, and devils, or bewitched and distracted by seductive female figures. There are, indeed, dangers and distractions. But let us not exaggerate them. Notwithstanding the difficulties, we know it to be true that each of us knows a great deal that is true.

The history of mankind may seem to some a history of errors. It is also a history of truth. The most uneducated and superstitious man knows the facts of everyday life, though he may also know a great many things that are not so. The highly educated humanist or scientist, who may put forward some quite mistaken theory, nevertheless knows not only the truth required for living in society, but also an infinite number of facts pertaining to his specialty. As a matter of fact, the body of sure knowledge is so great that no one can possibly know all of it.

The most convincing refutation of skepticism is our knowledge of so many factual truths. Relativism though less implausible is equally vulnerable. The technological and operative truths of a jet liner's construction and performance are identical for the men who construct them in America as well as for the Moslem in Egypt, the Buddhist in Japan and the heathen Polynesian, who repair them in their respective countries. Later analysis will examine whether skepticism and relativism—the idea that there are no objective rules for human conduct, which state what ought to be the case, and no truths about ultimate questions —are valid positions in the fields of ethics and religion.

In rejecting absolute skepticism, we are not discarding caution. A little skepticism is a healthy thing. Let us examine ourselves, our prejudices, and the facts we think we know. Even so-called "authorities" frequently neglect to do this. Reputable pharmaceutical concerns release drugs to the public before they have been sufficiently tested. Bridges designed by excellent engineers collapse. Scientific, economic and educational theories are presented as the last word on the subject before every angle has been thoroughly considered. The truth can be discovered only by more and more testing.

Finally, we should be constantly aware of the difference between truths that are almost indubitable and truths that are true within various degrees of probability. It is one thing to state absolutely that the earth has one moon and that its mean distance from the earth is 238,857 miles. It is quite another to speak with equal definiteness about the interior of the earth, nuclear particles, or about the nature of the learning process.

While we should cling steadfastly to the conviction that we can approximate the truth through tests, we should also be prepared to make pertinent qualifications whenever we assert anything, and should cultivate intellectual humility, which will keep us from claiming that *we* have attained the truth.

> Every judgment is no more than an approximation of the truth, subject to revision. . . . If we recognize our judgments as subject to revision, we shall be less inclined to force them down another people's throats, or to back them with bullets. . . . The mind has an enormous capacity for error, self-deception, illogic, sloppiness, confusion and silliness. All of these tendencies may be diminished by training, and that, of course, is the function of education. (John W. Gardner)

Our culture suffers from a split. In the ordinary situations of life we accept the facts as they are. We expect that the coffee pot will boil on the lighted stove, that a cut finger will bleed, and that small children will lose their milk teeth. No one is skeptical in such matters. Furthermore, scientists accept with confidence the vast body of established truths in the various fields of knowledge and the new findings that come out of their research. They are full of confidence. And therein lies a danger—the danger of transferring this confidence in the truths of their own fields to fields where they are not equally qualified to speak—of oversimplifying solutions to social, political, and moral problems.

Many intellectuals, however, are skeptical, and we, when we philosophize, may surrender to the same attitude and mood. Camus wrote: "Truth is mysterious, elusive, ever to be won anew." Some truths are indeed mysterious and elusive, but a great many are not, a fact with which Camus would probably have agreed. Skeptical generalizations are dangerous, for they undermine one of man's greatest gifts: his confidence in human reason. We have lost the confidence that animated Greek and Renaissance thinkers and the writers of the Age of Reason. It is the task of a good philosophy to recapture this confidence. Objective and untiring study in a free and self-critical community leads the way to truth "to the end of reckoning."

CHAPTER V

The Nature and
Role of Science

"The eternal mystery of the
world is its comprehensibility."
—ALBERT EINSTEIN

Common Sense and Science: Basic
and Applied

During our lifetime we acquire haphazardly a tremendous
number of miscellaneous facts that belong to the subject matters
of the sciences. We know about water flowing downstream;
about thunderstorms and rainbows; about the daily cycles of the
tides and the annual cycles of the seasons; about fires, electricity,
heat and light; about the structure of many plants and the habits
of many animals; about the organization of the human body and
its diseases; about human behavior; and about economics. But
what we know is unsystematic and inexact, and we are unable to
explain many of the events and regularities with which we are
familiar. Why do ice and iron melt and gasoline and wood burn?
What heats the sun millennia after millennia? How do plants
"know" when to bring forth leaves and when to let them fall?
Why do we die? What happens when we think? How does our
economic system operate? In far too many cases we do not know
what conditions cause what effects.

Science goes beyond everyday knowledge and common

sense. All of us know that water will boil when we heat it suffi-ciently for an extended period of time. We know how to produce the required heat with a wood or coal fire, a gas burner, or an electric stove. We do not need to know exactly how hot the fire has to be nor what the exact time factor is.

We usually take nature and technology for granted. The scientist, however, would study the boiling process, ask questions about it and try to find accurate and truthful answers. He would want to determine at exactly what temperature water boils and how much heat is required. Is what he finds true under all conditions? How is the transformation of water into steam ex-plained? These are questions with which the physicist deals.

These questions are of two kinds: (1) What, exactly, hap-pens when water boils, and why? The answer will be a scientific description and explanation. (2) What will happen when I put a lighted match to a gas burner under a pot of cold water? The answer will be a scientific prediction. Both types of answers give us factual knowledge.

This knowledge is gained by careful observation and de-scription of the facts and of the events that occur. The scientist, then, tries to bring systematic order to his findings. Some good examples of this are the description and systematic classification of chemical substances, stars, minerals and both fossil and living plants and animals. But an even more important concern of sci-ence is to find general rules (laws) showing what effects—for example, motion, heat, growth, pain—are due to what causes. In the performance of these tasks the scientist uses microscopes to see things too small for the naked eye, telescopes to observe the distant stars, and ever more complicated instruments to penetrate nature.

One of the scientist's most important techniques is the ex-perimental method. The scientist not only looks at nature as he finds it; he arranges controlled experiments in which as many conditions as are deemed necessary are held constant while others are varied systematically in accordance with a plan. All factors and changes are accurately observed and, when possible, measured. The experimenter can thus study what effects are caused by what changes in the surrounding conditions, and from the data he accumulates he tries to formulate general rules. Galileo is reported to have dropped substances of different weights from the Tower of Pisa and rolled them down inclined planes to establish the falsity of the prevailing Aristotelian assumption that heavy substances fall faster than light ones, as well as to establish the precise laws of free fall. We test the effect of sunshine and fertilizers on plant growth and the healing properties of complicated drugs in animal and human experiments.

Scientists go beyond the occurrences of everyday life. They study the sources of the sun's heat, the origins of the planets and the stars, the normal workings of our organs and the causes of their diseases. They examine the qualities and the composition of the substances that form the earth, plants, animals and men. A subject that seems utterly useless, yet which has fascinated the general public of recent years, is the ancestry of man and his slow development during the last few million years. Chemists and physicists have discovered through skillful experiments that all things consist of submicroscopic atoms, giving rise to the new task of investigating the nature and behavior of these infinitesimally small particles.

Pure, basic, or fundamental science, which I am writing about, should not be confused with applied science nor with technology. The inventor, engineer, architect, physician and agriculturist are not scientists as such. Most of the research in industrial laboratories, and in medical and agricultural institutions is for the improvement of technical processes, for the development of new and better products, or the study and cure of particular diseases; it does not concern itself with general underlying laws. However, the boundary lines between pure and practical research are fluid. The splitting of the uranium atom in a German research institute was a big step toward the making of the atom bomb as well as the use of nuclear energy for industrial purposes. The pure scientist makes discoveries in his laboratory that may result in new medical, military, or technical developments, and, conversely, physicians, military men, industrialists and agriculturists raise problems that may not only lead to practical solutions, but also into new areas of pure research. Man wants to know and comprehend; and he also wants to improve his life.

Let me quote a few eloquent remarks of Dr. Merle A. Tuve, Director of Carnegie Institute:

> The content of science is knowledge. Science is not airplanes and missiles and radar and atomic power, nor is it Salk vaccine

or cancer chemo-therapy. . . . These all are technological developments which have grown out of scientific studies. Science is knowledge of the natural world about us, it is a systematic ordering and interrelating of the huge body of information we already have acquired, it is the search for new knowledge about the marvelous world in which we find ourselves. Science is knowledge and the love of knowledge and teaching and research concerning nature.

We should note here that the acquisition of knowledge is only one of our intellectual activities. We hear complaints that science, in its pretentiousness, tries to monopolize or penetrate all man's intellectual occupations, but this is not so. The artist, musician, writer, entertainer use their intellectual faculties, just as the builder, technician, physician, educator and politician do. In fact, we all use our intelligence every single day. But that does not make us scientists. Because science deals with factual knowledge, philosophy, religion and mathematics are not part of it. Whatever knowledge these latter disciplines give us, or are supposed to give us, is not factual.

The Meaning of "Science"

The everyday usage of the term "science" is not very precise. Often, we mean only the *natural sciences*. Among these we distinguish the exact sciences (physics and chemistry), other sciences also dealing with the inorganic world (astronomy, cosmogony, geology, geography, etc.), and the various biological sciences (botany, zoology, physiology, bacteriology, genetics, psychology, etc.). The boundaries of the many proliferating specialties and subspecialities are not sharp; there are such interdisciplinary sciences as geochemistry, astrophysics, biochemistry and biophysics. Specialization developed historically and is necessary for the practical purposes of university organization and research. An additional reason for it is the obvious fact that the capacity of individual scientists to master a certain field of knowledge is limited.

There are, secondly, the *social sciences* (the study of man in society), to which belong such fields as anthropology, sociology, economics and political science. There has been a longstanding argument about the scientific character and objectivity of the social sciences, an argument which, to some extent, still goes on.

However, there is no question in my mind that these disciplines fall within the previously given description of science.

> In history and the social sciences, too, one deals with observations, inductive generalizations, hence theories; . . . every result is, in the last analysis, a proposition verifiable in experience. (Richard von Mises, *Positivism*)

Here the research instruments are naturally different, consisting, for example, of the study of artifacts and documents, the use of questionnaire and opinion polls, or the observation of human behavior in groups.* While the theories of the social sciences are often vague and their application sometimes temporally or geographically limited, they nevertheless attempt to be objective.

Some examples will clarify this point. Theories that apply to polygamous, feudal societies may find no application in a monogamous, capitalistic one. A highly industrialized, affluent society involves relationships which do not exist in a primitive agricultural community. A society with widespread birth control develops differently from one in which having numerous children is regarded as honorific. But these differences do not mean that sociology and economics are unscientific. We rely on specialized treatment in other fields also, in biology, for example. The study of an anthill, a beehive, a school of fish, or a herd of deer, and the isolated living of spiders and snakes result in quite different findings. Yet it should be noted that while the literature of the natural sciences infrequently strays from the exacting path of science, this is not equally true of the social sciences. Here personal bias, literary pretensions, political ambition, moral passion and the like often interfere with objectivity. It is therefore sometimes difficult to distinguish truth from subjective opinions.

Finally, what about *history*? Ordinary linguistic usage makes a sharp distinction between history and science. Most people might assume that these two intellectual enterprises are antithetical. But while we have to accept language as it is used, it does not have to rule our thinking. In fact, it would be a mistake to exclude history from the scientific field. In the first place there

---

* A convincing argument for the scientific character of the social sciences may be found in Ernest Nagel's *The Structure of Science* (New York: Harcourt, Brace & World, 1961), chaps. 13, 14, and 15. This lucidly written work is one of the relatively few contemporary books on philosophy that is neither an introductory college text nor a collection of technical articles; neither is it of such a specialized character that only philosophers can understand and benefit from it. However a few chapters of this book are quite technical.

are historical natural sciences describing chains of events, such as cosmogony, historic geology and evolutionary biology. Secondly, science shares some of its main characteristics with history. Historians endeavor to be objective. They use criteria for evaluating evidence, which, broadly speaking, resemble those employed in other scientific disciplines. History is systematically ordered even if it deals with only a one-run sequence of events. In explaining sequences it utilizes assumptions concerning regularities in human behavior. These assumptions, derived from either common sense or social science, appear implicitly or explicitly in the writing of historians. In this respect the historian is like the engineer or the physician, who makes use of (and contributes to the discovery of) laws and theories deriving from the physical and biological sciences.[1] Unfortunately, the historian as a social scientist is subject to the difficulties previously mentioned, and as popularizer, *litterateur*, or prophet à la Toynbee he may succumb to bias, sensationalism, artistic license, or religious fervor.

A definition that covers all the different fields of science must be quite general and abstract and each term must be carefully examined. "Science is a process consciously directed toward achieving knowledge that is explicitly formulated, general in scope, systematically ordered and dependable."[2] This definition is broad enough to cover the logical and mathematical sciences, but for us the term "science" refers to the empirical sciences. All sciences, as the word is used here, tend to be *empirical, objective, precise* and *systematic*, and except those which deal with the history of natural or social phenomena, they are *general*. Let us look at these characteristics in greater detail.

(1) That scientific knowledge is *empirical* means that its basis is observation of what has happened and is happening in nature, history, man's behavior and in the experiments which we set up. That this is the only way to discover the truth about these facts seems to us a matter of course. This predominance of the empirical attitude is one of the novel characteristics of our civilization. When we call this the scientific age, it is not merely because of the tremendous achievements of science, but because we have all become convinced of the superiority of the empirical method.

It was not always so. We are all familiar with the story that

begins thus: "When God began to create the heaven and the earth—the earth being unformed and void, with darkness over the surface of the deep and the wind from God sweeping over the water—God said, 'Let there be light'; and there was light." *
Past generations firmly believed until quite recently that this was a description of an actual event. Today, the overwhelming majority of Western people regard this magnificent story of the Creation as belonging to the realm of religion and myth. They are no longer uncertain: perhaps it is true, perhaps it is not. They are convinced that the narration of an event in the Bible is not sufficient evidence for its truth, unless other evidence, perhaps of an archeological nature, confirms it.

The Greeks and Romans too accepted speculation and myth instead of fact. In his *Timaeus*, Plato told a complicated story of the origin of the universe and its parts. There he wrote: "We ought to accept the tale which is probable and inquire no further." Such tales then became authoritative. However, the Greeks and Romans also studied nature though they did not make a sharp distinction between observation and speculation. In the Middle Ages the intelligentsia, a small group working mostly within the framework of the Church, almost completely halted the observation of nature. Instead they relied on the Bible, a few surviving Greek and Roman books, and the works of saintly authors (St. Augustine, St. Thomas) for their information.

An extraordinary change took place in the sixteenth century, when men such as Leonardo da Vinci (1452–1519),† William Gilbert (1544–1603),‡ and Francis Bacon became aware of the nature of the scientific method. Francis Bacon, in his *Advancement of Learning*, expressed the modern scientific creed in his recommendations "not to guess and divine, but to discover and to know . . . to examine and dissect the nature of this very world itself, to go to facts themselves for everything." [3] It is a matter of constant wonder that science as a great and systematic cultural endeavor is a comparatively recent development. The age of modern science really began with Galileo (1564–

* These are the first three verses of the Bible.

† "I shall test by experiment before I proceed further, because my intention is to consult experience first and then with reasoning show why such experience is bound to operate in such a way."

‡ Gilbert, who investigated magnetism, complained about those who build theories "on the basis of mere opinions, and old-womanishly dreamt the things that were not."

1642), the inventor of the telescope and great experimenter, who got into serious difficulties with the Church and characteristically complained about the "people who believe there is no truth to seek in nature, but only in comparison of texts"; with Johann Kepler (1571–1630), who formulated the laws of the movements of the planets around the sun; with William Harvey (1578–1657), who discovered the circulation of the blood; and with Isaac Newton (born the year of Galileo's death, 1642, died 1727) who is best known for his theory of gravity but who is almost equally important as a mathematician and for his work in optics.

But neither speculation nor respect for authorities has entirely disappeared in today's culture, not even in the scientific world. Speculation is still essential in the development of new experiments and new theories. Authoritative books still play a decisive role in our organized religions. The classical writers are more frequently quoted, discussed, and followed in the newly developed sciences, such as economics and psychiatry, than in fields in which the large body of established facts and laws seem beyond further controversy.

How do scientists find the empirical material with which they deal? A great many facts turn up accidentally. A fish regarded as having died out millions of years ago is brought to the surface in some fisherman's net. Fossil bones or a human settlement are discovered by a farmer ploughing a field, or by laborers excavating a building foundation. Our modern concepts of the structure of the atom and the advent of the nuclear age had their origin in Henri Becquerel's accidental discovery of atomic radiation in 1896, which was followed up by Pierre and Marie Curie. Penicillin, never noticed before, was detected by Sir Alexander Fleming in 1928. But most new facts are discovered in the controlled search for new data. New instruments and new experiments are employed to obtain a better, fuller, more detailed picture of the heavens, at the one extreme, and of subatomic particles, at the other. "Facts are elusive and you usually have to know what you are looking for before you can find one" (George G. Simpson). Scientists are engaged in a systematic enterprise of trial and error. Frequently, they are successful, sometimes they are not. Some theories are verified though later findings may necessitate modifications. Other theories are found to be wrong (a theory is falsified), and the search for new facts and explanations has to go on.

(2) The experimental method has definite criteria of measurement and of success or failure which make for the *objectivity* of science, making it independent of personal judgment. Unfortunately, the experimental method cannot be applied in large sectors of science, for example in anthropology. Consequently, it is difficult to settle the ardent controversies over the ancestry of man or the date of the coming of man to America. Every scientific finding is subject to analysis and test by every scientist willing and able to make the relevant studies. Science is an open book, except insofar as governments, for reasons of national defense, have classified certain scientific work. To publicize new work and discoveries there exists a tremendous worldwide organization of lectures, conferences, visits and, most important, periodicals. By means of this international, public network scientists in all sufficiently advanced countries can study, test, and criticize each other's work; science, insofar as it is true science, crosses all cultural, political, and religious barriers. This has brought about one of the most distinctive and fruitful accomplishments in modern history: the process of social self-correction through unrestricted criticism and the free exchange of information.* In the field of science the goal of "One World" has actually been reached. However, the qualification that it must be "true" science is important. The Communists have their own economics and we have ours. Prevailing ideologies may prejudice scientists, and it is not always easy to detect bias.

Unlike art and literature, science is progressive and cumulative. Greek art is admired, Greek epics are read, Greek tragedies are still performed. Little moral wisdom has been added to the teachings of Confucius, Micah, Isaiah and Christ, except that large groups of people—women, slaves, foreigners—are now regarded as equal to free men. Science works differently. Scientific knowledge not only grows, but it also improves. The progress of certain sciences is so rapid that great changes may come about in less than a lifetime. "Any scientist worthy of his salt labors to bring about the obsolescence of his work." (Th. Dobzhansky)

---

* Later, I shall discuss the reasons for controversies, errors, and wrong theories.

(3) Science is *precise*, or at least it tends toward precision. Ideally, its terms must be exact, not vague and ambiguous. When terms of everyday usage are employed, such as force, weight, pressure, time, distance, space, speed, they must be defined so that no confusion is possible. This is comparatively easy to do in what we call the exact sciences. It becomes more difficult in the biological sciences; a term such as "stomach" means quite different things, depending on whether we talk about man, cows which have four stomachs, or the body cavity of a polyp. It becomes even more difficult in economics (money, work, capital, inflation), and even more so in psychology (intelligence, affection, anxiety).

It goes without saying that scientists try to follow logical procedures in planning experiments, and in formulating proving, or disproving theories. But what is much more important is that wherever counting and measurement are possible, mathematics can be used in the formulation of findings: the speed of fall, for instance, which was one of the first exact laws discovered.[4] Mathematics makes it possible, first, to express and generalize experimental findings in a simple and precise manner, and second, to correlate one group of mathematically formulated findings with other mathematically expressed data and thus to suggest new theories and open up paths for new experiments. Today mathematics is used in almost every scientific field, including biology, psychology and economics. Without mathematical analysis and the experimental method modern science would be impossible.

The absolute need for higher mathematics in the scientific and technological fields is one of the most decisive factors in the unfortunate estrangement between scientists and non-scientists. Those of us who are not physicists can derive little intellectual satisfaction from the realization that the physicist understands, through the formulas of thermodynamics, what makes liquid water boil off as steam; or that biochemists are on the way to discovering the mechanisms and processes which make it possible for plants to transform the energy of sunlight into chemical energy so that they can live and grow. The books of today's scientists are written in a language which is totally incomprehensible for most people. Each scientist is a specialist, and when he writes or lectures in the scientific manner and not as a popularizer, he addresses himself to other specialists. The educated public can only admire from a distance what scientists know and do. At the same time we feel annoyed and cheated that we find ourselves standing in front of closed doors.

However, the great importance of the popularization of science should not be underestimated. Scientific findings have become so significant for political and managerial decisions that leadership in an industrial democracy has to know what scientists do. Moreover, scientific discoveries are fascinating. But popular books, for the most part, present merely the end results of scientific labor and deductions; they cannot describe all the experimental work and the mathematical derivations.

(4) Science is *systematic*. It is not merely an accumulation of descriptions and laws. The chemical elements have been arranged in the periodic table, underpinned by the knowledge of the atomic structure of the various elements. I have previously referred to the systematic arrangement of plants and animals in phyla, classes, orders, families, genera and species—fossils and living—which, in turn, is supported by the discovery of the evolutionary sequence. We endeavor to arrange all descriptions and laws into an orderly system, so that the sciences themselves appear "a patterned web." The laws of science form a hierarchy leading from limited generalizations to general, abstract and basic laws.

Our natural desire for synthesis, which has been strengthened by the success of modern science, has led many thinkers to look forward to the realization of the age-old ideal of coordinating all sciences into one unified system in which the basic formulas of physics would explain all past, present, and future events. This possibility has a practical and a theoretical aspect. Indeed, certain—though by no means all—matters with which chemistry and astronomy deal can be explained by the basic law of physics —quantum theory.* However, the extended use of this theory to throw light on chemical and physical phenomena runs afoul of the enormous complications involved in performing the appropriate mathematical derivations. The difficulties are even greater in biology, because we are dealing with different kinds of giant molecules built up of thousands and tens of hundreds of thousands of atoms interconnected in intricate organizations. While

---

* This theory states that all radiant energy (heat, light and other electromagnetic waves) consists of indivisible extraordinarily small packets of energy called quanta.

many processes of molecular biology can be analyzed and explained, we are far from being able to establish the laws of biological systems because we have not yet learned even to describe the thousands of different chemical reactions that go on simultaneously within each cell. Since a full biological understanding of psychological events—for example, seeing and hearing, having a headache or experiencing a psychotic episode, not to mention thinking, speaking, writing, loving and hating—is still far off, the possibility of explaining psychological processes through the laws of physics seems visionary at the present time. (I omit from consideration in this chapter the controversial question of whether man's inner life can ever be fully caught in scientific formulas, as his supposedly immortal soul makes him a unique creature.) More complex than the explanation of individual psychology is that of society as a whole, and as a consequence the social sciences are further removed from basic explanation. Starting at the top of a sequential order, we may envisage the possibility of "reducing" the social sciences to psychology, psychology to biology, and biology through biophysics to physics.[5] These steps may, in fact, go beyond our scientific capabilities, although many interdisciplinary links have been established. Indeed, it is a sobering thought that physics itself is not a complete science—a warning to our presumptions. In the prevailing situation, each discipline must continue to use its own vocabulary and follow its own specialized research in accordance with its own special methods.

Thinkers have occasionally given rein to their fantasies and envisaged a superhuman, godlike, perfect mind. By definition, a perfect mind would know everything and, with or without the help of a perfect computer, would be able to reduce all laws to certain basic ones. But this makes no sense in either practical or theoretical human terms. There are limits to the complexity of formulas with which we can operate. Today we still find elusive the formulas to explain large groups of events in the inorganic world, and the "why" of the life processes of even the simplest unicellular organism is, as previously stated, quite beyond our present capacity to fathom.

An additional systematic difficulty stands in the way of an exact description and prediction of events in nature. It is not sufficient to know all laws; we must also know the position and momentum of all particles in the whole world or at least in the systems we are studying, that is, the "initial conditions." This is far beyond the capacity of any mind imaginable. The following examples will point up the difficulty. Assuming that we could actually know the workings of the physiological system of any one individual, nevertheless, we cannot forecast his life history unless we also know the accidents that may happen to his car, the infectious diseases he may contract and countless other events to which he, as a human being, may be subjected.

It does not follow from these limitations, however, that the ideal of making theories more comprehensive and of absorbing less inclusive theories into more inclusive ones is unsound and unfeasible. I have already indicated some of the bridges that have been built. The earliest and one of the most famous is the incorporation of Galileo's laws of free fall and the laws of the movement of planetary bodies into Newtonian mechanics and gravitational theory. A contemporary example is the inspiring progress that science is making in uncovering the basis of disease and the mechanisms of genetics through biochemistry.

(5) All non-historical sciences make *general* statements. Scientists as scientists are not interested in the description and life cycle of an individual particle, stone, plant, animal, or human being.* This is the sort of thing with which artists and writers are concerned. The scientist makes statements about all particles of a particular nature, all oak trees, whales and human beings. All insects have six feet; all mammals nurse their young; mollusks have no bones; all animals need oxygen. All substances consist of electrons, protons, and, except for hydrogen, neutrons. The statements that scientists make are of differing degrees of generality. The last one above, for instance, is true not only of all inorganic, but also of all organic, substances. But what is true of plants is not necessarily true of animals. And even apparently obvious generalizations have their exceptions: the statement that all mammals give birth to living young is not true of the duck-billed platypus; not all plants are green; not all animals are bisexual. Consequently, the general statements regarding these matters need to be qualified—their generality must be restricted.

Much more important than general descriptions is the generality of scientific laws. A law describes what will always be the

---

* The scientific treatment of the sun and the several planets (including the earth) and their moons is in part non-historical, yet it does not generalize, for it deals with individual heavenly bodies.

case under identical circumstances. If stones, plates, or children are unsupported, they will fall from a height. If heat is applied to iron pots of water, then. . . . If our heart stops for a short while, then. . . . If a hot substance touches our skin, then. . . . Whenever a cat sees a mouse, then. . . . Scientific laws are characterized by this if . . . then structure. *If* certain particular conditions prevail—the cause—*then* certain specified effects will take place. Effects are related to causes and causes to effects. Scientific laws describe the processes of nature by singling out the unchanging relations between types of events. The fact that they do not deal with one particular occurrence (this cat, this pot of water), but with types of events (cats seeing mice, pots of water being heated), gives laws their importance.

A law tells us what has happened in all cases characterized by the same constants about which we know, and predicts what will happen in future cases when these constants appear together. We heat a pot of water, and we expect it to boil eventually. We throw a ball up, and we expect it to fall down again. Our garden is covered with snow, but we look forward to the miracle of spring. It seems, then, that laws predict what will happen. We go beyond the available evidence and forecast future unobserved instances.

Causality and Induction; Explanation and Prediction

We touch here on the problems of causality and induction, two of the most debated problems in the modern philosophy of science. The controversy began in the eighteenth century, when Hume stated that when we talk about the lawfulness of nature, we are dealing merely with the psychological expectation that we will again experience the same regularity we have noticed previously. There is no natural necessity for this recurrence, only our own disposition to expect the same event that we have experienced in the past. Kant, on the other hand, was convinced that the judgment, "Every event has a cause," is so general and our conviction of its truth so absolute that it goes beyond all experience and must therefore be part of the apparatus of our mind, of our "pure reason"; we do not discover causality in nature, we bring this idea to nature. Modern philosophy leans toward Hume: experience has taught us and teaches us every day that nature is regular and orderly. In our daily lives as well as in our scientific endeavors we follow the *general maxim* that the same causes will bring forth the same results. We operate as though there were a principle of "the uniformity of nature." But something must be said for Kant. Conviction of the uniformity of nature is so fundamental that even a toddler has implicit confidence in the regular recurrence of facts: a white liquid in a bottle is drinkable, a table is hard, a flame hot, mother will protect him. And what can be more tiring, exasperating, intriguing than a bright five-year-old with his day-long streams of whys, for which he is convinced there are answers. Why are you angry? Why did the glass break? Why does Happy bark? Why is it thundering? The search for causes has begun.

Without the actual regularities and uniformities which we experience as facts and thus take for granted, there could be no confidence in the stability of things and of the processes of daily life, nor would we be able to draw up scientific laws. But irregularities do exist, and we learn to cope with them. A part of a house that has been standing for years suddenly collapses. Immediately we ask: Why did this happen? We are sure that there are reasons: perhaps termites, faulty construction, or a sinking of the foundation. A second example: What causes the gradual darkening and even disappearance of the sun on a clear, cloudless day, an event which used to frighten people? Nothing miraculous has occurred. The moon, following its regular orbit, has temporarily come between the earth and the sun. Eclipses—of the moon, too, when the shadow of the earth covers the face of its satellite— take place with such regularity that we can calculate their occurrence thousands of years in the past and equal thousands of years in the future.

Certain irregularities in nature have led to sensational discoveries. From the earliest times five planets besides the earth were known, all visible with the naked eye (Mercury, Venus, Mars, Jupiter, Saturn). In 1781, Sir William Herschel discovered that an object, visible only with telescopes, was a planet, and that it was located further away from the sun than Saturn. To it was given the name Uranus. When attempts were made to determine its orbit, an approximation was arrived at, but there were serious deviations from the theoretical orbit in the actual motion of Uranus. Finally, two astronomers—one French and the other English—working independently, assumed the existence of another planet, whose gravitational pull disturbed Uranus' orbit. In 1845 both succeeded in computing "on the basis of grossly imperfect data on the motion of one planet, the location and motion of another whose very existence was unproved" (James R. Newman). The determination was so exact that in 1846 a search by German astronomers at the Berlin Observatory discovered the postulated planet. It was later called Neptune. Pluto, the most recently located planet in our system, was similarly deduced from irregularities in Neptune's orbit; after a twenty-five year search it was discovered in 1930. Theories of modern physics have led to the assumption of the existence of certain particles before they were ever observed. In 1928 the physicist P. A. M. Dirac, in formulating his theory of the electron predicted that a positively charged particle must exist corresponding to the negatively charged electron. Four years later the positron was discovered experimentally.

There are many phenomena which seemed inexplicable until a short time ago. For example, a clover field or a fruit tree begins to blossom, and suddenly it is surrounded by hundreds of bees. How did they find out? Who informed them? A few years ago the riddle was solved. The "language" of bees was found to consist in the performance of peculiar dances by the foraging bees in front of the hive, indicating to the other bees the direction and the distance of sources of honey. In a totally different area, Freud discovered that dreams, slips of the tongue, and the errors of everyday life, which seem to come about quite accidentally, in reality do not occur without cause. Underlying, hidden causative chains can be established in personality structure, prior happenings, worries, frustrations, suppression and other psychic phenomena, which, though they cannot be used to predict dreams, at least give us hints as to why they take the form that they do.

An astounding natural phenomenon is the migration of birds, extending thousands of miles over land and water. Many species leave the North in the fall to winter in a warmer climate; in the spring they return to the old localities. Banding has established that some birds come back to the identical forests and gardens. We are not certain yet how the birds find their way back; nevertheless, we are convinced that there *is* an explanation, that there exists a natural, lawful cause for this remarkable phenomenon, just as there is a cause for Uranus' peculiar irregularities and for the coming of the bees. In studying bird migrations

and other phenomena that we cannot explain, we concede that
we cannot explain them *now*, but we persevere in our search
until we do come upon an explanation. Difficulties in investigation do not compel us to surrender and turn for explanation to
the supernatural, to the assumption of mysterious forces and influences, miracles and divine intervention.

What does explaining really mean? First, we must distinguish between the explanation of an individual event and the explanation of a natural law. The water in the kettle boils because I
turned on the gas stove. A friend dies because of a heart attack:
a blood clot had formed in his coronary artery. People usually do
not search further, for they know from other cases that coronary attacks frequently are fatal. But for the medical scientist
this is just the beginning, he wants to know what the causes of
coronary attacks are, and then how they can be avoided. We are
constantly asking for explanations. Why did the car break
down? Why did the plane crash? Why did the stock market go
down? We look for the constellation of circumstances that are
responsible for an event and are usually content with superficial
answers. The scientist is not. He is not satisfied with the observational law that water boils when heated; he wants to find an explanation for this phenomenon. He begins by making exact observations. Then he tries to develop a general theory of boiling
(the transformation of certain substances into a gaseous state
when heated; some substances do not boil but burn instead). The
study of boiling leads the scientist to the theories of thermodynamics and from there to the still more general theories of quantum mechanics.

With this very general theory the scientist must be content,
as he cannot go any further, at least not now with the present
state of scientific knowledge. Why are the fundamental facts
(for example, that hemoglobin contains iron but chlorophyll
contains magnesium, or that the speed of light is 186,000 miles a
second) and laws of nature as they are? That is the way nature
is—the universe exists in a particular way. We do not have any
further explanation. Even the most successful investigation of
causes leads finally to a certain set of basic facts and laws beyond
which researchers cannot go with existing theories and instrumentation. If science should advance from this point, perhaps

still more basic general laws will be discovered. But then the chain of explanations would again come to an end.

Nature has the character we find it to have and to try to go further than we can go makes no sense. It has therefore been claimed that science does not really explain, for its explanations do not explain the nature of nature. Here we are confronted with one of the so-called ultimate questions. To answer it is impossible. How would one go about explaining why the world is as it is? The only answer to this ultimate "why?" which has been accepted by some, is the positing of a Creator of the world, who planned this universe. But then three new ultimate questions would arise: Where does the Creator come from, how did he create the world out of nothing, and why did he create this particular kind of world? Instead of ending the chain of explanations by accepting the nature of nature, we have now postulated a demiurge of a certain nature.

The above remarks about fundamental facts, general theories, and the limits that scientists reach may have given the impression that some sciences have reached terminal points. This is not at all the case. Most discoveries open up new fields for study. Quite recently, new disciplines have come into being: particle physics, radio astronomy, molecular biology, virology, the systematic study of animal instincts, and many more. There is no "last frontier." "Our knowledge is an island in the infinite ocean of the unknown, and the larger this island grows, the more extended are its boundaries toward the unknown." (Victor Weisskopf)

Natural laws not merely explain certain phenomena; they are also useful, as we have stated before, to predict events. We expect the sun to rise in the morning; the water in the kettle to boil when heated; a child to be born after the usual nine months of gestation, unless some modifying factor intervenes. We accept these events of everyday life with matter-of-factness, unaware of the reason for the certainty of our predictions—the underlying universality of natural laws which determine the future. An exceedingly complex set of laws and experiments made it possible to predict that the atomic bomb, never made before, would probably explode when the "two-billion-dollar gamble" was tested on July 16, 1945, at Alamogordo, N.M. And it did! [6] In general we can say that successful predictions can be made if we are able to apply laws to known and measurable circumstances. But if a prediction in a scientific realm is not confirmed, we may have failed to consider some relevant law, or the conditions are different from what we thought, or the law which we are applying requires modification or reversal.

Does this mean that nature obeys laws? By no means! Law as a scientific concept must not be confused with law as a moral or legal concept. Common and statutory law as well as moral law *prescribe;* they are commands, which we ought to follow. But the idea of "ought" makes no sense in connection with natural law, which merely *describes* the regularities that we find in nature. Nature cannot be said to comply with its own laws; we abstract its laws from natural occurrences, from the behavior of nature, so to speak.

Unfortunately, the prediction of many individual events of particular interest to us in our daily affairs is either uncertain or impossible. The weatherman is often right, but he is also often wrong. The difficulty here is that we are dealing with a vast number of factors that interact dynamically with one another, and these factors are hard to measure. I have spoken previously of the fact that when we drop a small piece of paper, we cannot predict its landing-place.* We all try to predict the reactions of others to what we say and do. Social intercourse would be impossible if everyone's thinking and action were accidental and unpredictable. However, it is easy to be mistaken about the reactions of others. Our educational activities as parents or in our tremendous system of schools, colleges and universities are based on the understanding of psychological facts and laws. But we all know how uncertain this field is. Everyone is interested in economic forecasting. Here, too, we are dealing with the interplay of innumerable factors, not all of which are determinable in advance, and yet it is precisely this exact advance determination of factors that is necessary for infallible prediction. We cannot foresee a sudden strike, a government move, an international incident, which would affect our economy.

There are, finally, certain classes of events which we can explain but not predict. Among these are earthquakes, the sex of animal or human offspring, the events of evolution, some dreams and the death of people. In these cases we may know the laws,

* Chapter IV, p. 69; see also chapter VI, p. 80.

but we cannot establish all the conditions—in the interior of the earth or of a human being, etc.—which we must know in order to make a prediction. Historical and current political events can be traced back to their causes, but predictions in this area are rarely possible.

In talking about scientific laws I have also occasionally used the term "scientific theory." There is no precise difference between the use of the words "laws" and "theories"; they are often interchangeable. It sounds trivial to say that a theory is more theoretical, that is, more abstract. Most scientific observations—that water boils, that heavy substances fall, that table salt consists of sodium and chlorine—are generalized in an experimental law, which is a single statement. We explain these experimental laws by theoretical laws, i.e., by more comprehensive theories: the theory of thermodynamics; the gravitational theory; the quantum theory; also the evolutionary, the genetic, the cellular theories.[7] A theory is usually "a system of several related statements," and from this springs "the greater generality of theories and their relatively more inclusive explanatory power." After a theory has been established, it is sometimes found that it can "cover fresh subject matter" originally not considered. As previously mentioned, the Newtonian theory embraces not only the laws of freely falling bodies and of planetary motions, but of tidal action and certain other natural occurrences as well. The quantum theory is one of the most comprehensive theories as it "can explain the experimental laws of spectral phenomena, of thermal properties of solids and gases, of radio-activity, of chemical interactions and of many other phenomena." (Nagel)

Instead of talking about laws and theories, scientists and laymen frequently use the term "hypothesis" to designate an explanatory conceptual scheme. Hypotheses are usually more tentative than laws and theories. What is stated is a conjecture, which must be examined further. The investigator speaks of a "working hypothesis" as a temporary basis for his experiments. Sometimes we formulate comprehensive hypotheses about the origin of the universe or of the planetary system or of life, which go beyond well-founded theories. But the boundary lines between what are called laws, theories and hypotheses are vague, and under many conditions the terms are interchangeable.

Problems Presented by Modern Physics

In discussing the fact that nature is governed by laws I have, as on other occasions, skipped over a considerable number of interesting and controversial problems because they have little bearing on the layman's world view, though they are important to philosophers, particularly to specialists in the philosophy of science, and to scientists interested in the underlying concepts. It is frequently claimed, however, in popular books and articles on philosophy, religion and science, that modern physics has had serious consequences for our world view.* I want, therefore, to discuss at some length several puzzling problems that arise from the theories of modern physics.

Several of the problems I have in mind came up in my White Mountains story. Are solid things such as mountains and rocks really solid or are they in some sense not real? Are they not practically empty space even though they contain trillions of particles (atoms) which themselves are almost empty? And how are we to regard these particles from the viewpoint of modern physics: are they real, are they particles or are they waves?

At this point there should no longer be any serious question about the reality of mountains. This was clarified in the third chapter on "Everyday Knowledge." That which we see when we see mountains and that which we can climb we call "real" or "solid," whatever it consists of. Not all real things are solid. Ice is solid but can change into a liquid or a gas. The different behavior of the water molecules explains whether the substance "water" is solid, liquid, or gaseous. The *physical object* (mountains, water, people) is real, and its kind of existence is explained by the *objects of physics* (molecules, atoms, electrons).[8] We are facing

---

* I commented briefly on the theory of relativity (p. 33). Victor Weisskopf makes the following pertinent comments about the relevancy of the theory of relativity to our world view in the Preface to his excellent small book, *Knowledge and Wonder* (Garden City: Doubleday Anchor, 1963, paperback): "The Einstein theory is one of the greatest achievements of physics and of all science. It has revolutionized our ideas of space and time to such an extent that without Einstein no exact quantitative consideration of space and time is possible. Einstein's ideas, therefore, play a decisive role in the *quantitative* formulation of many scientific problems." We are interested, however, in "the *qualitative* aspects of the picture of the world seen in science. The relativity theory is not absolutely necessary to this view."

There are many popular explanations of this theory, by Einstein himself in *The Meaning of Relativity* and by others.

one reality which we can describe in at least two different ways; in the manner of everyday language and in the framework of the formulas and particle concepts of modern physics. However, the space occupied by the mountains can hardly be considered empty when we realize that 1 cubic centimeter of water (about 6/100 of a cubic inch), which is equal to 1 gram of water, contains 30 sextillion atoms $= 30,000$ billion billion $= 3$ times 10^{22}.

A much more problematic question, considerably debated by the philosophers of science, is the question of the reality of particles, let us say the electrons. Are electrons real, so that we can *discover* them in nature, or are they merely the name of a mathematical notion appearing in the equations of the theoretical physicists, a useful shorthand expression, which the scientist has *invented* to make it simpler for him to talk to other physicists and also to engineers and laymen unfamiliar with the mathematical formulas of particle physics? Past experience has made philosophers cautious. To explain the propagation of light, heat and electricity through space, physicists had assumed the existence of an imponderable ether, omnipresent in the whole universe. But experiments at the end of the last century and modern theories have shown that ether does not exist and that the phenomena which it was supposed to explain can be explained without it. Does the same fate await the entities of particle physics? This is doubtful. The existence of the ether was a mere hypothesis formulated to make understandable that which seemed incomprehensible without it. It was never part of the mathematical formulas as are the nuclear particles and the electrons. Although most kinds of subatomic particles cannot be seen and only their effects can be made visible, very large protein molecules can be enlarged sufficiently to be photographed and the atomic structure of certain molecules and the molecular structure of certain materials can be made visible through X-ray and other modern techniques.

The question of the physical reality of scientific objects such as particles depends also on what we mean by the reality of objects which under no circumstances can be sensed.[9] All we can see are the natural and experimental phenomena that are explained by the quotations of quantum mechanics. These equations have demonstrated over and over again a remarkable capacity to account for an increasing number of phenomena. In these equations certain concepts appear, to which we have given the name atom, electron, neutron, proton, positron, etc.

Whether or not these names denote objects that are real in the ordinary sense of the word is quite unimportant for the theory. The physical theory works in either case.

Only a specialist can judge the controversial philosophic problems of modern physics. Nevertheless, I would be inclined to agree with Weisskopf that "atomic reality . . . is as good as any other concept of reality. It obviously exists in nature, and we can be proud of having discovered it despite its elusive character." Atomic particles are real for the simple reason that since the world as a whole is real, the particles of which it consists must be real too—even though we may be mistaken about one or the other entity. To further support this view let me quote a contemporary philosopher of science:

> If we are realists in regard to the physical world, we must assume that the concepts of theoretical physics, to the extent that they are instantialized in particulars, are not merely calculational devices for the predicition of observational data, but that they denote realities.[10]

Are the subatomic particles really particles or are they to be regarded as waves? While this problem is a consequence of the relatively recent quantum theory, a similar controversy goes much further back. Until the turn of the century, all physicists considered the theory that light is propagated through a minute wave motion firmly established. The brilliant physicist Christian Huygens, a contemporary of Newton, is regarded as the father of this theory, for which there seemed to be excellent experimental evidence. But Newton himself and a few later scientists inclined toward an emission, or particle, theory of light propagation. "Are not the rays of light very small bodies emitted from shining Substances?" [11] Present theory merges the two ideas, so that the physicist R. E. Peierls can say: "We know from the quantum theory that the light *wave* consists of light *quanta*, or photons . . ." (my italics) [12]

Is it possible to make sense out of these paradoxes: do light, heat, radiowaves, X-rays, and the like consist of waves or are they streams of corpuscles, and are the particles of atomic physics really particles or are they waves? The difficulty disappears when we remember that words can have many meanings depending on the context in which they are used. The economist speaks of the liquidity and turnover of money without thinking of water or the pages of a book. When we describe the particles of physics as *waves*, we are merely indicating that in certain circumstances they exhibit properties similar to those of waves; we do not mean to say that, though exceedingly small, they are in all respects like ocean waves or even like the invisible air waves of sound which we can actually feel when an organist plays a low pedal note. Likewise, in speaking of atomic *particles*, we do not mean infinitesimally small billiard balls, particles tinier than grains of sand or dust particles floating in the air.

In many contexts, however, it is practical to refer to atoms as particles, for under some conditions they behave as though they were particles. We know that atoms are composed of other moving entities (electrons, protons, and neutrons) organized like a planetary system. Under certain conditions these entities behave as though they were particles, but they are not particles in the ordinary sense. The wave-particle electron is neither wave nor particle; indeed, it cannot properly be described in the terminology of ordinary language or of classical physics. The words employed are merely "suggestive and heuristically valuable." The only true description of the dual nature of the wave-particle entities can be found in the mathematical language of quantum mechanics. Here the disjunction between wave and particle disappears. But when the physicist goes outside the theoretical vocabulary of formulas, he has to use ordinary language with all its inherent limitations. And when he popularizes his science, he must warn his listeners and readers that "no concepts drawn from the level of common-sense thinking are appropriate to subatomic, i.e., microphysical, phenomena." (L. Susan Stebbing)

Naively, we assume that all occurrences in nature can be visualized with our ordinary intuition and described in everyday pictorial language. This is a prejudice, albeit a natural one. Because we can visualize them, we regard growing, boiling, dissolving, as understandable processes. But we cannot visualize the transformation of mass into energy, that is, of exceedingly small masses into very large amounts of energy (in accordance with Einstein's famous formula $E = mc^2$), such as takes place in nuclear bombs, in the sun and other stars. Neither can we visualize the wave-particle entities of modern physics.

Finally, we must deal briefly with the most puzzling and controversial aspect of modern physics, "the alleged indeterminism of modern quantum mechanics," which is supposed to follow from the so-called *uncertainty principle.** This is a matter about which many popular philosophers, writers, and even theologians and moralists have made a great to-do, but our explanations of macrophysical happenings have not been changed by quantum theory.

The meaning of the uncertainty principle is the fact that the position and the momentum of sub-atomic "particles" (sometimes nicknamed "wavicles"), for example, electrons are so related to each other that the two cannot be determined at the same time. If we know where a wavicle is at a particular moment, we cannot know where it will be the next moment, because we do not know its momentum. And if we know its momentum, we nevertheless cannot know where it will be next, because while establishing its speed we cannot simultaneously establish the position from which it has started. But in employing the simple language we have been using here (frequently used by the physicists, too), we tend to forget that the words particle, wave, momentum, speed and position, are only analogous words in quantum mechanics and do not mean what they mean in ordinary language. Within the framework of quantum theory the simultaneous values of position and momentum cannot be meaningfully applied to an electron.

The factors I have just mentioned cannot be established in quantum mechanics, but other factors can be. Unfortunately, quantum theory requires such abstract and complicated mathematical formulas to state its laws that it has been found extraordinarily difficult to explain it in an intuitively clear and understandable manner.† This does not mean "that in quantum theory the laws of physics have become any less certain or less absolute. It is merely that the information to which the laws refer is of a different nature." (R. E. Peierls) A complete description of the interior state of an atom in the language of classical physics is impossible. We cannot determine therefore

> the state of an atom with such accuracy that its subsequent fate [is] completely predictable in the way in which an as-

* Most contemporary physicists accept the uncertainty principle, though there are a few who try to develop a different interpretation of quantum theory.
 † Because this difficulty besets attempts to explain quantum theory, it tends to limit the knowledge that a non-specialist can acquire about the theory.

tronomer can predict the future position of a planet in the sky. This does not prevent us from predicting the behaviour of bodies containing large systems of atoms with certainty, . . . with all the accuracy we shall ever require. (Peierls)[13]

This rule also naturally refers to the "large system of atoms" which make up a human being. Normally, the condition of our body is predictable. If something happens—say, we are tired or sick—then we look for ordinary causes. The same is true of our own mental behavior and that of others. To explain—as has been done—"miracles" of human action, such as the conversion of Saul to Paul, by reference to "quantum-indeterminate" brain-states, to the "play in the machine," is an unfortunate misconception and a misuse of quantum theory for religious purposes.

As though the various controversies surrounding the philosophic aspects of quantum theory were not sufficiently confusing, an additional one has been raised by the so-called complementarity principle, also known as the Copenhagen interpretation of quantum theory, after the great Danish physicist Niels Bohr. This principle means two things. On the one hand, it refers to the dual character of sub-atomic entities as waves and particles, which complement each other, as we have discussed. On the other hand, it means that the uncertainty principle is the outcome of an uncertainty introduced by the fact that atomic events involve such tiny entities that their behavior is influenced and disturbed by the laboratory instruments that measure them. But, the fact that measuring instruments disturb the objects being measured is insufficient to explain the significance of the uncertainty principle. It is not unusual for an observer and his instruments to influence that which is observed. This condition is not unique to particle physics. It occurs in ordinary life,* in classical physics, and in medicine, particularly psychiatry.

The uncertainty principle is part of the basic mathematical apparatus of quantum theory and is not the consequence of disturbing experimental devices. The mathematical formulations of the uncertainty principle cannot be paraphrased in ordinary language without leading to misunderstanding. For example, it

---

* In judging a person, for instance, we must take into account how much our love, anger, concern, or irony has contributed to the particular attitude or action of the person we are observing.

would be rash to conclude that the indeterminacy principle implies an indeterminacy in nature or is relevant to questions of freedom of will, as has often been maintained.

In view of the far-ranging consequences that are ascribed to the uncertainty principle, I shall conclude this presentation of the implications of modern physics with a lengthy quotation from Nagel's *The Structure of Science:*

> In consequence, the statistical content of quantum mechanics does not annul the deterministic and non-statistical structure of other physical laws. It also follows that conclusions concerning human freedom and moral responsibility, when based on the alleged "acausal" and "indeterministic" behavior of subatomic processes, are built on sand. Neither the analysis of physical theory, nor the study of the subject matter of physics, yields the conclusion that "There is no strict causal behavior anywhere."

Scientific Discoveries and Scientific Errors

I want to return now to the discussion of the nature of scientific laws in general. How are scientific laws discovered? Is there a particular method by which we can search for scientific laws, "some *one* master procedure underlying all scientific work"? [14] Yes and no. Yes, in the sense that all scientists strive for truth through accurate, objective fact-finding, generalizing, and rational reporting; they use "reflection, observation, experimentation, imagination, and a measure of intuition." No, because individual scientists work in ways peculiar to each of them. They differ from each other as do other human beings. Moreover, the separate branches of the sciences require different techniques, instruments and vocabularies. The technical methods of the archaeologist cannot be used by the sociologist or the economist. And their methods, in turn, are obviously useless to the particle physicist and the biochemist.

What is common to all scientists is to investigate factual problems, unanswered questions, and try to solve them. Various ideas and informed guesses which occur to them must be examined. It is only the fully prepared mind that can follow up a new truth. This procedure, which sounds so easy, perhaps even glamorous, in reality requires "a life spent in the laboratory, at the desk, or in field expeditions." The layman hears of the great accomplishments of Albert Einstein, Niels Bohr and Jonas Salk; he knows all too little of the tremendous amount of patient, tiring, hard and dull work that is involved in experimenting, testing, and applying mathematical methods. "The major clue may appear only at the end of a long investigation." The scientist can be compared with the performing musician or dancer. We take note of a few magnificent artists, forget the numberless minor performers and teachers, and ignore the endless hours that all performers, great and small, spend in tiresome practicing.

The cumulative and international character of science requires that all scientists be fully familiar with the present state of knowledge in their field. This is no easy task as great numbers of specialists frequently work on the same problems, and findings are published in hundreds of periodicals. Indeed, a unique concern has recently emerged, namely, how to keep track of the tremendous amount of material being published and make it available so that scientists can quickly lay their hands on it.

In the progress of science as well as in the evaluation of science as a career, we must distinguish between the typical and often routine but absolutely essential work of most scientists most of the time and the occasional revolutionary discoveries and theories. Of the latter John Dewey said: "Every great advance in science has issued from a new audacity of imagination." But patience, sweat, and money are just as important in the day-to-day operations of scientists.

In view of the accomplishments of the scientific method we may wonder how it is possible for science to make mistakes. Of course, it is not science that makes mistakes, but individual scientists. To err is human. "Science is made by people, and it has their style." It is as difficult for scientists as it is for the rest of us to free themselves from judgments once formed, from the prejudices of the period in which they live, from the theories that were in vogue when they did their early work. Individual scientists reveal themselves as normal human beings in finding it awkward to accept the idea that they are fallible. The historic development of science, however, corrects errors, especially today, when so many scientists are engaged in testing all observations and theories.

To laymen science looks more haphazard than it really is because of the publicity given to some scientific controversies

and because of occasional changes in scientific outlook. However, in all the important *older* sciences there exists a firm body
of knowledge of really extraordinary dimensions. One has only
to look at the voluminous standard works in physics, chemistry,
astronomy, biology, medicine, psychology and so on to realize
how much we know and how fatuous is the occasional diatribe
about "the bankruptcy of science." The newest fields, in which
matters are still in flux, are likely to be the most controversial,
cosmogony for instance, and the origin of neuroses and psy-
choses; or anthropology, where the discovery of a new skeleton
may upset previously held theories. Cultural "progress" sometimes raises entirely new problems, such as the relation of the
incidence of lung cancer to smoking, the danger of fall-out and
the causes of juvenile delinquency. Here too, commercial, political and military interests clash, intensifying the character of the
controversies. There are serious obstacles to the development of
a body of correct predictive laws about human society, and consequently, economics and sociology will probably not reach the
exactness of physics and will therefore remain more controversial. Certain aspects of psychology and psychiatry do not lend
themselves to the exactness of the biological sciences.

Some scientific controversies get into the daily press and become generally known because they concern matters that have
to do with our health—fall-out, smoking and water fluoridation
for example. Others are of interest to laymen because they touch
on his world view. The theory of evolution was a battleground
for scientists, clergymen and laymen for more than fifty years;
emphasis on sex made psychoanalysis anathema for a long time.
But with the acceptance of nearly all modern fundamental scientific theories by most organized religions, which I shall discuss in
the next chapter, the prolonged and intense disputes between
science and religion have been silenced.

Scientists frequently formulate speculative working hypotheses, which may later be overthrown. A tentative hypothesis, an idea, is propounded, and new facts are aligned in a new
way with already known facts when the factual material is not
yet sufficient. Good scientists know when they don't know and
when they are on uncertain, speculative ground. Science is an
unfinished, constantly growing enterprise, but its theories are not
being constantly changed.

However, there have been occasions in the history of science when well established, important theories have been overthrown. New facts are discovered, often because advances in technology make better instruments possible. What happens, then, to the facts on which the old theories were built? If they were facts, they remain facts and find their explanation in the newer theory. Newton's laws and formulas, as applied to free fall and planetary movements, have not been overthrown, but have become a special case within the wider frame of the theory of relativity. Atomic theory of the eighteenth and nineteenth centuries assumed indivisible atoms. Today we know that the atom can be split. But the old theory is still useful as a practical tool in describing the chemical structure of various substances and their chemical interactions. The newer picture of the atom, in turn, explains not only how and why different atoms interact with each other but many additional facts. Finally, certain theories, such as the theory of the ether, have been completely abandoned because nothing like the ether could be found and because other explanations accounted for the relevant phenomena.

The more stable and important aspect of scientific inquiry is found, not in any particular conclusions reached, but in the methods employed to attain them. Though scientists make mistakes, the methods they use have led to reliable knowledge. It may be appropriate at this point to repeat a statement I made at the end of the last chapter: "Objective and untiring study in a free and self-critical community leads the way to truth 'to the end of reckoning.'"

The Aim of Pure Science

I touched briefly at the beginning of this chapter on the different natures and goals of pure and applied science. However, the purpose of pure science deserves further observations. One of man's most remarkable characteristics is his tremendous desire to understand his own and nature's behavior, to find explanations for everything that happens, to penetrate nature's secrets. Nevertheless this impulse of human nature has been neglected, almost forgotten, during many centuries. The days of Greek antiquity and our own post-Renaissance era have been the outstanding periods for the flowering of science. The great French mathematician and thinker, Henri Poincaré indicates why scientists value science as an absorbing "ideal good":

The scientist does not study nature because it is useful; he
studies it because he delights in it, and he delights in it because
it is beautiful. If nature were not beautiful, it would not be
worth knowing, and if nature were not worth knowing, life
would not be worth living. Of course, I do not here speak of
that beauty which strikes the senses, the beauty of qualities
and of appearances; not that I undervalue such beauty, far
from it, but it has nothing to do with science; I mean that
profounder beauty which comes from the harmonious order
of the parts and which a pure intelligence can grasp. This it
is which gives body, a structure so to speak, to the iridescent
appearances which flatter our senses, and without this support
the beauty of these fugitive dreams would be only imperfect,
because it would be vague and always fleeting. On the contrary,
intellectual beauty is sufficient unto itself, and it is, for its
sake, more perhaps than for the future good of humanity, that
the scientists devotes himself to long and difficult labors.[15]

Merle A. Tuve, whom I have quoted before, expressed himself as
follows:

I believe that science must firmly be included among the
liberalizing humanities in any honest assessment of modern
thought and knowledge. The beauty and simplicity of the
laws of nature which govern the world in which we find ourselves, the fantastic range today of man's ideas and studies and
measurements, from the countless galaxies in the distant reaches
of outer space far beyond the faintest stars of our own Milky
Way, down to the structure inside the atomic nucleus, this is
vision enough to humble the most arrogant. The poetically
beautiful patterns of modern scientific knowledge bear fresh
witness in a whole new range of thoughts and qualities and
dimensions to the Psalmist's ancient cry: "The heavens declare
the glory of God and the firmament showeth His handiwork."
Lest anyone here has lost sight of it, let me tell you that this
attitude, all too rarely spoken in these days of secular support,
is historically and still today the essential spirit of all scientific
study and research. This spirit of wonder and exaltation is the
ancient root and the modern strength of all our Western search
for new knowledge.

Most of the eminent scientists have felt the spiritual greatness of science. In a more religious age it was assumed that a direct proof of the workings of a beneficent Deity could be found
in the orderliness of nature which science disclosed to us and
which seemed to show up especially in the laws of planetary
movements. But whatever the relation between science and religion may be, the appeal of science can be felt by all of us.

The pursuit of well-ordered knowledge is one of the greatest pleasures in which man can indulge:* the scientist in his daily work, and the rest of us indirectly, through the vast number of excellent popular books on all phases of science, one of the most praiseworthy of contemporary developments. The intricacy and variety of nature's processes can keep us pleasantly occupied during a long lifetime, yet there is always more to learn; the chain of secrets to be probed is never-ending. Poets and singers have immortalized the beauty of nature as it appears to our untutored eyes, but there is another kind of poetry and beauty in the appreciation of the inner workings of nature.

On this level, science exerts a humanizing influence on those who study and practice it. The greatness of nature and the difficulties of the scientific enterprise teach us humility. Science also has a directly moral value. It is an enterprise that demands the cooperation of many people. Honesty, reliability, carefulness and objectivity in performance and reporting are absolute requisites for all scientific work; they are the necessary conditions for determining factual truth. However, scientists are not necessarily all-around better people, any more than clergymen. The philosophic friends of science like to think—hopefully— that "the organization of science as a community of free, tolerant, yet alertly critical inquirers embodies in remarkable measure the ideals of liberal civilization." [16]

There is a tendency among some scientists and laymen to overestimate the usefulness of science in shaping our lives. Scientists can be teachers of science, they are not medicine men, high priests, or "how-to" experts. More than exact analysis and scientific knowledge are required for the competent conduct of affairs. The creation of a useful harmonious life is an art, not a matter of scientific calculation. However, this does not relieve us from carrying the scientific, objective study of all personal and communal affairs as far as it is possible to do so.

The importance of science in society should go beyond technological significance—"better things for better living." Many questions of public policy ought to be liberated from old-fashioned prejudices and the partisan bias of political passions and subjected to more objective, thorough, scientific investigation. At the construction site of a large bridge and in the oper-

---

* Aristotle's famous praise of philosophy would today be transferred by many to science; see above, p. 24.

ating room of a hospital the scientifically trained expert is in control, but the public policies of the nations of the world are influenced too little by experts trained in economics, political science, social welfare and public health.

In making use of the scientist, however, we must be careful.

> Scientists sometimes forget that they cease to be experts when they leave their laboratories, and that in deciding questions foreign to science, they have no more (but, of course, no less) claim to attention than anyone else.[17]

Scientists are not supermen. They can be vain about their dignity and reputation, too interested in their personal power, oversensitive about their standing in the academic hierarchy. In short, scientists are people.

Science: Pro and Con

What I have said about science so far may give the impression that science is and ought to be regarded as an enterprise that is in general beneficent. This evaluation of science has been seriously questioned. As early as 1921, Norman Campbell wrote that it had been "seriously urged . . . that science, being responsible for the horrors of modern warfare, is a danger to civilization." What should we say today, when atomic bombs have been dropped, supersonic missiles with hydrogen bomb warheads have been built and nuclear submarines armed with missiles secretly cross the oceans? I am afraid that as long as the nations of the world do not get together and realize the age-old ideal of Isaiah—"nation shall not lift up sword against nation, neither shall they learn war anymore"—just so long will scientists lend a hand not merely for the civilian but also for the military benefit of their country. Fortunately, many scientists are in the forefront of educational and political efforts to cope with the extreme dangers that confront us as the result of the originally peaceful and purely scientific undertaking to split the uranium atom. It seems to me that it is the particular moral and civic duty of experts to do their best to overcome the harm that their work may cause, not because they have brought it about but because they are the most knowledgeable people in this field.

We are frequently unprepared when new technologies bring about novel and troublesome, if not dangerous situations.

Here, of course, the scientist ought to show foresight and cooperation in finding remedies. But our society is so ramified and its
decision-making power so diffused that it is difficult for scientists to make themselves heard. The words of knowledge penetrate, but slowly.

Science and Religion

One of the most decisive consequences of the advance of
science has been its impact on religion. Practically all educated
people today regard many of the Biblical stories as myths, while
superstition, which ruled the healing arts, has been replaced by
scientific medicine. The vast cosmic spaces that seemed to be the
realm of God are subject to scientific investigation. The atmosphere of our age has become more and more permeated with the
spirit of science, while belief in the truth of the theoretical and
metaphysical teachings of the great religions has gradually dimin-
ished. Science seems to have pushed religion aside or passed it by
and in some degree to have taken its place.

Has science, then, perhaps become the religion of modern
man and contemporary society? The relation between science
and religion is a problem that has been debated ever since
worldly philosophy and science have existed together. Today
the heated arguments of the last century and early part of this
one have ended. The churches in general have stopped attacking
science as such and most scientific findings. The scientists, in
their turn, leave the churches and the theologians alone and concentrate on their scientific work. Nevertheless, there are a considerable number of people on both sides who try to build
bridges and to eliminate the differences. Many of these attempts
—through conferences, books and sermons—are illusory, if not
deceptive, because they employ ambiguous vocabularies. Key
terms—God, devotion, idealism, spirituality, faith, science, religion—are used in such a way that the distinctions between them
are lost. Analogies are confused with identities. The issues, instead of being clarified, become clouded. One of the most paradoxical men is the scientist when he tries to put on clerical garb.

> It is odd how readily a few scientists abandon life-long habits
> of buttressed reasoning and cautious utterance once they
> leave their circumscribed fields and take a fling in the wider
> realms of mysticism. (Ernest Borek)[18]

Whether science is one of the religions of contemporary intellectuals is to some extent a semantic problem. If we regard religion as that to which men are devoted and that which is central to their lives, then science may be called a religion for those scientists who know no other interest, to whom science is both occupation and hobby. The truly religious person, in the usual and dictionary sense of the word, is one who is devoted to God. It will only create confusion if we call that which preoccupies a man's heart and mind his religion. If we were to use the term in this sense, then farming, flying, skiing, money-making, power, could be called the religion of some people instead of merely their primary or perhaps even exclusive interest. Because certain scientists glorify science above everything else, we should not call science a religion. These scientists might very well be agnostics or atheists.

An equally unfortunate semantic confusion ensues if we use the term "religion" for what is usually meant by idealism and spirituality. Many scientists find an outlet for their idealism in their scientific work. We can readily sympathize with this attitude, especially in those, for example, who are doing successful work in the elimination or cure of disease. Other scientists, too, have idealistic and spiritual feelings about science (see the quotation from Henri Poincaré, p. 112). But profound devotion to science is not devotion to God.*

Science does not give us any assurance that there is a beneficent God who has created the world, and man as a special creature in it. Unlike religion, there is no absolute certainty in science. When it is equated with religion, its self-critical nature is disregarded. But the venerated teachings of the various religions can never be proved either correct or false, as they are based on faith, authority and revelation. Science is not concerned with accounting for existence in general. It does not say *why* the world is as it is; it tells us *how* the world is and explains how it operates. It does not discuss the purpose of man and the final ends of the

* Other definitions of religion have been arbitrarily formulated to muddle the relation between science and religion. "Religion is man's effort to orient himself in his total environment." "Religion is man's effort to promote advance." These definitions, to which innumerable similar ones could be added, are from *Science Ponders Religion*, edited by Harlow Shapley (New York: Appleton-Century-Crofts, 1960), an astounding effort revealing the philosophic ineptness of scientific experts, yet culturally and psychologically interesting as a manifestation of the anxiety of many intellectual leaders not to be regarded as irreligious.

universe. It does not follow from this disavowal, however, that we can find an answer to these "ultimate questions" and a non-scientific, religious way to account for the world and its purpose.

Some apologists for religion, believing that religion and science have common aspects, have claimed that science, too, rests on faith. But to equate religious faith and so-called scientific faith is to reveal either a lack of real religious faith or ignorance of the true nature of science. We use the term "faith" in everyday language. We speak of faith in our physician, in our spouse; we even say "faithful car." In this sense it indicates our confidence. It is a pragmatic faith, which can be tested and even overthrown. But when Job says, "Though He slay me, yet will I trust Him," and St. Paul writes of faith as "the assurance of things hoped for, the conviction of things not seen," they are not talking about pragmatic, testable faith, but absolute, unconditional faith in Him who is in or beyond the universe in a manner that *transcends* experience. But science deals with experience, and its findings are tested by experience. The scientist's "faith" goes no further than what he can establish by experiment; it is not an absolute faith. "Faith" in the truth of the statement, "There are people here now," or in the formulas of the general theory of relativity does not give us assurance when our faith in God is shattered. The scientist's "faith" is really his drive for factual truth, his constant endeavor to explain reality through laws and theories and, on the basis of them, to make predictions about future events.

To this last point it has been countered that the scientist has faith not in any particular scientific fact or theory, but in the orderliness of nature or in the scientific method. The orderliness of nature is something we can discover and test. As far as the scientific method is concerned, it is merely an extension of the ordinary, everyday procedure we follow to find the truth.

The "orderliness" scientists find in nature is frequently presented as an argument for the existence of a great and apparently mathematically-minded God. But the orderliness of nature is deceptive. Orderliness in the sense of regularity is what the scientist finds and what his formulas cover. There are no exceptions to it, no room for God's intervention. But order can also be used as a value term, in the sense of harmony. The poet, John G. Whittier, speaks of "the calm beauty of an ordered life." But it is doubtful whether nature is orderly in that sense or whether it is not rather disorderly, lacking harmony. The terms order and disorder presuppose a scheme, a purpose, or an ideal; they have nothing to do with the scientist's work, even though they can be applied to nature. If we do apply them, the question arises, how nature measures up and what it proves about God's beneficence. The spider web and the wasp's nest hanging in the tree seem beautifully ordered. But how do they appear to the fly caught by the spider or the child stung by the wasp? And what role do we assign to the storm, which destroys the web and tears the nest from the branch? A virus works according to the laws of its nature, but it can kill a young mother. The solar system seems a paradigm of eternal order, but it was born in a most disorderly manner, perhaps in a stellar explosion or out of a tremendous stellar fog—scientists are not sure, and one day it will come to an end. It is a completely arbitrary matter, depending on our mood and esthetic sense, whether or not we call the universe orderly in the sense in which we use the word here. The observations of the scientist and his complicated equations, as such, do not bolster religious faith. Whether the feeling of awe and reverence which nature may inspire in us can establish the existence of a supernatural realm and of God is a problem which is better left for the later discussion of religion.

Science, accused of having usurped the place of religion, is then belittled as unable to serve the functions that religion supposedly does. But science *per se*, as an investigating and theorizing activity, has neither undertaken religion's presumed role nor intends to do so. Science as an absorbing interest and hobby may, for some scientists, fill needs which, for other men, are met by the contemplation of God, prayer, church-going, holiday celebrations. In this restricted sense science may be called a substitute for religion.

But science cannot fill all the needs of our mind and our emotions. Nor does it want to range far from its field, which is the increase of knowledge. One of the charges against it is "its failure to minister to the needs of the soul." For some individuals it does—this is merely accidental—for some it does not. The belittlers of science and the champions of religion erect a straw man when they complain that "it does not seize the ultimate truths. . . . It does not soothe [man's] fundamental disquietude or fulfill his needs to evolve a moral law, to rest secure in the faith that death opens the door to another life," that it lacks relevancy "to the one necessity, our salvation." (Henri Peyre commenting on Blaise Pascal.) But these criticisms cannot disturb science or scientists, for they are analogous to the complaint that a portrait of George Washington does not advise us in our present political predicaments. The portrait, nevertheless, does not lose its value for us. Science is not metaphysics, religion, psychotherapy, or ethics; not politics, art, music or literature; nor is it feelings. There are dimensions of our mind and heart that are beyond science. And still it is true, as C. P. Snow, with some exaggeration, says:

> The scientific edifice of the physical world [is] in its intellectual depth, complexity and articulation, the most beautiful and wonderful collective work of the mind of man.

I want to make an additional point here about another limitation of science, which scientists are sometimes accused of overstepping. It ought to be obvious that the biochemical explanation of the nature of a rose or of a woman's lovely face does not account for their beauty, nor does the scientific description of our neural apparatus make clear to us why we esteem beauty in nature and the arts. The biophysical description of the workings of our glands does not make clear to us the nature of love or anger. Science does not *reduce* knowing, feeling and appreciating, to biophysics. Such reductionism, also called the "nothing-but fallacy" must be avoided. A scientist who "falls for" a "reductionist scientism" is rightly accused of narrow-mindedness. But most scientists, in Nagel's words, exhibit "an unequaled and tender sensitivity to the aesthetic and moral dimensions of human experience," and they appreciate to the same degree as non-scientists —and sometimes more so—"the role of moral idealism and of intellectual and aesthetic contemplation in human life."

CHAPTER VI

"Man's Place in Nature"*

Several of the sciences mentioned in the preceding chapter deal with man. They have, therefore, a great deal to offer in answer to Kant's question: What is man? This is not to say that only the sciences are competent to discuss man. Every religion deals with the problem of man's nature, as do the arts—Shakespeare and Dostoevsky, Rembrandt and Rodin, Mozart and Verdi, all give us deep insights into man's situation—and philosophers, too, have devoted their thoughts to the subject of the "essence" of man. Man is on the one hand a part of nature, an object, an "it" in the universe. On the other hand, he is both a spectator and an actor, one who values what he experiences and creates new values, through art, science and the devices he fashions for his daily life. Each of us is not just an "it" but also an "I." It can be said of man that though he is made of dust, he ponders things eternal. Clearly, then, our view cannot be based on the sciences alone. However, it is important to know the facts of man's nature, and these facts we learn from the sciences.

* The title of this chapter has been taken from the distinguished biologist Thomas Huxley (1825-95), grandfather of the brothers Aldous and Julian Huxley. In 1863 he gave an epochal lecture entitled "Man's Place in Nature," a defense of Darwin's theory of evolution, then recently published.

The Biblical Version of Man's Nature and Its Overthrow

Let us first take a look at what used to be the generally accepted theory in the Western world of man's place in nature. We find it in the Bible, in the first three chapters of Genesis,* a majestic and wonderful story, glorified by Michelangelo in the Sistine Chapel, by Haydn in his oratorio *The Creation*, and by innumerable artists and poets.

The Biblical story, believed by most Western people from the time they converted to Christianity until fairly recently, has three important aspects:

1. There is *a creator*, God. "God said, 'Let there be light'; and there was light."

2. God created *a finished world*. All things in the universe —the stars, the sun, all living plants and animals and man—were created in the shape and manner in which they now exist. The Bible describes the creation of animals, for example, as follows: "God said, 'Let the earth bring forth every kind of living creature: cattle, creeping things, and wild beasts of every kind.' And it was so. . . . And God saw how good this was."

3. For us a most important facet of the creation story is the pleasing idea that God gave man a special character and a special position in the universe. (This, by the way, is much less significant in the more playful and somewhat confused stories of Greek mythology.) "And God created man in His image, in the image of God He created him; male and female He created them. God blessed them and God said to them, 'Be fertile and increase, fill the earth and master it; and rule the fish of the sea, the birds of the sky, and all the living things that creep on earth.'" The idea of man's kinship with God is still fundamental to Western religion.

But the unearthing of thousands of varieties of fossils demonstrated that something was wrong with the Biblical creation story, for these fossils revealed that plants and animals once existed which have become extinct, that many plants and animals which exist now, man in particular, are of comparatively

* Every people has conceived myths on the origin of man. The Biblical story has roots in the mythologies of several Oriental people who lived in the Near East long before the Jews made their appearance in history.

recent origin, and that the earth has undergone a slow and gradual development over several billions of years. Under the impact
of these discoveries, culminating in the theory of evolution,
modern religions have given up the idea of a creation according
to a static pattern and substituted a creation developing in time in
an evolutionary process. This change in thinking has eliminated
the second aspect of the creation story enumerated above but not
the other two.*

The idea that man was not created on the sixth day but appeared on earth rather late seems not necessarily in contradiction
to what is essential in our religions.

Most modern naturalists and humanists, however, have gone
much further and have abandoned all aspects of the creation
story. Man is now regarded as one of the products of natural
development, albeit a rather unique and complicated one, thanks
to his brain.

This overturn of the creation story or, for many people, at
least a weakening of belief in it, was a startling experience in the
intellectual growth of Western mankind. Until a few generations
ago the earth was pictured as the center of the universe. Over-
head, in the canopy of the sky were the sun, the moon and the
stars, and beyond was heaven, God and the angels. Somewhere
below were hell and purgatory. Man ruled on earth as a special
child of God. This anthropocentric, geocentric and heliocentric
(man-, earth-, sun-centered) view, however, has been replaced by
a decentered view: our great, life-supporting sun is merely an
average star in one of myriads of galaxies, and we are one of
numberless "beasts" on a minor planet. We may not even be the
only thinking beings in the universe. (This is not science fiction
but a theoretical possibility which I will describe later.) Our
pride has been deflated. But though each one of us is naturally
egocentric, as well as family-, nation-, and humanity-centered,
we are bound to adjust our philosophies, our world view, our
creeds, to the universe as we actually find it. Our "place in nature" cannot be discovered through speculation, but only
through fact-finding, i.e., observational, scientific thinking.

* It is not generally known that the Catholic Church too has adopted a
tolerant attitude toward the evolutionary theory. See the Encyclical *Humani
generis* of Pope Pius XII (August 12, 1950).

The Universe

I will now try to marshall the most significant facts from the fields of astronomy, biology and anthropology for a portrayal of man's place in nature. The earth, our home, is "one of the smaller planets of a typical star. . . . Our solar system is minute by cosmic standards." [1] The sun is 93,000,000 miles away from us. Its light, moving at the speed of 186,000 miles per second, reaches us in eight minutes and reaches the planets that are farthest away in a few hours. However, "the nearest star is so far away that light from it . . . takes four years to reach us." * Thus we see that by earthly standards solid bodies in the universe are exceedingly far apart. The solar system is part of a still larger system, the spiral galaxy, which appears to us as the Milky Way. A galaxy is a group of hundreds of billions of stars that belong together. The universe contains many billions of such galaxies, the nearest ones, such as the Andromeda nebula, being a few millions of light years away, the more distant ones, many billions of light years off. Distances are inconceivably large, as is the number of stars. The universe contains more stars than there are grains of sand on all the beaches of the earth. This world picture, Lovell says, "is not seriously questioned today." The stars and galaxies are incredibly far away and the messages they send us have to be interpreted from their light, and from radio and other waves that we can either see with the naked eye or observe through optical and radio telescopes. The vastnesses of interstellar space are not empty but contain particles and radiation.

Unfortunately the cosmogonist, who studies the origin of the universe, cannot answer with a high degree of certainty the question we ask of him, which men have asked since time immemorial. Taking the known facts into consideration, the preponderant theory today is what has been popularly called "the big-bang theory," that is, that our universe had a beginning in time and evolved through the explosion of an incredibly dense cosmic globe some ten to thirteen billion years ago. The resulting

---

* Astronomical distances are frequently expressed in light years. One light year is 186,000 miles times 60 times 60 times 24 times 365 equal to 6 trillion miles or 6×10^{12}. The nearest star, Alpha Centauri, is 24 trillion miles away. Because of the distances involved, it is highly improbable that our spaceships could ever reach stars outside our own planetary system, even if present technology improved tremendously.

development and expansion of our universe will continue for
many billions of years. Several astronomers have suggested that
the universe will then return gradually to the state of the primeval atom, whereupon it may undergo other cycles of explosion,
expansion and congealment. This hypothesis describes the universe as a pulsating affair. However, some scientists speak of
present theories of cosmogony as mere conjecture and speculation.[2]

If this state of affairs seems unsatisfactory, if one of our
most interesting "ultimate questions" cannot be definitively answered by the astronomers, if the origin of the universe is still
uncertain, then why not return to the simple mystery of the religious solution? But it would be a hasty abdication of our reasoning power to substitute the word "God," with whatever hazy
ideas are attached to this word, for a real explanation of the numerous important astronomical facts that have become known.
We are here dealing with events that we cannot investigate experimentally and about which basic knowledge is quite recent. We
should not therefore become impatient or draw prematurely pessimistic conclusions about the limitations of the human mind. We
should accept the temporary fact that at this particular moment
in the history of science we cannot say with certainty whether
the universe has always existed or whether there was a first in-
stant of physical time, a concept that we may find difficult to
grasp.

As the sun, the other planets and our own earth are much
closer to us, we know more about the history of the solar system
than we do about the history of other parts of the universe. It
probably was born four and a half billion years ago out of a
cloud of hydrogen gas containing a mixture of heavier elements.
To a large extent the planets consist of the heavier elements in
that cloud. The earth gradually cooled and developed the peculiar set of conditions which made life possible: the proper atmosphere and temperature, water and soil. Of our earth Stuart Chase
has written: "If we do not blow ourselves up with foolish atomic
experiments, or waste our resources . . . we can be reasonably
sure of a pleasant and stimulating home in a hospitable universe,
for a long time to come.[3] Astronomers calculate that the raw
materials of the sun are sufficient to keep it hot for another five
billion years. (What possibilities are thus open to man, who is
only a million or so years old!)

New technologies and those still in the developmental stage such as television cameras and other instruments sent through the solar system and space, and telescopes placed on the moon and on orbital platforms, will make possible astronomical observations that are free from the interference of the earth's atmosphere. This may well lead to the clarification of numerous problems concerning the nature and origin of the universe. Moreover, the investigation of the geology of the moon will help in the determination of the origin of the earth and the sun's planetary system.

Our sun does not seem to be the only star that is surrounded by a planetary system. If there are planets orbiting around other stars, we have difficulties observing them with our present instrumentation. But if only one star out of one million in our Milky Way Galaxy had a planetary system, there would be more than 100,000 such systems. And there would be over one trillion in the part of the universe within the reach of telescopes. Planetary systems and life on them arise under certain conditions. The sun and its planet earth obviously developed the necessary conditions. If similar conditions prevail in other parts of the universe we may conjecture that life will develop. "If you start with a universe containing protons, neutrons and electricity, life will eventually appear. It will pursue evolution. And this gives man his place in the universe. He is the most complex being, the first matter which has begun to contemplate itself." (George Wald) Is it far-fetched to assume, as some astronomers and other scientists in fact do, that among the vast number of probable other planets in the universe there are some that are suitable for living organisms, perhaps even including thinking beings? [4]

One may ask: How can man help but feel humble in the incomprehensible vastness of the universe? Is he not an insignificant little beast rushing about over the face of a small planet that goes whirling around an average sun somewhere out there among billions of much larger ones? Cosmically speaking, man is indeed not significant, but he ought never be insignificant to himself. The realization of the immensity of the universe and its complexity should free us from arrogance and pretense and teach us modesty and patience; it should not lead to self-deprecation. The impression of the star-studded sky has always appealed to the poetic or the philosophic streak in man. The mathematician, Frank Ramsay, puts it well when he says:

> I don't feel the least humble before the vastness of the heavens. The stars may be large, but they cannot think or love; and these are qualities which impress me far more than size does.

Similarly, the philosopher Harold Titus replies to "astronomically speaking, man is insignificant," with "astronomically speaking, man is the astronomer." Pascal, on the other hand, expressed what would now be called our existential fear:

> When I consider the short duration of my life, swallowed up in the eternity before and after, the little space which I fill, and even can see, engulfed in the infinite immensity of space of which I am ignorant, and which knows me not, I am frightened, and am astonished at being here rather than there, . . . why now rather than then.

I find Kant's attitude, quoted earlier, more profound and more meaningful:

> Two things fill the mind with ever new and increasing admiration and awe: the starry heavens above me and the moral law within me.

Everything in the universe consists of radiation of various kinds and certain fundamental particles that are manifestations of energy: electrons, protons and neutrons. The last two, in turn, consist of still smaller entities whose nature and relations to each other are not yet fully understood. The combinations and physical processes of the particles in the stars, in the nebulae, and in space are comparatively simple, but they occur at enormous temperatures and under conditions not merely unknown on earth, but difficult, if not impossible, to duplicate in experiments. Knowledge about these processes is relatively recent.

The ninety-two chemical elements that are found on earth (and the artificially created ones) are combinations of atomic particles which can exist in the earth's moderate temperatures. Normally, most of these combinations are stable. Many of the elements are commonly known: hydrogen, oxygen, carbon, sulphur, uranium, the various metals, etc. The elements can combine chemically with each other to form countless substances, which, in various compositions and combinations, make up the earth and organic matter. There is thus a certain unity in the universe: a few identical nuclear particles make up everything that exists in it. On the next level of organization, we find that some of the same elements that form rocks are also in plants, animals and man. The idea that man is made of stardust sounds quite romantic, but it states a fundamental truth. The biochemical processes, however, which make life possible, are distinguishable from most other chemical processes in the universe by their extraordinary complexity.

What Is Life?

What characterizes a living organism? How does it differ from a rock or a crystal "growing" in a solution? All live organisms, plants and animals alike, absorb certain substances from their environment, break them down chemically and from them synthesize their own complicated material. *They have a metabolism.* Of the higher animals we say that they eat, drink and digest. "The essence of living matter is an arrangement of chemicals capable of reproducing the pattern." (Stuart Chase) Organisms grow and die.* One of the most significant characteristics of all organisms is the fact that they propagate; that is, they multiply, either by cellular division or the splitting off of parts, or by a great variety of sexual processes. Hence, an organism is endowed both with the faculty of living and creating new life identical with its own pattern.

The question, "What is life?" has been one of man's most important and intriguing problems. Does life require, as the so-called vitalists claim, a special energy, a unique life-principle or life-force, some imponderable life-stuff, perhaps a spirit or a soul? These speculations became academic when scientists learned in the first half of the nineteenth century how to synthesize a few of the substances that are essential to life. Since then biochemists have made tremendous strides in synthesizing innumerable organic substances, including certain proteins. Thus, the "uncrossable chasm [which] was supposed to separate the realm of the living, organic world and the realm of the nonliving, inorganic world" [5] has vanished. We now know that established laws of physics and chemistry govern life processes. It is not merely the evolutionary idea, taken from its original biological realm and

* However, one-celled organisms may be regarded as immortal. The mother-cell divides and the daughter-cells, each a part of the original organism, go on living.

applied to the whole universe, which has revolutionized our thinking. The discovery of the unitary lawfulness of nature also is an influential element in our modern naturalistic outlook.

Returning to the question, "What is life?" we find that the term "life" does not designate a thing or a special entity, a force or apparatus or substance. The word "life" designates the functional process of being alive; it is used very much like such terms as manufacture, digestion and reproduction. ". . . [Life] is a word used to describe the properties and activities of living substance, as observed in animals and plants." (Julian Huxley)

The philosopher calls "reification" (from the Latin word for material thing, *res*) the mistake of regarding as a thing something that is not a thing. It is the fallacy of misplaced concreteness, to use an expression coined by Alfred North Whitehead. Consequently, the question, "What is life?" can be answered only by referring to the process of living.

Something that is alive is called an organism. All organisms have a cellular structure, visible under the microscope. The most primitive ones (plants and animals difficult to distinguish at that level) are unicellular. Man consists of something like fifty trillion cells of many different kinds and purposes. All organic processes, such as the production of energy, the manufacture of new material for growth, the processes leading to locomotion and propagation, to sensations and direction of the organism, take place in cells. The chemical operations within each cell are unbelievably complicated, as a typical cell contains something like one trillion atoms. Their "wonderous efficiency is a never-ending source of awe and admiration." (Ernest Borek)

In describing cellular activities we tend to use such expressions as chemical factory, apparatus, mechanism, machine, instrument and the like. We must bear in mind, however, that nothing man has devised so far compares even remotely with the living cell in complexity. In a cell of microscopic size thousands of chemical reactions take place simultaneously, with infinite precision, and at considerable speed. We are far from building a living cell or an organism.

The last twenty-five years have seen the most exciting development of what at first was called biochemistry and biophysics and is now embraced by the term "molecular biology." New techniques have been invented to look inside the cell and to analyze the nature and molecular structure of the proteins, nucleic

acids, and the processes of intracellular interactions. Many riddles have already been solved, and we are at the threshold of
solving many more. While nuclear and space development are the
sensation of today's technical and scientific activity, here is another field of extraordinary theoretical importance and potential
fruitfulness for genetics and medicine.[6]

We take it completely for granted that all plants and animals
have organs that reproduce only their kind. An acorn produces
an oak; out of spider, or salmon or chicken eggs come spiders,
salmon, and chickens. A fertilized human ovum develops into a
human child. Throughout the living world this pattern prevails
—the offspring is basically like its parents. The germ cell of each
plant and animal must therefore contain the complete pattern for
each species and each particular individual. In the last twenty
years we have learned a great deal about the structure of the
"blueprint" and about the mechanism whereby millions of deter-
miners (genes) work together with "exquisite precision, keeping
step with one another in time and place as they guide the unfold-
ing of a normal embryo and do not lead instead to somatic
chaos." (E. W. Sinnott) The trillions of cells which constitute a
human being are produced by forty to fifty consecutive divisions
in accordance with the plan represented by the exceedingly intricate macromolecules of the tiny fertilized ovum.

Is it possible to explain the existence of life and of man without assuming the miracle of creation? Hypotheses formulated in
the last forty years seem to have solved this difficult problem.
Three billion years ago the earth was surrounded by an
atmosphere very different from its present one containing meth-
ane, ammonia, water vapor and other substances. Through it
passed tremendous lightning flashes and other powerful radia-
tions. The temperature was much higher than it has been for
hundreds of millions of years. The co-occurrence of these conditions made it possible for more complicated organic substances of
many different kinds to form in certain seas.

In the early seas these complex chemicals accumulated over
the eons because there were no living things to break them
down or consume them. The seas became a thin "soup" of
the fundamental organic compounds that today make up living
things.
Gradually, in this "soup" more complex aggregations took

place [and] some of the resulting structures acquired the ability
to make copies of themselves. (Harold M. Schmeck, Jr.)[7]

To be sure, any statement about the early stages of life must
be conjectural, but this theory has found some important confir-
mation in experiments that have been going on since 1953. Scientists filled closed vessels with a mixture of gases resembling the
primordial atmosphere and then sent electrical sparks through it
for many days. These conditions produced certain amino acids—
the building blocks of the proteins—and other organic molecules
important for living organisms. True, no protein and no living
organisms have been created in this way; nevertheless, current
theories give us a persuasive explanation of the emergence of living things on earth. Scientists have gone further and assume that
if planets outside the solar system have conditions similar to those
on earth, then organic life may very well have developed in
other parts of the universe. However, considering the enormous
distances between stars, it is quite uncertain that we will ever be
able to verify this.

Some thinkers have taken the position that the development
of life as well as of thinking beings goes beyond the possibilities
of regular natural development and that something qualitatively
wholly new and apparently completely unpredictable and mysterious *emerged* when first life and then mind appeared.[8] But
the emergence of new qualities, unexpected by the uninformed,
is not limited to the realm of living things. From the combination
of a poisonous greenish gas (chlorine) and a shiny soft metal (sodium) emerge the white crystals of plain salt. What could be
more mysterious to a non-expert than the skillful combination of
a great many different parts of metal, glass, plastic and so forth,
from which emerge pictures and sounds of distant events in our
living rooms? However, we are able to investigate the causes of
the new qualities which do not go beyond nature's physical and
chemical regularities.

It is the same with living processes. We cannot create a man;
neither can we create stars, tornadoes, or glaciers, but we can
explain them. We have made tremendous progress in understanding the processes that go on in living cells and in organisms as a
whole, and there is no impenetrable curtain which would make it
impossible to continue further progress.

Yet life, the whole world in fact, seems mysterious. A
flower, an anthill with its ordered regime, a new-born baby are,

indeed, astounding and wonderful, but they are not really mysteries. Flowers, anthills and babies are essentially understandable; they are not inexplicable as are ideas that transcend experience, such as God and His love, or as are the existence of God's Son and His resurrection. We can accept these ideas only as revealed by Divine inspiration, if at all.

The intellectual confusion associated with the idea of an unexplainable emergence is encouraged by the idea of wholes, which are supposedly more than the sum of their parts. Thus, it is claimed that an organism is more than the sum of its various components, that some undefinable entity, unknown to chemistry and physics, has to be at work, for otherwise life could not emerge. It is indeed true that a one-celled bacterium as well as a trillion-celled man is not merely the sum of the chemical elements of which it consists. The rule that a whole is equal to the sum of its parts is true without exception in arithmetic, but we must stop talking of sums if we go beyond arithmetical problems or situations. I refer again to the television set. A particular connection of the parts, their *configuration*, gives to the whole certain novel properties which are not possessed by the parts themselves. What is important is the relation of the substances to each other. Under certain specific conditions, processes and qualities have emerged which lead to the existence of a living organism.

We are inclined to simplify things in our thinking and system-building. An error frequently committed is that of reductionism, otherwise known as the nothing-but fallacy. An organism is nothing but a machine (it can be reduced to a machine); our brain is nothing but a computer; man is nothing but a "naked ape"; the child is nothing but a miniature adult. Yet anyone who has ever observed a child knows how differently from an adult he thinks, feels and behaves. Notwithstanding similarities, there are deep qualitative differences, as between organisms and machines, brains and computers, man and ape. It is important to keep this in mind if we are to have a proper perspective on ourselves.[9]

Evolution

To explain man's place in nature it is not necessary for us to go into the particulars of evolutionary theory and sequence, or the processes and causes that bring about evolutionary changes.[10]

Now, more than a hundred years after the appearance of Charles Darwin's *On the Origin of Species* in 1859, there is no longer any doubt about the fact of evolution. Thomas Huxley was ridiculed when, in 1863, he gave the lecture after which this chapter is named. Since then the climate of opinion has become completely adjusted to the idea of evolution and the unity of the organic world. It is accepted that plants, animals and man evolved from pre-existing simpler types and that their development came about through innumerable modifications in successive generations. Such disputes as persist concern the details of the organic mechanisms that set the evolutionary processes in motion, which in turn give rise to the development of new species. It is assumed that the main factor of evolution is mutation (change) of the genetic material (chromosomes) in the germ cells. We do not know yet, I believe, why certain changes are directed toward greater complexity. However, some very old species and primitive orders still survive, while others have died out. What role climatic and geological changes have played at various stages of evolution is still uncertain. In any case, as Julian Huxley writes:

> [It] is remarkable . . . that the blind and automatic forces of mutation and selection, operating through competition and focused immediately on mere survival, should have resulted in anything that merits the name of advance or progress. When looked at on the large scale, biological evolution *has* resulted —not universally, but regularly—in the overcoming of limitations, and has led to a steady rise in the upper level of life's achievements. It has produced co-operation as well as competition, and it has led finally to the emergence of values as operative factors in the process.[11]

The oldest traces of life (primitive algae and bacteria-like specimens) have been found in rocks that are calculated to have existed more than 3 billion years ago. Between the records of "these primitive plants and the broad array of oceanic plants and animals that suddenly appear in the fossil record of about 600 million years ago" (Walter Sullivan) there is a great gap. All major types (phyla) of animals are roughly that old. For a long time animals lived only in the seas and rivers. Land animals appeared about 350 million years ago, and the first mammals are about 200 million years old. The most primitive primates (primates embrace prosimians and monkeys; also man) evolved about 70–75 million years ago. These were, in all probability, not particularly intelligent. The hominoids (the higher primates: apes, protomen, and man) started about 28 million years ago. Creatures resembling living man are newcomers—possibly two million years old —and underwent a comparatively rapid evolution. A great many questions relating to the time between early man's first appearance and the beginning of our historical period still remain unanswered. "It is a history that begins with rival genera and species, then narrows to the races of *homo sapiens*." (Jacquetta Hawkes)[12] Fossils of *homo sapiens* can be found for only about the last 70,000 years.

Man did not descend from any living ape nor can apes be regarded as "our cousins"; man's evolutionary ancestry branched off from the hominoid stem at an early date. There is no point in pussyfooting about the fact that we are descended from primitive monkeys.

Sufficient fossil links have been found to establish the main line of human development, though there are still large gaps in the detailed sequence of the evolutionary chain. In order to grasp man's position in general, the non-specialist need not know the details of our evolution. It is immaterial to us which species of monkeys is closest to what prehuman skeleton and to modern man, or how the various fossil precursors of *homo sapiens* are related to each other and us, or what primitive manlike skeleton or tooth represents the main line, and which branch has died out. To the anthropologist these are questions of great importance, and the subjects of heated controversy; for us the major fact is the establishment of the evolutionary chain of man in broad outline:

1. Man is more closely related to animals than to plants.

2. Man is more closely related to vertebrates than to invertebrates (sponges, worms, molluscs, insects, etc.).

3. Man is more closely related to mammals than to fish, amphibeae, reptiles, birds.

4. Man is more closely related to primates than to other mammals (mice, lions, horses, whales, etc.).

At the same time that we place mankind in its proper relationship, we should realize what George Gaylord Simpson expresses so well:

> Not only are all men brothers; all living things are brothers in the very real, material sense that all have arisen from one source and been developed in the divergent intricacies of one process.

The fact that man is part of nature's great chain of being should warn us that mankind is subject to natural extinction, a fate that has befallen millions of other species. Like the dinosaurs they flourished and then disappeared from the face of the earth. However, there are no indications that man is undergoing a biological change that may interfere with the continuation of his life on earth. There are more people alive now than ever, and the species has skillfully adapted itself to the hazards of life in all parts of the earth.

Although we may regret our own mortality, we must nevertheless realize that death plays an important constructive role in organic development. In a later chapter I will have more to say about the problem of death as it presents itself to the philosopher. Here I would like to point out that evolution could never have taken place if the earth had remained full of primitive organisms. Death cleared "the way for fresh starts." If primitive pre-man had been immortal as a species, higher man could not have developed. Some species must make room for other species and each generation for the following one. To paraphrase Huxley, death is the price life has to pay for progress.

Some people have complained that the evolutionary theory, which is an essential part of a naturalistic world view, debases man. If we are a purely accidental product, are we not, therefore, without significance since we are merely one of the creatures that happened to be brought forth by the processes of evolution? Here, the terms "accident" and "significance" only lead to confusion. In the first place, evolution obeys natural laws; things do not happen accidentally in nature. In the second place, we usually use the word "accident" when, in a chain of occurrences having some relation to a human order or plan, a chance occurrence, an accident, interferes with the order or plan. A house collapses accidentally; a man is accidentally shot; another suffers an accident while driving. But there is no human order and purpose in evolution; it just happens. Man was not planned. It therefore makes as little sense to speak of man as an accident as it does to speak of stars, the earth, trees and dinosaurs as accidents.

The term "significance" indicates either that something has meaning or importance or that it stands in a characteristic relation to something else. Our evolutionary origin neither gives nor deprives us of meaning and significance; these our lives can acquire only through our own activities. In its second meaning the word "significance" requires a relationship: something signifies love, an uneasy conscience, a vitamin deficiency. In neither meaning does it make much sense to say that our lives are without significance because we evolved through unplanned natural processes. In any case, accidental and insignificant though he may be, man is still *homo sapiens*, "the most highly endowed organization of matter that has yet appeared on the earth." (G. G. Simpson) He has the gift to philosophize and to live by a sense of values. "No matter how man came to be, he is no less than what he is—a self-conscious person with unique characteristics. . . . Man's upward reach gives him his place and his importance." (H. H. Titus) We would do well always to remember the famous words of the Chorus in Sophocles' *Antigone:* "Wonders are many and none is more wonderful than man."

The Special Traits of Homo Sapiens

What are man's special characteristics, biologically speaking?

(1) Man's erect posture and locomotion on two feet; the structure and use of man's hands and particularly the size and complexity of his brain, that is, not its absolute size but its size relative to man's body weight (whales and elephants, for example, have larger brains). A unique characteristic of the adult female *homo sapiens* is the fact that biologically she is always sexually receptive—a human trait that is the cause of much pleasure and grief—and is not bound by regularly recurring periods of being-in-heat.* The human child is helpless and much longer dependent (6–8 years) than the offspring of any other creature. Consequently, the family normally survives mating and birth, an important factor in man's cultural development.

Let us return to man's brain. The bee, which is one of the most highly developed "lower" animals because it uses its dances as a "language" by which to communicate with other bees, has a brain consisting of 900 brain cells. Man's brain has 10 billion cells. His brain capacity is about three times that of the great apes and of some early protomen.

---

* There is an interesting enumeration of the traits which monkeys, apes, and man share and do not share in Theodosius Dobzhansky, *Mankind Evolving* (New Haven: Yale Univ. Press, 1962, paperback).

Man is distinguished as the highbrow or egghead of the primates. Here, housed within the curved boneplates of the skull, is the most subtle and complex instrument in the world, which, at the command of the whole man, has created the rich and varied cultures, the superb individual works of art, the inspiring if never final systems of thought, that make the history of mankind.[13]

We must take note here of the striking fact that though the great apes (which, I repeat, are not our ancestors) still roam the tropics, all our direct ancestors or other early species of man, with brain capacities intermediate between that of early proto-man and modern *homo sapiens*, have disappeared from the earth —perhaps *homo sapiens* outwitted and killed them. There is only *homo sapiens!*

(2) The special cultural traits of man are naturally conditioned on the new and enlarged centers of his brain. "Man is not simply a very clever ape." (Dobzhansky) He uses tools to a degree no animal can. Man can think and man can learn. Finally and most important man uses a symbolic language to communicate his thoughts and feelings about things that are not here, that are long past, or that may occur in the future. Man has always been a social creature, and it is presumed that in the more recent eras of the Stone Age, when tools and weapons became more complicated and visual art was born, people must have been able to talk to each other, to name things, discuss cooperative action, and pass on to their children what they knew. Then, when man became settled and new techniques and still more complicated social organizations developed, language must have advanced very rapidly.

As we grow up, we are not only influenced by our total natural environment, but are educated and nourished by the transmitted experience of generations of ancestors and associates. Our culture is not instinctive; it must be handed down from generation to generation, each generation having the potential of improving on its cultural inheritance. This capacity for improvement arises from the fact that man "is the most educable, the most intellectually malleable, the most plastic of all creatures." [14] However, "the world of culture can endure only so long as most of mankind possesses genetic equipments which are favorable for culture." (Dobzhansky)

There is today—and there has been for tens of thousands of years—only *one*, though polytypic, human species: *homo sapiens*. All humans can interbreed. There are obviously different body types, varieties and ethnic groups, usually—perhaps unfortunately—called races. The problem of race differentiation is scientifically complex (and politically charged with emotion). The racial picture of mankind has changed considerably in the course of time. Neighborhood relations, peaceful migrations of whole peoples, or invasions have, since time immemorial, mixed population strains and cultural achievements. A good example is the present Negro population of North America, which, through slow inter-breeding with various Caucasian groups and with an admixture of American Indian, has become noticeably different from the original, forcibly transported Africans.

We can assume that, given the same cultural environment, "the average person in any human society is able to learn just as much as the average person in any other society." (Montagu) This is the only proper, pragmatic rule by which the various peoples and races of mankind can live together peacefully and fruitfully. All healthy individuals are endowed with the genetic inheritance which makes it possible for them to learn a language and acquire a culture. Dobzhansky, however, wonders whether this genetic basis is "completely uniform in all populations." As Jacquetta Hawkes points out:

> [It] seems likely enough and should certainly not be denied
> [that the many races] have developed abilities and weaknesses
> peculiar to themselves. . . . Without this variety our future
> would be less abundantly promising just as our past would
> have been infinitely the poorer. No one can claim that a violin
> is a better or worse instrument than the clarinet; what is glorious is a whole symphony orchestra. So it is with mankind.

I wish to add here what Stuart Chase phrases so well: "All men are brothers under the skin. From Chicago to the Congo, from Sidney to Kamchatka, there is a common way of life below the surface differences."

All living human groups have a language, a family system, they obey some community rules, they make tools and have some healing techniques, they trade, they play games, engage in artistic activities and they hold certain cosmological beliefs.

Cultural Development

Up to this point I have been dealing in a highly simplified manner with the cosmological evolution of the universe and with the biological evolution of man. Let me now consider very briefly the major steps of our cultural evolution. The beginnings of our cultural development go back perhaps two million years, to the age of primitive man, to a time before the rather recent appearance of *homo sapiens*. In unraveling the pre-history of man we must rely entirely on ruins, excavations and accidental finds of materials that were able to survive the millennia. Consequently, a great many questions cannot be answered satisfactorily. Prior to 5,500 years ago we are dealing with non-literate groups. How recent this seems, as compared with the spans of time with which we have been dealing up to this point, yet how much has happened in the last few thousand years, how much has our way of life changed, how much has the face of the earth changed through us! And now we have landed on the moon.

Primitive men were hunters or fishermen, while women gathered other types of food: roots, berries, fruit. The ingenuity our ancestors must have used in order to bring down great wild beasts with their primitive weapons and traps is an indication of their cunning and intelligence. For the most part, families and small bands led a nomadic existence. Populations were small; it is estimated that as comparatively recently as 25,000 years ago roughly 3,000,000 people were sparsely distributed on all inhabited continents. Primitive people were acquainted with the use of fire at least half a million years ago. Through the several hundreds of thousands of years of the Old Stone Age (Paleolithic Era), while life continued from generation to generation with monotonous sameness, primitive man nevertheless very slowly learned to improve his stone and wooden weapons, tools and ornaments. Later, bone and ivory were added as raw materials. Burial cults indicated the presence of some ideology (belief in continued existence after death or fear of death). Statuettes of primitive female nudes—probably goddesses of fertility—have been found, among them the famous one called Venus of Lespuges, about which Jacquetta Hawkes writes that it was "carved perhaps 25,000 years ago," and that she is "lovely and harmonious of form, massive and yet full of grace." The cave paintings in Spain and France, mostly of wild animals, represent an astounding new cultural development. Painted probably 15–20,000 years ago, they are exciting and, even to modern eyes, beautiful. Man's artistic sense is manifestly very old.

Depending on one's point of comparison, it was that long ago or that recent in prehistoric time, perhaps about 40,000 years ago—the time is very controversial [15]—that various peoples, predominantly but perhaps not exclusively of Mongoloid origin began to cross from Siberia to Alaska. As glaciation changed in North America, they gradually moved east and south, until they finally covered both Americans. About 8,000 years ago they had reached the southern end of South America.

Approximately 10,000 years ago (in the Neolithic Age) a great change began gradually to take place in parts of the Old World. It was at that time that the first of the two great revolutions in human productivity occurred: the beginning of agriculture with the domestication of plants and animals.* (The dog had become man's companion still earlier.) Man could give up his nomadic life and settle down in villages and small towns and later in larger cities. In the course of the next few thousand years (up to this point we have reckoned in billions, millions, and hundreds or tens of thousands of years) the plow and wheeled cart were invented; rowboats and sailboats made their appearance; pottery, baskets, and textiles helped to make life easier and more pleasant; bricks were used in the construction of houses. About 6,000 years ago the technical culture of the long periods of the Stone Age reached its zenith and gave way to metal-using cultures, first the Copper and then the Bronze Age, and still later the Iron Age. It must be noted, however, that these cultural stages spread very unevenly from their Near-Eastern sources over the rest of the world. (It is presumed that the development of civilization in the Americas took place independently.) There were flourishing cities all around the Mediterranean Sea at the same time that tribes in Europe were still leading a barbaric life. (Such a difference in timing, in a relatively short period, also characterized the advance of the Industrial Age from one country to another. By now it has spread over all continents but still has hardly touched certain primitive peoples.)

Life in the Americas developed somewhat differently. "Be-

---

* The second great revolution in productivity is that of the last two hundred years, the coming of the Industrial Age.

cause there were no sheep or cattle, the Indian had no pastural
life and no milk and butter. He had no beast of burden except
the dog and the llama; he invented no wheeled cart." (Macgowan) Yet by the time of Christ he had developed the great
Mexican and Peruvian cultures.

Ruins of the oldest villages or cities can be found in Iraq and
Palestine. Nelson Glueck says of Jericho that "about 6,000 B.C.
Jericho already had experienced several millennia of what by all
counts must be considered civilized history." * The first written
records—Sumerian cuneiform is the oldest written language—
date back to about 4,000 B.C. Egyptian writing is almost contem-
poraneous. Alphabetical writing was invented in the region of
Syria-Palestine two thousand years later, about 1800–1500 B.C.[16]

The origins of English, one of the Indo-European languages, go back to some unknown tribe living in the Temperate
Zone to a time when agriculture was already being carried on
and animals had been domesticated. The problem of dating an
ancient language can be solved, not through excavations, but by
tracing the *common* ancient vocabulary of the living languages
and thus establishing the cultural level of the tribe employing the
basic ancestral language.

Our narrative has now gone beyond what we usually
understand as man's place *in nature*. We have entered the period
of recorded history and of the great ancient civilizations. We
who trace our technical, artistic, intellectual, moral and religious
culture back to the ancient Jews and Greeks must realize that
both these peoples are the successors and inheritors of advanced
civilizations that had flourished for thousands of years before.
Mesopotamian history begins about 4,000 B.C. (the famous Code
of Hammurabi dates from 1780 B.C.); Egypt's First Dynasty
reigned about 3,200 B.C.; India's history goes back to approximately 2,500 B.C., China's to about 2,000 B.C. It is possible that
certain climatic changes and geographic modifications played an
important role in providing an environment that produced the
magnificent Oriental civilizations.

In dealing with recorded history we pay attention, first, to
centuries and decennia; later, certain years become important,

* With respect to these ancient periods, one must carefully distinguish between dates "B.C." and the time indication "x thousand years ago." The difference, of course, is two thousand years.

and finally, we pinpoint particularly decisive days. The history of man's activities during the last 6,000 years presents an infinite variety of fascinating stories: the history of empires, kingdoms, and republics; of wars, art, literature, religion, economics and technology, science, and philosophy; of culture and society as a whole. We humans are to such an extraordinary extent interested in the description of the past that it would not be wrong to call us the history-minded creature.

Here our story of man's development comes to an end. While man's culture is in constant development, his organic development seems to have come to a standstill. Man, to whom I have referred as "the tool-using creature, the playing, the laughing, the talking and the symbol-making animal. . . . *homo sapiens,* wise man," has been established as the terminal point of a cosmic and organic evolution that lasted billions of years, ending 50,000 or so years ago—at least for the time being. "Man is very young." Since then cultural evolution has taken over.

Man's Future

What of the future? Man will continue to evolve. Can we foretell the direction he will take? Naturally, we have a burning interest in what may be the fate of our children and children's children, of our nation and culture, of mankind as a whole. What could possibly be more fascinating than to discover an outline of what is ahead of us! Here the prophets of doom, on the one hand, and the optimistic utopists on the other, have had and are still having a field day. Scientists, too have gotten into the act. I suggest that we remain skeptical in regard to man's prophetic talents. I was a young boy in Germany when, in August of 1914, everyone—that is, in Germany—believed that "our" invincible armies would enter Paris by Christmas. But the First World War lasted four years, and they never got there. I have always remembered that lesson. When you study political events, economic swings, or the ebb and flow of cultural movements, some predictions are borne out (otherwise planning and the conduct of family, business, political and cultural life would be impossible), but we must never forget the uncertainties implicit in the infinite possibilities of the future. As the old proverb so wisely says: Man proposes, God disposes.

The descriptions of life in the classical Utopias make for fas-

cinating reading; Aldous Huxley's *Brave New World* and
George Orwell's *1984* are terrifying. Utopias may represent
goals to be aspired to; *1984* and similar forebodings should serve
as warnings, though none of them should be taken literally.

Two quite different serious attempts to look into the future
deserve closer attention; one of these is based on history, namely,
the cycle theory of civilizations, the other deals with certain theories and speculations in the field of genetics—some of which
prophesy impending degeneracy, while others hold out the hope
of possible improvement in man's inheritance.

The cycle theory of history rests on the fact that all past
civilizations seem to have developed in accordance with a certain
pattern. They begin, they flourish and they die, either by internal collapse and disappearance, or through conquest and absorp-
tion by another civilization. Some civilizations, however, attain a
plateau or long stagnant phase lasting for hundreds, if not thousands, of years (the Byzantine and the Chinese empires)—quite a
modification of the "regular" cycle. Repeated attempts have
been made to discover great cyclical laws in the reputed regularity of human history. These studies, though they have presented interesting, and indeed grandiose, schemes, all suffer from
the same defect: broad conclusions are drawn from insufficient
data, while troublesome data are often ignored. There is, of
course, a sequence in cultural developments, and there are occasional parallelisms in the growth and decay of civilizations; however, the development of each and every civilization is different
and of a special kind.

Lacking the certainty of a universal law of cyclical development, we cannot conclude from past events what will happen to
our Western civilization. It does not follow that, because Sumerian, Egyptian and Greco-Roman civilizations did not endure, the end of our civilization is in sight. The decline of the
Roman Empire is often held up to us as a frightening example of
the moral decay to which Western civilization has supposedly
sunk, with the implicit or express warning that a fate like Rome's
awaits us—our civilization, too, will expire. Although this analogy is meant seriously, it cannot be emphasized too strongly that
history does not lend itself to such predictions.[17]

Closely related to the attempt to find a basis for forecasting
in the supposedly cyclical character of past civilizations is the
search for causal regularities in the development of unique pe-

riods, for example, our present period characterized among other features by industrial capitalism, advanced technology, science and democracy. Events in history are governed by particular causal sequences which we can elucidate. But it is impossible to discover general laws that explain and predict their development.*

The theories of geneticists are to be taken more seriously. Certain trends have been traced which purportedly make for a weakening of man's genetic structure. Our physical structure, our mental and thus cultural capacities depend on our inheritance—the genes we inherit from our parents. Radioactive fallout from atomic explosions is frequently mentioned as one cause of detrimental mutations and of our possible biological damnation. Another trend regarded as dangerous derives from the fact that people who are physically weak, if not actually sick, mentally feeble, or intellectually incompetent are protected and supported by modern society and are permitted to produce children who may inherit their parents' poor genes. This is one of the "achievements" of modern medicine and a result of contemporary social work and legislation. Warnings of the adverse consequences of this situation are by no means new, and belief in the possibility of a gradual deterioration of our human stock has found a number of proponents.

On this controversial matter I am not competent. However, I would like to quote Theodosius Dobzhansky, a leading geneticist, who discusses these problems at length in his masterly book, *Mankind Evolving*, previously mentioned.

> Neither prophecies nor refutations of an imminent biological doom are convincing while our knowledge is in no way commensurate with the gravity of the problem on hand.

> We simply do not know enough about the influences on fitness of most human genes in present-day environments, let alone in environments that may be contrived in the future.

A further concern has been the fact that the educated middle and upper classes produce fewer children than the laboring classes, whose lower socio-economic status seems to signify that they are less suited to bear and rear children. But it is fallacious to correlate success in the economic struggle with cul-

* See the remarks about sociology of knowledge in Chapter IV.

tural potentialities. The slum child who does not "amount to anything" may merely lack the opportunities available to the child in the middle-class suburb. Given the proper nurture, he might have done very well. The great majority of the people in the world (peasants, laborers, women, untouchables) have remained uneducated or have received no more than a rudimentary education, and "the many [have served] as a manured soil in which to grow a few graceful flowers of refined culture." (Dobzhansky) Who can foretell what would happen if these masses of people participated fully in the cultural life of the future?

Geneticists have also examined the opposite possibility, that science may find ways to improve nature and create a better human stock. They have drawn up eugenic plans involving the fertilization of preselected egg and sperm cells originating in outstanding females and males. Although this seems theoretically possible (similar procedures are carried out with animals, though the breeder is usually interested in developing *one* particular *measurable* quality), this scheme involves so many factors of a private and social nature that at the present time it cannot be considered seriously. Without prejudging the wisdom of such breeding experiments, it can be said that we are certainly not ready for them.

However, we are now able at least to envision the control of the biological nature of man. In the last few years biologists have learned a great deal about the molecular blueprints of inheritance, so that they can speculate on the possibility of modifying and perhaps improving human genes by inducing planned mutations. But in this field of molecular biology we have just begun to unravel the workings of nature; up to now scientists have concentrated on the most primitive one-cell bacteria and viruses. It will be quite a while before we can think in practical terms of redirecting the natural methods of transmitting inheritance in higher organisms, so that the results will be beneficial. We cannot determine at present whether and when this science-fiction will become realizable.

In the meantime, however, an almost immediate biological danger threatens mankind: the population explosion and the resulting crisis of starvation. This is not something that may occur in fifty or a hundred years; it is with us right now. Although the living standard of white people almost everywhere is constantly improving, living standards among some of the non-white peoples of Africa and Asia and among the Indians of South America are actually declining today. The reasons are well known. The medical sciences have rapidly reduced infant mortality and have improved public health generally through the elimination of endemic diseases (malaria, for example) and epidemics. More children grow up to marriageable age and bear ever more children who survive. The world population increases by more than 60,000,000 a year, so that it will grow from more than 3 billion now to more than 4 billion by 1980 and to 6–7 billion by the year 2000. This is within the lifetime of most people today.

At the same time, the mere subsistence farming that prevails in a large part of the world has not been able to keep up with current population increase, so that millions of people in the underdeveloped countries suffer from acute under-nourishment. It should be noted however that the food imbalance is lessening at present due to greatly improved varieties of wheat and rice. The distress in the rural areas still spreads to the ever-growing cities, to which thousands upon thousands migrate, driven by hunger and despair. But there no better fate awaits the swelling unemployed masses who starve on the streets of India's cities just as they did in the villages from which they came. Dire poverty engulfs practically the entire population of China, India, and large parts of Africa and South America.

The remedies seem to be remarkably simple, yet they are exceedingly difficult to execute: fewer children and more food! To achieve both goals requires the cooperation of billions of individual people, not merely the plans, laws, consultations, and votes of a limited number of statesmen, parliaments, and economists. Most of mankind traditionally regard having children— many children—as their greatest blessing. To accept an artificial limit on the number of children one may have requires a cultural sophistication that can develop only gradually, especially in the poor countries where birth control is most needed but where the necessary educational tradition is largely non-existent.

Here we have a vicious circle: education requires a higher standard of production and a higher standard of production requires more education. How difficult it is to break out of the circle can be seen from the fact that up to now only Japan of the countries outside the European tradition has succeeded in this effort.

Here mankind faces its greatest crisis, not in the distant future, but in the next decennia.

> Given both population pressure and political pressure, is it possible to live peaceably in a world where such inequalities are being aggravated rather than attenuated and where dreams of development are sometimes frustrated? (Asa Briggs)

Given sufficient time, however, these problems can be solved. Birth control pills are successful; some educational and economic aid is being extended to underdeveloped countries; better agricultural methods and control of water resources are being introduced. But crash programs are not possible, for traditional ways, physical unfitness and general indifference will only change slowly from generation to generation. On the horizon appear the possibilities of synthetic foods, of "farming" algae in sea water, of making the Sahara bloom, of weather control and other methods to increase substantially the world's food production, but so far these are still in the theoretical stage. Those who are knowledgeable are concerned, but this cannot be said for the Western peoples as a whole; otherwise they would be less interested in the conquest of space and very much more interested in the conquest of hunger and the population explosion. This is a burning contemporary issue. Billions of dollars and rubles should be diverted from defense and space spending to an anti-starvation budget.

If the combined wisdom of mankind succeeds in solving these problems, and if we are spared nuclear war and destructive pollution of our environment, then man faces a future of great potentialities. There has been considerable acceleration of cultural change in the last hundred years and particularly since the 1940's. No one can prophesy where it will lead us. We are aware that almost everywhere the educational enterprise suffers from serious limitations. Perhaps we can learn to overcome them, to educate for excellence, give opportunity for creativity, and inculcate brotherliness and thus bridge racial, religious and national prejudices. Our natural and social sciences must be placed at the service of a humanistic idealism so that we may be able to exploit all the rich endowments given us by nature. Only then will man find his proper place in nature.

CHAPTER VII

Man's Mind and Freedom

I
Abilities of the Mind

To elucidate the problems of truth and knowledge I described an imaginary philosophic conversation in which one of the people present made the non-controversial observation, "There are people here now." I want to begin the discussion of man's mind and freedom with an equally obvious statement, "All readers of this book are able to think." We are also certain that all other people can think as long as they are alive and are not unconscious. Furthermore we are able to remember statements made in previous chapters. Our memory can be prodded. In addition we are endowed with feelings: pleasures and pains, love and hate to mention only a few. Finally, it is clear that you made up your mind to read this book. You decided not to look at television, not to play cards, not to go for a walk, or to bed. You were free to engage in other activities, but you chose to read. We all have this capacity to make choices; we have what is called free will.

Let me condense what I have said so far into one sentence. Human beings are able to observe, to think, to recall; they have feelings, and they can make choices. These are our mental abilities. We can also talk and read. Dreaming, too, is a mental phenomenon. All of this is quite obvious, straightforward, factual, and in agreement with common sense.

In the area of mind and free will, however, we encounter some of the most difficult and controversial of philosophic problems, which have been and are still being endlessly debated.* The difficulties are of a special kind. It is quite understandable that the esoteric ideas of quantum mechanics and the new biological discoveries should pose previously unknown philosophic perplexities. But why should our mental powers, with which we and all philosophers since time immemorial are well acquainted and which can be readily observed, lead to uncertainties and controversies of a peculiarly philosophic nature?

There are three basic philosophic problems involved. They are old problems, and to some extent most readers, I am sure, are aware of them. (1) There is something essentially personal about thoughts, dreams, memories, feelings and decisions. One person cannot discover what is going on in another person's mind, unless he is told, or draws conclusions from facial expressions and gestures. We can see smiles and tears, we can hear what other people say, but we cannot see or feel what goes on "inside" another person's mind. We can introspect ourselves, but we cannot introspect others. How, then, can one be so sure that others have mental powers? (2) How can an organism, which consists of organic chemicals—the offspring of mere stardust—the processes of which obey the laws of molecular biology, how can such an organism be conscious, philosophize, compose songs, find itself in moral dilemmas, act heroically or cowardly and even write books about itself? How can a body house a mind, and what is the relation between body and mind? What place ought we to allot to mind in nature? (3) Finally, if man is able to decide freely to act in certain ways, how does this accord with the regularity and lawfulness of nature? Was it a deliberate decision that made you read this book or was this activity determined by some molecular brain processes of which one is not aware? If you do something because you regard it as sensible and interesting, how can this decision originate from mere biologic interactions? This seems quite incredible. The answers to these problems are controversial, and I can only skim their surface in one chapter.

* Take any current volume of any philosophic journal, and you are almost sure to find several essays on mind and on freedom of will.

Before discussing the three problems in detail, let me return briefly to some matters touched on in the last chapter. Man is unquestionably able to engage in more multifarious activities than any other creature. This is a fact, not a philosophic theory. The higher up we go on the evolutionary ladder, the more complicated are the things that organisms can do. Some plants turn themselves toward the sun, others catch insects and digest them. Corals build large reefs and islands. Spiders spin intricate, regular webs; the organization of beehives and anthills is proverbial. Birds build nests, each kind in its own particular way. Rats, dogs, elephants, dolphins, apes and other mammals, as well as some birds, definitely show intelligence and can learn through training. But man not only builds "nests" for himself, he does it in an infinite variety of styles; he also builds schools, temples and monuments. He prepares his food in innumerable and different ways, using a great many kinds of products. Only man has the ability to speak, using words to characterize and refer to objects. I have mentioned man's artistic and literary abilities and his capacity for speculation, which has led him to worship gods and has brought forth science and philosophy. Man has eaten "of the tree of the knowledge of good and evil"; he has a conscience and can pursue ideals. He has met the rigors and scarcities of nature with clothing, houses, agriculture, and, finally, he has transcended his own limitations through instruments and machines. Man is indeed wondrous, and even in this age, so full of despair and self-denigration, we may confidently claim numberless remarkable achievements. It is our mind that has made this possible.

"Mind" here means more than just intelligence, intellect and reason. We use this term for all of man's mental powers,* thinking, perceiving, imagining, remembering, feeling, wanting and deciding, "the whole of man's inner nature." (A. C. Ewing) † "Mind involves the vague but real power of the 'human spirit,' which seeks the good, the true, and the beautiful and inspires the exalted idea of soul. Immediately it also involves less agreeable possibilities. Because man can make conscious choices, he may

* "Mind" (Latin: *mens*) and "mental" come from the same word root.
† The broad sense in which "mind" is used here is the same as that in which modern philosophers use the term, for example, Gilbert Ryle, in his *The Concept of Mind* (New York: Barnes & Noble, 1960, paperback), a well-known study much debated by modern philosophers.

make unintelligent, ridiculous, even fatal choices. No other animal is so stupid as the human fool." [1]

On Knowing the Minds of Others

I know that I have all the enumerated powers of mind. I
know that I am thinking. But do others have mental capacities? I
certainly cannot observe them directly. I know that I can make
decisions and can study my underlying motives. I intuitively
know that I still love my wife. But does she still love me? If my
wife tells me about her dream, how do I know that her story is
true, how do I know that she dreamed at all? There is no way to
make other people's dreams observable to me or to anyone else.

We had better distinguish two questions. First, how do we
establish in our everyday contact with other people—family
members, associates, strangers—what goes on in their minds?
And, second, the basic philosophic question: Where do we find
justification for our assumption that other people have mental
powers, that there are other "minds" besides our own?

Let me stress the peculiarity of this situation. I can see and
feel my own body, and I can also see and feel the bodies of others. I can hear my own voice, as well as many others. But my
mental phenomena are accessible to me alone and yours to you
alone, and not to anyone else.

In a way, this seems like an artificial, almost perverse puzzle,
which a non-philosopher would be most unlikely to recognize.
Of course, I am confident that someone is thinking when we
speak to each other. The littlest toddler notices when Mama feels
good about him and loves him or when she is angry or generally
in bad humor. And when the widow of a close friend of mine
tells me with tears in her eyes that she does not know how she
can go on, I have no doubt whatever that her grief and despair
are genuine. I know that she has mental powers, and I am sure
that she is not pretending. We get to know other people's
thoughts and feelings, not by study in school or elsewhere; we
pick up the faculty very early in life in much the same way that
we learn to walk and talk.

Our knowledge of other people's thoughts, feelings, dreams
and motives are based on what they tell us and on how they
behave. When we listen to people speak, we pay attention not
merely to their words, but to the tone of their voice, and we

watch them, though for the most part not with any particular concentration. Normally, there are no problems in finding out what those who communicate with us think. It goes without saying, however, that though it is often easy to see through deception, we can nevertheless be deceived, and it is sometimes impossible to discover the truth. A child who has fallen down and is screaming at the top of his voice but suddenly quiets down when a playmate appears was merely seeking attention, not suffering severe pain. People simulate, lie, put on an act. The young woman to whom eternal love was sworn may discover that her "boy friend" was merely a charmer out for sexual adventure. A considerable degree of maturity and experience is necessary to fathom the thoughts and feelings of the men and women with whom we come in contact. But the fact that one is being misled does not make one disbelieve in the mental power of others.

There are two justifications for our confidence in the existence of "other minds." There is the fact that the overt behavior of people would make no sense if they were mindless. A father discussing his son's plans with him and getting meaningful answers, a teacher conducting a class and listening to a student's questions, would be engaged in totally absurd behavior unless father and son, teacher and students were thinking. Words and actions would be beyond explanation unless we were able to understand and follow remarks addressed to us and to act accordingly. All social intercourse, all conversation, books, rules and regulations, schools and courts of law, would be completely unexplainable, unless they were regarded as phenomena originating with and used by intelligent and feeling, i.e., minded, creatures.

The second justification is twofold. (1) Other people look at us and listen to our remarks, and then *they* say: "You are upset"; or, "Obviously, you enjoyed the movies"; or "You seem to love her very much," etc. From what we say and the way we act they draw conclusions about our mental state. Sometimes we do not even have to talk. The knowledge that others can usually draw valid conclusions about our minds convinces us that we have the same ability regarding theirs. (2) We note the similarity between our own behavior and that of others, and we therefore assume that their behavior is caused or accompanied by the same mental events that we can introspect in ourselves. When I see my wife balance her checkbook, laugh at a joke, play with a grandchild, or get annoyed at something or other, I infer from the way she acts and from what she tells me that mental processes are going on in her mind very much like those which, under similar circumstances, would go on in mine.

Neither with our senses nor with instruments can we inspect another person's mind; what we do is to assume that other creatures who are built and behave in a manner similar to ourselves have minds that resemble our own. We draw an *analogy* from our mind to the minds of others, yet we are usually not consciously aware of making this analogical inference, which leads us to the conviction of the basic sameness of human minds. This inference is an important argument for the philosopher.* We can be sure of our dream and pain, our uncertainty or our good humor— these are our own immediate experiences; by analogy we understand when someone else talks about *his* dreams, pains, joys. By paying attention to what we hear (a cry, a laugh) or are told and observe, we are able to intuit particular mental states of others.

However, we also have observed ourselves in hiding or simulating feelings and saying things about ourselves which we know are not true, and we therefore assume that others have similar skills and can deceive us about their thoughts, motives, and feelings. As we find others making mistakes about the processes of our minds, we understand our own difficulties in interpreting their mental activities. Even when others do not consciously try to deceive us, we often have difficulty in evaluating their mental behavior. Others may face situations which we have not encountered. In addition, each one of us is a particular kind of person, and other people differ from us in some respects. Age may interfere with understanding. A troubled adolescent may not notice the anguish of his parents, nor they his. Nevertheless, a sensitive imagination may make it possible for us to understand feelings and empathize with others in circumstances with which we may not be familiar. There are limits, however, to our ability to share in another's feelings or ideas. Consequently, our analogical conclusions may be faulty. Yet even though we may sometimes remain dubious about the feelings or ideas of another person, we do not doubt that all people are minded. We are firmly and correctly convinced of the existence of "other minds."

* While A. J. Ayer, in "One's Knowledge of Other Minds" *Philosophical Essays* (New York: Macmillan, 1954, paperback), calls this "a normal type of inductive argument," others have attacked the logic of the argument from analogy. But the critics of this particular argument do not doubt the existence of the mental faculties of others; they merely substitute other arguments.

Body and Mind

We now turn to the second question regarding the relation of body and mind, and the place of mind in nature. But first let me make a terminological clarification. What I have called "mind" has been and still is frequently called man's "soul," to which all our mental powers are ascribed, the totality of our inner life. "Soul" is a term that has definite religious connotations, whereas "mind" sounds more psychological, scientific and modern, and for these and other reasons is preferred in contemporary philosophic discussion.

The belief that man's consciousness is due to a noncorporeal entity, to his soul (the Greek *psyche*) or spirit, has a long history in primitive, early Near Eastern, biblical and Greek thinking, and in one form or another has also been part of Christian philosophy and theology. That human minds are immaterial and immortal separate entities or substances, interacting with our bodies, was the established view not only in all Western religious thought until only a short time ago, but also in Western philosophy, where Descartes is regarded as its major proponent. The dualistic idea, that man represents the union of a material, visible body and an immaterial, invisible soul, or mind, probably is still the view of most "men in the street." It is the view entrenched in our everyday thinking and speech.

Are our bodies and our minds entirely independent of each other, nowhere interacting, or are our bodily and mental activities related in some manner? We need neither science nor philosophy to decide this question. We all know that we cannot see, hear, smell, or taste without the physiological apparatus of our sense organs. We also know that we can move our arms and legs, shake our heads, speak and think when we make up our minds to do so. It would thus appear that our sense organs produce mental episodes and that we can move our muscles because we have a mind. But many bodily activities (breathing; the beat of our hearts; the activities of our kidneys, liver, digestive apparatus; the temperature control of our body, etc.) go on without any conscious involvement whatsoever; we notice most of our organs only when something goes wrong.

All our mental activities are dependent upon our nerves and our brain. We could not see without the optic nerve, which leads from the eye to the brain. Nerves and their respective brain centers are equally necessary for all the other senses. We could not talk without the brain's speech centers and the nerves leading from these centers to the muscles that move our speech organs. Animal experiments and brain disorders and injuries have shown the close relation between certain mental faculties and processes (such as memory, sensing, thinking, feeling) and particular parts of the brain. The brain is active when we are quietly thinking or daydreaming, even though there is no outward action. We know this because all brain and nerve activity is associated with electrical currents, and these can be measured by the electroencephalograph. Through this electrical activity we can determine whether a sleeping person is dreaming or not. Every act of ours, every experience, every thought, is dependent upon electrical signals pulsating through our nerve cells. "Whether or not we are conscious depends solely on whether a suitable pattern of electrical activity exists in a specific center of the brain stem." (Dean E. Wooldridge)

It is the task of neurology, not of philosophic analysis, to describe *The Machinery of the Brain*.[2] However, it is worth mentioning the most remarkable feature of the biology of the brain. All neural events are comparatively similar electrochemical transformations of similar cell masses in different parts of the brain, yet they are correlated with our most diverse experiences: seeing colors and shades, hearing speech and melodies, feeling hot or cold, being excited or being cheerful, thinking and dreaming. All these exceedingly varied episodes correspond to different patterns of the brain. As yet we know little about the various neuron patterns; we have to accept as a matter of fact their correspondence to certain mental episodes and states.

It is important to be very clear about the great difference between nerve happenings and sensations. When I burn my hand, I find that "the throb of pain experienced" is not "like anything described in textbooks of physiology. . . . [It is] quite distinct from anything that other people could observe if they looked into [my] brain." (Ewing) C. D. Broad, a well-known English philosopher, has illuminated the difference with great clarity in a repeatedly cited argument:

> Whenever it is true to say that I have a sensation of a red patch it is also true to say that a molecular movement of a

certain specific kind is going on in a certain part of my brain. . . . It is plainly nonsensical to attempt to reduce the one to the other. There is something which has the characteristic of being my awareness of a red patch. There is a something which has the characteristic of being a molecular movement. . . . These 'somethings' . . . are two different *characteristics*. The alternative is that the two phrases are just two names for a single characteristic, as are the two words 'rich' and 'wealthy'; and it is surely obvious that they are not. If this be not evident at first sight, it is very easy to make it so by the following considerations. There are some questions which can be raised about the characteristic of being a molecular movement, which it is nonsensical to raise about the characteristic of being an awareness of a red patch; and conversely. About a molecular movement it is perfectly reasonable to raise the question: 'Is it swift or slow, straight or circular, and so on?' About the awareness of a red patch it is nonsensical to ask whether it is a swift or a slow awareness, a straight or a circular awareness, and so on. Conversely, it is reasonable to ask about an awareness of a red patch whether it is a clear or a confused awareness; but it is nonsense to ask of a molecular movement whether it is a clear or a confused movement. Thus the attempt to argue that 'being a sensation of so and so' and 'being a bit of bodily behaviour of such and such a kind' are just two names for the same characteristic is evidently hopeless.[3]

That our mind constitutes, to some extent, a separate sphere can be seen from the way in which we generally deal with it. When we want to learn something, we use intellectual processes. (This does not mean that learning does not also involve physiological occurrences.) When we want to find out what members of our family, friends, or business partners think, we discuss these matters with them; we do not study their brain processes. The apparatus of modern biology gives us knowledge—thus far quite limited—about what goes on in the brain, but it does not enable us to discover what is going on in people's minds, the thoughts and emotions they entertain.

Apart from the ordinary relationships between body and mind, there are others I should mention briefly. Certain chemicals affect the mind: stimulants, opiates, depressants, tranquilizers. Shock treatment and drugs have become important tools in the hands of psychiatrists (physicians of the psyche). "Electrical stimulation in appropriate small regions of the brain" can artificially induce "the peculiarly personal sensations of fear, horror, rage, pleasure, and ecstasy." (Dean E. Wooldridge) Certain states of the body can made us feel depressed, while others may cause euphoria.

Psychic conditions, in turn, exert an influence on our body. The excitement of a love affair can rob us of sleep, fear can give us clammy hands and pounding hearts. Emotions cause us to blush, cry and faint. When we lie, our pulse may become sufficiently irregular to affect a lie detector. And of course, there are such well-known psychosomatic disorders as ulcers, eczema, asthma and certain cardiac conditions.

Monistic and Dualistic Theories

Showing that body and mind are closely connected does not solve the riddle of their relation to each other, i.e., how this relationship is to be interpreted and explained, nor does it answer the question of the place of mind in nature, "one of the most perennially baffling problems of metaphysics." (Lewis Beck) The history of philosophy has produced monistic and dualistic theories about the mind-body relationship, which I want to describe very briefly before spending more time on the contemporary empiricist view. Reductionist monistic theories claim that only one of the entities, body or mind, exists. Thus we get materialistic theories—only bodies exist—and idealistic theories—only minds exist. Impelled by "the philosophic craving for unity," both these theories succumb to the nothing-but fallacy: they deny some facts.

Materialistic theories, in claiming that there are only physical events, disregard consciousness. Obvious facts of our existence, our mental events, are denied and made to disappear as though by magic. The mind-body problem is not solved; it is evaded. While it is true that physiological conditions are correlated with personality factors (intelligence, gentleness, courage, conscience, scientific or artistic talent) and with mental processes, we have to keep firmly in mind that these mental characteristics and activities do exist as such and are to be distinguished from electrical and chemical happenings. They are also to be distinguished from behavior patterns that accompany certain emotional states. Tears are not the same as sadness. Wincing and "Ouch!" are not the same as pain. The non-identity of behavior and inner, that is, mental, episodes seems to have been overlooked by some extreme behaviorists.

Idealistic theories rest on the fact that it is mind that shows us the world and makes us know it. If we were mindless, like rocks, we would not know that there is a world. Therefore, mind is primary, and man is a spiritual being. Matter is merely a manifestation or expression or appearance of spirit. No modern philosopher takes this kind of idealism seriously any longer. Yet notions like these have not completely died out; they continue to live, for example, in Christian Science. Mary Baker Eddy wrote:

> All is infinite Mind and its infinite manifestations, for God is All-in-All. . . . Man is not matter; he is not made up of brain, blood, bones, and other material elements. . . . Man is idea, the image of Love; he is not physic.

This has an inspirational sound. But it is an emotionally induced denial of plain facts, thus reductionism.

In dealing with dualistic views, I will take as my point of departure the common sense view, which distinguishes body and mind or soul, and which is still dominant in our religions. This view is also embedded in our ordinary language usage. We talk of our mind as if it were a separate entity. We make up our minds. Someone loses his mind. We engage in research on the mind of the child, or of the aborigines, or of the neurotic or psychotic personality. But though this is the language with which we grow up and which naturally influences our thinking, it should be regarded critically and should not necessarily govern our world view. It is one of the main tasks of philosophy to clarify language and free us of its deceits.

Let us then ask ourselves what these minds or souls are that we have been talking about. We know of what substances bodies are made, but of what do souls consist? Are they a special kind of immaterial substance? Some ethereal entity, a spirit (and what is that?), within our bodies, a separate little creature inhabiting our skulls? What is this "ghost in the machine" which Gilbert Ryle tries to exorcise in his book, *The Concept of Mind?* [4] Most modern thinkers agree that it does not exist. (Theologians and many religiously inclined people, however, adhere to dualism.) There are no separate substances, entities, or objects inside of bodies. Mind, or soul, is no existing *thing*. This is the fallacy of misplaced

concreteness, or reification, which we discussed when we talked
about life in the preceding chapter. Just as the term "life" stands
for the processes of living, for the totality of our physical and
mental activities, so the terms "mind" and "soul" stand for the
totality of our mental events, faculties and activities. We are not
organisms which have, or house, a mind. Rather, each "I" is a
minding organism, an organism that not only moves, makes
sounds and digests, but also thinks, feels, loves, hates, memorizes,
is motivated and decides.

This is, again, a kind of monism. However, it is not a reductionist theory. Mental processes are neither denied nor reduced
to physical processes, though we find empirically that they are
dependent on neural activity. We acknowledge the existence of
both these processes in nature. In a famous essay, "Are Naturalists Materialists?" by John Dewey, Sidney Hook, and Ernest
Nagel, published in 1945, the authors wrote:

> Naturalists most emphatically acknowledge that men are
> capable of thought, feeling, and emotion, and that in conse-
> quence of these powers (whose existence is contingent upon
> the organization of human bodies) men can engage in actions
> that bodies not so organized are unable to perform. . . . To
> the naturalist, at any rate, there is no more mystery in the
> fact that certain kinds of bodies are able to think and act
> rationally than in the fact that cogs and springs arranged in
> definite ways can record the passage of time or that hydrogen
> and oxygen atoms ordered in other ways display the properties
> of water. "Things are what they are, and their consequences
> are what they will be; why then should we desire to be de-
> ceived?" [5]

Although I heartily concur in the scientific spirit of the above
statement, I wonder whether we can, and perhaps even should,
regard the human mindedness of "certain kinds of bodies" as entirely without an element of mysteriousness.

The history of monistic naturalism, of the assumption that
we are dealing with one entity, the minded organism, has roots in
antiquity, just as the history of dualism does. The oldest parts of
the Old Testament have no special word for "soul." Aristotle,
among the Greek philosophers, regarded the soul as the equivalent of the principle of life and its various forms. This realistic
view, however, was overthrown by the Platonic and later by the
religious view affirming that we must distinguish between man's
material body and his immortal soul. The blossoming of science

in the last four centuries raised doubts in a minority of thinkers about the speculative dualist theories and led them to propose either a materialistic monism or a naturalistic monism,* the latter finding more and more adherents among contemporary scientists and philosophers. Naturalistic monism is unlike materialism in that it does not deny mindedness. It is a fact of nature that mindedness exists as a function of those organisms which possess the most complex nervous systems.

The modern viewpoint settles many serious difficulties that are inherent in the dualistic view. The dualistic assumption that a mind (soul) is a something raises many questions. Where do these objects, or entities, come from before they join our bodies? Why did a particular soul enter my body, and what happens to it when I die? Do souls as entities independent of bodies nevertheless live only as long as bodies? And of what do they consist? Our Western tradition has answered these questions by assuming immortal souls. But with that theory new problems present themselves. Why did it take so long for my mind to develop, assuming that it was truly immortal and thus pre-existed? And again, what happens to our souls when we die? The naturalist takes it for granted that when life ends, mindedness ends too. But assuming immortality, that is, the continuous existence of souls, we want to know what differentiates individual souls; we are puzzled about how your soul and my soul are identified and distinguished. Do some fare well and others badly in accordance with Christian beliefs? Where are all the souls of our ancestors, and how far down the line of early and proto-human creatures can we go and still regard their perceptive and instinctual powers as manifestations of immortal souls? The answer that souls are somehow with God is religious imagery, but it is so vague that it does not resolve any honest question.

Many people today realize this. Belief in immortality is no longer held very strongly, less strongly, it seems, than belief in God. On the other hand, no clear idea about the place of mind emerges from common sense. Even if we accept in principle the idea of the minded organism, we still face considerable difficulties. But though naturalistic monism does present certain puzzles,

* The meaning of these and other -ism terms in philosophy is imprecise and flexible, being applied to various philosophies with some arbitrariness. They are thus confusing. It is the theories that are important, not the names we attach to them. I mention these -ism terms only because they are frequently used in intellectual discourse by philosophers and others.

most educated people and also most philosophers are thoroughly convinced of its factual correctness.

There is, first of all, the difficulty of language. However, all the expressions enumerated above, which speak of mind as an entity, remain meaningful even though we realize that when we use the word "mind," we do not designate special entities within people, but certain features, qualities, or actions of people, of minded organisms. Though fully convinced of the non-existence of minds as real objects, I nevertheless use the noun "mind" throughout this chapter, as other contemporary philosophers also do. We must employ the established language which everyone understands.

The second difficulty is still the basic one of the relation of our mindedness to our body. We have discarded monistic materialism and idealism, and we have given up dualism, which has been well entrenched for some two thousand years. We have purged our terminology, and we have solved some but not all of the problems by substituting minding for mind. The question, now rephrased, still remains: How are our mental episodes and faculties related to the physiological events in our neural system? There appear to be two chains of events—the mental and the electro-chemical—which we know to be somehow interrelated or to belong together, but how?

Here, too, several theories have been put forward. First, there is the theory of *epiphenomenalism*, which holds that mental events are mere accompaniments of bodily events. The body acts on the mind, but minding as a mere accompaniment cannot act on the body, nor can any one mental episode influence future mental episodes, as the latter are mere accessories of later neural events. But this seems an unsatisfactory description of what we find on observing ourselves and others. Mental events certainly appear to be interconnected with and to influence each other, for example, the lengthy deliberations that result in a plan of action, or the warm affection and thoughts that "produce" a friendly letter. Mental processes seem more than mere shadow play, particularly since we know that our worries, excitements, passions, affect our physical condition. Epiphenomenalism would thus appear to be a poorly chosen description.

Psycho-physical *parallelism* is a second theory. According to this theory, there are two *independent* chains of events, the bodily and the mental, which run parallel to each other. Not all physical occurrences, not even all cerebral events (not the nervous control of our breathing and heartbeat, not the flow of blood nourishing our brain), but only a select group of neural events are accompanied by parallel mental activity, though for every mental event there must be a parallel event in the neural organ. According to this theory, there is no causal connection between neural and mental events; they merely occur parallel to each other. Yet why this mysterious parallelism of all mental events with some physical ones exists and how it is preserved remain unexplained. Recondite terminology does not make a theory. Furthermore, "parallelism" does not seem to be an apt term to describe what happens when physical and mental events are related, for example, when we see (nervous activity leads to sensation) or when we move a limb (motive, decision bring about movement).

The Identity Theory

All the mind-body theories so far mentioned, except reductionist materialism and idealism, have one feature in common, the assumption that we have to deal with two substances, or, if only one substance, then with two different processes whose relationship to each other must be described and if possible explained. The newest theory—not yet fifteen years old—held by a number of contemporary philosophers, tries to do away with all duality elements and assumes the *identity* of every mental event with some particular neural state.[6] It has the great merits of philosophic simplicity and intellectual economy. It is both attacked and defended with considerable sharpness.

Let me first try to clarify the application of the identity concept. One of the obvious examples of identity, used in philosophy texts, is the identity of the author of *Hamlet* and the author of *Macbeth*. Now, a more complex example. We know that something that is called a cloud is "a mass of tiny particles in suspension."[7] When we talk of clouds, we use the descriptive language of everyday visible objects. But when we speak of a "mass of tiny particles in suspension," we express ourselves in an entirely different framework. Nevertheless, a particular cloud is identical with a particular mass of tiny particles. Here is another example, that I devised. Let us assume that an art critic, an anatomist and a chemist study Picasso's *Guernica*. The critic will comment on the meaning of the picture, the anatomist may be highly critical of the artist's distortions, the chemist may wonder about the chemical formulas of the materials used. Each studies the identical picture but uses an entirely different terminology to describe the features he is interested in; each speaks of the picture in a different frame of reference.

The mind-body or psycho-neural identity theory claims that my seeing a chair is identical with a particular neural process that goes on in the optic nerve and brain center. The act of seeing consists, not of two events, the visual and the chemical-electric, but of only one. All sensations and all inner episodes are identical with certain corresponding cerebral events. We cannot at the present stage of science—and perhaps we never will—distinguish the brain process connected with seeing our fathers from the brain process connected with seeing our mothers, though we can easily distinguish the experience of seeing father from the experience of seeing mother. This lack of knowledge about neurophysiology in no way impairs the principle of the identity of the particular neural processes which we cannot describe accurately and the personal experiences which we can describe. We may know the identical thing well in one frame of reference and not well at all in another frame of reference. People were aware of and talked about clouds long before they knew that clouds are identical with masses of tiny particles in suspension. *Guernica* does not change its identity when discussed by the art critic, the anatomist, or the chemist. Thus, in answer to Broad's point that a molecular movement and seeing a red patch are two quite different things, we could say with J. J. C. Smart: "I'm not claiming that 'experience' and 'brain-process' mean the same. . . . All that I am saying is that 'experience' and 'brain-process' may in fact refer to the same thing." In reporting our mental happenings or states, we have at our disposal a tremendously developed language as well as the advantage of dealing with that side of the identity equation of which we are automatically aware with respect to ourselves and indirectly with respect to others. We know very little about the details of our neural processes—the other side of the identity equation. These would have to be empirically investigated, but unfortunately, the personal brain viewer ("an autocerebroscope," a term used by Herbert Feigl) is at present in the realm of science fiction rather than science. The fact that in the equation, inner episodes = neural processes, we know the left side intimately and the right side only to a limited extent does not nullify the equation. Nor does the fact that physiological descriptions and descriptions of inner episodes have utterly different meanings disturb the identitists. Statements about clouds also have meanings different from the meanings of statements about masses of tiny particles. And statements about the chemistry of ethyl alcohol (C_2H_6O) have meanings different from the meanings of statements about alcohol control, craving for alcohol, cure for alcoholism and the like; nevertheless, "alcohol" in these statements refers to the identical substance.

The logical simplicity of the identity theory is very appealing, but it leaves many philosophers dissatisfied or puzzled. Another example should illustrate what I mean. When Beethoven wrote his famous last quarters, he was totally deaf. Nevertheless, he somehow "heard" them. Any good musician has this same ability to "hear" a composition merely by reading the score. The quartet that the deaf Beethoven "heard" was identical with the quartet that we hear rendered by four players in the concert hall. If a musician took the score of Beethoven's last quartet with him to a performance, he could simultaneously hear and read the very same quartet. But actually hearing a piece of music gives us an experience "over and above" that of merely reading it. Yet in both cases the composition is identical.

I have a feeling that inner experiences also possess qualities "over and above" the qualities of neural processes. I find it difficult to accept the idea that talk about my seeing my father or about my anxiety denotes talk about a certain neural process. Cases such as these are different from the identity relations exemplified in talk about clouds being the same as masses of particles. The statement that "the physical property . . . is one and the same thing as (the) phenomenal property" which Brandt calls "the heart of the Identity Theory" is not clarifying and is even paradoxical. For this reason, such noncommittal expressions— used by numerous philosophers—as mental occurrences *accompany* or *correspond to* or are *correlated with* neural processes seem preferable. We thus openly recognize the twofold "irreducibly different aspects" (A. Pap) of experiencing our living activities. The identity theory does not explain any facts of nature. It is merely a name for a simple but unusual relationship which is just as comprehensible, if not more so, without the use of the identity characterization.

Perhaps the relationship of mental and bodily happenings can be better understood if we compare it with the so-called complementarity of the wave and particle aspect of subatomic particles ("wavicles"). (See V pp. 107.) [8] In talking and thinking about man one can on the one hand pay attention to his inner, mental experiences and, on the other hand, to the complementary neurophysiological happenings. Even the layman realizes that the language of mental and of physiological events must be kept distinct. In self-observation and ordinary social intercourse we usually deal with the mental sphere alone; the psychologist might study both mental and bodily aspects, while the neurophysiologist concentrates on bodily happenings.

Whatever theories we have, we must remember that "a general theory of the relation of mind and body has no bearing upon any specific problem that arises in the communication of human beings with each other or in their transactions with things in their environment." (Sidney Hook) Also, we will always have to deal with two sets of observations, those of neurology and the molecular biology of brain processes, and the descriptions and theories of sensual impressions, feelings, thoughts, desires and dreams; as well as all other manifestations of our mindedness such as philosophy, science and the creative arts.

The problems of language and theory are, to some extent, created by the fact that we are trying to describe and explain a unique relationship in nature, that matter on a certain high level of organization develops mental activities. "This property of mind is something given: it just is so. It cannot be explained," Julian Huxley writes, "it can only be accepted." It is a fact of nature, an astounding fact, yet there stands man—and any theory that attempts to account for him seems inadequate and pale. However, as I pointed out previously, mindedness is not limited to *homo sapiens* alone. It is he who has the most varied "chemistry of the intellect" and also the most complicated neural system, consisting of approximately 10 billion nerve cells, as compared, for example, with "250 neurons in the brain of an ant and 900 neurons in the brain of a bee." [9] How far down in the animal kingdom we must go to discover the first traces of mentality and consciousness is a factual question of animal psychology.

The Evolution of Mindedness

The evolution of mindedness in the animal world buttresses our disbelief in souls and other mind-substances. Mindedness is an evolutionary development that was of decisive importance in man's survival. Man is a relatively slow creature, without great physical strength or size, lacking natural weapons such as claws, horns or poisons. It was his resourcefulness that protected him from enemies and helped him in hunting, fishing, and foraging. Unfortunately, as all links between monkey-like creatures and early man, as well as early man himself, have died out, we cannot follow the gradual evolution of mind through the last few million years.

It goes without saying that the evolution of mind from primitive beings without mindedness or, still further back, from inorganic substances, does not establish the non-existence of mind. To use the genesis of mind as an argument for the non-existence of mind is to fall into the trap of our old enemy the genetic fallacy. We must never forget the consequences that result from very different and more complex levels of organization and functioning. Things are not the same as their origin. As C. D. Broad says so well:

> You have no right whatever to say that the end is just the beginning in disguise if, on inspecting the end as carefully and fairly as you can. you *do not* detect the characteristics of the beginning in it and *do* detect characteristics which were not present in the beginning.

The uniqueness of the development of mindedness has sometimes been evaded by assuming that all physical reality is conscious, that it has a psyche. This theory is called panpsychism (*pan*, all, everything). But the analogy induction, which makes us confident that all other people are conscious and which makes us wonder whether the family dog, apes, dolphins, or elephants have "minds," comes to a complete stop with the lowest forms of animal life and with plants and minerals. There is no indication whatsoever that the stone or bullet that hits a man feels sorry or triumphant, or that a tree or a house destroyed by a hurricane is brokenhearted, though we may experience these emotions. In poetry and fantasy we can give full rein to our imagination, but neither common sense nor science can accept panpsychism.

"Electronic Brains"

A much more serious question is the "mindedness" of robots, computers, and "electronic brains." [10] Here a distinction must be made between performance and consciousness. Today's computers can execute certain tasks much faster and better than man can: complicated and lengthy arithmetical calculations, storing and retrieving information, lining up and following up alternatives, whether in chess, engineering, or strategic planning. If instructions are clear and correct, the machine "thinks" faultlessly. Since computers can make millions of calculations in one second, certain complex problems, which formerly could not be handled, can now be solved, be they technical, scientific, medical, economic, or strategic ones. It is man, however, who makes the computers and draws up their detailed programs. I might add that as far as the operational aspect is concerned, the human brain is in certain respects the superior "machine": for all its outstanding feats, it consumes exceedingly little energy and occupies a very small space. As for the creativity and learning ability of computers, I lack the specialized knowledge to take sides in the controversy on whether computers really can learn from experience and improve their performance. Norbert Wiener, one of the pioneers in modern computers, has written: "Computers can learn to improve their performance by examining it. . . . Whether you call that thinking or not is a matter of terms." This is, I believe, the prevailing opinion among computer experts.

That a computer can even realistically be imagined as capable of writing *King Lear*, Dylan Thomas' poetry, Plato's *Republic*, or Verdi's *Requiem* is pure science fiction. Computers lack the life situations and emotions on which art and philosophy rest. They are not curious—it is we who ask the questions which the computer helps to answer. Men have often speculated about artificially created *homunculi*. Similarly, if we give free rein to our fantasy, we can envisage computers which, through the use of billions of circuit elements, act and react like people. But there is nothing in the behavior of existing and of actually planned computers to make us wonder whether they are conscious. This does not mean that those who are interested in the mind may not benefit greatly from studying computer operations. The philosophic implications of the operation of computers is a rather new and perplexing subject, one on which only limited work has been done. Continued research calls for the cooperation of two quite different disciplines (always a difficult matter): philosophy and computer theory.

The ability of computers to follow logical sequences and do arithmetic makes it clear that one argument raised against the naturalistic theory can be refuted with relative ease. This argument is very well put by W. T. Jones,[11] in his criticism of the Greek atomists.

> In the kind of thinking which goes into the fashioning of a theory, the mind is developing and pursuing a logical "chain of reasoning." So far as the mind is reasoning well, the order of the propositions which are successively before it is determined by the compulsion of logic, not by mechanical motion of atoms. There is a compulsion, but it is a logical compulsion, not a physical compulsion.

But if man-made dead aggregates of tens of thousands of electronic components can "think" logically, there is no reason why nature should not be able to fashion an instrument which can perform equal feats of correct thinking through "the mechanical motion" of the differently organized atom system in man's brain.

I have sufficiently emphasized how very much greater and how qualitatively different and more varied are the accomplishments of the human mind than those of machines. We marvel at these wonderful talents. However, there is no theoretical reason why nature could not develop a thinking organ in the ascent of living matter. Plotinus (205–270 A.D.), a late Roman philosopher, who exerted a profound influence on the foundations of Christian theology, commented: "The most irrational theory of all is that elements without intelligence should produce intelligence." Yet we know that this has actually come to pass, illustrating the incredible creativeness of nature.

II

Man's Freedom to Choose

The most remarkable of our gifts—a uniquely human characteristic—is our ability to plan and to act freely on our plans.

Within certain limits we can choose the activities we engage in and the patterns of our lives. Only a few of us are creative in the strict sense of the word, and are capable of producing important works of technology, art, science and speculation, but unless he is a slave or a prisoner, every man and woman, to some extent, creates himself as a unique person. He can and must choose between the alternatives that are open to him. For people living in abject poverty, the opportunities are very limited. But for middle-class and upper-class men and women, growing up and living in a modern, industrialized country, the range of choices is remarkably wide—so wide, in fact, that choice might well be burdensome for certain people. In this atmosphere of freedom and with an income considerably above the minimum, whether on a farm or in a kitchen, in an office or in a factory, in a minor or in an executive position, it is at least in some measure our own choices that have put us there. Once we have chosen a career, a spouse, a home, and have settled into a routine, we are prone to forget the freedom we have had and indeed still have (though few would want to give up the responsibilities they have assumed and the security of a known pattern). Yet we still must make innumerable choices in our relations with others, in religious and political affairs; and in our use of ever increasing leisure time.

However, the extent of our freedom must not be exaggerated, as has been done, for example, by Sartre who wrote: "Man is not to be defined as a 'reasonable animal' or as a 'social' one, but as a free being, entirely indeterminate, who must choose his own being." Man is not "entirely indeterminate." * Man's freedom to act has certain definite biological, political and economic limitations. He cannot fly like an insect, run as an antelope, swim as well as a fish, or carry burdens like a camel. Each person has individual limitations, of a physical or intellectual nature. In addition, a young person's social milieu, his racial origin and his economic condition may severely limit his dreams, the fulfillment of his aspirations and consequently his freedom. But except for prisoners, some psychopaths and some retarded people, everyone may act freely.

Our ability to choose freely, that is, our so-called free will, is still one of the most discussed problems in philosophy, perhaps

* There is a more detailed analysis of Sartre's idea of freedom in chapter XIII.

the most debated one.* Yet we all have no doubt about our free will and are certain that we can freely move our hands and feet or that we can talk when we want to (unless we suffer from special affliction).

> "The man in the street" may well wonder why anyone should ever have denied the existence of free will since the difference between freedom and compulsion appears to him a fact that he finds exemplified every day. To his mind, there is no particular problem here; some of his actions are free, while others are compelled or constrained.[12]

We also realize that we cannot hold ourselves or others responsible for a good or an unfortunate deed unless each of us has freedom to act and is not forced. Common sense tells us that man is not like the ocean, which we do not blame for raging, or the car, which we do not scold for not working properly; man is not a machine. He can be praised or condemned; he can feel regret or remorse, because he is an agent who chooses to do what he does and as such is accountable for his deeds. All of this we take, perhaps somewhat naively, for granted. It might seem, then, that the problem of free will is an artificial one, dreamed up by philosophers. This is not so. The problem of the existence and the nature of free will has a certain relationship to everyday life and community affairs and to generally held religious and theoretical views.

When a small baby, sitting on its mother's lap, kicks her, we smile; we certainly do not make an issue of it. A baby does not have free will, it is not responsible for what it does. But when a ten-year-old youngster throws rocks at a playmate, we feel justified in scolding him and holding him responsible. Where do we draw the age line between having and not having free will? A drunken driver is responsible for an automobile accident in which some people lose their lives. But can we justify this position? Under the influence of alcohol, he was perhaps not aware

---

* The question of free will has a theoretical side, namely, whether or not it is true that man has free will, and, if it is true, how is free will possible. But, more important, it has an ethical aspect, too. One of the decisive tasks in ethics is to determine under what conditions an acting person is responsible for what he does. The power to act freely is one of the conditions of responsibility. Practically speaking, as ethical problems are the more important ones, free will is usually discussed in ethics. I have chosen to deal with it here as part of my description of the nature of man's mind. In my discussion of free will, I shall use certain ethical concepts and ideas, but I shall do this only to the extent that they are part of everyday language and thinking.

of his actions. If he was deprived of his free will, can we nevertheless hold him responsible? And what about the psychopath, or
the person acting in insane passion? There are some practical
solutions to these problems, which moral and legal systems have
found. But the philosopher must examine and clarify this situation in all its theoretical ramifications. This is a difficult, controversial challenge, which has not perhaps been entirely solved.

Besides the practical questions of the free will of children,
drunkards, psychopaths and people acting in the heat of passion,
about which I will say more later, there are two additional aspects of a more theoretical character. First, there is a religious
question: How can the freedom of man be reconciled with the
omnipotence of God? Second, how can human beings have free
will when everything in nature happens in accordance with
regular laws?

St. Augustine (354–430 A.D.) was the first thinker to consider, in detail, the difficulty of combining a belief in the existence of an all-knowing and all-powerful God, who governs the
universe, with a belief in free action. "If God foreknows that a
man will sin, he must necessarily sin. But if there is necessity
there is no voluntary choice in sinning, but rather fixed and unavoidable necessity." There is also the further question: Why
did a merciful, loving, and just God endow man with the freedom to sin and did not, instead, make him a necessarily good
creature? "God both blames us and punishes us for the sinful acts
of which it now appears He is the sole author." (W. T. Jones)
As naturalists, we need not discuss here the complicated theological, historical, and personal reasons that have led highly intelligent men of all Western religions to become involved in these
religious paradoxes. Nor need we discuss the tortuous, apologetic
arguments of theologians from St. Augustine to the present day,
and we certainly do not have to accept the obscurantist defense
that we are faced here with mysteries transcending human
understanding. The religious questions raised by the problem of
the free will naturally disappear if the existence of an all-
powerful and omniscient God is not assumed.

The Bible itself gives no indication of the difficulties arising
from the contradictory assumption of God's power and omniscience and man's free will. In telling the story of Cain's murder
of Abel, in the fourth chapter of Genesis, the Bible takes the com-

mon sense position that man has control over sin, and later, in Deuteronomy (30:19), God admonishes man: "Choose life by loving the Lord your God, heeding His commands, and holding fast to Him." There are, however, other places where God interferes in man's choices, for example, when He hardens Pharaoh's heart (Exodus 7:3; see also Deut. 2:30).

Greek philosophers did not treat the free will problem systematically. In the old myths, gods and fate directed and intervened in human affairs. But in the Classical Age, belief in the Homeric gods had been abandoned, and man's ability to act freely did not seem to present a problem to the philosophers. While Aristotle examined a related issue, the difference between voluntary and involuntary acts—involuntary through ignorance, compulsion, or fear—neither he nor others discussed the problematic of voluntary actions, which is the central issue of the contemporary free will discussion.

The rise of science in the sixteenth and seventeenth centuries added a new dimension to the free will problem. As it became possible for scientists to show that mechanical and astronomical happenings occur in accordance with universal laws, a firm belief in a *general* determinism grew among some scientists and philosophers, in which the universality of natural lawfulness took the place of the omnipotence of God. According to this belief, it is not God who directs our will; antecedent causes determine our decisions in accordance with natural laws, and this is still the framework within which the contemporary free will discussion takes place. This is indicated by the title of the book, *Determinism and Freedom in the Age of Modern Science.* [13]

We know that man is a part of nature, a mammal, and that the activities of man's body and mind are governed by universal biological and psychological laws. Voltaire, in his *Philosophical Dictionary*, explained:

Everything happens through immutable laws. . . . everything is necessary. . . . "There are," some persons say, "some events which are necessary and others which are not." It would be very comic that one part of the world was arranged, and the other were not; that one part of what happens had to happen and that another part of what happens did not have to happen. If one looks closely at it, one sees that the doctrine contrary to that of destiny is absurd; but there are many people destined to reason badly; others not to reason at all, others to persecute those who reason. . . .

. . . I necessarily have the passion for writing this, and you have the passion for condemning me; both of us are equally fools, equally the toys of destiny. Your nature is to do harm, mine is to love truth, and to make it public in spite of you.[14]

If everyone's behavior is governed by "immutable laws," then free will is an illusion, and we are all similar to the young children, drunkards, and psychopaths; people without free will. If natural laws in fact govern our behavior, and the story of our lives is written by outside forces, then the novelist Morris West was correct when he wrote, "a man's death sentence is written on his palm the day he is born," and we might just as well resign ourselves to our fate.

Determinism and Criminality

Determinism also seems to dispose of the difficult problem of the criminal. Could he have avoided committing his crime? Not if we accept the strictly determinist view. The fatefulness of crime has been a frequent theme of novels, which describe in detail the vague, merciless social and psychological forces that seem inexorably to determine a tragic end.[15] The neurotic or psychotic basis of deviant behavior plays a remarkable role in modern literature. Dynamic psychology has shown that a complexity of suppressed drives and antagonisms are present in each of us, and when too strong, boil over into murder, rape and other crimes. All this is in accordance with deterministic laws. Consequently, criminals are unfortunate but not guilty; and what the Apostle Paul wrote long ago is true: "For I do not do the good I want, but the evil I do not want is what I do." (Romans 8:19)

But doesn't something seem very wrong here? We don't consider the student who studies industriously and the student who copies another's homework as equal, the hard-working storekeeper and the bank robber, the hunter who inadvertently shoots a companion and the assassin who deliberately plans a murder. Even though these personalities and events may be determined by natural law, we do differentiate in certain cases, such as those just cited.

We differentiate between a two-year-old toddler who grabs another child's toy and a four-year-old who takes a few pennies from his mother's kitchen money. We explain to the four-year-old why he should not do this. But, when an adolescent "steals" money from his parents or from a store, we become concerned about his criminal tendencies. The baby has no idea at all of what he may or may not do. The four-year-old is just beginning to distinguish between what belongs to him and what belongs to others and to respect the latter. But the healthy adolescent is in a different class; he is approaching maturity, and we regard him as a free agent.

The distinctions we make in evaluating the actions of adolescents apply also to adults. We draw a line between the normal, healthy individual, whom we regard as free because he should be able to control his behavior by his deliberate decisions, and the abnormal or ill person who lacks the ordinary capacity to make decisions and to act freely. Under what intellectual or emotional conditions a person is regarded as having the "normal" capacity to act freely, in the usual sense of the term, is frequently a difficult question, which only a psychiatrically trained expert can handle. It is a factual question, not one to be decided by the philosopher; but the philosopher must recognize the categories of the free acting and the not-free acting person. People may also be not-free because they have been hypnotized, brain-washed, tortured, manacled, or forced at gunpoint.

The question has been much discussed in recent years whether children growing up in extreme poverty or in a segregated environment, which gives them little or no incentive to become educated, perhaps without one or both parents, lack certain prerequisites of mental health. To what extent a criminal standing before the bar of justice can use the neglect of society as a legitimate excuse is, again, a practical, not a philosophic question. It is a question generally minimized in criminal procedure.

Free Will in a Lawful Universe

Even though there is merit in the distinctions we have just made between mental normality and disease, between babies who react instinctively and older children and adults who have self-control, we have not yet tackled the major difficulty of the free will problem. How is free will possible in a universe in which all events are determined by natural laws as the necessary consequences of previous conditions? If my action—say, wanting to look at television—is fully determined by my personal physical and mental conditions at the time I turn the knobs of the set, then how can we justify the conviction that I freely decided on what I actually did do? Self-observation shows us that our desires, the purposes we have in mind, determine our actions. But these desires, as natural events, are an inevitable outcome of all the forces and events of our previous life. "Men are sometimes free to do what they wish," the English philosopher Hobbes wrote in the seventeenth century, "but they are never free in their wishes."

Historically, there have been three proposals to solve the problem of the existence of free will in a lawful universe. First, there is the old dualistic idea that man has a soul that is free from the restraints of natural determination. Descartes transferred this idea from theological speculation to Western philosophy. In one form or another, the assumption of the existence of a separate spiritual substance in man became part of the dominant philosophic view until the nineteenth century. Kant regarded the soul as a necessary idea and part of the free realm of things-in-themselves, which transcends nature. While similar doctrines are, of course, still held by religious philosophers, this view now can claim few friends among wordly philosophers, and it is rejected by empiricists.

There is, secondly, what has been called the libertarian view.[16] According to this view, there are certain occasions in our lives, particularly in moments of conflict, when our character or our natural desires tend one way and an ethical command directs us to act in a way contrary to our inclinations. At these times man, by a creative choice, may free himself from the bonds of natural law and do the right thing. Contrary to the deterministic view, which holds that antecedent circumstances condition all our choices, this theory postulates the existence of a "contra-causal type of freedom." (C. A. Campbell) Determinism maintains "that no man could have acted otherwise than he did"; libertarianism assumes that we have a special spontaneity which permits us to rise to duty by the exercise of our will.

> It lies with me here and now, quite absolutely, which of two genuinely open possibilities I adopt; whether, that is, I make the effort of will and choose X or, on the other hand, let my desiring nature, my character as so far formed, "have its way," and choose Y, the course "in the line of least resistance." (Campbell)

We could have acted differently than we did, though all the antecedent events and conditions of our lives and environment had been the same. Our free will could have substituted another action.

Several points may be raised against this view. Why should this non-causal free choice, which is an exceptional interruption of the natural course of events, take place only in the special case when duty and inclination conflict? What about all the other cases of deliberate choice, when we buy a particular book, or when we consider really important matters, such as whether to accept a certain new position? What is different about these decisions? If we assume the occurrence of contra-causal, spontaneous decisions at all, then why not in the cases just mentioned?

There are other difficulties with the libertarian position. Generally speaking, people have certain dispositions and characters and act accordingly. When an entirely novel situation arises, of course, we cannot anticipate what someone will do; and in some situations people do very surprising things. But generally, people act in accordance with their personal characteristics, and even so, we ascribe free will to them. Has the man who swears every morning when the alarm clock rings, exercises before he gets dressed, stops at a bar before he comes home and asks his children night after night what happened at school, lost his free will—he *could* stop acting in this manner if he wanted to, although it has become second nature to him. The same is true of the man who has always been honest; we expect him to resist temptations. But there are other people of whom we are not at all surprised to learn that they cut corners in business or indulge in extramarital affairs. Habit and free will are not mutually exclusive. We do not limit the idea of free will to the unusual cases, when someone's decision seems to be "out of character." Viewing the matter from this angle, we realize that free will is not incompatible with predictability and regularity. Our decisions about what we do always seem to lie with us, except when we are subjected to overpowering outer or inner forces.

Quite aside from these special problems, which are raised by the libertarian view of a unique area of uncaused decisions, scientists and naturalistic philosophers see no valid reason to accept a breach in their deterministic view, which holds that there are no uncaused events and that every event, including human activities, can be explained in principle by an earlier state of affairs. Most philosophers, however, agree with our everyday thinking and assume that our actions are under our control, that we are free. In other words, we combine the basic deterministic conception of science with the assumption of free will.

This, then, is the third proposal for dealing with free will. In one form or another it has become the theory held by many contemporary philosophers.[17] Let me restate the idea. Like everything in nature, human beings are subject to natural laws, but at the same time they are free to the extent that they are mentally healthy and not under duress or outside restraint.

How can such a view be upheld? (While I have no doubt whatsoever about the meaningfulness of this apparently contradictory combination, I, along with some other philosophers, find it puzzling and some of its ramifications difficult to understand. Articles on this issue are full of remarks indicating that "this needs further clarification.") The basic factor that has made the modern theory possible is an analysis of the meaning of the notion "being free." Let us first distinguish involuntary and voluntary actions. Among the involuntary actions, or acts as some call them, certain ones involve only ourselves, such as giggling, weeping, uncontrollable rage, or other explosive emotional outbreaks, and certain actions of psychotics. Then there are influences from the outside, which may restrain us or force us to do what we do not wish to do; prisoners, and people being tortured, brainwashed, or hypnotized, cannot act freely.

Most voluntary actions, despite the fact that they are voluntary, are based not so much on decisions, as on habits we have acquired. We decide to get up, wash, dress and have breakfast. These activities take place more or less automatically, without much, if any, deliberation. After we have decided to go walking or swimming, we walk or swim without giving much thought to our leg or arm movements. Of course, we can, for one reason or another, decide at any time to interrupt any of these actions, and this would require a decision. The fact that we can make such decisions is one of the aspects of our free will.

In the course of these everyday actions, however, there are numerous times when we do have to make decisions; what we are going to eat for breakfast, or where we are going to walk. When we talk or write we are constantly engaged in deciding on the arrangement of our thoughts, and we may have to search for the right expression. Our life, while we are awake and active, is a constant mixture of important and unimportant choices and more or less unpremeditated actions.

Free will means nothing more or less than that we have the capacity to act voluntarily, that we could have decided to act differently than we did. We have the ability to choose how we shall act. "The voluntary would seem to be that of which the moving principle is in the agent himself, he being aware of the particular circumstances of the action." (Aristotle) No action we want to engage in comes of itself. Our bodily movements depend on us. We must consider and select. If we had decided differently, we could have acted differently. We are not like a player piano; we must play the music of our lives ourselves on the keyboard of the possibilities that are open to us. "A man is not the 'mere spectator of the play of forces' within him. We say not merely 'I may do right, and I may do wrong,' but 'I *can* do right and I *can* do wrong.' " (H. D. Lewis, in part quoting David Ross) Each normal individual is capable of self-government, and our minds work like "a parliament or deliberate assembly." (H. J. Muller)

Our decisions naturally depend on the strength of our wants and desires, our motives, our insights and our impulsiveness. These factors, in turn, depend upon our inherited characteristics, as they have been influenced or redirected for better or worse by education and life experiences. Here we seem to be back again at a determinism that denies free will. Schopenhauer has said: "A man can surely do what he wills to do, but he cannot determine what he wills." This sounds persuasive because of an unclear use of the word "determine." However, we know that we can determine ourselves, we are not compelled. We can control our behavior. There is a scene in *Huckleberry Finn*, in which Huck is torn between his conscience, which tells him he ought to turn in the runaway slave Jim, and his memories of the wonderful experiences he and Jim had together on their trip down the Mississippi, which make him reluctant to do so.

> I'd got to decide, forever, betwixt two things, and I knowed it. I studied a minute, sort of holding my breath, and then says to myself: "All right, then, I'll *go* to hell"—and tore it [the note to Jim's owner] up. It was awful thoughts and awful words, but they were said. And I let them stay said; and never thought no more about reforming.[18]

When you speak to me and I speak to you, it is we ourselves who determine what we are going to say. "It is just incredible to say that I could not, simply of my own volition here and now, choose to alter the next word I shall write after this sentence." (D. D. Raphael) When someone is criticized for looking sloppy, or making an offensive remark, killing a competitor for his girl-friend's love, he may try to excuse himself with an I-could-not-help-it. But if he is a normal person mentally, one may very properly retort: Indeed, you *could* have helped it; you *could* have acted differently. To excuse an act because it is the result of unfortunate circumstances is valid only in certain cases; it does not negate free will in general.

The determinism that supposedly governs our behavior is often sought in the lawfulness of the biophysical processes of our neural system, which, in a manner unknown to us, are related to the mental activities of decision-making. But these purely mental activities cannot be made more understandable as biophysical events. Biophysics does not explain our choices. When we dis-cuss free will, we deal solely with problems in the mental realm of "the two-fold 'irreducibly different aspects' of experiencing our living activities." (Discussed above, p. 163) In this realm we call free will our normal ability to choose voluntarily what we think, say, write and do.

> Nothing we have discovered or will discover about the physiological and psychological *conditions* that make delibera-tion and choice possible can be used as evidence (except on pain of a fatal incoherence) for denying that such deliberative choices *do* occur. . . . A person is correctly characterized as a responsible moral agent if he behaves in the manner in which a normal agent behaves; and the characterization remains cor-rect even if the organic and psychological conditions that make it possible for him to function as a moral agent are not within his control on any of those occasions when he is acting as a responsible person. (Ernest Nagel)[19]

Our free actions are not uncaused events, but their causes are neither constraint nor compulsion. It is our *mental* make-up which is the working basis of the decision-making of each of us. When something occurs that inclines or requires us to do some-thing or to discontinue doing something, then it is we who must decide.

It is fruitless to try to escape the necessity for choice, for we cannot live without choosing, without exercising our free will. It is impossible to sit back, proclaim a wait-and-see policy and leave everything in the hands of fate. Fate does not feed, clothe, house and protect us. It is man's lot not to be like "the lilies of the field . . . [which] neither toil nor spin." We ourselves must take care of our affairs, and we can do this only if we choose our everyday activities and our long-range plans. It goes without saying that our projects often do not work out according to our expectations. The goddess of fate may smile on our endeavors, or she may frustrate our plans. In either case we may be confronted with the necessity of making new decisions. Each individual may also regard as fated his physical and mental endowments and limitations, and the family, social and historical situation into which he is born, as well as the further course of these events during his lifetime, all of which are beyond his control. These are matters that we have to learn to live with. And intelligent adjustment to that which we cannot change is a sign of wisdom.

The powerful, ineluctable role which fate plays in our lives should not lead us to believe in a general fatalism. Fatalism is, according to the dictionary, "a doctrine that events are fixed in advance for all time in such a manner that human beings are powerless to change them." It claims that our destiny is independent of our desires and of whatever we may do; God's or Allah's predestination, or the causality of natural forces or of a miserable upbringing have predetermined our lives. But the events of our lives do not occur according to a prearranged plan. We are not powerless to decide what we want to do and how we want to live. In fact, we must decide. "Men at some time are masters of their fates: The fault, dear Brutus, is not in our stars, But in ourselves . . ." (*Julius Caesar*)

When we are choosing, we do not know what we are going to do until we have considered the question. Even in such a trivial matter as selecting the tie I am wearing today, I could not know which it would be until I had chosen.

> Making a decision . . . implies, by the very meaning of the term, uncertainty as to what one is going to do. (A. Pap)[20]

> A man in making up his mind how he is going to act does not and cannot do so by reflecting on his previous mental history and what he knows of his own character. He is to go through

the process of coming to a decision before he knows what that decision is going to be. (A. K. Stout)[21]

The idea of my predicting in advance what my as yet uncertain decision will be is contradictory. Even a fully rational person, facing a problem, is often not aware of all his thoughts and desires regarding the particular matter to be decided until he has brought them into consciousness; only then can he weigh what he wants to do.

A person, before he has decided, is in a position similar to that of the physicist E. O. Lawrence, who is supposed to have answered when asked what he expected to discover with a larger cyclotron, "Why, if we knew that, there wouldn't be any sense in building the damned thing." No psychological or physiological law or combination of laws can tell me or anyone else, in advance of my coming to a decision, what *I* will do. This is not in contradiction to the fact that we *usually* can count on people to act "in character." An honest man will be honest; a tardy man will be late; a Don Juan will chase women; a typical teen-ager will resent being asked, "Where are you going?" But even these forecasts have an element of uncertainty. In every one of these cases an agent may decide of his own free will to act atypically. Prediction is even more difficult, if not impossible, when one faces a new situation. Take Sartre's example. During the German occupation of France a man "had the choice between going to England to join the Free French Forces or of staying near his mother and helping her to live. He fully realized that this woman lived only for him and that his disappearance—or perhaps his death—would plunge her into despair." (*Existentialism Is a Humanism*)[22] Until the young man had deliberated and determined what he would do, no one could know what would happen with him. Not fate but he decided; he *had to* decide when his conscience or his friends appealed to him: Won't you help Free France; won't you avenge your brother, whom the Germans killed?

The Grand Inquisitor of Dostoevsky's famous story of that name speaks of freedom as a "terrible gift that had brought such suffering." Because decisions are often difficult and their consequences may be tragic and people are weak, some of us are afraid of freedom and try to avoid it (see Erich Fromm's *Escape from Freedom*). They join orthodox churches, fascist movements and military organizations in order not to be burdened with the "dreadful freedom" with which we are endowed. But try as we may to escape, we can never really get away from our free will. It is inherent in every normal person, and it is up to us to make the most worthwhile use of our freedom.

CHAPTER VIII

Are There Ethical Norms?

"In all the world and in all of life
there is nothing more important
to determine than what is right."
—C. I. LEWIS[1]

Ideological Chaos

The preceding chapter ended with the idea that "it is up to us to make the most worthwhile use of our freedom." Unfortunately, today nothing is more in dispute than what is worthwhile and what ought to be the goals of our actions; nowhere is skepticism more in evidence than in the realm of ethical values. There was a time, not too long ago, when people believed in eternal values such as those set forth in the Ten Commandments, the Sermon on the Mount, or the Declaration of Independence. Indeed, there is serious doubt whether an ethical philosophy is possible at all, whether we can say anything meaningful about moral judgments. Over and over again we are told that we are living in a moral vacuum because life is absurd, or, as one young writer put it, "all things are equal and equal to nothing."

People seem to be living forlornly in "a world of shattered and shifting values" (Gladys Schmitt), a world of value-lessness, pessimism, frustration and fear. A sense of insecurity, turmoil and impending disaster pervades today's outlook, radically affecting the arts, the theatre, literature, moral and religious thinking and behavior.

This agonizing attitude can be examined from two different viewpoints, the philosophic and the sociological. The philosopher asks whether it is correct to assume that belief in personal and political ideals is unjustified. On the other hand, it is the task of the sociologist to study the reality and the causes of the prevailing social atmosphere. The following is an outline of some of the main features.

1. One basic cause of our contemporary malaise is the fact that we are living in an age of terror and destruction. A sense of total insecurity has been generated by the atom bomb, which has the capability to destroy all human life. Nothing like this had ever been feasible before. In this connection, Freud's profound insight of 1930 has great validity for us:

> Men have brought their power of subduing the forces of nature to such a pitch that by using them they could now very easily exterminate one another to the last man. They know this—hence arises a great part of current unrest, their dejection, their mood of apprehension.[2]

This is also the age of genocide by the gas chamber, of the leveling of cities by aerial bombardment, of assassinations and "crime in the streets."

2. Our existence seems disoriented and unstable because we are at the conjunction of several rapid and decisive transformations in many spheres of life.

a. Important historical changes have followed each other in quick succession since 1914. Wars and revolutions have been almost constant. The position of the United States—its foreign policy and influence on the political stability and economic welfare of the rest of the world—has undergone a fundamental change in this century. There are only two great powers today, Russia and the United States; they face each other in an almost unendurable and foreboding equilibrium. The resulting competitive arms race has caused the so-called "military-industrial complex" to gain a dominant influence over our foreign policy and our society, a factor quite novel in our history. The book title, *World Politics and Personal Insecurity*, aptly describes our situation. What is each individual's position and responsibility in the "one world" of today?

b. Advances in science and technology have revolutionized our everyday existence. We can hardly imagine what life was like a few generations ago without automobiles, airplanes, telephones, television and all the numerous labor-saving machines and gadgets in our homes. Changing styles of living create fresh moral issues.

New agricultural techniques have driven millions of farm laborers from the farms to the slums of the big cities. The progress of medicine has greatly reduced child mortality, thus contributing to the population explosion. This has, in turn, intensified problems in developing countries and caused increased problems in our country. The automobile and the pill have critically altered the character of courtship and liberalized sexual behavior. There is talk of a *new* sexual morality. In this area, standards, or the lack of them, are much discussed by young and old and have caused much uneasiness. Tension between the generations is created by the fact that today's children are growing up in an environment quite unlike that of their parents and grandparents. The moral standards of one generation are not necessarily those of the next.

The great productivity of modern industrialism has brought about other significant social transformations. The shrinking farm population, the blue collar and the ever increasing white collar class all aspire to the middle-class standard of living. Home ownership and suburban living, which has its own multiple social problems, have changed the face and the manners of America. Commerce and industry, the rich and the poor, have taken over the metropolitan cities.

However, we are far from eliminating poverty for 30–40 million people living in our midst. The traditional individualistic values of our politics and economics are not suited to cope with our grave social ills. The scandalous discrepancy between our productivity and our social progress weighs—or should weigh—upon our conscience and it reveals the hypocrisy behind our tireless professions of adherence to social and religious ideals. Does not the sickness of our society and "the moral depravity" of war indicate the hollowness of these ideals? This is the question so many of the younger generation are asking and answering in the affirmative.

c. After some three centuries of comparative apathy, we are now involved in a frequently bitter struggle to achieve the political, social and educational equality of 22 million Negroes. Young people, because of their restlessness and fervor, have been particularly drawn to activism for racial justice and against the senselessness of the horrible Vietnam war.

d. Authoritarian structures in society have weakened and traditional bonds have loosened, as is exemplified by strikes of teachers, policemen and other public employees and by the turmoil in high schools and colleges.

Great changes have also taken place in the old-fashioned character of the American family, so well described in Clarence Day's *Life with Father*. Children and adolescents have acquired greater freedom in the more permissive home. With greater flexibility in standards of behavior and obedience, parents must constantly ask themselves when they should criticize, when they should punish, and what their role should be vis-à-vis the adolescent sub-culture.

e. Millions of children and teen-agers who formerly had to go to work on farms or factories are able to continue their education. Large groups of young people living and studying together in small citylike campuses vent their restless energy in sometimes violent protests against authority and against a society they regard as totally misdirected. However, their goals are often unclear to them. Unfortunately, affirmative ideologies and the utopian ideals of traditional socialism and communism have lost their luster. The general trend is frequently to non-conformity and rebelliousness for its own sake. The ferment is increased because the sexual revolution has contributed to the uncertainty regarding standards of personal behavior in this particular age group.

f. Finally, there has been a great shift in the intellectual climate, and this affects our moral consciousness. The hold of organized religion and the belief in God as moral lawgiver who punishes man for his sins have gradually weakened. We are "sickled o'er with the pale cast of thought." For those who reject their father's faith there seems to be no new set of commandments and consolations to take its place. The non-religious ideologies and directions that are developing do not have the organized strength and visibility of the churches. We seem to have lost our way in this era of disbelief.

A new psychological perspective has become all pervasive and what it seems to reveal is not pleasant. It stresses our aberrant drives, our troubles and weaknesses, and thus adds another ingredient to our pessimism. To some it seems to indicate that everything is permissible and must be tolerated.

Volumes have been written about the numerous social and political problems in our bureaucratic mass society, about the contemporary cultural situation and the modern zeitgeist, and about our disturbed youth, but I have to limit the description of our skeptical moral climate and its varied and complicated causes to these brief remarks.

In the foregoing summary of disturbing elements I have said nothing about the very substantial benefits of increased productivity, advancements in science and medicine, progress in race relations, mass education, more natural sexual behavior, liberation from religious superstitions and the new insights of psychology and psychiatry. The picture I have drawn to explain contemporary uneasiness is purposely one-sided. There are, however, very positive aspects to life in today's era of transition. Daniel Bell has quite correctly remarked:

> Modern society is, for the mass, more differentiated and life-enhancing, in its cultural aspects, than traditional society.

However, our young people, living in the midst of rapid change in every aspect of human concern, have for the most part discarded historical perspective. Such perspective is needed for a just comparison between the quality of life today with the quality of life in an imagined better past.

Murder: Cain and King David

As a philosopher, interested in moral theory, I now must ask whether it is really true that moral values are non-existent and that human reason is unable to distinguish right from wrong and inferior values from more lofty ones. In answering this question I prefer to begin, not with an abstract analysis of the reality or nonreality of moral values, but with a review of a very old and well-known case of clear-cut fratricide, the murder of Abel by Cain as described in the fourth chapter of Genesis. First I would like to make some remarks about the Bible itself. I do not cite the Bible because of its religious character or even because it is the basis of our religious tradition, for it is more than that. Even if today it is the "unknown book," as is often deploringly maintained, it is nevertheless the expression of one source of Western intellectual civilization. Obviously an understanding of modern culture is impossible without some knowledge of the nature and content of the Bible.

The Bible confronts us with the One God, in whom both Jews and Christians believe, and with Christ; it describes their activities and sets God's commandments before us. It also records the history of the Jews as the people of the Book. The Bible accomplishes these things by relating exciting old myths and beautiful, dramatic stories; through historical narrative, much of it quite accurate; through ethical injunctions, laws, philosophy and theology. Religious ceremonies are prescribed in great detail. Finally, there is inspiring and delightfully sensuous poetry. However, there are also long dull stretches.

The Bible with its varied content is not a book in the usual sense of the word. It is more like a gradually growing anthology. What should go into the first part of this anthology, that is, that part we now call the Old Testament, was long debated, and was settled only in the first century of the Christian era, long after the various parts had been written down; the final canon of the New Testament was decided in the second century. Some parts of the Bible are very old and represent the primitive tribal beliefs, customs and law of a nomadic people. Others were written hundreds of years later. The Biblical text does not distinguish between what is old and what is not. The Torah, that is, the first five books, contains, for example, the old law of retaliation, often cited as evidence of the primitiveness of Mosaic Law ("Life for life, eye for eye, tooth for tooth, etc." [Ex. 21:23–24]). But the statement of this law is only one chapter removed from the Ten Commandments (Ex. 20) and only a few chapters from the statement of the Golden Rule ("Love your neighbor as yourself: I am the Lord." [Lev. 19:18]), a commandment of love which most Christians and Jews ascribe to Jesus. Thus the Bible does reveal evidence of ethical advancement.

Let us now turn to the Cain-and-Abel story, which reads as follows:

> Now the man knew his wife Eve, and she conceived and bore Cain, saying, "I have gained a male child with the help of the LORD." She then bore his brother Abel. Abel became a keeper of sheep, and Cain became a tiller of the soil. In the

course of time, Cain brought an offering to the LORD from
the fruit of the soil; and Abel, for his part, brought the choicest
of the firstlings of his flock. The LORD paid heed to Abel and
his offering, but to Cain and his offering He paid no heed.
Cain was much distressed and his face fell. And the LORD
said to Cain, "Why are you distressed, And why is your face
fallen? Surely, if you do right, There is uplift. But if you do
not do right Sin is the demon at the door, Whose urge is toward you. Yet you can be his master."

And Cain said to his brother Abel ("Come, let us go out
into the field") and when they were in the field, Cain set upon
his brother Abel and killed him. The LORD said to Cain,
"Where is your brother Abel?" And he said, "I do not know,
am I my brother's keeper?" Then He said, "What have you
done? Hark, your brother's blood cries out to Me from the
ground! Therefore, you shall be banned from the soil, which
opened its mouth wide to receive your brother's blood from
your hand. If you till the soil, it shall no longer yield its
strength to you. You shall become a ceaseless wanderer on
earth."

Cain said to the LORD, "My punishment is too great to
bear!" (Gen. 4)

These few Biblical verses present a number of important
problems. We dealt with one of them previously, the problem of
the freedom of man's will, a freedom that is affirmed in God's
assertion that man *can* master sin. A further problem, and one
that must be a matter of constant concern to all religious people,
is the equivocal role of God in neglecting Cain's offering and
thus being Himself responsible for subsequent events. This phase
of the story is a particular aspect of the general problem of why
the all-powerful, all-loving and omniscient God allowed sin and
evil to exist among His creatures, and probably the most difficult
for theism to deal with. But since our concern is not theology,
we do not have to look for a solution. The dilemma disappears if
one is not a theist. Nor must we discuss the problem of punishment now.

But we are still left with the murder story as such. I am sure
that every one of us knows it is wrong to kill his brother from
mere envy; we condemn fratricide. It is interesting to note that
Cain himself feels guilty; otherwise he would not have answered
God's question, "Where is your brother Abel?" with the lie, "I
do not know." Since we find ourselves in accord with Biblical
thought here, as expressed by God and felt by Cain's uneasy con-

science, we can say that at least within the narrow framework of this particular situation, an ethical rule dating back thousands of years has not changed and that skepticism and relativism have no place here. We will not go into the question of what may be the basis of our own conviction now. Whether the commandment not to murder one's brother out of envy can be justified is another question; age-old custom and current thinking do not constitute a justification. In any case, we seem to have found an absolute here, a rather self-evident one to be sure, but still "a truth till the end of reckoning." If we modify the situation slightly by omitting the fact that the killer and his victim are brothers, I am sure we will all agree that this will not change our moral judgment. The owner of a small grocery store put out of business by a large, newly opened supermarket, may have good reason to hate the owner or manager of the supermarket, but he would commit a great wrong if he killed his competitor.

There are many actions and events in the Bible which we view quite differently than the Bible does. Just as views about heavenly bodies and many other natural phenomena have changed, so have ethical evaluations. Yet it is noteworthy that certain commands which the Bible upholds are still regarded as valid.

Let us take a look at another, lesser known Biblical murder story, King David's successful maneuvering to bring about the slaying of his general Uriah (II Sam. 11 and 12). David had observed Uriah's beautiful wife, Bathsheba, bathing. He thereupon sent for her and "he lay with her." David then attempted a "perfect crime," ordering his commanding general to so conduct a battle that Uriah would be left alone to face strong enemy forces, who would kill him. And so it happened. David then "fetched Bathsheba to his house, and she became his wife . . . But the thing that David had done displeased the Lord. And the Lord sent Nathan unto David," who reproached David in the Lord's name, and David confessed, "I have sinned against the Lord."

We have here, not an unpremeditated murder committed in the heat of passion, but a cold-blooded planned killing. As in the case of the Cain-and-Abel murder story, we do pass an ethical judgment of condemnation, which has gone unchanged since Biblical days. Like Cain, David feels guilty, and we agree with both that they were wrong-doers. It should be noted that when this story was written, even kings were regarded—as they are today—as subject to the moral law forbidding the murder of one man by another merely because the latter lusts after his wife. Similar crimes still occur today.

There are certain moral facets of the second story, however, which have changed greatly. If we read the story carefully, we cannot help wondering about Bathsheba's attitude and behavior. When David first sent for her, the Bible says simply, ". . . and she came in unto him . . . and she returned unto her house. And the woman conceived, and sent and told David." After Uriah's death "she mourned for her husband. And when the mourning was passed, David sent and fetched her to his house, and she became his wife, and bore him a son." Nowhere is there the slightest indication that Bathsheba felt that she was doing any wrong, nor is there any condemnation of her whatsoever. It was the king who had sent for her, and she did as he commanded her. Since the days of this love story, kings have lost what was then considered their right to call on the women of their realm to share their bed, a right that still existed to a certain extent even in the eighteenth century, as Mozart's opera *Figaro* shows.

What is much more important than this particular change is the fact that the whole position of women has gone through a revolutionary change. In most pre-modern civilizations women had few rights; often their status was not much better than that of serfs. That they are full-fledged members of humanity and that their rights and position ought to be the same as those of men is a comparatively recent notion. Most of us would regard the modern viewpoint as morally superior. In our acceptance of this point of view we have discovered another valid moral goal, in the sense that no thinking person can help but consider it an objectively more desirable ideal, an ethical truth.

It may be argued that to condemn murder and the second-class status of women—one-half of humanity—is trite and does not solve any of the moral problems which actually affect us here and now. That may be so. What these examples and their interpretation show, however, is that we do believe in the truth of some ethical rules. Thus, to maintain that we are living in an era without any moral guideposts is erroneous. We regard as ethical truths the statements: murder is wrong; a king ought not to command women to have sexual relations with him; women ought to have the same rights as men. Perhaps we shall discover many other ethical truths, and they may be as obvious as the three just stated. Nevertheless we may very well find that the subject-matter of ethics is, in any event, of some interest.

Changing Customs and Ethical Truth

It will be useful to examine more closely how it is possible to assume the existence of ethical truths, even though what was and is affirmed as ethical truth by various peoples and individuals can differ. This situation has been the source of much confusion. We have had occasion in previous chapters to deny the meaningfulness of the idea that there are different truths for certain people or for other cultures. The Hebrews, the Greeks and the Indians had or have different beliefs and opinions from ours. But there is only one truth, and our opinions, or the opinions of the Hebrews, the Greeks and the Indians are either true or false. In certain cases the decision with respect to truth or falsity may be difficult. It is no different with ethical principles. It does not require an analysis of philosophic ethics to accept this. Every one of us believes that prescriptions such as "life for life, eye for eye" are barbaric. Our moral and common sense denies that men have the right to treat women as chattels and laborers as slaves. Whatever a dictator may proclaim regarding the propriety of torture, brainwashing, or concentration camps, there is no doubt in our minds that he is a malefactor.

If there are such ethical rules as the few obvious ones we have discussed so far, then we must hold contrary rules to be false. Nevertheless, we do not regard the Greeks, or the biblical Jews immoral because they owned slaves, just as we do not consider them stupid because they did not know that the earth revolves around the sun and not the sun around the earth. In both fields, astronomy and ethics, advances have been made in the last two thousand years and new insights have been gained. Mankind has developed. To single out one important example: there has been a constant enlargement of respect for the individual and of the sphere of equality, though it is a process which has by no means reached the perfect state.

In general, people do not become skeptical because theoretical beliefs have undergone, and are still undergoing, great changes. New but eventually well-confirmed scientific findings are normally accepted after a while as truths. The number of those who maintain a Barbusse-like skepticism toward scientific findings is rather small. It is different with ethics. We are fully convinced of the immorality of murder, slavery and concentration camps, but when we theorize about ethics we become uncertain for reasons mentioned at the beginning of the chapter.

I shall discuss one additional reason here. A plethora of anthropological discoveries, and treatises and their popularity at the end of the last and the beginning of this century made people aware of the many different ways and cultures of mankind. Thoughtful men hesitated to proclaim our morality as *the* right one. But it is necessary to discriminate here. Many differences between cultures are merely matters of a practical nature: adaptations to different climates, terrain and economies; others are esthetic or ceremonial. In so far as moral differences are involved, it is legitimate, and not a sign of intolerance to question whether or not certain practices, such as polygamy or human sacrifice, are in accordance with good moral standards.[3]

The Nature and Uses of Ethics

What does ethics mean? The dictionary defines ethics as follows: "1. the discipline dealing with what is good and bad and with moral duty and obligation. 2a. a set of moral principles or values, b. a theory or system of moral values. c. the principles of conduct governing an individual or a group." * As is evident from this definition, the rather vague terms "ethics," "ethical" and "moral" may frequently be used interchangeably, like the words "sick" and "ill."

Ethics deals with the second of Kant's four questions: "What shall I do?" And not only what ought you and I to do or not do, but also what ought you and I to have done or not done. It judges the rightness or wrongness of human conduct—past, present and future. It tells us "what it is we believe to be worth the seeking" (L. Susan Stebbing) and thus deals with the goals of our lives. Ethics contains commands, rules, imperatives. Do this! Don't do that! Ethics is, therefore, a normative discipline. It evaluates what is good, what is better, what is bad or worse, what should or should not be and how we ought or ought not to act. It follows that ethics also deals with the question of what actions

* *Webster's Seventh New Collegiate Dictionary,* 1963.

and what people are worthy of praise or worthy of blame, which deserve reward and which punishment.

We know that people, including ourselves, have certain rules of behavior and morality, and our intellect in general and sometimes our conscience in particular—if I may use this old-fashioned term—tell us to do certain things and abstain from certain other things. These rules may vary from individual to individual, from country to country, and from civilization to civilization. The factual story of what people think, what their values are, and how they actually behave is not part of ethics but of the social sciences, such as psychology, anthropology and sociology.

Ethics is part of every life and not merely an esoteric, philosophic discipline. The denial of ethical thinking, which is a widespread fashionable attitude, is completely contrary to actual life and to everyday reasoning.

> No one can avoid ethics. . . . We are moralists willy-nilly. The only question is whether, since we are committed to ethics anyhow, the views we have shall be reflective and clear or uncriticized and muddled. (Brand Blanshard) [4]

Even a murderer, like Shakespeare's Richard III, acknowledges ethical concepts in his outburst: "And every tale condemns me for a villain."

Ethics plays an important role in life. Ethical considerations, however, are not involved in all of the choices of our ordinary life. Many are without ethical relevance. Much of our conduct is routine, much habitual, or related to quite unimportant matters, such as what to wear, what to eat, or which friend to visit. Some actions depend on esthetic considerations (how a room is to be furnished), others on the pleasure we expect to derive from them (what movie to see, where to go in the summer). Certain crucial practical choices, such as what occupation to enter, what college to attend, or whom to marry, have emotional as well as practical aspects, and in addition, to the extent that these decisions are related to our life-goals, they may also be influenced by our ethical preferences. Finally, there are decisions that turn on such ethical values as honesty, decency, gratitude, charity, justice, fortitude and such ideals as excellence, harmony and beauty. Often several of these aspects—the practical, emotional, esthetic and moral—have to be taken into account in weighing a particular action.

> Moral talk is not intended just to describe our world but primarily to criticize and *alter* it. The intent of moral language is to *intervene in the world*, to alter actions and attitudes concerning what is to be done. [Italics mine] (Kai Nielsen) [5]

Ethical philosophy, therefore, has been called practical philosophy, and it was for this reason that Kant entitled his basic analysis of ethics *Critique of Practical Reason.* Philosophic ethics is rather impractical, however, for several reasons; and in this respect it is no different from the theory of knowledge or the philosophy of science. Everyone is acquainted with the world and knows a great deal about it without studying the theory of knowledge, and most scientists attend to their particular field without bothering about the philosophy of science.

Most of us do give thought to moral problems. Even the doubter knows and lives by a great many moral principles without studying ethics. Everyone receives some kind of moral education, beginning in his earliest youth. Don't be rough . . . don't grab . . . help your sister . . . don't pick the flowers in Mrs. Smith's garden . . . be polite! And it continues through childhood, adolescence and adulthood. In our civilization a well-educated person becomes familiar, in one way or another, with many ethical ideas. What philosophic ethics teaches may not seem new, but it will at least contribute to a systematic order of the ethical ideas we have acquired and will clarify puzzling problems and contradictions.

Unfortunately, ethical common sense is often confused. It ". . . guides some people in one direction and others . . . in the very opposite direction. We may ourselves be torn this way and that by contradictory feelings. Which of these shall we follow? . . . We need a yardstick which would enable us to decide which of the contradictory feelings should be regarded as the correct, sound, unperverted, authentic feeling." (Leonard Nelson) [6] Not only individuals, but whole nations often follow wrong ideals, which a *proper* philosophy could rectify. A yardstick will make it possible for us to defend our views when we are asked for advice and to convince others of what they ought to do. It may also show up our own ethical sophistry and rationalization, that is, our self-deceptions, whereby we ascribe worthy motives to unworthy actions or to actions which, in reality, were done for questionable, or purely egotistic reasons. Hypocrisy is the tribute that immorality pays to morality. "One can never be quite certain whether the disguise is meant only for the eye of the external observer or whether, as may usually be the case, it deceives the self." (R. Niebuhr) The study of ethics may deepen our moral understanding and enlarge our moral horizon and demonstrate goals that we have not seen. The "sense of justice is a product of the mind and not of the heart." (R. Niebuhr)[7]

Philosophic ethics suffers from the generality of its principles. We know that we ought not to steal, murder, or rape. We do not have to study ethics to acquire *that* knowledge. But we would like to have some help in handling situations that really puzzle us. For example: Shall we demonstrate for integration or for peace; should one resist the draft; how much energy, money and time should we devote to good causes? We know we should not cheat the government, but the line between legitimate business expenses and those that are not is very tenuous. (I am referring to the moral aspects, not the legal aspects.) What is legitimate exaggeration in advertising, and where does misrepresentation begin? Philosophic ethics does not offer us formulas with which to resolve such problems.

Or let us take a much more serious and age-old dilemma, the pregnancy of an unwed, immature adolescent girl. The contemporary version has found its way into many plays and movies. A pregnant high school girl tells her parents that she is in trouble. What advice should the parents give their daughter? How ought they to help her? An earlier strict, Puritanical morality might have inclined the parents to throw the girl out of their house. Or the girl, overcome with fear and shame, might have committed suicide. But today we evaluate this situation differently—and, I believe, in a better way. Should the girl undergo an illegal abortion? Should she have her baby in her home town, with her family standing by, and keep it? Or should she go away, have her baby in secrecy, and give it up for adoption? These are difficult questions. Many factors enter into the decisions that are made, and their relative importance is difficult to assess. General ethical principles shed little light on the "right" answers.

Unfortunately, since it is true that we still face perplexities even after we have studied philosophic ethics, we may come to doubt the usefulness of ethics; for in the complicated situations of actual life, when we most need moral clarification, the practical assistance it can give us is limited. The final outcome of an ethical evaluation cannot be determined with the definiteness of an answer to an engineering problem, to say nothing of a mathematical problem, and it is possible that the prevalent ethical skepticism has one of its roots in this uncertainty. In addition, as I have previously pointed out, there are important life decisions in which passions, interests and preferences of a non-ethical nature play the decisive role.

This uncertainty prevails in many areas, not only with respect to our own personal decisions. It is just as bothersome when we try to judge the behavior and character of our friends and acquaintances or of public figures, whose actions are detailed in the columns and pictures of our mass media. What are we to think of the divorces of Miss X, the well-known film star; the behavior of our friends when their son was expelled from college, the demonstrations in front of Y's house, or A's lawsuit against B, his former partner and friend? Acquaintances and neighbors are often all too ready to condemn, but how do we know that they are justified? When answers are most important, we seem to be left in the lurch. Is not ethics therefore meaningless! A little while ago I mentioned some counterarguments to this complaint. But I think an outline of ethics will be the best refutation.

There is another, very important factor which diminishes the importance of philosophic ethics in human affairs. Ethical knowledge alone does not make for a just life. Right motivation is essential. I have quoted St. Paul's well-known self-reproach: "For I do not do the good I want, but the evil I do not want, is what I do." (Rom. 8:19) We often know what ethics teaches, but we do not follow its prescriptions.

> We can no more learn to act rightly by appealing to the ethical theory of right action than we can play golf well by appealing to the mathematical theory of the flight of the golf-ball. The interest of ethics is thus almost wholly theoretical. . . . (C. D. Broad)[8]

Let us note that even Professor Broad grants that the interest of ethics is not entirely theoretical. (Saul would not be *St.* Paul if he had done only evil.) There can be rational moral control of our behavior but there are limits to our willingness not to "fall into sin." The Ten Commandments, the Sermon on the Mount and other similar ethical prescriptions have, in theory, been mankind's guiding stars. But our actual behavior has never even come close to our proclaimed morality. Our deficiency in ethical motivation does not mean that ethical philosophy serves no purpose and should be done away with. On the contrary, we should do everything to strengthen the moral point of view. Knowledge alone may not suffice, but it is one prerequisite to the moral improvement of individual man and of society. Our self-observation will probably tell us that the perversity St. Paul saw in himself frequently applies to us, too, but many will also find that at the same time they are considerably influenced by ethical learning, which strengthens efforts to live a good, useful life. What men learn is the basis on which they act; it contributes to their virtues, and to their vices. Ethics *is* important. Theory *does* have a bearing on our moral life. "Thought or knowledge may not only influence impulse but even extirpate it." (Blanshard)

It has been said by disheartened people, by writers and thinkers despairing of human goodness, that ethics is a vacuous idea in a world where more than half the inhabitants never get enough to eat, and in an age of mass murder and terror. And indeed there is cause for despair. Yet we cannot live without moral thinking, for it is as much a part of our existence as observing and thinking about nature. Let us therefore do it well! We of all nations whose political institutions are based on the philosophy of the seventeenth and eighteenth centuries—the period of Enlightenment—have much reason to be grateful to ethical thinkers.

Ethical philosophy is almost as old as philosophy itself. Socrates' interest was mainly moral, and some of Plato's most famous dialogues (*Crito* and *The Republic*) deal with ethics. Aristotle's major contribution, his so-called *Nicomachean Ethics*, proclaiming the idea of the harmonious life, is an important work in the history of ethics. Greek philosophy was continued by the Romans, and the well-known schools of the Stoics and Epicureans flourished, finding numerous adherents to their rational ethical teachings. In the subsequent Christian era, the ethical teachings of the Bible, expressed not in philosophic arguments but in commandments and in the preachings of the prophets, merged with the Greco-Roman stream to form the theology and philosophy of the Christian Church. Finally, in modern philosophy, beginning with the Enlightenment, ethics began to make itself in-

dependent of religion, though Kant and his disciples continued
to maintain that a close relationship existed between ethics and
religion. Contemporary ethical philosophers are not of one opinion on how to establish ethics, but generally speaking, the foundation of their systems of ethics is not a supernaturalistic Deity,
but man's reason, his interests, nature, emotions, or existential situation.

Whatever their differences may be, *all* philosophers agree
with our common sense opinion and belief that there *are* moral
preferences. Far from regarding values as absurd, they hold
firmly to a position which is not too different from that of the
American Dream expressed almost two hundred years ago in the
Declaration of Independence: "We hold these truths to be self-
evident, that all men are created equal, that they are endowed by
their Creator with certain unalienable Rights, that among these
are Life, Liberty and the pursuit of Happiness." Although the
ideals expressed in these phrases may require modification and
clarification, most philosophers and laymen applaud and support
their essence.

"Thou Shalt Not Kill"

We now turn back to the first story I used to demonstrate
that we all believe in at least one ethical command, that expressed
by the Sixth Commandment, "Thou shalt not kill." * This prohibition is necessarily basic, to most of us it is a self-evident, or
prima facie, duty. Apart from those with suicidal tendencies, we
all want to continue to live, since our existence is the necessary
condition for the pursuit of all our other interests. We don't
want our lives to be ended, and certainly not by the arbitrary act
of another.

The prohibition of killing a person is by no means absolute,
and it is here that great difficulties arise. In any case, even the
most basic rule is not unqualified. If a robber or a person with
murderous intentions attacks us, we have the right to fight him
off and, if necessary, kill him. The question of whether it was

---

* The Ten Commandments are to be found in Ex. 20 and Deut. 5. I have
been told that the principal word of the Sixth Commandment, the Hebrew
word *retsach*, means murder, and accordingly the Jewish Bible gives the commandment as "Thou shalt not murder." The King James Version, however, as
well as the Revised Version say "Thou shalt not kill." This latter is the generally known formulation of the Sixth Commandment.

actually necessary to take this most drastic step is not considered too closely as long as it seemed that our life and property were unlawfully endangered at the time. We also have the right, and in fact sometimes the duty, to come to the defense of others, be they members of our family, friends, or strangers, when they are attacked. In that case, too, the thief, rapist, or murderer might forfeit his life. The policeman who shoots at a person running away from the scene of a crime has not only a legal, but a moral right to do so, and even, under certain circumstances, to kill him. There is general agreement with respect to these situations even though there may be some argument in a particular case.

But a great deal of disagreement exists with respect to several other situations in which killing is involved, such as abortion, mercy killing, capital punishment, suicide and war. I shall comment briefly on each of these, in an attempt to clarify the general character of ethics and some of its important principles.

I do not see any moral problem in abortion. An embryo at the usual time of abortion is only a small growth; it is not a child. Why should a pregnant woman be deprived of her freedom to decide whether she wants to have the child? Her reasons may be of a kind with which others would sympathize—the probability of bearing a deformed child, too many previous children, illegitimacy, etc.—or they may be quite arbitrary. No woman ought to be forced to give birth to a child she does not want, especially in an age of overpopulation. A law is immoral (and its consequences tragic) that forces a teen-ager who has had too good a time at a wild party or an ill woman to go through such an ordeal.

Mercy killing (euthanasia) presents a more difficult question. Anyone who has watched a person linger in terminal cancer, or a person disfigured by surgery and kept alive by transfusions and ever stronger doses of drugs, seriously questions the wisdom of prolonging a situation that is hopeless, that is agony for the patient, demoralizing for the family and frequently financially ruinous. The morality of mercy killing in such a situation seems clear-cut. This is also the view of many leading churchmen. No one ought to be made to suffer against his wishes and without purpose. We ought to be able to devise some practical way of deciding when enough is enough, perhaps through a committee of physicians and legally trained neutral parties.

Capital punishment is a survival from the more barbaric systems of punishment which have persisted until fairly recent times. (Less than 200 years ago about 350 offenses were punishable by death in Britain.) We will not go into the morality of punishment in general here. We will assume that criminals ought to suffer some form of punishment for their offenses. The only question is whether capital punishment is moral. It has been abolished in several states of the Union and in some countries abroad. In most countries that still use it, certainly in the United States, the question of whether or not to keep it is actively debated. The literature in favor of its abolishment is enormous.[9] Experience has demonstrated that it is not an effective deterrent. It is not in accord with a humane age because it makes society a participant in a cold-blooded, revengeful legal "murder." In many cases the neglect of society has contributed to the making of a killer. However, the strongest argument against capital punishment is the fact that time and again men have been executed who were later proven innocent. A prison sentence can be commuted or terminated when new facts are brought to light or when society modifies its attitude, as might well have happened in the case of Sacco and Vanzetti. Capital punishment is final and irrevocable.

It is difficult to take a fixed position regarding suicide as people resort to it for many and diverse reasons. Neither general permissiveness nor general prohibition seems proper. As our interest here is the Sixth Commandment, we only need to examine the question of whether it is ever permissible to kill oneself. A case of permissible suicide is movingly described in Lael Tucker Wertenbaker's *Death of a Man;*[10] it deals with the suicide of the author's husband, who was suffering from incurable cancer. This is a self-chosen and self-inflicted mercy killing. We shall not discuss here the broad question of whether each one of us has the absolute right to end his life.

Willful killing reaches its greatest magnitude in war. That war as such is immoral requires no lengthy discussion. If there is any place for the application of the commandment, "Thou shalt not kill," it is here. It is a sad indication of man's lack of rationality that organized mass murder was not done away with long ago. However, the ideal of peace between nations is a subject of political philosophy; here we are discussing individual morality, and we must ask, what is the duty of an individual when his country is involved in war? Being a fighting soldier in wartime may mean violating the Sixth Commandment. But in general, men take the position, so ably defended by Socrates in *Crito*, that a person must do what his country orders him to do, and it is normally not left to the individual citizen to decide whether or not a war is justified, whatever this may mean. Hence, this kind of killing is commonly not regarded as murder but as a valid exception.

However, the moral problem seems a rather dubious one to many people in our country at the present time. They wonder whether the concept of a "just war"—an old philosophic idea— is not self-contradictory. How can war be just, and particularly the present war in Vietnam? Young men are now faced with the grave quandary of conscience—do they have the right, perhaps even duty, not to submit to the draft and fight?[11] The universality of the old rule "right or wrong, my country" is put in doubt. Nevertheless, the general opinion of most people, including ethical thinkers, is that some wars, at least, are fought for just causes, as, for example, wars of liberation such as the American Revolutionary War, or the war of the Allied Powers against Hitler and the Japanese militarists.

Pacifism is a most commendable principle, but under the conditions that have actually prevailed in the world from the beginning of history to this day, a nation that will not defend itself will be swallowed up by aggressive neighbors. The defense of our relatively free society is a vital matter (comparable to self-defense) and the refusal to bear arms in a defensive war may be regarded as a serious moral mistake. Nevertheless, this viewpoint should not be carried too far. In view of the strength of our society and our traditional tolerance for divergent opinions, we can —and do—permit conscientious objectors to play a non-arms-carrying role even in time of war.

We come, finally, to a situation not mentioned so far, one that I shall call the lifeboat situation. Let us assume that after a disaster at sea, lifeboats are launched and filled with survivors to more than capacity. There are still people in the water holding on to whatever they can find, screaming to be picked up. What is our duty in this calamity, when not everybody can be saved? Common sense, even though it may sound brutal, tells us that the lifeboats should be filled with as many people as possible and those for whom there is no room must be left to their tragic fate. In a situation like this we must distinguish between morality and sentimentality.*

Compare the lifeboat situation with certain unusual situations described by anthropologists where people living under primitive conditions have killed either their old people (who, they believe, continue life in the next world) or some of their newly-born children (who are not yet regarded as properly human). Where there is not enough food to keep everyone alive, some must be sacrificed so that the rest may survive. The fact that this has been done indicates neither the absence nor the relativity of ethical principles. General principles require different application, when economic conditions limit survival and when "differences in the comprehension of the situation" prevail.[12]

In modern society we tolerate a large number of accidental killings, many of which would not occur were it not for modern technology. Notwithstanding constantly improved precautionary measures, people suffer critical accidents in factories and laboratories, on construction jobs, in farm work and at home. In this country alone over 50,000 people are killed annually by cars. We punish the drunken and the negligent driver, but "if cars were prohibited entirely, there would be no fatalities resulting from automobiles. What should be done? How much inconvenience balances against the loss of one life?" (Hospers)

It is obvious then that even as fundamental and indisputable an interdiction as that against killing presents considerable difficulties in its application to various situations.

* This confusion or a false sense of duty was perhaps the doom of the Scott Antartic expedition in 1912. John Hospers' *Human Conduct*, (*op. cit.*) gives the following condensed report: "When Scott's famous journey to the Antartic met with disaster, the only chance for the survivors was to reach the coast at once. But on the way one of them was injured and had to be carried on a stretcher. Though this delay seriously imperiled all their chances of survival, the captain decided that he should not abandon the man to die. The result was that all the men died." Hospers' book is a clearly written, detailed and comprehensive introduction to the many problems of modern ethical philosophy, clarifying the subject by a wealth of well-chosen examples. See Hospers, p. 422, regarding the lifeboat situation, and Lucius Garvin, *A Modern Introduction to Ethics* (Boston: Houghton Mifflin, 1953), p. 442, for a description of the exceedingly difficult choice of whom to throw overboard in order to lighten an overloaded boat.

General Rules, Exceptions

Similar uncertainties exist with respect to other general commands. I have previously mentioned obedience to the laws of one's country as an important tacit obligation defended by Socrates in Plato's *Crito*.* "We have a duty to observe the laws of the state faithfully, even if we have not explicitly promised to observe them." (Leonard Nelson) However easy-going our personal attitude may be toward traffic and certain tax regulations, theoretically at least, we would regard it as improper behavior to disobey the law of one's country, in accordance with the old Socratic rule. Any other position would lead to the breakdown of law and order and thus to the destruction of society.

Here, too, we find that there are important exceptions. We honor our Founding Fathers and all those who instigated the American Revolution and participated in it. In so doing, these men and women violated the laws of the jurisdiction under which they were living. They claimed, and we agree and honor them, that a *higher law* commanded them to throw off the yoke of the colonial power and make themselves independent. As Thoreau said, "We should be men first, and subjects afterwards. It is not desirable to cultivate a respect for the law, so much as for the right." Gandhi learned from Thoreau, and the Reverend Martin Luther King and his followers learned from both, adopting civil disobedience as their weapon in the fight for racial equality and justice. The demands of the legal system "must in the end be submitted to a moral scrutiny," as H. L. A. Hart, a contemporary English jurisprudent and legal philosopher, has written. "There is something outside the official system, by reference to which in the last resort the individual must solve his problems of obedience." [13]

All the other simple rules that most of us have learned as children lead to similar difficulties. We feel that we ought to adhere to them, but we find ourselves frequently coming upon situ-

---

* The short dialogue *Crito* is one of Plato's most beautiful and simple ethical arguments, it is highly recommended as an important work in world literature and moral philosophy. Plato's *Apology*, *Crito* and the first and last few pages of *Phaedo* describe the trial leading to Socrates' death sentence, his resolve to suffer his unjust verdict, and his actual death. Socrates' death is one of the most important events in the history of philosophy, for it inspired Plato's philosophic writings. His willingness to die for his ideals and his death have often been compared with the death of Jesus.

ations where some of the rules do not seem to fit. The Eighth
Commandment tells us, "You shall not steal." But what should a
ship's crew do that runs out of provisions on a vessel that is
carrying a cargo of foodstuffs? We regard honesty and telling
the truth as important duties, but what is one to do when a
mother, who is critically ill, inquires about her daughter, who
has just been killed in an airplane accident? Here we face the
difficult problem of "white lies." We feel that in certain cases
deception is justified, but where do we set the limits?

We thus find that there are critical, accepted exceptions to
whatever rules religion and common sense have laid down, creating duties by which we feel ourselves bound in general. We are
convinced that there is some merit in the specific ethical principles, and we are under the impression that we ought to do what
these imperatives tell us to do. However, in certain definite circumstances conflicts arise, and we realize that we cannot follow
the generally accepted moral rule because another self-evident
(prima facie) duty that is more important intervenes.

In these cases we know that "there is *some* act that in the
circumstances would be the right one for me to do" (Brand
Blanshard), and there are also some acts that would be wrong.
We regard these judgments as not merely subjective. What is
right for me to do in certain circumstances is also right for any
other person to do, assuming that the circumstances are really
the same and that the other person does not differ from me in
any relevant details. In other words, duties are universal.

As we have pointed out, the situation we are to decide or
judge is sometimes so complicated or beclouded that we are not
sure what is right. It is impossible to formulate a code containing
rules of right and wrong so detailed that they would give us a
specific norm for every situation we encounter, and tell us what
we ought to do whenever we are faced with an ethical dilemma.
Nevertheless, even in difficult cases most people have a feeling
that certain choices are morally preferable to all others, and we
endeavor to find the right solution.

What, then, is the importance of the Ten Commandments
and similar guides to moral conduct, often regarded as God-
given and therefore eternally valid? Briefly, they are rules of
thumb representing the wisdom of the ages. But they are no
more than that; they are not absolute commands. Rather, they
are signs telling us to stop and think, warning us that we are

taking on a heavy responsibility if we kill or steal or lie or violate the laws of our country.

The fact that there are alternatives in the application of the traditional moral commandments is an additional source of skepticism. If the truth of the hallowed injunctions of the Sixth and Eighth Commandments is open to doubt, what are we to believe of values in general? Indeed, are there any real values? An inconsistency exists between our natural inclination to make decisions of a moral nature when confronted with choices and our tendency toward skepticism when we theorize about ethics. We feel that without a detailed, specific moral code, laying down a rule for every possible situation, all we can do is flounder through life.

But this is not really so. We have broad rules that point to the general direction in which we should go. The Bible presents certain general and often quoted rules. There is the so-called Golden Rule, "Love your neighbor as yourself." (Lev. 19:18, Matt. 22:30) Many Jews regard the prescription of the prophet Micah as the quintessence of ethics: "It hath been told thee, O man, what is good, and what the Lord doth require of thee: Only to do justly, and to love mercy, and to walk humbly with thy God." (Mic. 6:8) Isaiah expressed the highest ethical rule of the Old Testament in even fewer words: "Keep ye justice, and do righteousness." (Is. 56:1)* The Sermon on the Mount combines a number of specific commands with some general ones, such as the injunction to love your neighbor, including your enemies. The Golden Rule, the rule of fairness in dealing with others, is a sufficient general guide for the solution of some of the situations we have mentioned, including those involving conflicting prima facie duties. Both Cain and David acted unjustly. Justice is better served if, as in the lifeboat situation, some survive rather than all drown. When someone attacks us or others without reason, he is acting wrongly, and justice gives us the right to interfere with the attacker.

* The Talmud discusses the change from innumerable specific commands to a few general ones in an interesting passage quoted in Milton Steinberg's *Basic Judaism* (New York: Harcourt, Brace & World, 1947, paperback).

Relativism in Ethics

There are, in addition, certain other issues which I would like to clarify before discussing the general norms. The fact that ethical insight has changed in history and between cultures has already been analyzed. This should no longer be a problem. The mere fact that the Aztecs and others honored their gods through human sacrifices does not make the ethical evaluation of this religious custom meaningless. There can be ethical truth, notwithstanding different beliefs and customs. But what of the truth of the norm not to kill, when, as now, it is considered morally desirable to apply the norm in some cases and in others not, as, for example, in self-defense or in legitimate police actions. Here we must distinguish the *relativity of the ethical judgment* and *the relativity of the situation*. The former we disclaim, but the latter is, of course, a fact we encounter constantly. We must act in accordance with the well-established rule: "Treat like cases alike and different cases differently." (H. L. A. Hart) Changes in the situation bring different commands, permissions and prohibitions into play. A sailor does not have the right to throw people out of a lifeboat that is not filled just because he dislikes them. But the situation is changed when the boat is overcrowded. And even in this case the sailor's dislike is not a proper basis for the selection of those who have to be sacrificed.

When we weigh an action, we apply our moral insight, the norms we regard as true, to an infinite variety of circumstances, and the judgments, therefore, vary. We may compare this difficulty to the findings we derive when we apply the laws of mechanics to actual cases of falling bodies. The results must differ, depending as they do on the original speed of the moving body, its shape and the friction of the substance through which it falls. In choosing our actions we must consider all the circumstances that are relevant in the particular situation. It may be difficult to decide what is relevant and what is not, but many actual cases are clear-cut. We demand of a good swimmer that he help a drowning child, whereas under otherwise identical circumstances we would regard as a fool a poor swimmer or a person with a cardiac condition who dared to swim out.

Assuming that another man and I each find ourselves facing a situation in which all relevant circumstances are similar, then what is right for him to do is also right for me, and what is wrong for him is also wrong for me. And this is so, although the idea is sometimes expressed that everyone's personal ethical code is valid and that "right you are if you think you are." It is indeed true that we all have our own maxims of action, just as everyone has an individual totality of opinions and beliefs. Few people engage in murder, theft, rape, or other criminal activity. But one man may be charitable, another man not at all. One man may regard it as his duty to devote practically all his waking hours to his business or occupation; another man will spend a considerable time with his family and enjoy hobbies with them. Relations to co-workers, spouse, or children may be handled in many ways. But the ethical question is quite different, should there be distinctions in right and wrong for you and for me where there are no relevant differences in our situations?

To say, "all things are permissible," * is completely contrary to our reason, our convictions and our ideals. While there are many cases of perfectly legitimate variations, nevertheless—and I want to repeat this with great emphasis—we all *do* condemn murder, robbery, rape, slavery, war, torture, gas chambers and the harem-like subjection of women. Although some social critics claim that our society is being ruined by moral relativism, no ethical philosophy defends relativism. Rather, the moral decay and uncertainty that actually prevail are caused by the difficult historical conditions and crises of modern society.

In times of great political, economic, technological and cultural change new situations arise and new ideas emerge. While some groups or an older generation acknowledge only the long established standards, other groups and younger people may be evolving new values. As a consequence, moral ideas may seem to be in flux or relative. We are living in such an age. We observe how, within the span of just a couple of generations, our labor, race, family and sex relations have altered. This does not mean, however, that ethical truth does not exist or is relative. Perhaps previous patterns of conduct ought to have been discarded. We cannot say whether, in general, the developing ethical insight is right or wrong; each of its norms must be examined individually. Let us consider labor relations, for instance. Is it not better to prohibit child labor and to give protection to the masses of laboring men and women through laws and unions than to leave them

* Smerdjakoff in Dostoevsky's *The Brothers Karamazov.*

helpless vis-à-vis their employers, as was their miserable lot early in the industrial age? Incredible as it may seem to us today, this was a much debated political and even moral issue until fairly recent times. Is it not better to settle wage rates and working conditions through negotiations rather than through violent and bloody strikes, which were the workers' only recourse until the late thirties? Is not equality of races, religions and sexes better than inequality? These questions answer themselves. But, it is not problems such as these that are of the greatest concern to the "moralists." The "moralists" stress lack of regard for excellence, poor use of leisure time by the "masses," juvenile delinquency, and with the deepest alarm, the apparently complete breakdown of sexual morality in an age of hedonistic promiscuity.*

Let me make a few concluding remarks about the prevailing moral uncertainty. One factor is the skepticism, the various sources of which I touched on earlier in this chapter. An additional factor is our great range and freedom of choices, greater now than ever before in history. This is a feature of modern life which affects young people particularly. This freedom, when properly used—perturbing as it may be—is quite in accord with our individual striving and our highest ideals. Man ought to be free and permitted to determine his own fate within the limits of the possible and the permissible. But "the fearful burden of free choice" (Dostoevsky's *Grand Inquisitor*) presents problems. The security of fixed patterns of life and of detailed moral codes has disappeared. We all can and must choose the path we will follow with respect to education, occupation, sex, marriage and family life. But we have to pay for this abundance of opportunities. As Charles Frankel has so well said:

> The increased freedom of choice which intellectual progress has given to modern man has undoubtedly added to his sense of strain, to his consciousness of his failures, and to his feelings of guilt . . . If there is a dynamism and restlessness in modern culture, it is in part because that culture has a wider sense of its limits, and a more imaginative view of what it is possible for human life still to become.

* I shall deal later with the possibility of an ethics of sexual relations.

CHAPTER IX

Ethical Norms and Conduct[1]

> "I have taught men how to live."
> —CONFUCIUS

The Moral Point of View

Let us now try to discover whether it is possible to bring systematic order into moral feelings and judgments and to organize them into a limited number of general principles. In this process I will indicate the uncertainties and controversies that are involved. It is not possible to present a complete picture here, and I cannot avoid doing something I mentioned at the close of Chapter I; that is, I "cannot teach philosophy without teaching *a* philosophy." I shall do so although I feel like the contemporary English moral philosopher R. M. Hare, who wrote in the Preface to his *Freedom and Reason:* "I am still far from clear on many matters." My view—that the goal of moral conduct, in its widest sense, is the greatest possible reconciliation and furtherance of the interests of all men—is probably shared by most thoughtful and conscientious people, including many contemporary philosophers. But different ethical ideals are possible, and I will refer to them when appropriate.

When we consider and evaluate actions and judgments from the moral point of view, we must examine what we expect of ourselves, and what standards we hope others believe in—even

though none of us may live up to his own high ideals. We want
to be fair and to be treated fairly; we want to be helpful when
our help is needed, and, in turn, want others to help us when we
are in need; we want to be able to enjoy life in freedom; we feel
that everyone ought to strive to develop his talents and to participate in the promotion of the general good, and to contribute to
the richness of life of the larger community of which we are all a
part. These aspirations are summarized in the principles of justice, benevolence and excellence.

Moral philosophers have differed in the stress they have laid
on these principles: the Prophets, Plato and Kant emphasized justice ("Justice, justice shalt thou pursue" [Deut. 16:20]); the
utilitarians (a term I shall explain presently) placed great weight
on helpfulness and the common good; philosophers as unlike as
Aristotle and Nietzsche stressed excellence. Another differentiation must be made among the ethical philosophers of the last two
hundred years. One group, the formalists, lists a finite number of
classes of duties and stresses obedience to a multiplicity of definite rules; rules such as, act justly, be honest, grateful and helpful. The other group, the utilitarians, look at the results of our
actions, and regard "utility as a test of right and wrong" (John S.
Mill); they proclaimed as their only goal "the greatest happiness
of the greatest number" (Bentham), later they modified it to
"the greatest good of the greatest number." * The idea of the
greatest good (*summum bonum*) and the principle of excellence
present us with the important task of examining what we should
regard as the greatest good and the goals of excellence. Finally,
there is an additional and quite different ethical problem: What
are we to do when men violate ethical commands? Is it right to
punish wrongdoers?

Duty

Whatever our ethical viewpoint, we single out certain actions which we think we ought to perform and certain ones
which we think should be prohibited. We use the term "duty" to
indicate that which we are obligated to do or not to do for moral
reasons. There are situations in which we are commanded to

---

* The three English philosophers, Jeremiah Bentham (1748-1832), John
Stuart Mill (1806-1873), author of the small book *Utilitarianism*, and G. E.
Moore (1873-1958), are the most representative thinkers of this school.

carry out an action because it is right. "Duty is a thing which may be *exacted* from a person." (Mill) Ordinarily, we do not earn special praise for doing what we are duty-bound to do or for not doing what we ought to refrain from doing; duty is the ethical minimum. But this holds only if the performance of our duty does not require the overcoming of great difficulties.

Kant made the idea of duty central to his "practical" philosophy. It was he who coined the well-known expression "categorical imperative," referring to the command that we do certain things, not because they are means or instruments which bring about good consequences, but because they are necessary obligations, because their fulfillment is intrinsically right—to carry out justice, for example. As they are frequently cited, I will state the formulations Kant gave to his categorical imperative:

> Act as if the maxim of your action were to become through your will a universal law of nature.

In other words, an ethical norm is valid only if we are able to generalize or universalize it for all mankind. This is a very basic idea in ethics, one which we dealt with briefly in the last chapter.* Kant also proclaimed another version of the categorical imperative:

> Act in such a way that you always treat humanity, whether in your own person or in the person of any other, never simply as a means, but always at the same time as an end.†

In arguing for the categorical imperative Kant describes humanity as "an end in itself," as something that has "absolute value." Thus, man, having intrinsic value, deserves our respect. However, I do not wish to pursue Kantian ethics any further, nor discuss the relation between the two formulations of the categorical imperative; this goes beyond our task.

As far as duties are concerned, we must distinguish actual duties from prima facie duties, a term introduced by W. David Ross in his *The Right and the Good*.‡ Ross's terminology was

---

* See Chapter VIII, p. 204.

† Kant, *The Fundamental Principles of the Metaphysics of Morals*, quoted in *Value and Obligation, op. cit.* Hardly any other philosophic book made such a deep impression on me or gave me such pleasure as did this book by Kant when I read it as a first-year university student. I have never lost—fortunately, I think—my Kantian bent in ethical philosophy.

‡ Brandt calls Ross "one of the outstanding figures among writers on ethics in the present century." Two lengthy excerpts of this book are reprinted in Brandt, *Value and Obligation, op. cit.*

intended to clarify the situation in which two or more so-called
duties are in conflict with each other. We feel we ought to lie if
we can thereby prevent the Gestapo from murdering a Jew who
is in hiding. The *conflict of duties* (prima facie) can arise only in
a formalistic moral philosophy that believes, as most of us actually do, that a multiplicity of rules and duties regulate our lives.
Something "tends" to be our duty when it falls under one of the
rules; it is then our prima facie duty or responsibility. It "holds
not absolutely and unconditionally but only in the absence of a
superior conflicting obligation." (Ewing) As we have seen, an
act that we are weighing may contain "various elements in virtue
of which it falls under various categories." Being an *actual* duty
is an "attribute which belongs to an act in virtue of its whole
nature." (Ross)* This still leaves open the question of how to
determine the actual duty when several prima facie duties conflict. We shall consider this question later.

Just as there are no duties that prevail under all conditions,
but only actions which tend to be duties, so, conversely, there
are no inalienable rights (for example, life, liberty, or property)
but only reasonable rights. Whatever rights we have may be restricted by the conditions of particular situations. By law we
may be drafted into the army and thus not only be deprived of
our freedom, but also be subjected to an enormously increased
risk of losing our lives. The taxing authorities deprive us of part
of our property, and the free use of our remaining property is
restricted for the benefit and protection of our neighbors and of
the community as a whole.

Not all the praiseworthy acts we perform are duties. When
I contribute money to my political party or send a book or flowers to a sick friend, I do more than my duty. I do something that
is over and above what is called for; I would not be acting immorally if I did not do these things.[2] It is sometimes difficult to
decide where duty ends and the optional good begins. How
much should a well-to-do person give to charity or his alma
mater? How often should a "dutiful" son visit his ailing parents?

---

* Ibsen's hero Brand, in the moving tragedy of that name, holds to one
particular prima facie duty, his unswerving "all-or-nothing" goal—his interpretation of the manner in which he can serve God—rejecting compromise
and blinding himself to his other prima facie obligations: regard for the welfare
of his mother, wife, child and congregants. He refuses to see the "whole nature"
of the various situations in which he finds himself.

What is obligatory and what goes beyond obligation? We will come back to this problem in another connection, but it is not possible to lay down hard and fast rules in this area.

We all recognize that there are worthy actions which are not obligatory and therefore not duties. Ideals set goals for us outside the realm of duties. We ought to use our leisure intelligently, engage in worthwhile activities, help others to achieve excellence. These are ethical oughts but not of the same categorical character as the commands to be just or honest. We are unhappy when a man of great intelligence wastes his abilities, but we do not regard him as immoral, as we do regard a rapist or a murderer. In short, we find commendable actions that go beyond our normal obligations: good deeds that are not commanded, but that we are called upon to perform in the service of cultural ideals.

Justice

Let us take a look at some general maxims. We can begin with the Golden Rule: "Love your neighbor as yourself." Actually, this is a utopian injunction, if we take the term "love" in its everyday emotional sense. The feeling of love in this sense arises in the intimate contact of men, women, and children, in family life in general and among others who are in close contact with each other. Although we may treat our neighbors politely, fairly, respectfully and, as Kant would say, not as means or instruments, we do not usually "love" them; indeed, we often hardly know them. Nor can we "love" the numberless people with whom we work, whom we meet in the street and in other places.

The Golden Rule has therefore been converted into two commands by which we can abide, as it is possible for us to apply them in our relations with other people. There is, first of all, a negative form: "Do not do to others what you would not want them to do to you." This formulation is not to be found in the Bible but it is, nevertheless, part of Western ethical thinking and, as a matter of fact, was proclaimed by the famous Talmudic scholar Rabbi Hillel (a contemporary of Jesus) and by the Chinese sage Confucius (551–479 B.C.). It is the command to be just. The positive version of the Golden Rule goes much further in commanding us: "Whatever you wish that men would do to you, do so to them." (Matt. 7:12) Just as *we* want to be well treated, so we should treat *others* well.

The first of the above two commands that we not treat others as we would not want to be treated by them directs us to give the same weight to the interests of others as to our own. In weighing whether or not to take certain actions we should consider the impact our plans may have on the affairs of others. When my interests conflict with those of others, I am enjoined from preferring my interests over and above those of others. But we cannot be just unless we are also peaceable and trustworthy. Because the following acts would violate the interests of others, we are forbidden to lie, to break promises, to commit fraud, to interfere unnecessarily with the freedom of others, to steal, to rape, or to kill except when there are special, morally significant circumstances overriding these prima facie or conditional duties. We are under a *duty* to treat others with fairness, and they have the *right* to expect fair consideration from us. This gives us the principle of equal personal dignity. "All men are created equal." As the English moral philosopher Henry Sidgwick expressed it:

> It cannot be right for A to treat B in a manner in which it would be wrong for B to treat A, merely on the ground that they are two different individuals, and without there being any difference between the natures and circumstances of the two which can be stated as a reasonable ground for difference of treatment.[3]

From this it follows that if there are significant differences between people, then differences in treatment are not only permissible but sometimes commanded. I am obligated, in certain circumstances not to treat the President of the United States or a mother of several young children as my equals. They are entitled to special consideration on my part. This does not contradict the principle of equality, which says: "Each person *as such*, i.e., only in so far as we abstract from his individual qualities, has a dignity equal to that of every other person." (Leonard Nelson) Arthur Miller's too often forgotten cry holds for every human being: "Attention must be paid." (*Death of a Salesman*)

Opposed to the principle of equality is a standard which we as children jokingly expressed as "First comes I, and then comes I, and then comes I again, and then you don't come by a long shot." This is the principle of egoism: Always look out for Number One, for oneself. If this should become a general rule for everybody, it would create widespread conflict in which the strongest and trickiest would win. This is the very negation of an ethical idea. If egoistic conduct is proper moral conduct, then all the idealists of mankind's history and of the contemporary scene have been guilty of a tragic mistake. It may indeed be *clever* for an individual or a group to be egoists as long as everybody else is decent, but from the moral point of view this kind of behavior is wrong.

Two defenders of egoism, who appear in Plato's Dialogues, are famous in the history of ethics, Callicles of the Dialogue *Gorgias* and Thrasymachus of *The Republic*. Let me quote the latter's well-known remarks:

> What I say is that "just" or "right" means nothing but what is to the interest of the stronger party. . . . To be "just" means serving the interest of the stronger who rules, at the cost of the subject who obeys. . . . Socrates, you must see that a just man always has the worst of it. . . . Injustice, on a grand enough scale, is superior to justice in strength and freedom and autocratic power; and "right" . . . means simply what serves the interest of the stronger party.

Later Socrates asks, "That justice is a defect?" and Thrasymachus answers, "No; rather the mark of a goodnatured simpleton." Socrates: "Injustice, then, implies being ill-natured?" Thrasymachus: "No; I shall call it good policy."

The history of mankind bears witness to the tragic results of this glorification of injustice. The right of the stronger to dominate the weaker was advanced in this country to justify slavery; the idea of the right of a "master race" to oppress a so-called "inferior" race is put forward to this very day as an argument by segregationists. A similar power ethics has, in recent times, been ardently proclaimed by Fascists and National Socialists, causing the annihilation of millions of "sub-men"; it has gone hand in hand with the glorification of war, another cause of tens of millions of deaths.

In modern times Friedrich Nietzsche (1844–1900) seemed to revive the arguments of the two Platonic defenders of "master morality" as opposed to "slave morality," proclaiming the aristocratic and heroic idea of the "superman." German nationalists interpreted Nietzsche's philosophy as a bugle call to make themselves the masters of the world, and they adopted his aggressive slogans: "will to power," "break the good and the just," "live dangerously," "become hard." Nietzsche, in arguing for the "re-valuation of all values," severely criticized Christianity and utilitarianism, the former because of its defense of meekness and sympathy for the mass of men, the other because of the stress it placed on pleasure and pain rather than on creativity. Nietzsche, however, was opposed to German nationalism; what he was fervently interested in was human greatness, what Walter Kaufmann[4] translates as the overman (Übermensch):

> Man is something that shall be overcome. . . . The overman *shall be* the meaning of the earth! (*Thus Spoke Zarathustra*)[5]

> The goal of humanity [lies] . . . in its high specimens.

> One task [is assigned] to every single one of us: to promote inside and outside of ourselves the generation of the philosopher, the artist, and the saint, and thus to work at the perfection of nature. (*Untimely Meditations*) [6]

This call to creative and artistic greatness was for Nietzsche the essence of morality; for us it is only one of the three pillars of morality.

Altruism is diametrically opposed to egoism as it reads into the Golden Rule the duty of self-sacrifice and sets the welfare of one's neighbor above one's own. Obviously, this goes beyond the principle of equality. There is, however, an important difference between the evaluation of egoism and that of altruism. Egoism is wrong. We condemn the man who acts solely in his own interest, disregarding his neighbors', but we admire him who does more than mere fairness demands, who makes personal sacrifices for the benefit of others.

Jesus and other holy men have been held in great esteem because of the "high" ethics of altruism which they preached. Their precepts probably have not helped mankind. By asking men to "be perfect" and to behave in a manner far beyond their natural moral inclinations and strength of character, they put morality on such a high plane that ordinary people have despaired of ever attaining it and thus have neglected the more earthly task of striving for that which is within reach—justice.

Utilitarianism

Philosophers, motivated by their striving for unity, have either attempted to derive the command to be fair and the command to do good from the same source, or they have endeavored to draw the one principle from the other. Kant and those who have followed him derived the duty to be helpful and to do good from the mere principle that we ought to universalize the maxim of our actions. This principle, however, leaves unclear the goal we are to universalize. Utilitarians, on the other hand, incorporated the duty to be just, which also embraces the duties of honesty and trustworthiness, into their rule of "greatest good for the greatest number of people." For myself, I believe, along with other contemporary thinkers, that it is better to structure our ethics around the three previously mentioned separate principles of justice, benevolence and excellence. Having clarified the principle of justice, I turn now to the principle of benevolence, which is the basis of utilitarian thinking.

Utilitarianism is a goal-directed, teleological theory (*telos:* end, purpose). It does not require us to conform to a catalogue of prima facie duties; rather, it sets us only one task, the promotion of the general good, thereby bringing about maximum human satisfaction and the least possible suffering for all people concerned with our actions. When in a specific situation, we ponder what we should or should not do, we should keep in mind Mill's observation that "a person may cause evil to others not only by his actions but by his inaction." The simplicity and generality of the utilitarian principle obviates—except when justice overrides utilitarian advantages—the possibility of a conflict of duties (an unfortunate idea which has long raised havoc with common sense moral thinking). In every situation there are certain actions or one particular action that we may or ought to perform and others which are prescribed, and these are governed by the principle of the maximization of human benefits.

Human satisfaction does not consist solely or even primarily in the pursuit or the attainment of pleasure, as the previously quoted slogans indicate. (The detractors of utilitarianism disparagingly accused it of teaching this hedonistic view.) Mill speaks of "utility in the largest sense, grounded on the permanent interests of a man as a progressive being." He realized that "some *kinds* of pleasure are more desirable and more valuable than others," and it was in this connection that he made the often quoted statement about the satisfaction of a pig and the dissatisfaction of Socrates:

> It is indisputable that the being whose capacities of enjoyment are low, has the greatest chance of having them fully satisfied; and a highly endowed being will always feel that any happiness which he can look for, as the world is constituted, is imperfect. . . . It is better to be a human being dissatisfied than a pig satisfied; better to be Socrates dissatisfied than a fool satisfied. And if the fool, or the pig, are of a different opinion, it is because they only know their own side of the question. The other party to the comparison knows both sides. . . .

> A cultivated mind—I do not mean that of a philosopher, but any mind to which the fountains of knowledge have been opened, and which has been taught, in any tolerable degree, to exercise its faculties—finds sources of inexhaustible interest in all that surrounds it; in the objects of nature, the achievements of art, the imaginations of poetry, the incidents of history, the ways of mankind, past and present, and their prospects in the future. (*Utilitarianism*)[7]

Everyone strives to some extent for his own happiness. How am I to weigh my happiness against that of others? What should I do if I can effect a substantial increase in my own happiness only at the expense of others? Mill was too much of a humanitarian not to apply the principle of justice, and so he maintained that:

> The happiness which forms the utilitarian standard . . . is not the agent's own happiness but that of all concerned. As between his own happiness and that of others, utilitarianism requires him to be as strictly impartial as a distinterested and benevolent spectator.

Justice is thus a second independent principle and must be regarded as a modification of strictly utilitarian ethics, where only the magnitude or intensity of pleasure or happiness counts. In fact, Mill goes further and makes an eloquent plea for altruism and self-sacrifice, but it "must be for some end; it is not its own end." It is not a virtue unless it produces some "fruit for any of [the hero's or martyr's] fellow creatures."

Because of the multiplicity of interests and goals which individuals have or strive for—sensual and esthetic pleasure, knowledge, power, love, self-development, creativity—modern utilitarian ethics has been called pluralistic and ideal utilitarianism. Its imperative is expressed succinctly by Moore in his *Ethics:*[8]

> It must always be the duty of every agent to do that one action whose *total consequences* will have the greatest intrinsic value.

How can we discover what action in a given situation will produce total consequences of the greatest intrinsic value? How are we to measure the various pleasures and values, pains and dislikes of any number of affected people and balance them against each other? To say, "Do what is best," sounds almost too simple, and yet it is the correct commandment. But there is a complication.

The application of the rule that we should always produce the greatest total amount of satisfaction leads, in certain situations, to rather peculiar consequences. Here are two examples taken from the philosophic literature, and one from a modern play.

> [Utilitarianism] implies that if your father is ill and has no prospect of good in his life, and maintaining him is a drain on the energy and enjoyment of others, then, if you can end his life without provoking any public scandal or setting a bad example, it is your positive duty to take matters into your own hands and bring his life to a close. (Brandt)[9]

If you freed yourself of the burden of caring for your father and could still your conscience, how much better life for your family would be! But this apparent consequence of utilitarian thinking seems the very opposite of good morals. The other example leaves us equally dissatisfied with the correctness of utilitarianism.

> You have borrowed money from a well-to-do man and promised to return it on a certain day. On the way to return it, you meet a friend who is unemployed, ill, or distressed, and who would, in all probability, use the money to much better advantage than the man to whom you owe it. (Blanshard)[10]

As your friend needs the money much more than the rich man, shouldn't you give it to him? But what, then, of your promise to return the money?

The third example comes from Tennessee Williams' *Suddenly Last Summer.* A wealthy widow promises a young doctor

a large sum of money for a much needed hospital if he will perform a brain operation on a young woman which would make
her lose her memory. The young woman knows certain facts
about the widow's son which the widow wants to make sure will
not be divulged. Wouldn't the greatest common good be best
served by the construction of the hospital, even if this requires
the ruin of one life? The plan may indeed confer a great benefit,
but is it moral?

Treatises on ethics give many situations in which individuals
and even whole communities could derive considerable advantages from "bad" actions such as those in our examples.

Utilitarians have overcome this difficulty by going back to
Kant's idea that whenever we plan an action, its character should
be such that the maxim of our action could be established as a
universal moral principle. In other words, we ought not weigh
the advantages or disadvantages of an action as an isolated phenomenon but should consider what would happen if everyone
acted as we did. We should evaluate each act, not by itself, but as
a case falling under a general rule; then we must weight the *utility
of the rule*. If the rule is good for the general welfare, we can go
ahead, but if the rule itself is harmful, then the contemplated act
is perforce immoral, however advantageous it may be for certain
people or in certain circumstances. This theory, called rule-utilitarianism in contradistinction to act-utilitarianism, has been fully
developed only in the last twenty years, and has found considerable support.

When we apply rule-utilitarianism to the examples just described, we find that the greatest good would not be attained in a
society which did not prohibit killing burdensome parents,
breaking oral agreements and depriving others arbitrarily of certain mental faculties. A general moral chaos would prevail if we
did not honor certain moral rules.

> Each act, in the moral life, falls under a rule; and we are to
> judge the rightness or wrongness of the act, not by *its* conse-
> quences, but by the consequences of its universalization—that
> is, by the consequences of the adoption of the *rule* under which
> this act falls. (Hospers)

If we adopt ideal rule-utilitarianism, then we can incorporate
Ross's system of prima facie duties (be truthful and trustworthy,
protect lives, be grateful, honor your parents, do not injure
others) into utilitarianism. In a specific case we must consider the

intrinsic good that would follow by weighing the utility of the various rules against each other. We thus discover our actual duty when prima facie duties are in conflict. "Rule-utilitarianism is in a sense an organic theory: the rightness of individual acts can be ascertained only by assessing a whole social policy." (Brandt) In applying this policy we must always remember the importance of the demands of justice—promote the general good in a fair way. It is generally held that in weighing the claims of utility and justice we must grant priority to justice. As slavery and the subjugation of women are always unjust, they are morally wrong, whatever the economic advantages may be.

The name "ideal rule-utilitarianism" sounds complicated and technical. Actually, it not only means the simple injunction "Consider what happens if everyone acted like you," but also indicates a method which we all use in practice when we are puzzled about moral behavior.

Moral Decisions

Let us assume that we decide to be decent people, guided by moral principles. How do we proceed? In most cases, when we must make moral choices, we do not have to think very hard. When I cash a fifty-dollar check and the cashier gives me sixty dollars, I don't wonder about what I ought to do. When a motorcycle policeman drives in front of my car and signals me to stop, presumably to give me a ticket, I know that I ought not to run him over, even if I would not be seen. In court, after having sworn to tell the truth, I know I ought to tell the truth. I do not leave restaurants and stores without paying for my purchases even when I can get away with it, nor do I pick up other people's coats or pocketbooks when they are not watching. When a small child tries to run across a busy intersection, I try to grab him even though I may endanger myself. We probably do not realize how many "decisions" we make automatically day in and day out, which have some moral implications.

When we are puzzled and uncertain about a moral decision, the process is quite different. We try to put ourselves in a sober, dispassionate frame of mind. And since one of the preconditions of moral action is the application of intellect and insight to the particular situation, we must familiarize ourselves with the moral values at issue and with all the pertinent facts of the case. We then weigh the moral pros and cons, wondering what is the best rule in our difficulty. What would we expect others to do in a similar situation? What would we like them to do? What would be best all around, even though it may not be the most advantageous for us? We must distinguish between moral and prudential considerations; sometimes they lead to the same result, at other times they do not. In short, we search "for the soberest and steadiest judgment of which, in the light of all relevant obligations, we are capable." (Aiken) But the capacity to arrive at good judgments is acquired only through life experiences; theory is of little help.

Moreover, most of us, when faced with the necessity of making difficult decisions, do not have the complete objectivity and the vision required for a true appraisal. In such situations it is often well to turn to others with more experience to gain a more detached point of view and different insights.

Considering all the circumstances of a situation, we must take into account not only pleasure, happiness and satisfaction, but also pain, unhappiness and dissatisfaction. These negative factors cannot always be avoided. At other times, the choice may only be between two or more evils, as for instance when a pregnant teen-ager and her parents consider the best possible solution to the predicament, giving thought to the possible and probable future of the yet unborn child. In such situations, the task is to discover the lesser evil.

Obviously, we can evaluate the consequences of our actions only in accordance with the probability of future events. Our duty, then, is to perform that act which, under the circumstances known to us, is the most likely to produce the maximum good or the least evil. But no *exact* calculus of probabilities and values is available to aid us. We cannot be held responsible if unforeseeable events upset our good intentions; however, we neglect our duty if we act irresponsibly, failing to use proper care in assessing relevant evidence.

Whatever we do or do not do influences the future. But the future always contains elements of uncertainty. The student who receives a scholarship may turn into a drug addict or he may become a famous actor.

Moral dilemmas do not always lend themselves to ready solutions. Circumstances are often very complex, and a particular action may affect hundreds or even thousands of people. This is true not merely of the activities of those who govern nations or preside over great corporations and educational institutions, but also of the acts of lesser individuals, such as discoverers, inventors, or traitors or assassins.

The moral correctness of a choice may be as indeterminable as the landing place of a falling piece of paper. We may face a problem so complex that we cannot imagine anyone else besides ourselves in this kind of situation. "For I am the only person sufficiently 'like me' to be morally relevant and no situation could be sufficiently like 'this kind of situation' without being precisely this situation." (A. MacIntyre) This is the material that drama and novels deal with. Who can advise a God-fearing Abraham when the Lord commands him to sacrifice his only son; a Socrates in prison; a couple considering either marriage or divorce; a young promising scientist who plans to join the Peace Corps?

It is this kind of perplexing situation that Sartre uses in his well-known lecture "Existentialism is a Humanism"; it is the one and only example he employs to elucidate his ideas on ethics. The question is, which should a young man choose, who is the only moral and financial support of his mother during the German occupation of France in the Second World War: to stay with his mother "helping her to live" or to go "to England to join the Free French Forces."

> Which is the more useful aim, the general one of fighting in and for the whole community, or the precise aim of helping one particular person to live? Who can give an answer to that. . . ? No one. Nor is it given in any ethical scripture. . . . No rule of general morality can show you what you ought to do: no signs are vouchsafed in this world.

Sartre concludes, therefore, "that the moral choice is comparable to the construction of a work of art." The young man was "obliged to invent the law for himself. . . . Man makes himself . . . by the choice of his morality." On the one hand, Sartre denies "that certain values are incumbent upon me" (which sounds dangerously like moral nihilism or capriciousness), but, on the other hand, he claims that man "is responsible for all men." [11] There is argument against Kant as well as agreement with Kant. In conclusion, man is told that it is only "by pursuing transcendent aims that he himself is able to exist."

Not ethical norms but the anguished freedom of the individual decision is at the center of existential thinking. Yet we do not surrender one particle of our freedom when we give consideration to ethical ideas. Inevitably we must decide for ourselves, not merely in occasional important matters but continuously in every day matters, whether non-moral or moral. This facet of our existence in no way denies the generality of ethical rules, which each man obeys or violates by his own free choice, nor does it argue against the possibility of rational discussion of ethical problems. We and the situations in which we find ourselves are, for the most part, sufficiently similar to other people and their predicaments to make the important moral principles and ideals meaningful for humanity in general.

Regarding himself as a law unto himself is also characteristic of the adolescent. The young person leaving the restrictions of childhood, trying to separate himself from his parents and finding his own "inner identity" goes through a period of restlessness when established values appear "phony" to him. He, a unique personality, wants to live his own life by his own values. Or he may just drift and say with Holden Caulfield, the hero of J. D. Salinger's *The Catcher in the Rye:* "How do you know what you're going to do till you *do* it?" (This is a condition, which, unfortunately, may also afflict an emotionally disturbed or despairing adult.) We hope and expect that the youngster, as he achieves maturity, will learn to accept proper values, that his irrational rebellion will change to rational idealism.

One does not have to be an adolescent or an existentialist to realize that however general ethical formulas are, each life situation is unique. Unquestionably, freedom and responsibility can be burdens, but they are inescapable. The moral man tries to do the best he can.

The moral theory I have presented deserves much more explanation as well as defense against its critics. Here we find ourselves in a quandary. However brief or even wrong I have been when discussing theory of knowledge and science, our actual knowledge of the world and of science is little affected by a superficial or wrong philosophy. But in ethics, which ought to give one a system of guidance, the situation is different. I must limit my discussion to only a few dilemmas; two were mentioned previously, Socrates' argument in *Crito* and the problem of the so-called "white lie."

In *Crito*, Socrates defends the general rule that "you must do whatever your state or country bids you to," which in this particular case meant submitting to an unjust sentence of death. Against this rule I quoted H. L. A. Hart as saying, "There is something outside the official system, by reference to which in the last report the individual must solve his problems of obedience." (above, Chapter VIII.) This the Greeks had already realized. When Antigone, in Sophocles' tragedy, breaks the law of Thebes to bury her brother, Polynices, she claims a duty toward the dead and takes her stand upon a higher law (Hart's "last resort"), "the infallible, unwritten, everlasting laws of Heaven."

How does rule-utilitarianism reconcile the conflict between the Socratic rule and Antigone's resort to the "everlasting laws of Heaven"? Under certain conditions the choice may be a very urgent one. Ordinarily, we certainly would agree with Socrates, for "every violation decreases the effectiveness of law, and we are surely better off having law than not having it at all." (Hospers) There are situations, however, in which refusal to obey a given law, or take part in revolution, or tyrannicide may be for the best and therefore morally commanded. This is especially true when great moral issues are at stake and recourse cannot be had to lawful procedures. Then we can justify the actions of the leaders of the American, French and Russian revolutions, of Simon Bolivar and the other champions of South American liberation, of the participants in the "underground railway," of Gandhi and the many other nationalist leaders against colonialism, of the anti-Nazi underground resistance in Europe and of all those who, with technically illegal methods, fight against the immoral second-class position of the Negroes.* Of course, "if anybody ever has a right to break the law, this cannot be a legal right under the law. It has to be a moral right against the law." (Charles Frankel). Consequently, an exceedingly heavy responsibility rests on those who engage in civil disobedience, and the consequences ought to be carefully weighed. What about a man like Klaus Fuchs and others who, in the name of idealism, betray their own countries for the benefit of the Soviet Union? Legally we condemn them. Furthermore, *we* think that these men made a morally wrong choice, for we regard the cause of democracy

---

* The above remarks apply also to those who engage, for moral reasons, in illegal protests against the Vietnam war.

as the better one, since it respects the dignity and freedom of the individual. And yet in so far as these men acted on moral grounds, can we withhold from them a certain respect? As Frankel warns, however, "the man who chooses to disobey the law on grounds of principle may be a saint, but he may also be a mad man." At the same time, the person who obeys the law, that is, nearly everyone in normal times and most people even in times that are "out of joint" (the average citizen in Mississippi, white as well as Negro; the quiet Germans during the Nazi Regime), should realize that he, too, has made a choice, the choice to obey the law and thus to compromise with evil.

When we tell a so-called white lie, two prima facie duties, i.e., two moral maxims, are in conflict, the prima facie duty of honesty and the duty to protect some other interest. The theory of prima facie duties and of many different maxims leaves us without a yardstick to decide which maxim ought to be followed. Rule-utilitarianism abolishes the idea of several, possibly conflicting, duties; instead it tells us to follow that rule which would produce the maximum good. But, of course, as someone has so well put it, we should not ask: " 'May I deceive in this case?' But: 'Must I deceive?' " "A single lie spreads. It is difficult to draw the line around it. It spreads in the habits of him who tells it, and it spreads in the community as soon as it is openly defended." (Blanshard) *

So far I have avoided discussing the exceedingly important ethical problems that arise for people who head governments or government agencies, or administer businesses, unions, or political parties. It is regrettable that the textbooks on ethics—those I have mentioned and most others—which are addressed to young students, are quite silent regarding these questions, which are of the utmost concern in modern society. The same problems do not, to the same extent, plague professional men, who work more or less as individuals, and white-collar and blue-collar employees, who do not play a directive role in large corporate or political entities. There are certain ethical problems that everyone faces who works with other people in any kind of an organization, be it a school, a university, a hospital, a municipality, a store, a bank,

* There is much debate among laymen and physicians as to whether patients suffering from a fatal illness should be told this fact. All we can say here is, it depends. See Hospers, *op. cit.*, p. 208 f., and numerous books on medical ethics.

or an industrial enterprise. While adhering to ethical standards, how shall I relate myself to those who rank with me, below me, and above me? How can I advance my status?

Hospers points out quite correctly that the ethical problems of business and politics are not covered by childhood teaching, nor are they dealt with in Sunday School and only occasionally in church. Consequently, they are, in many instances, erroneously not related to morality. "That's just politics," people say. Or, "You've got to do that if you want to stay in business." [12] Businessmen and statesmen usually do not feel guilty when they sail close to the wind in doing what seems advantageous or necessary; but should they experience a twinge of conscience over something they have done or not done, they justify their behavior on the ground of necessity or rationalize it by reference to the general standard in politics or in their line of business. General ideas of justice and benevolence ought to prevail here, too, as strategic directives, but to apply them in business and politics is a difficult matter. These two fields contain large gray areas of uncertainty, making it difficult to say what is right and what is not right from the moral point of view.

There is an important difference between political leaders and businessmen. The former hold elective offices and are controlled by parliamentary bodies. But the power exercised by the great business empires is *de facto* completely uncontrolled, although the decisions they make affect the fate of thousands of other dependent business firms (suppliers, dealers, agents), the lives of hundreds of thousands of employees, customers and depositors, and indeed of the whole economy. To the extent that companies like the large international oil and ore concerns are important factors in foreign countries, they even influence or interfere with our foreign policy.

In considering business and political matters, and every day affairs, we must be careful to distinguish between success and morality. We operate here with two different scales of evaluation. On the one hand, we value success, wealth and power. Yet these things may have been brought about through tough and ruthless behavior. Personal integrity may be a costly luxury. The successful man and the great conqueror—regardless how he got his wealth or won his conquest—may be considered as clever and admirable and is envied. On the other hand, we respect integrity, considerateness and helpfulness. We also hold in profound esteem the moral heroes and saints. "A good life is equivalent to a just and honorable one," said Socrates in *Crito*, and Isaiah declared, "The work of righteousness shall be peace, and the effect of righteousness, quietness and confidence forever."

Ends and Means

What does ethics have to say about making compromises and about the much criticized maxim that the end justifies the means? Whether we ought to compromise our principles and what means we ought to use depends on the total situation.

> Only a man who does not act can avoid compromises, and thus preserve inner purity. . . . Compromise is not reprehensible if it denotes a concession made to secure the most valuable result possible in the given circumstances. . . . Willingness to compromise is a test of the seriousness of a man's idealism. (Nelson)* [13]

The saintly rigorism of the "higher" ethics preached, for example, by Jesus (Matt. V) cannot be applied to everyday life. "There is no cure in high moral precepts. . . . We need an ethics which is moral and which works." (Bronowski) Or as Jefferson said: "What is practicable must often control what is pure theory." Radical, youthful idealists frequently condemn this mature wisdom.

Consider the person who lives in an outrageously unjust environment. A decent white man in South Africa or Mississippi may lose his life or be imprisoned or economically ruined if he speaks up for his ideals. What should he do? In these "existential" situations an inflexible ethical view might dictate one course of action, while a more understanding view of the frailties and limitations of human nature might suggest another. How arc are we to judge a clergyman in the Deep South who, appalled by segregation, feels he ought to do the work of the Lord even if he cannot preach against the most immediate sin? From the utilitarian point of view, can we argue that it is better to uphold religion (whatever this may mean in the particular environment) than for churches to be closed? Finally, what about the powerless, ordinary good man in a totalitarian dictatorship, living a life of compromise, whose political choices are limited to silence or

---

* Regarding the problem of ethical purity and "opportunism," see the example of Ibsen's *Brand* referred to above, p. 212.

death or the terrible dangers of underground work, which can be successful only if the dictatorship is eventually overthrown by revolution, military defeat, or perhaps—in the long run—by internal reform? It is easy for people in a free country, far away from danger, to condemn the large silent masses who face such tragic choices.

In reality we, too, belong to "the large silent masses." We who are not confronted with perilous alternatives are nevertheless passive in the face of the evils around us, to which we close our eyes. Most whites have quietly tolerated segregation for a century, and poverty seems to be a recent "discovery" although it has always been with us. We make little effort to change things because we feel we are powerless, so we remain inactive, impotent and indifferent. We compromise our sense of the moral for the sake of our comfortable lives.

The ethics of compromise is really part of the larger problem of achieving good ends through expediency (a loaded term), that is, the use of seemingly unethical means. When a policeman shoots a burglar who attacks him, or when, in the lifeboat situation, some people drown, an unfortunate means has had to be used to produce desirable results. Now let us take a very different example. Is a businessman right in falsifying his tax return in order to save his small manufacturing concern and thereby protect the jobs of his workers? An act-utilitarian might say "yes," but a rule-utilitarian would regard a rule according to which weak enterprises might properly cheat the government in order to remain in business as against the public welfare. Our country defended its democratic ways against Japan and Nazi Germany and now protects these values against those who want to destroy them; war and atomic armament were and still are the deplorable means leading to a beneficial end: the bringing about and the preservation of peace. (We "arm to parley"—Churchill.) But people all over the world still ask whether, on the basis of utilitarian considerations, the ends were and are worth the use of the terrible means.

In choosing means we must guard against the contingency that their use will make the achievement of the end impossible. Whatever means we employ, they become part of the general effects. All parents and teachers use certain tricks, disciplinary measures and commendations in the education of children. But they must strike a happy medium so as not to destroy the initiative, independence and strength of character of the youngsters entrusted to them. Shortly after the Bolshevik Revolution some radical socialists pointed out to Lenin that the means he used, a totalitarian dictatorship, would make the achievement of his goal, a classless society, impossible. History has justified this prediction.

All of life is a constant compromise between many divergent goals and we have constantly to determine what are the best means of achieving them. "Some compromises are desirable; some necessary; others are dishonorable." (Henry Aiken)

Many, particularly young people, resist making the necessary adjustments to the situations in which they find themselves. Frequently we have to revise our goals because we cannot escape the consequences of prior decisions we have made—the past cannot be lived over again. We can change study plans, jobs, friends, get a divorce, move to other places, but what was will remain, with all its consequences, part of our lives. Even if we change our living conditions radically by running away to some tropical island "paradise," perhaps only in our dreams, we are still the same "we" and we cannot avoid becoming adjusted to the conditions of our new environment. The necessity of compromising, of resorting to "impure" means, is an inescapable burden that some tortured souls protest against all their lives. But most of us gradually acquire sufficient wisdom to make peace—either cheerful or grudging—with the limitations of our existence. Nevertheless, protest is healthy as long as it finds constructive outlets.

In defending certain compromises and accommodations I am not suggesting a philosophy of quiescence or of maintaining the status quo. It goes without saying that we ought never cease to improve the moral conditions of the institutions with which we have to work. But how far should we go? How much energy, time and money ought we, as individuals, to spend on good public causes? If altruism is not commanded, how far does our duty extend and what is supererogatory? Quite frankly, I do not know, and all I have read in the literature does not sufficiently clarify the problem for me. There is, on the one hand, the formula of utilitarianism to maximize welfare, to do what produces the greatest intrinsic value for the greatest number of people. But is there any limit to the good we ought to do? In a society where injustices and poverty prevail, ought I stop taking occasional pleasure trips, going to concerts and theater, or living in a nice home in a pleasant suburb? Ought I to stop lecturing on philosophy and devote my time and financial resources to changing life in Harlem, or demonstrate day in and day out against nuclear arms? I believe this is what Christ would have asked of us. Leonard Nelson comments:

> Under certain circumstances . . . it may be unworthy of an educated man to take up a scientific or artistic vocation—ideal vocations otherwise—because what is ordinarily only a challenge to his love for justice becomes under such circumstances a duty, an unconditional obligation to set all other interests aside, no matter how strong or worthy.

And J. O. Urmson, in his previously cited essay, *Saints and Heroes*, says:

> From the agent's point of view it is imperative that he should endeavor to live up to the highest ideals of behavior that he can think of, and if an action falls within the ideal it is for him irrelevant whether or not it is a duty or some more supererogatory act.

The very opposite view is taken by the American philosopher, Kurt Baier:[14]

> We do not have a duty to do good . . . [so] that it produces the greatest possible amount of good in the world. We are morally required to do good only to those who are actually in need of our assistance. The view that we always ought to do the optimific act, or whenever we have no more stringent duty to perform, would have the absurd result that we are doing wrong whenever we are relaxing, since on those occasions there will always be opportunities to produce greater good than we can by relaxing. For the relief of suffering is always a greater good than mere enjoyment. Yet it is quite plain that the worker who, after a tiring day, puts on his slippers and listens to the wireless is not doing anything he ought not to do, is not neglecting any of his duties, even though it may be perfectly true that there are things he might do which produce more good in the world, even for himself, than merely relaxing by the fireside.

Most formalistic and utilitarian writers are quite vague on the question of how far we ought to go in bringing about "the biggest possible stockpile of what is good. . . . Being beneficent is considered praiseworthy and virtuous," Frankena writes, "but it is one of the things that are beyond the call of moral duty."

The Talmud admonishes us: "Whoever is able to protest against the transgression of the people of his city and does not do so is punished for the transgression of the city."* But after protesting and even after sending out a few checks to protesting and charitable organizations, may I then return to philosophy and my television set?

Let me put this quandary on a somewhat different basis, using the distinction, made by Urmson, between what we ourselves ought to consider as our obligation—"to live up to the highest ideals"—and what others can demand of us:

> A line must be drawn between what we can expect and demand from others and what we can merely hope for and receive with gratitude when we get it; duty falls on one side of this line, and other acts with moral value on the other, and rightly so.

From this, I suppose, it follows that the Negro child in Birmingham or the hungry family in India have no moral right to my assistance; their rights are only against their immediate neighbors and their particular electoral district or commonwealth. But what about poverty-stricken families and slum children in my own community? Urmson might argue that they have no moral right against me either, that I have done my duty vis à vis the stranger if I have voted for the best possible administrations and legislatures in my city, state and nation. How much further we *ought* to go I do not know. Except for fanatics and saints, we all, including philosophers and churchmen, take the position that we have the right to be frivolous at times despite the fact that life on this earth and right in our neighborhood is full of terrible injustices. After all, we do have to relax and replenish our energies. Who can be serious all the time? We do not want to put nature and beauty, fun and sports out of our lives altogether. Most of us lead a normal, "unsaintly" life, whether good or egotistical, without much compunction; only a few feel the need to rationalize their lighthearted behavior to themselves. But this still leaves us with Sartre's acid question: "Why do you want to alter the way in which postage stamps are made rather than the way in which Jews are treated in an antisemitic country?"

* Charles Morgan, Jr., author of *Time to Speak* (New York: Harper & Row, 1964), brands every citizen of Birmingham as guilty in the bombing of a Negro church in September, 1963, in which four Negro girls were killed.

Subjective and Objective Rightness.
The Moral Person

Thus far, in evaluating behavior from the moral point of view, I have not emphasized two important distinctions. One is the distinction between what objectively is the proper act to perform under certain circumstances and what the actor subjectively thinks he ought to do. The actor's view of the situation or of his moral obligation in it may be correct or it may be mistaken. The second distinction is that between the evaluation of an action as such and of the moral character of the actor. For example, a selfish person may be very good to his parents, not for any moral reasons, but because he wants to impress his political friends with his good character. On the other hand, an unselfish person may hide a criminal from the police because he pities him.

With respect to the first distinction, let us assume that while out sailing, I see a boat in trouble, which capsizes, throwing two men into the water. Naturally, I do not investigate who these men are but go quickly to their rescue. From pictures in the next morning's newspapers I see to my horror that I have saved two murderers escaped from prison. My act was most unfortunate and objectively wrong; unwillingly, I had become an accessory to the flight of two criminals. I will not be blamed for a moral misdeed, however, if I did what under the circumstances seemed my duty and obviously the best thing to do.

> There are two kinds of problems upon which [critique] may be directed. One is that of answering the question what it will be right to do in a given case; and the other is that of assigning praise and blame to doers, and perhaps of meting out reward or punishment for what is done. . . . Any doer . . . will hold himself responsible for *right thinking* as well as for conforming to what he thinks is right. (C. I. Lewis)

If we then ask with L. Susan Stebbing, "If I act conscientiously, can I be sure that I shall be doing the best that could be done in the situation in which I now have to act," the answer must be that we cannot be sure. Our conviction that we are acting rightly does not guarantee objective rightness, just as our certainty of the correctness of our judgment on everyday matters or on natural or historical facts and events may be completely unjustified. The moral man can do no more than try his best to find out what is objectively right and then do it.

This differentiation between subjective and objective rightness removes the difficulty we encounter in judging the peoples of other civilizations whose customs we regard as immoral. I have mentioned previously that there were ages when slavery was looked upon as quite legitimate,* and we do not condemn the Greeks as individuals; they followed what they regarded as proper. Similar considerations prevail with respect to cannibalism, human sacrifices, and the historical role assigned to women.† Thus, through the ages and all over the world intelligent and decent people have had and still do have erroneous opinions about morality just as they have had about nature.

We ask of an action that it be ethically correct, that is, in accordance with the principles we have outlined. But we ask of an acting person not merely that again and again he perform proper acts and abstain from misdeeds, but that he be a conscientious person, a person of good character, who makes it his firm goal never to do what ethics forbids. This is a tremendous undertaking, a demand transcending human strength. No one is *always* good. Yet that is what we ought to strive for. The task is made easier by the fact that it is not necessary, in order to be a moral person, to perform the right action *because* we are motivated by its rightness, or *because* we have considered the situation rationally under the aspects of justice and beneficence. Kant seems to have thought that we ought to act morally, motivated by our "good [i.e., moral] will." But such moral rigor is not required of us. Love and affection may be the motives that make a man be good to his family or his friends. Gratefulness for having succeeded in his country may make him be a good citizen. Impulsive courage may lead a bystander to risk his own life in order to save a perfect stranger from a burning building. A man's business dealings may be honest and equitable because he would like to be

* Aristotle wrote: "The use made of slaves and of tame animals is not very different, for both with their bodies minister to the needs of life. . . . It is clear, then, that some men are by nature free, and others slaves, and that for these latter slavery is both expedient and right." *Politics* I. Ch. 5, 1254–55. Nor does the Bible condemn slavery.

† According to Aristotle, "The male is by nature superior, and the female inferior; and the one rules, and the other is ruled" *ibid*. Likewise, the Bible: "And he [the husband] shall rule over you [the woman]" (Gen. 3:16).

respected as an honorable merchant. Unlike Kant, we are satisfied when actions are in conformity with duty, whatever the motive may be. But, our respect for the doer may depend on the quality of his actual motives.

The moral person is characterized by the fact that he has made up his mind once and for all to follow ethical principles even when he would rather do otherwise. All of us, if we are in good mental health, have many habits and desires and presumably also passions—particularly when young—which are not all moral. As our will is not saintly, conflicts arise between our impulses and our duty. We are then enjoined by what Nelson called "the imperative of character" to show sufficient self-mastery "to make the sense of duty the preponderant motive." A feature of moral character is "moral autonomy, the ability to make moral decisions and to revise one's principles if necessary, and the ability to realize vividly . . . the 'inner lives' of others." (Frankena) It goes without saying that an unwavering moral character is a state of goodness which we only more or less approximate. We all know that "the heart of man is the place the Devil's in."*

Besides conscientiousness, there are other *character traits* which are important and commendable, while still others are condemned as weaknesses or as being deplorable, evil, or vicious. We applaud honesty, reliability, kindness, generosity, tolerance, openmindedness, love of goodness paired with aversion to evil and particularly moral courage. In anticipation of what I shall discuss in the next chapter I would like to add here three vital human qualities which enrich life: love of knowledge, love of beauty, love of excellence. To some extent all these virtues (to use an old-fashioned term) are under our voluntary control. We say they can be cultivated, so that we may ask of ourselves not only what we ought to *do* but also what we are to *be*. Having these qualities of inner strength (and suppressing their opposites as reprehensible traits) makes it easier to act "virtuously"; without them we cannot be counted on in moments of trial. The "virtuousness" of the agent determines his moral behavior; its earnest cultivation leads to *spontaneous* right action.

* The problems of "the heart of man" (see the book with this title by Erich Fromm [New York: Harper & Row, 1964, paperback] subtitled "Its Genius for Good and Evil") have been "dissected" by clinical psychology and psychoanalysis.

Even though someone has searched his conscience and investigated the facts of a particular situation to the best of his ability, he may nevertheless decide that he should do something that we think is objectively morally wrong. We must always be careful when condemning. A friend of ours divorces his fine wife, to live with a much inferior woman, leaving her and several children. To us his action may seem not merely foolish but immoral, yet wisdom dictates that we follow the Biblical injunctions: "Be not righteous overmuch" (Eccl. 7:16) and "Judge not, that you be not judged" (Matt. 7:1). Or, as James Couzzens writes:

> On people as people, I try never to pass judgment—we can seldom know what the real truth about them is. Yet on acts, acts of theirs, I see no reason to hesitate in passing judgment—this is good; this is bad; this is mean; this is kind.

This is a matter for personal restraint and humility, and many of us lack humility.

> For with the judgments you pronounce you will be judged. . . . Why do you see the speck that is in your brother's eye, but do not notice the log that is in your own eye? (Matt. 7:2–3)

Finally a remark of the Jewish philosopher Franz Rosenzweig: "What anyone is able to do, he alone knows; the voice of his own being, to which he is to listen, can be heard only with his own ears."

When we condemn as wrong, an act by someone who claims that he sincerely believes that he did the right thing, the extent to which we can respect his sincerity depends on the nature of the act. When a mother kills her imbecile child because she sincerely believes it would be better dead than vegetating in some state institution, we may sympathize with her, but I personally feel that we should not grant her the right to take the law into her own hands and commit murder. As Blanshard remarks: "Nothing is more obvious than that we may do the wrong thing with the best and purest of motives." But Blanshard also cautions us, quoting Sidgwick as follows:

> When we contemplate Torquemada torturing a heretic for the eternal good of souls . . . a Nihilist murdering a number of innocent persons in order to benefit his country by the destruction of an emperor, a pastor poisoning his congregation in the sacramental wine in the hope of securing their eternal

happiness, we recognize that such acts are . . . done from the very highest motives; still common-sense does not therefore hesitate to *pronounce them profoundly bad.*" (My italics) [15]

Even assuming that Hitler and many of his followers, particularly the younger ones, may have had idealistic motives, we cannot absolve them from the gravest moral guilt.

Is he [Hitler] to escape all moral blame because he somehow deluded himself into thinking that all the abominable things he wanted to do were right or actually his duty? (A. C. Ewing) [16]

Sincere conviction is not an admissible defense if the deed strays too far from recognized morality. No exact demarcation is possible here. Everyone who disobeys recognized morality, calling upon the "infallible, unwritten, everlasting laws of Heaven," must be aware of his grave responsibility (see above, p. 225). Heretics and revolutionaries have played a tremendous and fine role in the development of mankind but they have also done many pernicious things. We respect reformers ("It is not safe or right to act against conscience. God help me. Amen."—Martin Luther at the Diet of Worms), but though we may admire their heroic morality, we must also consider that society is under the moral necessity to protect itself against disturbers of the peace, even the most high-minded.

The Wrongdoer. Punishment

In considering "ethical norms and conduct" we must also take a look at unethical conduct, at behavior that violates the norms set forth. We impose blame on the immoral agent, condemn his actions and may even punish him. However we can do this only if an action can be ascribed to a responsible agent. Only a free agent is responsible; only of such an agent can we say that it is his choice which determines what he does. Two problems must concern us in regard to immoral behavior. First, why do we, who are free to act rightly, nevertheless violate the norms, although we frequently are quite aware of what proper conduct is? And second, what should be done with wrongdoers?

Why the will of man, who is capable of the deepest love and the greatest sacrifices, is also capable of avarice, selfishness, deceit, destructiveness and hideous cruelty is a riddle no philosophy can answer. Investigation of the darkness of man's heart is a task for psychologists, psychiatrists, sociologists, and for novelists and dramatists too. We who do not believe in Original Sin, an idea revived by some modern theologians,* must accept the ambivalence and complexity of human nature as a basic fact of the structure of the universe.

Unquestionably, man has improved his conditions for living through the centuries, as well as his social life. Slavery, personal revenge, and cruel criminal laws have generally been done away with. The suppression of women has almost disappeared or has been ameliorated in most cultures. And there are other notable improvements. Universal peace, on the other hand, is still far off. As far as man's *personal morality* is concerned, it is quite problematic whether we have made any progress in the past three thousand years. There were good people in the old days, too, as the stories of Ruth and the Prophets, and Jesus and the saints show. And in the Greek world we have the fidelity of Penelope, the dignity of Hector and the moral courage of Socrates in the face of death. Today we are very conscious of the fact that mankind cannot simply be divided into good and bad people, but that the man of good repute and generally honorable behavior also harbors a capacity for evil and elements of barbarism and savagery, which may or may not be translated into deeds.

> There is no man so good, who, were he to submit all his thoughts and actions to the law, would not deserve hanging ten times in his life. (Attributed to Montaigne)

And yet we also find people performing deeds of helpfulness, love and heroism of whom it was never expected.

In certain cultural periods man has held an optimistic and idealistic view of himself. This was true in the Renaissance and again during the Enlightenment, and to some extent during the Victorian Age. This view finds rather naive expression in a religious New England verse of the middle of the eighteenth century:

> The great eternal God, who made
> The World and all therein,
> Made Man also upright and just,
> And truly free from Sin.

* About the belief in Original Sin, Herbert Muller has well said: "The doctrine of Original Sin may inspire a needed humility, it may also be a way of avoiding personal discomfort and responsibility, a too facile, selfrighteous reconciliation with folly and evil."

This idealistic view, when it is disappointed, as it must be, because it is unrealistic, can easily change into bitter cynicism. Frequently this happens to young people when they become aware of the "phoniness" of adult life, of the "dirtiness" of commercialism and of politics. But cynicism is as unrealistic as the overly idealized view; it is blind to man's better qualities and embitters his life.

Fifty years of terrible history have seemingly destroyed all illusions. Since Dostoevsky and Strindberg, novelists and dramatists have vied with each other in giving us a perspective of the seamy side of man's nature. The ultimate seems to have been reached by a considerable group of writers, whose point of view Ionesco articulates when he cries that there is "nothing in the world but 'evanescence and brutality, vanity and rage, nothingness or hideous, useless hatred . . . cries suddenly stifled by silence, shadows involved forever in the night.' " (Ionesco, quoted by John Gardner) The sick, perverted, criminal, weak un- and anti-hero, the helpless victim of circumstances, of his unconscious,* of the absurdity of life, has become the protagonist. He is not free and cannot choose. How, then, can we feel sorry or guilty for what we are doing? (A modernized, unreligious version of the idea of Original Sin) This excuse is in its turn absurd. We all know that we *can* choose. The pessimistic view of man, although it prides itself on its realism, is one-sided. It is significant that William Faulkner, who wrote some of the most powerful novels of degradation and degeneration, in his Nobel Prize Acceptance Speech (1949) spoke of the "old universal truths lacking which any story is ephemeral and doomed—love and honor and pity and pride and compassion and sacrifice." And in the same vein Bernard Malamud ten years later declared:

> I am quite tired of the colossally deceitful devaluation of man in this day. . . . In recreating the humanity of man, in reality his greatness, he [the writer] will, among other things, hold up the mirror to the mystery of him in which [sic] poetry and possibility live, though he has endlessly betrayed them.

A special trap for man's morality lies in his involvement in and his protective attitude toward the social organizations of which he is a part: family, business, social class, labor union,

---

* It was Freud's view that man could control the drives of his unconscious. In "normal" man reason can govern emotional patterns. In the neurotic or psychotic person, however, this is not possible; it is the purpose of psychoanalysis and other psychiatric procedures to help people gain rational control.

church, army, country. Their standards of responsibility or expediency, of industry or sloth, of modesty or aggrandizement, become his standards. (This is a very complicated matter, but this brief observation must suffice.) People follow the "outer direction" of their environments and he who dares to become a heretic, an outsider, is rare. Have people of "individual rectitude" died out? No questionnaire or poll can answer this question. The Puritans and Victorians—that is, the generation of our grandparents and great-grandparents—talked a great deal about high morality and tried to present an impeccable front. But behind this façade they repressed their wives, their children, servants and laborers; prostitution and poverty were rampant and taken for granted; colonials were treated like sub-humans. Standards of morality may not really have deteriorated, instead, the deceptions of hypocrisy may be more apparent.

There are many reasons for the present moral disillusionment.* However, the significant fact remains: *The moral structure of our civilization has not collapsed*. I see a great many hardworking and decent people around me and wherever I go. Traditional values have not been destroyed, even though they were ignored by the Nazis and the Stalinists and are ignored by us in our activities in Vietnam and our lack of proper concern for social justice; they are violated daily, as they have always been, by criminals, derelicts, and certain abnormal and deviant unfortunates. While we do not have to probe deeply to determine man's capacity for evil, neither do we have to look far for men and women of great courage and compassion. We have all read about such people, and I regard it as a high privilege to have met a few in my lifetime. Let me close this side trip to man's "sinfulness" with Saul Bellow's affirmation:

> We are called upon to observe our humanity in circumstances of rapid change and movement. I do not see what else we can do than refuse to be condemned with a time or a place. We are not born to be condemned but to live.

What is the moral situation of the wrongdoer? You will immediately think of the possibility or perhaps the ethical necessity of punishment. But punishment applies only to comparatively infrequent and extreme cases, whereas unpunished and unpunishable wrongdoing is a commonplace event in all our lives. The

---

* I do not have to repeat what I have previously said about the tremendous historical, technical, and cultural changes disturbing man's equilibrium.

many incidents of selfishness, disloyalty, deplorable impatience and frequent lovelessness which occur in our homes between husband and wife, parents and children, and between siblings, to say nothing of those between friends, associates and acquaintances, are more or less tolerated by the parties concerned; if there is any punishment at all for these transgressions, it is experienced as guilt feelings and remorse. The heartless or ruthless sinner, however, may be little disturbed by the suffering he has caused. Many of us are avaricious and power-hungry in our private dealings. Wherever people are in contact with each other, be it accidentally or socially, in commercial, political, or educational activities, ethical misconduct is, for the most part, too subtle to be covered by a criminal code. And what about the indifference to the grave social evils around us!

Only if wrongdoing goes beyond certain limits, upsetting order and peace in the community, does it become subject to criminal laws. In such cases we wonder whether the evil that has been done should be balanced in some equitable manner with an evil imposed on the agent. In other words, does justice require that the malefactor be punished in retribution? Or shall we, with respect to wrongdoers, be governed entirely by considerations of utility, that is, by the result we desire: the attainment of the greatest good, including the betterment of the criminal? The whole apparatus of moral education and of praising, blaming and punishing is supposedly directed toward that end. Apart from education, the most important means of securing the orderly life of society against criminal activity is the threat that those who violate certain prescribed rules will suffer disagreeable consequences (fines, imprisonment, or sometimes death). When, nevertheless, a serious crime has been committed, we endeavor to protect society by imprisoning or even killing the criminal agent. In so far as these agents are mis-educated or abnormal, they ought to be re-educated and given treatment; if they are dangerous and cannot be cured or rehabilitated, they should be isolated from society in mental or penal institutions. There are thus two views on the treatment of wrongdoers: the retributive, which is grounded on punishment alone, and the utilitarian, which maintains that punishment should be used to deter crime, protect society, and treat the wrongdoer.

The imposition of punishment by a public body (tribe, state government, or the like) is an outgrowth of and a civilized advance over the more primitive form of private revenge by individuals or families against those who have injured them. To leave punishment in the hands of the aggrieved parties was a dangerous procedure, and even primitive civilizations established tribunals, regulations and codes of law to handle disturbers of the peace of the community. At first, criminal codes were harsh: "If anyone maims his fellow, as he has done so shall it be done to him: fracture for fracture, eye for eye, tooth for tooth. The injury he inflicted on the other shall be inflicted on him." (Lev. 24:19–20) In the course of time, however, under the influence of humane considerations, punishments have gradually become less and less cruel.*

The retributive function of punishment seems to satisfy a strong feeling natural to most people. Why should a thief, crook, or killer, who has done physical or financial harm, not suffer more or less equivalent pain rather than get off scot-free to glory in his misdeeds? Does not a Simon Legree or a Göring deserve to be punished? How else can we restore the moral balance? In modern times retribution as *the* purpose of punishment has been strongly defended by Kant:

> Juridical punishment can never be administered merely as a means for promoting another good either with regard to the criminal himself or to civil society, but must in all cases be posed only because the individual on whom it is inflicted has *committed a crime*. For one man ought never to be dealt with merely as a means subservient to the purpose of another. . . . He must first be found guilty and *punishable*. . . . The penal law is a categorical imperative.

Kant continues with an often quoted warning, striking evidence of his extraordinary evaluation of morality, which was shared by Leonard Nelson:

> If justice and righteousness should perish, human life would no longer have any value in the world.

The retributive attitude, which regards punishment as an end-in-itself, has had many adherents among philosophers until quite recently. At the present time, however, utilitarian considerations predominate. This attitude is not new. Plato wrote: "No

* There is a complex interrelationship between ethics and criminal law, as there is between ethics and other branches of the law. This is a technical problem, which I shall not discuss except to make the broad and not very informative statement that ideally the laws of a country should promote ethical conditions in the community.

one punishes the evil-doer under the notion, or for the reason, that he has done wrong. . . . But he who desires to inflict rational punishment . . . has regard to the future. . . . He punishes for the sake of prevention." Jeremy Bentham, taking a position diametrically opposed to that of his contemporary, Kant, expressed the utilitarian view.

> All punishment is mischief; all punishment in itself is evil. Upon the principle of utility, if it ought at all to be admitted, it ought only to be admitted in as far as it promises to exclude some greater evil.

In a similar vein Mill wrote:

> If any one thinks that there is justice in the infliction of purposeless suffering; that there is a natural affinity between the two ideas of guilt and punishment, which makes it intrinsically fitting that wherever there has been guilt, pain should be inflicted by way of retribution; I acknowledge that I can find no argument to justify punishment inflicted on this principle.

The literature dealing with punishment is enormous and controversial.[17] Before a writer on ethics defends the legitimacy of punishment, he should be sure he is on firm ground, for, with the exception of small fines, punishment is frequently quite drastic. A short prison sentence may be routine for a hardened criminal, but a devastating experience for a young person. Freedom is one of man's highest goods, and before we deprive a human being of it, we ought to have excellent reasons for doing so.

There are, then, the following problems: Who is subject to punishment and what excuses may exculpate a person who has committed a harmful act? What is the philosophic ground of punishment? What kinds of punishment best serve whatever purposes we wish to accomplish?

We should punish only those who have committed a crime. What is a crime is a legal, not a philosophic question. We may, however, inquire whether the law itself conforms to sound ethical principles. Without arguing specific examples, let me mention a few controversial questions. Should attempted suicide or abortion, prostitution, or homosexual acts performed in private between consenting adults be prosecuted under criminal laws? How far should the criminal law go in limiting the free speech of radical right-wing or left-wing dissenters or agitators? How far down the ranks should German criminal prosecution go in punishing men who participated in the mass murder of Jews and others? There are also criminal aspects to certain provisions of the United States anti-trust laws. Each one of these examples deserves thorough philosophic and practical examination.

Only the guilty should be punished. We may ascribe guilt only to a person who has acted voluntarily and is responsible for his actions. I covered this subject in my discussion of free will. In determining guilt we have to take into consideration exculpating or mitigating circumstances.*

> Those whom we punish should have, when they acted, the normal capacities, physical and mental, for doing what the law requires and abstaining from what it forbids, and a fair opportunity to exercise these capacities.

> No simple identification of the necessary mental subjective elements in responsibility . . . can be made. . . . No one should be punished who could not help doing what he did (H. L. A. Hart).[18]

We should never forget John Dewey's admonition with respect to the "social partnership in producing crime." However, we ought not, I think, regard all reprehensible actions as merely the outcome of unfortunate circumstances, just as we do not ascribe all praiseworthy actions to fortunate circumstances, but to human merit.†

In our relationship to a person who has violated the moral code, as set down in the codes of law, there are both backward-looking and forward-looking elements.[19] When a crime has been committed, the principle of justice ought to prevail with respect to the actor who is "guilty and punishable," to use Kant's phrase. If he is to suffer punishment, he brought it on himself.

> The main element in anyone's right to life or liberty or property is extinguished by his failure to respect the corresponding right in others.

> [We cannot leave out of consideration] the moral satisfaction that is felt by the community when the guilty are punished, and the moral indignation that is felt when the guilty are not punished. (W. David Ross)[20]

* The drunken driver referred to in the free will discussion can be held accountable for the fact that he drank intoxicating liquor and nevertheless undertook to operate a potentially dangerous machine.

† Even a retributivist may feel sorry for a human being who has gone astray, and, if he is the wronged party, may forgive him unless to forgive is detrimental to society.

But what of the future—the future of the criminal and of the community?

> Punishment is the simplest method of reaction to offences and one strongly supported by the natural instinct to hit back, it is therefore the first refuge of the mentally lazy, whereas it should be almost the last. (Ewing)

We should turn to the *principle of utility* and let it determine what ought to happen. "We must take care that social life is not made worse by the medicine than by the disease." (Michael and Wechsler) Against Ross's defense of the propriety of feeling a certain satisfaction when criminals are punished "it is urged that the desires for revenge and for retribution are themselves anti-social and, therefore, ought not to be encouraged by law." (Michael and Wechsler) The infliction of unnecessary pain is itself a moral wrong. Punishment, therefore, should be appropriate to its goal of "deterrence, incapacitation and reformation."

In considering what kind of punishment should be meted out, the believer in the retributive theory finds himself in less of a quandary than the utilitarian. The former will argue that the malefactor has violated the dignity of others and ought to suffer some violation of his own dignity and be deprived of some of the benefits that living in a society offers. The utilitarian must establish the deterrent, preventive, protective and educational usefulness of blame and of various forms of punishment. Whether punishment really achieves the goal of deterring anti-social behavior and whether a term in prison really reforms the character or, at least, the behavior of a wrongdoer are social and psychological questions that are difficult to answer. Consider the following skeptical warning:

> Common sense suggests that [it is the first duty of the prison administration] to ensure that a man on emerging from prison is not more depraved than when he entered it. Within his cell he may degrade himself, within the wall he may be degraded by others. Prison can so easily become an unhealthy little cess-pool. It is unnatural that men should live apart from women and children, unnatural that they should be solitary for so many hours in so small a space, that their movements should be so confined and their daily doings so minutely routined. In such an artificial surrounding it is difficult for men to develop or retain a normal social habit and attitude of mind. They may well become more hardened and antisocial. . . . The man

who comes in as a criminal is made into a prisoner. All initiative and self-reliance are lost. (Michael and Wechsler, quoting Alexander Paterson.)

The philosopher is troubled. Prisoners are unseen, forgotten people, frequently badly treated. They are powerless and voteless. They cannot speak up and lobby on their own behalf. And yet we feel that sanctions are necessary within a legal system "if it is to serve the minimum purposes of being constituted as men are." They are "a *natural necessity*." (Hart)

CHAPTER X

Ideals to Live By

Happiness Through Pleasure, Through Peace of Mind

In the previous chapter I touched several times on the aim of achieving the greatest happiness, the greatest good, or the greatest intrinsic value as the basis of utilitarianism, and on the principle of excellence. However, I did not spell out these ideas in detail. Although I have already discussed an advanced and now widely accepted form of utilitarianism—the pluralistic, *ideal* utilitarianism of Mill, Moore and their successors—it will be helpful to go back a bit and spend some time on the original, basic idea of utilitarianism, happiness.

The Declaration of Independence contains the confident assertion that one of man's unalienable rights is the pursuit of happiness. The same year that this document was signed (1776), Jeremy Bentham wrote that "it is the greatest happiness of the greatest number that is the measure of right and wrong." This emphasis on happiness was an important aspect of the thinking of the Age of Reason.[1] When, during the Age of Enlightenment, religious ethics—obedience to God's commands—began losing ground, happiness was much discussed by English and Continental moralists and the very formulation of Bentham's utilitarianism had already been set down before. (What a contrast to today's emphasis on anxiety, loneliness and guilt!)

"Happiness" is a seemingly plain, innocent word of every-day language, but in reality it is ambiguous and tricky like many of the other key words and phrases in philosophy.

1. For Bentham, happiness means pleasure. If we base ethics on a search for the greatest pleasure—taking this word in its narrow sense of sensual pleasure and other forms of enjoyment—we arrive at Hedonism (*hedone*, pleasure), a philosophy propounded by Greek thinkers as early as the time of Plato. Although the drive for pleasure is often called Epicureanism today, Epicurus' idea of happiness was actually different, as I will show presently. The essence of Hedonism is well expressed in the famous lines from Ecclesiastes:

> Then I commanded mirth, because a man hath no better thing under the sun than to eat, and to drink, and to be merry; for that shall abide with him in his labor all the days of his life.

Ezra Pound's poem "An Immorality" charmingly sums up the spirit of Hedonism:

> Sing we for love and idleness,
> Naught else is worth the having.
> Though I have been in many a land,
> There is naught else in living.
> And I would rather have my sweet,
> Though rose-leaves die of grieving,
> Than do high deeds in Hungary
> To pass all men's believing.

To derive some pleasure from life and to avoid pain and misery is, of course, a natural urge. We want to eat, drink, sleep, make love, laugh, dance, play and do many other things, in short, to have a good time. Unfortunately, owing to the perversity of the human heart, man may also derive pleasure from crime, cruelty, harmful drugs and the misfortune of others. But a life of continual and unmixed pleasure and laziness soon palls. As Lin Yutang points out: "No one's life can be happy unless . . . the deeper springs of character are touched and find a normal outlet."

To consider sensuous pleasure as the paramount purpose of life is unworthy of us. The hedonist wastes his life; there should be some "high deeds." Ernest Hemingway is right in calling the amoral, pleasure-seeking group of men and women of his *The Sun Also Rises* "a lost generation." Pleasure and joy—happiness in that sense—are a valuable part of life but not its be-all and end-all, any more than an ascetic Puritanical self-denial. For the "monkish virtues" (Hume) of the "higher" religions and their saints, I give you Nietzsche's counsel: "Remain true to the earth."

What does the foregoing mean for ethics? We do not need a command: Seek pleasure! A normal person, unless he holds a one-sided ascetic view, seeks it as a pleasant and refreshing aspect of the healthy life. As for our neighbor, we must, in all fairness, respect his "pursuit of happiness" as deserving the same consideration as our own. And in accordance with the command of utilitarianism to do good, we ought to remind ourselves that great masses of people—a considerable percentage in our country and almost everyone in the Southern Hemisphere—enjoy little or no happiness, living in grave, if not desperate, poverty and near starvation. Our duties toward them spring from the good fortune in our own lives. The romanticists may see bliss in the supposedly simple life of the poor, but the reality is cruel and stark.

2. Realizing that pleasure cannot be the foundation of happiness but, at most, only one phase of it, other thinkers have laid more stress on the absence of painful experiences. Our natural pleasure-drive makes us avoid physical pain as much as possible. Even one who exposes himself or is exposed to possible pain in sports, adventure, financial operations, love, idealism, or as a soldier, will nevertheless try to reduce to a minimum his experience of physical harm and pain. But physical pain is not the only kind; there is also mental pain, to which we are all subject. Unhappiness spoils much of the satisfaction we might derive from life.

Several different ways of life have been proposed which are designed to reduce our mental pain and make us happy by bringing us "peace of mind." The nature of each depends on what its proponents regard as the major torment. As I have mentioned previously, many people find the necessity of constantly making decisions and choices agonizing.

What better protection against this torment than turning all important decisions over to a revered authority, which will direct our lives? In his story of *The Grand Inquisitor*,* Dostoevsky gives a most stirring and grandiose description of a life marked by the abandonment of individual freedom. In this story

* *The Brothers Karamazov*, Book V, Chapter V. Freud said of this book, "*The Brothers Karamazov* is the greatest novel that has ever been written, and the episode of the Grand Inquisitor one of the highest achievements of the world's literature, one scarcely to be overestimated."

the Grand Inquisitor, trying to win a silent Christ, who has reap-
peared on earth, to his ideal of happiness, argues:

> Man was created to rebel; and how can rebels be happy?
>
> I tell Thee that man is tormented by no greater anxiety than
> to find some one quickly to whom he can hand over that gift
> of freedom with which the ill-fated creature is born.
>
> No science will give them bread so long as they remain free.
> In the end they will lay their freedom at our feet, and say to
> us, "Make us your slaves, but feed us."
>
> Now [freedom] is ended and over for good. . . . But let me
> tell Thee that now, today, people are more persuaded than
> ever that they have perfect freedom, yet they have brought
> their freedom to us and laid it humbly at our feet.
>
> We have corrected Thy work and have founded it upon
> *miracle, mystery* and *authority*. And men rejoiced that they
> were again led like sheep, and that the terrible gift that had
> brought them such suffering was, at last, lifted from their
> hearts.
>
> Too, too well they know the value of complete submission!
> And until men know that, they will be unhappy. . . . We
> shall give them the quiet humble happiness of weak creatures
> such as they are by nature. . . . Child-like happiness is the
> sweetest of all. . . . We shall set them to work, but in their
> leisure hours we shall make their life like a child's game, with
> children's songs and innocent dance. Oh, we shall allow them
> even to sin. . . . They will be glad to believe our answer, for
> it will save them from the great anxiety and terrible agony they
> endure at present in making a free decision for themselves.
> And all will be happy, all the millions of creatures, except the
> hundred thousand who rule over them.

This sounds like the exaggerated ambitions of the medieval
Church, but is the idea really so far-fetched? Is it not in the nature of modern totalitarian governments to approach the pattern
of George Orwell's *1984*? As a matter of fact, all through history there have been regimes and philosophies that maintained
the superiority of dictatorship, be it by an aristocracy, a hierarchy, an officers' class, Plato's philosopher-kings, an autocratic
party, or power-usurping leaders. Dictatorships by ruthless,
sometimes charismatic individuals, are numerous today among
the countries of the world. We, however, believe in freedom,
i.e., the right and the ability of the large majority of people to
live their lives in their own way, and condemn every unnecessary

infringement of individual liberty. It is the glory and the fate of
man to make his own decisions, whether for good or for evil.

3. Epicureanism was a philosophy of life that combined individual choice and "peace of mind." * Far from being an Epicurean in our sense, Epicurus preached a simple, tranquil, frugal,
almost ascetic life "far removed from the disturbing turmoil of
politics or the harassing anxiety of economic strife and competi-
tion" (Robert F. Davidson),† unburdened by the cares of family
life (no wife, no children), free from anxiety, the fear of death,
and brightened by the enjoyment of simple pleasures and the delights of friendship. But let Epicurus speak to us in his own
words:

> When we maintain that pleasure is the end, we do not mean
> the pleasures of profligates and those that consist in sensuality
> . . . but freedom from pain in the body and from trouble in
> the mind. For it is not continuous drinkings and revellings nor
> the satisfaction of lusts, nor the enjoyment of [the] . . .
> luxuries of the wealthy table, which produce a pleasant life,
> but sober reasoning, searching out the motives for all choice
> and avoidance, and banishing mere opinions, to which are due
> the greatest disturbance of the spirit. Of all this the beginning
> and the greatest good is prudence.
>
> It is not possible to live pleasantly without living prudently
> and honorably and justly.
>
> We must release ourselves from the prison of affairs and
> politics. . . . Nothing is sufficient for him to whom what is
> sufficient seems little. The greatest fruit of self-sufficiency is
> freedom.[2]

Epicurus' sane attitude toward death was similar to that previously taken by Socrates, who, however, believed in immortality.
This attitude was characteristic of many Greek and Roman
thinkers.

> Life has no terrors for him who has thoroughly apprehended
> that there are no terrors for him in ceasing to live. . . . Death,

---

* Epicurus was born in 341 B.C., six years after Plato's death, and died in
270 B.C. See Hospers, *Human Conduct, op. cit.*

† Besides important differences in their metaphysics, the most significant
distinction between Epicureanism and Stoicism consists in the active interest that
Stoics took in the social and political life of their day. Stoicism became very
influential in the great era of classical Rome. The Stoic attitude toward public
life is similar to that of the modern Western World. Epicureanism, properly
understood, shows, I believe, parallelisms to classical Buddhism and some
tendencies of Zen.

the most awful of evils, is nothing to us, seeing that when we are death is not come, and when death is come we are not.[3]

We who believe in the life of engagement cannot ignore the strong tendency among some of our contemporaries either to abdicate responsibility and turn it over to others or to escape from the market place and the public arena. Catholicism has had a definite attraction for certain romantic non-Catholics, who see it as an old-established, authoritarian Church offering a refuge from modernism, enveloping life in resplendent, solemn and mystifying ritual, and with a priesthood that supposedly directs and gives absolution from sin. This, however, is a false conception of Catholicism; it does not relieve men of responsibility in the manner described by the Grand Inquisitor.

The authoritarian and escapist aspects of a "peace-of-mind" way of life are expressed in the lovely song by Franz Schubert, "Die Junge Nonne" (The Young Nun). The following is a paraphrase of the text:

> Loud is the tempest and wild the night. The thunder and lightning rock the convent walls. Rage, thou storm, as once it raged in my heart. But now all is calm for there is peace at last. My bridegroom comes, the heavenly Savior! Softly the Angelus tolls, calling like a voice from on high, to Heaven, my home! Alleluia!

Withdrawal from civic responsibilities runs counter to the command to do good. A monkish life of nothing more than contemplation and prayer—whether Christian or Buddhist—is useless though it may seem saintly, unless it produces something of value for the "saint's" fellow creatures. (See Mill, Chapter IX above.) Equally questionable is the life-style of some members of the affluent class, who seek repose and mild pleasures and engage in barren activities, paying merely passive if any attention to the problems of the society of which they are a part. We may envy their "peace of mind," but at the same time we know that such a leisure class, by not realizing its potentialities, violates all human ideals.

Epicurean "peace of mind" suffers from another defect: it tends to dull the mind. If we believe in the intrinsic value of man's drive for truth and knowledge, then we cannot rest but must continue to search. This idea is well formulated in two quotations from Emerson:

People wish to be settled; only as far as they are unsettled is there any hope for them.

God offers to every mind its choice between truth and repose. Take which you please—you can never have both.

A similar thought was humorously pictured in a cartoon some years ago which showed a young woman angrily shouting at her psychiatrist, "I'm fed up with being adjusted. How do I get my neurosis back?" Herbert J. Muller, one of my favorite contemporary thinkers, wrote in an early work:[4]

> The sign of spirit is doubt, disquiet, endless seeking and not finding; this is also its dignity. Almost all the great writers have told this same story, and told it . . . with irony and with reverence. . . . The great spirits have typically been wanderers, the great ages unstable ages and . . . as Whitehead has said, it is the business of the future to be dangerous.

"Peace of mind," however, can mean something quite different from either "escape from freedom" or withdrawal from family and civic life. It can mean a life that is at one and the same time active and serene. Just as we ought to seek a mode of life that is neither a constant eat-drink-and-be-merry nor an ascetic sacrifice of all pleasures, so we should attempt to achieve an *equilibrium* that permits us the commotion of family life and the restlessness of a full round of various activities and at the same time imbues us with an inner steadiness, balance and harmony.

In order to achieve this goal we must adopt some of Epicurus' wisdom. Time should be set aside for contemplation, for quiet leisure and repose. For this, private and public life must be so organized that men and women can free themselves or be freed from the necessity of constant labor. (Even in our society many have to work from morning to night—working mothers, for example, and men who cannot support their families without "moonlighting.") On the other hand, exhausting vacations filled with strenuous sightseeing and weekends crowded with competitive sports and visiting are not "quiet leisure." We need to meditate, to introspect and think. It is here that the poet, writer, artist, musician and even the philosopher may help. And the sea and the mountains, gardens, woods and meadows invite us to share their grandeur and their peacefulness.

Most important of all is, of course, the way we handle the

temptations and tribulations of life and the drive for wealth, social standing and power. Gnawing ambition and other passions should be controlled as well as the tendency to become excited and upset in the face of the constant minor "crises" of everyday life, particularly those that arise when we live with others. Whenever we find ourselves stewing and worrying, we should ask ourselves: what it really is that we are so disturbed about. Frequently we will find that the magnitude of our distress is entirely out of proportion to the matter at hand. In this age of transition, with varied intellectual and moral forces driving us hither and yon, we must learn to accept the fact that a "certain disorderliness and ambiguity of attitude are a part of the good life." We must acquire the ability to "move in different directions, to be unintegrated to a degree, to operate on discontinuities." (David Riesman) And yet we must maintain our mental and moral balance. Finally, few lives are spared calamity: grave illness, serious family conflict, economic and political misfortune, accidental or natural disaster, the death of dear ones. At these times we need fortitude and resignation. Inasmuch as none of us escapes death, we can benefit from Epicurus' and Stoic wisdom. And notwithstanding today's atomic danger and general insecurity, we must overcome fear and uncertainty and find "the courage to be." Controlling our restlessness and anxiety in the presence of a threat of danger may not make us happy, but it can give us profound peace. This is a gratifying state, though rare and difficult to attain.

Happiness Through Fulfillment

4. There is, finally, a very different way of achieving happiness: to forget completely the search for it and devote ourselves to the activities we have chosen; then perhaps one day we may experience a sense of satisfaction, joy and happiness coming over us. This happiness of fulfillment is something quite different from the kinds of happiness we have been discussing, that is (a) the enjoyment of pleasures and (b) the "peace of mind" gained through submission to an authority or through an Epicurean way of life.* The activities that may bring about the satisfaction

* Although there is a certain "family-resemblance" between the several meanings of the term "happiness," that is, all involve an agreeable state of mind, they must nevertheless be distinguished.

I am dealing with here need not be related to great achievements. Everyday life—work, love, children—can give us a deep feeling of pleasure, contentment and gratitude.

A sense of joy is probably more readily experienced when a person does something important that engages his highest faculties: the scientist working on a new experiment or theory; the artist, writer, or composer creating a new work; the businessman preoccupied with a difficult but promising piece of business. The sportsman and chess player may also feel this happy satisfaction when absorbed in what they are doing. We experience "a joy that we have accomplished the thing, that we are making headway, that obstacles are being surmounted, a joy of victory—and, corresponding to it on the negative side, there is a sorrow of failure, of defeat." (Karl Duncker) Willa Cather, the novelist (1876–1947), had this sentence from her beautiful story *My Ántonia* inscribed on her gravestone: *"That is happiness, to be dissolved into something complete and great."*

I do not want to decide whether the happiness of those who are "dissolved" into something "great" is greater than that experienced by the average person when he is successfully handling occupational or family tasks or other chosen pursuits; I am not sure whether there are varying magnitudes of inner satisfaction. Unfortunately, most people do not find the satisfaction of creation in their work. The white-collar and blue-collar worker participates only in a minuscule segment of the total work process, an unavoidable consequence of industrial, commercial and governmental organizations. For most people the happiness of achievement is found in their hobbies and family life.

It is a distinctive characteristic of the joy of fulfillment that we cannot prepare for it or pursue it. It follows a particular activity but does not motivate it. It springs from investing our vital powers to strive toward meaningful goals. Without any prior notice a feeling of fulfillment, of worthiness may come over us, and we say with Goethe's Faust (when he envisioned the building of a great settlement of free people around him):

> Then, to the moment I might say:
> Abide, you are so fair. . . .
> As I presage a happiness so high,
> I now enjoy the highest moment.
>   (Walter Kaufmann's translation)

Here we are confronted with what has been called the hedonistic paradox ("Pleasure to be got must be forgot"), a paradox very well described by Mill in his *Autobiography*:

> Those only are happy who have their minds fixed on some
> object other than their own happiness; on the happiness of
> others, on the improvement of mankind, even on some art or
> pursuit, followed not as a means, but as itself an ideal end.
> Aiming thus at something else, they find happiness by the
> way. . . . Ask yourself whether you are happy, and you
> cease to be so. The only chance is to treat, not happiness, but
> an end external to it, as a purpose of life.

Mill, notwithstanding his insight that happiness ceases when
we aim for it, nevertheless made the idea of happiness central to
his ethics and not those other objects or ends he refers to as "the
purpose of life." The modern utilitarians, on the other hand,
have abandoned the attainment of happiness as the primary goal
of the moral life and speak instead of realizing the greatest intrinsic values. L. Susan Stebbing writes: "Happiness is not an end to
be chosen instead of Truth, Beauty, and Goodness; it is a character of experiences of knowing something to be true, contemplat-
ing something beautiful, fulfilling one's duty."

Flaws in the Happiness Doctrine

The importance of happiness in Mill's ethical doctrine is
strange for another reason. In his early twenties Mill suffered a
severe attack of depression ("I seem to have nothing left to live
for"). He recovered fairly quickly, but he learned "that many
others have passed through a similar state." Mill and the other
early utilitarians should have known from their own observation
and experience that a great many people suffer periods of depression. Men as outstanding as Michelangelo, Beethoven and Freud
were melancholic personalities. Goethe told Eckermann that in
the course of his then 75 years there had not been even four
weeks when he was in a pleasant frame of mind. If you look
among your acquaintances and friends, the chances are you will
find that some usually exude a good and happy feeling while
others are dejected, discontented and pessimistic a good bit if not
most of the time. All of us frequently feel worn out, miserable
and sad. Because we are human, we know sorrow, anger and
guilt; these are unavoidable experiences.

Unquestionably, there can be happiness in life, but usually it is only a fleeting experience. Our great literature expresses this. How little joy and satisfaction there is in Homer; Shakespeare shows us good fortune but also much misery; Chekhov's and Ibsen's protagonists are ill-starred and frustrated people—happiness has passed them by.[5] Moreover, modern writers constantly stress the idea that the world, or rather their world, is a place of emptiness, despair, alienation, absurdity, nothingness, a "killing ground." There is a happy world for the happy and an unhappy one for the unhappy.[6] Since, therefore, happiness depends on our life experiences and our general mental state, it cannot play the role in ethics assigned to it. (Happiness is of course to some extent quite independent of physical and financial conditions. A crippled person may be quite cheerful and view his lot philosophically. On the other hand, one who lives comfortably may be bored and dissatisfied.)

It is commonly held that we normally make happiness the goal of our actions, that we are engaged in "the pursuit of happiness." But this is either a truism or it is an erroneous psychological observation. If by happiness we mean simply the fulfillment of our desires (still another meaning of the term) then all our strivings—whatever the objective—become strivings for happiness. Whether we want to eat a good meal or a quick meal; whether we want to marry a lovely girl, or a rich girl, or not marry at all—whatever alternative we elect, we fulfill our wishes. Happiness in this sense is useless as a basis for deciding between alternatives. If by the term happiness we mean wish-fulfillment, then the sentence, "We pursue our happiness," which looks like a factual observation, is not an observation at all but a truism, i.e., it is true by definition. According to this definition we are always "happy" when we act freely. This is, of course, not true at all if we substitute the other definitions.

Let us now examine whether the statement, "We are always engaged in the pursuit of happiness," is true, when we mean by happiness not merely wish-fulfillment but either pleasure or the satisfaction of achievement. In all our free actions we do what we most wish to do at every stage—we follow the preponderant motive. The question is whether this motive is our own happiness.[7] A great many of our daily activities are done routinely, without much thought. But there are quite a few choices in which happiness, that is, pleasure, is indeed decisive. When we look at a menu or a list of plays; when we consider vacation plans, our choice is presumably conditioned by the weight we give to the pleasures we hope to derive. Even when we are choosing a college or a job, we may very well give some consideration to such factors as climate, environment and entertainment possibilities.

There are, however, many choices in which the pleasure factor does not play the decisive role. John, a high school senior, is debating whether to go to a mediocre college, where he would get good grades without too much work and would have ample time for sports and fun, or to a college with high scholastic standards, where he would have to study hard. In this situation John is probably asking himself, "Where will I be happier?" This is the usual way of putting such problems of personal choice, but it is a deceptive one. John is choosing between pleasure—one kind of happiness—on the one hand, and acquisition of knowledge, on the other hand, leading to whatever satisfaction—another kind of happiness—he may derive from it. The primary element of the second alternative is the value John puts on learnings.

Susan's parents are wondering about their co-ed daughter, who wants to tutor slum children. They may shrug their shoulders and exclaim, "Oh, well, if it makes her happy!" But Susan is not out for happiness. Susan finds herself challenged by her idealism. She does not know, nor can anyone tell her, whether she will be happy doing what she regards as her duty. Indeed, the last thing she thinks of is her own happiness. When we wonder at the activities of a Gandhi, a Martin Luther King, a Buddhist monk in South Vietnam immolating himself, or the Dutch people who dared to hide Anne Frank and her family, we often think as Susan's parents do: people do what makes them happy, which really means: people do what they prefer doing after weighing practical (prudential) and hedonistic and ethical preferences against each other. But happiness was far from their minds when these heroes searched their consciences. Of course, they did what they wanted to do—that is the truism I referred to above; as long as we are free, we always do what we choose to do. But the choices of these agents were inspired by their idealism, by the categorical imperative. They did not "seek the victory in order to enjoy the feeling." (Duncker) If they experienced the happiness of achievement, it was quite incidental.

You may protest that these are all rather heroic deeds. But this is not the case with John, for example. Nor am I thinking of *my* happiness when I buy a gift, visit a sick friend, or write a check for a charitable organization. I choose as I do because I think it is the proper way to act.

It is apparent, therefore, that *voluntary* is not identical with *pleasurable*. As long as we are free, we always act voluntarily—that is true by definition—but we do not always choose for our benefit and pleasure. We are not necessarily selfish egoists, as is sometimes claimed, just because we do what we have chosen to do.

Winding up this argument, we must realize that the happiness doctrine suffers from two fundamental flaws. In the first place, the achievement of happiness is to a decisive extent dependent on the personality structures of people. I believe that most adults are rarely either happy or unhappy. They are busy and harassed. They have things to do and pay little or no attention to their frame of mind. Naturally, if we thought about our moods, we would prefer to be happy because it is more pleasant to be happy than not. Naturally, too, a cheerful person (other conditions being equal) is better company than a gloomy one. But when we evaluate the merits, the worth, of a person, we give little thought to his happiness; rather, we concentrate on his intelligence, character, achievements and even his or her attractiveness. A happy disposition is a likable personality trait, but not one that particularly elicits moral respect, an indication of the fallacy of the notion that happiness ought to be our ultimate goal.

In the second place, while there are, indeed, occasions when choices are made in the pursuit of happiness (pleasure), most ordinary choices are governed by family and occupational obligations, and certain important choices are dependent upon the pursuit of other, "higher" values. They are made in accordance with ethical standards and illustrate Kant's assertion that "morals is not the doctrine of how to make ourselves happy but of how to be worthy of happiness." Now we are back to the question, How do we become worthy of happiness; how do we fulfill ourselves; where do we find Willa Cather's "complete and great"? This is what I like to call the problem of excellence.

The true meaning of the unalienable right to "the pursuit of happiness" proclaimed in the Declaration of Independence is the right of every person to live his life in his own way, restricted only by the rights of all other people to follow their own legitimate life goals. It is uncertain whether this will lead to happiness, but in any case each person must be free to follow his own judgment regardless of whether it is good or poor.

Humanistic Excellence

Here we approach the final step in our analysis of what we ought to aim for in life. I want first to mention some ideals which do not appeal to contemporary humanists. In his book, *Issues of Freedom*,[8] Herbert J. Muller refers to John Stuart Mill's

> distinction between the active and passive type of man: the one seeking to bend circumstances to his own will, to struggle against evils, to improve his earthly condition, and so promoting the values of enterprise, initiative, independence of spirit; the other seeking to adapt himself to circumstances, to bear any lot, and so promoting the values of patience, obedience, resignation, humility. To most Westerners today it may seem self-evident that the active type of man and life is superior. But as Mill pointed out, most of the great moral and religious teachers of mankind have held up the passive ideal. . . . There is wisdom in the passive ideal. It has helped millions to endure a hard lot with fortitude and some measure of grace. . . . In its entire manifestation—of contemplation, composure, self-denial, non-attachment—it is a mode of self-knowledge and self-realization that may yield a deep or even rich contentment.

Buddha and Christ both upheld ideals of poverty, humility and non-resistance. Muller continues:

> Yet it is undeniable that the active type of man has promoted the growth of freedom, as in his discontent he led the rise of civilization. . . . One may add with Mill that the active ideal is positively superior in one respect, that an energetic spirit can more easily learn patience than a passive spirit can acquire energy.

All of us, to a greater or lesser degree, desire the quiet, passive life. I touched on this longing when I discussed Epicureanism. Our evaluation of the ideal of passivity as against the active ideal of *humanistic excellence* depends on our scale of values. We do get tired of progress, of the dynamic restlessness of our society, which constantly forces change on us—and change not always for the better. If the world would only leave us alone! If we could only escape to some faraway Shangri-la! Yes, there is something attractive about a community of gentle people, bound by traditions and customs, enjoying their festivities, apparently happy and serene. But how long would it be before this "paradise" began to pall on us? The most decisive question still remains: What besides goodness do we value in man? Is it not freedom, in the first place, and then the striving for knowledge, for betterment, for beauty? If these are our goals, then we cannot escape the instability of progress and the "costs of freedom," as Muller calls the sources of our discontent.

There is a passive way of life which I would like to call the ideal of meekness. Until fairly recently this ideal had a certain influence on the education of women. "Be good, sweet maid, and let who will be clever." Brand Blanshard, in mentioning this verse, comments: "The trouble with such advice is that the person who is *merely* good is likely to be good for nothing." Mere meekness is unproductive and therefore useless. It kills healthy ambition; it narrows our horizon. David Riesman quotes from a recent novel the remark of a nun to a gifted young pupil: "It is a hundred times better to knit a pair of socks *humbly* for the glory of God than to write the finest poem or symphony for mere self-glorification." (My italics) We think otherwise. We prefer a world in which human creativity flourishes, where poems are written and symphonies composed, and whether or not they are done for self-glorification does not matter. The tremendous panorama of medieval art and architecture, celebrating Christianity and its symbols, could never have been realized if men had devoted themselves completely to humble tasks. We rate active striving higher than the sacrifice of all ambitions.

> Self-respect is healthier than self-contempt, courageous endeavor is more admirable than meek submission, highminded independence is nobler than innocence. . . . Pride remains a moral necessity, the spring of all personal dignity and responsibility. (Herbert J. Muller)[9]

Here, it seems to me, Muller expresses the salient ethical point very well. Courageous endeavor and high-minded independence are held in greater esteem than their opposites. While it is not a sin or a crime to be passive or meek, it is a pity if one is too submissive; it is a fault not to use one's gifts and to stand still if one can move.

When Muller recommends pride, he does not mean arrogance, conceit, or vanity. He suggests the opposite of meekness as a virtue. We ought not to think little of ourselves. We should have confidence to make decisions, confidence that we can do what we ought to do, confidence that what we are doing is worthwhile. To be sure, confidence is not easily achieved by everyone. Aristotle's idea of the mean between two extremes—"neither too much nor too little"—can be properly applied here: neither self-disparagement nor conceit ought to be our attitude. We should value our personal dignity. By the same token, others should respect our dignity just as we should respect theirs, whatever their standing in an arbitrary social scale. To humiliate another person is intolerable.

The direct opposite of the ideal of meekness may be called the ideal of aristocracy. It is an old notion that some are born to be kings and others are born to be slaves. Some people regard themselves or build themselves up as supermen. I touched on this idea in the last chapter when I talked about Callicles, Thrasymachus and Nietzsche. In its contemporary, less exaggerated form, our feeling of superiority manifests itself when we somewhat contemptuously refer to "the masses" or when we say "they" don't know or understand or have no taste. However, the idea of aristocracy and the arrogance of an elite are not very significant in the present-day thinking of American society. The lines of the nineteenth-century hymn,

> The rich man in his castle,
> The poor man at his gate,
> God made them high or lowly
> And ordered their estate.

sound laughably old-fashioned. And yet a certain snobbism is quite widespread—the drive to be better than anyone else in some respect. Some people experience this agreeable feeling of pride and superiority from driving a Rolls-Royce, from hanging a few Cézannes and Picassos in their living rooms, from having a library named after them. This sort of thing is quite innocent and indeed may often produce beneficial consequences.

The idea that the government of states should rest, not in the hands of the mass of people, but rather with an aristocracy distinguished by birth, wealth, social virtues, or, like Plato's philosopher-kings, specially trained for their functions, has been important in the planning of undemocratic Utopias from Plato to the American philosopher, George Santayana. Even certain of our Founding Fathers, "convinced of the superior influence and capacities of 'the rich, the well-born, and the able' " (David Spitz, quoting John Adams), regarded democracy as "a demonstrably false—because unnatural—theory of state."

Let me mention briefly another so-called ideal way of life. Most people prefer to be much like their neighbors, but there are many too, who would like to be different in some respect from the general run; they want to be something more than a carbon copy. Regrettably, these feelings are suppressed most of the time. However, some people, Bohemians, beatniks, some artists and writers make a cult of unconventionality. This pursuit of the peculiar is a negative ideal since the only value it recognizes is deviation from the socially accepted. It is more desirable to demonstrate one's independence in more positive ways.

All the ideals described above and rejected as inadequate have one feature in common—they are not evil, and they do not violate our ordinary moral feelings regarding justice and goodness. But there are some ways of life—we can hardly call them ideals—which are either totally immoral or so reprehensible that we do condemn them as evil. They represent disvalues. The "life-values" of criminals and gangsters belong in this category, as well as the degrading activities of gamblers, drunkards, drug pushers, procurers and others who pander to men's "lowest" instincts. Some of these practices are perhaps caused by physical or mental disorders.

In this connection I would like to refer back to what I said about Hedonism: living merely for pleasure, frequently for low pleasure. The Italian film, La Dolce Vita gives an excellent picture of the pointless and wasteful life of ostentatious pleasure-seekers, which has a particularly destructive influence on the younger members of society.

The distinctions here made between high and low values and disvalues is a moral one. This fact is sometimes obscured by the use of the terms "natural" and "unnatural." Everything we do has its origin in human nature and in that broad sense is natural. Only when we apply ethical or esthetic value systems—and thus philosophy—can we distinguish the natural from the unnatural. Neither cannibalism nor polygamy, slavery, sadism and drug addiction are foreign to human nature; if they were, they would not exist. We condemn them, not because they are unnatural, but because we regard them as immoral and degrading.

The often repeated admonition to listen to the voice of our "real self" or Polonius' "true self" is equally deceptive unless we mean by our real and true self our *good* self.

Let us now go from one extreme to the other, from disvalues to our highest values. Here we have finally reached the capstone of ethics and can now take up the question, previously raised, as to what it is that deserves to be called "complete and great." We ask: In what does human excellence consist? It is not merely the idealist or the philosopher who feels the *moral urge* to strive for higher values. Most men living above the starvation level realize that there are higher "goods" which are worth pursuing; even the poorest endeavor to help their children to higher horizons. But excellence is not merely something that we can or do pursue. I use the term *moral urge* to indicate that we are upholding an ideal, i.e., a goal, which can be and deserves to be pursued, which presents an ought to our will, a task which Nelson calls "a categorical optative." We *ought* to like and dislike rightly, or, to paraphrase Kant, we *ought* to learn how we can properly fill the place assigned to us in life and what each of us "must be in order to be a man." Or, as Nietzsche more daringly puts it, in the previously quoted admonition:

> One task [is assigned] to every single one of us: to promote inside and outside of ourselves the generation of the philosopher, the artist, and the saint, and thus to work at the perfection of nature.

Ideals represent standards of perfection for beings who are human and fallible and not angelic; we can do no more than try to approach these goals.

> Ideals are like stars—you will not succeed in touching them with your hands; but like the sea-faring man of the desert of waters you choose them as your guides and, following them, you reach your destiny. (Carl Schurz)

Both ideals and duties are "grounds on which we commend or condemn actions." (R. M. Hare) Duties are "connected with the interests of other people": we should be fair, we should be good to others. This social morality is an ethical minimum. The ideals praised here refer to our own excellence; yet some pertain to our excellence in our relations with others—the ideals of benevolence, neighborliness, friendship and love. An ethics that embraces both the duties we have discussed and the ideals we will discuss is a *humanist ethics*.

By humanism I mean a way of life centered on human dignity and values which each of us can pursue through his own free endeavors. Humanism stresses many values, not just one *summum bonum*. Humanist thinking is a this-worldly philosophy; it does not look to heaven or to any other supposedly better world transcending our sphere. Traditional Western religious thinking, on the other hand, is God-centered and stresses faith in, love of, and obedience to God as man's highest excellence. Developments during the last two hundred years, however, have softened these differences. Humanist ethics, like the notions of science, has exerted a strong influence on our living religions.

Love of Truth, of Good, of Beauty

Humanism is not new. It can be traced back to the writings of Plato and Aristotle.[10] Today it is an attitude widespread among educated people and not restricted to philosophers, even if the name is not always used.

Although excellence may be achieved in many ways, there is a large area of agreement among humanists regarding ideal activities. This is, therefore, not a very controversial subject and I can deal with it by touching on some high points. Familiar though the subject is, and even trite in some respects, an outline of the content of humanism is necessary in order to complete our system of ethics. Furthermore, the goals of life are too important to be passed over entirely.[11]

We can agree with Ewing when he says, "It is doubtful whether we can produce any tidy list of things good-in-themselves." Nevertheless, we can bring some clarity and order to our ideas if we make use of the old Platonic triad and designate our ideals as love of truth, love of good and love of beauty.[12]

1. *Love of truth.* Love of truth requires intellectual honesty, and honesty, in turn, requires courage. Superstition and prejudice have reigned for a time in every society, but from Socrates to the present day men have risked their welfare and even their lives proclaiming what they held to be the truth.

The desire for truth and for intellectual freedom is so strong and enduring that even when the free search for knowledge has been suppressed, truth has usually triumphed in the end, and the efforts of Grand Inquisitors and other spiritual dictators have met with defeat. Socrates and Galileo have been vindicated, the Catholic Church has acknowledged evolution and Marxian orthodoxies have been greatly diluted.

We learn and acquire knowledge with two purposes in mind. Learning may be a tool with which to make a living, or it may be an end-in-itself; we read and study because we are interested in, and enjoy, some field of knowledge. For scientists and many other professionals this either/or may not exist: their work may at the same time be a wonderfully satisfying activity.

Others have expressed themselves so eloquently on the importance and pleasures of learning that I will let them speak to you.

> The intelligence of every soul rejoices at beholding Reality and, once more gazing on Truth, is replenished and made glad. (Plato)

> Thought makes the only dignity of man; therefore endeavor to think well—that is the only morality. (Pascal)

> The man whose mind mirrors the world becomes in a sense as great as the world. (B. Russell)

> To know, to discover truth . . . is a desire whose fulfillment does not lead to disappointment and boredom, as does the fulfillment of almost every other human longing. For there is no end to truth; each part of it reveals, when found, yet other parts to be discovered. The man who desires knowledge knows no satiety, for the knowable is perpetually new. He might live innumerable lives and never grow weary. (Aldous Huxley)[13]

It is obvious from these quotations that when these writers speak of the acquisition of knowledge, they do not "mean the random accumulation of mere data." To be knowledge, what is learned must be ordered and assimilated and should contribute to the enhancement of an individual's culture.

Because thinking and knowledge are important for a worthwhile life, it is up to us not merely to educate ourselves, but also to arouse others and educate them. This task has sometimes been regarded with a jaundiced eye. Romantics have wondered whether it is not better to allow a primitive, superstitious, poor but happy tribe to retain its traditional ways. But this point of view not only represents a questionable ideal, it has also become an idle dream. Jet planes, movies, radio and television have brought modern knowledge and a technically advanced life to practically all corners of the globe. All peoples are restless and want to share in modern science, medicine and technology. For this education is a prerequisite.

In all Western countries, education is involved in an extraordinary number of controversies concerning organization, techniques and goals. Of the many fundamental problems, two are of special philosophic interest. First, there is the question whether we are to give our young people a general, or so-called liberal, education or educate them exclusively as specialists for occupational competence. As a philosopher, the only thing that I ought to say here is that some measure of general education is a basic requirement of the "good life." A broad base ought to be laid for a lifetime of continued learning and growth. An affluent society like ours ought to organize and finance its educational undertaking in such a way that every educable youth may acquire a general awareness of our literary, artistic and scientific culture, and of politics and history. He should have an overview and a comprehension of life. However, we must adapt our educational enterprise to the varied interests and the emotional and intellectual qualities of young people. General education, indeed, gains in importance as working hours become fewer and retirement comes earlier. Our increasing leisure demands that we develop our inner resources. Adult education and stimulation are thus confronted with a big task.

The second problem I have in mind is a conflict resulting from the co-existence in our society of "two cultures," a much debated controversial idea of C. P. Snow's. In the field of education this means the conflict between a humanistic education and an education in a scientific discipline (taking the words "humanistic" and "scientific" in their narrow sense). The social sciences share in both parts of this dichotomy. From what I have just said, it is clear that I favor some liberal education for everyone, combined with an understanding of the way science views the world. In addition, of course, there should be special training in the young person's chosen occupation. A progressive modern society needs people, both generalists and specialists, who can work and learn together to further individual excellence. However, only a limited amount of learning can be squeezed into a limited number of years, and most young people are anxious to go out into the world, be independent and prove their mettle.

2. *Love of goodness.* Love of goodness goes beyond doing one's duty and acting with justice and benevolence. It means pleasure in doing good, "with malice toward none; with charity for all." The humanist ideal becomes a humanitarian ideal. "Be thou a blessing," God said to Abraham. In an ethical sense, we are all neighbors and brothers and one another's responsibility. John Donne expressed this thought with moving simplicity in the passage that Ernest Hemingway used as the epigraph for his book, *For Whom the Bell Tolls:*

> No man is an Iland, intire of itselfe . . . any man's death diminishes me, because I am involved in Mankind; and there- fore never send to know for whom the bell tolls; It tolls for thee.

We ought to strive to express loving-kindness, compassion, pa- tience, understanding, even graciousness in dealing not only with those who are dear to us, but with everyone—a noble and diffi- cult precept, unfortunately more honored in the breach than in the observance.

Most of us have a small or large circle of friends, and we applaud one who has a talent for friendship, feeling an esthetic satisfaction in knowing him. We find that the man who keeps everyone at a distance lacks something. Love goes beyond friendship, though it may very well be combined with friend- ship. We may love our friends, and we may be friends of those whom we love, our adult children, for example. High tribute is paid to love on several grounds; here we esteem it as an ideal value, as something that is good and beautiful.

The opposite of friendship and love is contempt and hatred. We hold these feelings in low regard unless they are directed against matters which deserve our contempt and enmity. It is fashionable in certain circles of today's intellectual world to dis- play contempt for, or at least disenchantment with, mankind. It is more praiseworthy, natural and useful, however, to love our fellowmen, if by love we mean an active interest in others, and in improving the lot of all the world's peoples. This, too, is an ideal value, perhaps the highest. The world cannot be saved without our "intelligence and energy and good will" applied in the public affairs of our local community, and for the benefit of our nation and humanity as a whole. As Edmund Burke said a long time ago: "The only thing necessary for the triumph of evil is that good men do nothing." Reinhold Niebuhr has stated it another way: "We cannot build our individual ladders to heaven and leave the total human enterprise unredeemed of its excesses and corruptions."

Only an analysis of a particular historical situation can determine whether political ideals can best be realized through a revolution or a patient, yet stubborn, drive for piecemeal reforms. The perpetual injustice of political arrangements tends to incline idealists to radical solutions. However there is wisdom in the saying of Marcus Aurelius, the great Stoic Roman emperor (161–180 A.D.): "Dream not of Utopias but be content if the least thing go forward."

This is the place to remind ourselves of what Urmson calls "the higher flights of morality," of the saintly and heroic deeds that have all too rarely been done. We admire the courage of the physician who voluntarily joins the depleted medical forces in a plague-stricken city (one of Urmson's examples). We are all better off because of the men and women who freely sacrificed life and position in the many fights for independence, liberty, freedom of conscience and justice. They are symbols of our ideals.

3. *Love of beauty* is the third member of the triad. Here again I can be brief as so much has been said and written about beauty. It is impossible to define or describe what it means, for the concept of beauty cannot be analyzed into other generally applicable characteristics. Nevertheless, we *know* what it means. From the prehistoric men who painted animal pictures on the walls of caves and ornamented their tools and presumably sang and danced, to sophisticated modern man, people have appreciated beautiful objects and activities. I cannot tell you why we are sure that a Greek statue or temple, a Rembrandt painting, a Beethoven quartet, or the face of a friend is beautiful. It just *is*. All I can do is refer or point to a number of objects and say of them: This one and that one are beautiful, or I regard them as beautiful. It would not be useful for us to go any further into esthetic problems.

Among the various forms of beauty there is, first of all, the beauty of nature. We thrill to the scenic grandeur of nature: snow-covered mountains, a raging ocean, a tremendous thunderhead cloud. We derive great pleasure from a colorful sunset and

the stars on a clear night. Many quiet and intimate things gladden
us: a flower or a whole garden, a butterfly, a bluebird, a brook
in the woods flowing among moss-covered rocks. And let us not
forget the sweet, rambunctious beauty of a small child and the
sensuous and alluring beauty of a lovely woman.

> The contemplation of Beauty, and especially the Beauty of
> nature, is an immense solace and joy, calming and cheering.
> It is sharable by all. . . . The contemplation of Beauty is a
> form of living that involves no competition, interference, con-
> sumption, or destruction. . . . The contemplation of Beauty
> sometimes induces ecstasy, and ecstasy is a happier state, a
> humming perfection of the whole person.[14]

The realm of nature and its beauty, which seemed inde-
structible and eternal to our ancestors is today being severely attacked by the ever-expanding encroachments of pleasure-seeking
people, of cities, roads and industry. They need to be protected
from their human enemies.

We cherish too the beautiful things created by man's imagination: temples and churches, statues, paintings, literature
(poems, stories, and plays), dance, music. But it is not sufficient
to pay tribute to the men and women who conceive these works
or execute them; they deserve our active support and financial
backing. A society without artistic, literary and musical activities
(both professional and non-professional) is indeed impoverished.

Personal Harmony

Looking back, we can say that we find, in activities motivated by our love for the true, the good and the beautiful, Willa
Cather's "complete and great" which will give us the inner satisfaction of real happiness. From this springs another idea of
beauty, having an esthetic ideal in fashioning our own daily
lives.

> Moral ideals have a very close resemblance, in some ways, to
> aesthetic ideals. . . . It is as if a man were regarding his own
> life and character as a work of art, and asking how it should
> best be completed.[15]

"Harmony" is a favored term used to express the esthetic
vision in the shaping of our lives. Plato asked: "Will the good
soul be that in which disorder is prevalent, or that in which there

is harmony and order?"* Harmony is not a precise concept, but it has been used by several philosophers. Other philosophers have employed other words for the same or a similar ideal. It can be as little explained as beauty. Aristotle refers to the great-souled man; Spinoza to nobility. Modern writers speak of self-realization.

To bring about inner order and harmony is not easy, as we are entangled in various incompatible impulses and activities. Some of these impulses are wicked, and we would no doubt find grave faults in the hearts, and sometimes the deeds, of practically everyone. In spite of this, we ought to try to achieve a viable integration and ethical balance of our many ambitions and drives, and of those aspirations which serve ideal goals. Admittedly, this is an almost impossible task. Parker states that, "The aesthetic balance . . . is for life an ideal, not a reality." And he therefore speaks of "the conception of tragic harmony . . . recognizing not only the inevitableness but also the persistence of conflict and waste . . . of frustration and pain."

The goal of harmony in our lives challenges us to overcome the threats of alienation, disorder, destruction and despair in ourselves and thereby to secure the peace of mind which I have previously referred to, not the Epicurean peace of mind but the peace we find through inner "fortitude and resignation." (above, p. 254) Thus we may finally attain what Blanshard calls "the rational temper," distinguished by equanimity and serenity.

What are some of the qualities we expect of the ideal person? We expect him to have the moral and ideal character traits (virtues) previously mentioned. His mind should be well-informed and flexible. ("Only those who continue to change remain my kin"—Nietzsche.) The ideal man should show tolerance, modesty and reliability; he should be a constructive and stimulating force in his community; in short "a productive personality" to use Erich Fromm's expression. The ideal person must have an affirmative attitude and believe in his own worth and the worth of others. An active, adventuresome and occasionally lighthearted person, he should also appreciate interludes of quiet and contemplation. Finally, the ideal man should recognize that there are others who deserve his support.[16]

* *Gorgias*, quoted in DeWitt H. Parker, *Human Values* (Ann Arbor: George Wahr, 1944, paperback). The last chapter of this book, entitled "The Supreme Value," deals with "the good life [which] would be the beautiful life, beautiful like a work of art."

The ideal of excellence and of the beauty of life is not monistic; it can be represented in a rich variety of personalities.
"People are different and what they are likely to succeed in
achieving is different (it is sheer waste when a man who could
have been an artist of genius becomes an indifferent civil servant
—and vice versa) . . ." (Hare) No totalitarian regime ought to
enforce a uniform ideal on its subjects nor should an individual's
career be governed by examinations and computers. "Any doctrine that the pattern of the ideal life should be the same for all is
intolerable. . . . Any diminution of this variety would impov-
erish the human scene." (P. F. Strawson)

Play, work, family and sex relations are important features
of the full life and deserve some special comment.[17] Games, sports
and entertainment contribute to our relaxation and enjoyment,
and often to health. My particular pleasure is walking and hiking. Hiking is good for body and soul. It encourages
contemplation and shows us the beauty of nature with its magnificent variety of plants, animals and rocks. We are privileged to
live in a beautiful country, and it is sad that so few people ever
get to know more of it than can be seen from their cars as they
speed along the highways.

The fact that man must work to obtain the bread he eats,
and everything else, too, gives rise to numerous economic and
sociological problems, among them, the question of remunera-
tion which has an ethical as well as an economic aspect. However, we cannot discuss *distributive justice* here, or "justice in
the allocation of income." (Brandt)[18]

The dullness of much work and the fragmentation of the
work process greatly diminish the conditions for an ideal life. It
is rather widely thought that the monotony of blue-collar and
white-collar labor is something new, resulting from the rise of
the industrial society. But this is not the case. Agricultural labor,
the work most peoples of the world have been and are still engaged in, is equally monotonous, although it may be regarded—
because it is performed outdoors—as more pleasant. We cannot
get away from the fact that labor has always been a drudgery.
The blueprints of socialists and utopists designed to change this
condition have been unrealizable wish-dreams. All we can do,
and indeed have done, is to make the conditions of labor health-
ier and more pleasant, and to shorten the working period, not

only by cutting the number of hours in the work day and work week, but also by reducing the number of years of his life a person must spend in a factory or office.

These developments impose two previously mentioned tasks on us, which are of the utmost importance. First, we must revamp our high school curricula to include challenging courses for the academically less gifted teenagers. And, second, we must devote more community effort to the creation of meaningful leisure activities for older people.

Everyone needs to feel that he performs a useful function in the economy or in other aspects of community life and thus most people have a natural desire to do well whatever they are doing. But unfortunately, modern industrialism gives most workers little room within which to demonstrate good craftsmanship. Modern economic life requires that most people specialize. Time alone makes it impossible to realize all of our potentialities. We have to select—a necessity often resented by young people. For creative self-fulfillment "a dominant center" is necessary "to which the rest is subordinated." (Nelson)

Modern developments have created the much discussed problem of the proper specialization of academically trained married women. Should they take on only the "feminine" role of making a harmonious home? What happens, then, when the children are in school most of the day, or have left the parental home? However, to enter the ardent contemporary discussion of "the feminine mystique" would take us too far afield.

The Ethics of Family Life and of Sex

What can be said about the ideal of family life was implied in what I stated previously about duties and ideals. Here as elsewhere, we ought to apply the principles of fairness, goodness, loving-kindness and excellence. The fulfillment of the ideal is by no means easy even in the best of marriages. As far as children are concerned, it is the parents' duty to see that their offspring develop healthily and freely, that they receive the best possible moral and intellectual education and become independent. Children, in turn, should not consider the Fifth Commandment: "Honor thy father and mother" as out-of-date. A healthy nation can be built only on healthy family life, grounded on loving, reciprocal relationships among the members of the family.

Mankind has organized its family life in an infinite variety of ways. The present-day American family, consisting solely of parents and children, is a recent development and the smallest type of family that has ever existed. Among its drawbacks is the fact that it isolates young adults from younger and older family members, gives them unlimited freedom and deprives middle-aged parents and grandparents of many family functions. We may well question whether this family setting, or one embracing a wider circle of members would offer the better arrangement for the various generations involved.

Monogamous marriage is an ideal that is gaining predominance all over the world. An acquaintance with a Nigerian Muslim gave me an indication that even where the present generation of men have several wives they expect their sons to have only one wife.

Young married people are often surprised and perturbed to discover how difficult the first years of marriage are, however much in love they may be.

> Compatibility is a process and not an accident . . . it depends upon the maturing of instinctive desire by adaptation to the whole nature of the other person and to the common concerns of the pair of lovers.

> A successful marriage depends wholly upon the capacity of the man and the woman to make it successful. They have to accomplish wholly by understanding and sympathy and disinterestness of purpose what was once in a very large measure achieved by habit, necessity, and the absence of any practical alternative. It takes two persons to make a successful marriage in the modern world, and that fact more than doubles its difficulty. (Walter Lippmann, *A Preface to Morals*)[19]

It takes time, patience and understanding for two people, who have been independent and who are of equal dignity, to learn the self-discipline, mutual regard and willingness to compromise that the du-archy of modern marriage requires.

> The American marriage ideal is one of the most conspicuous examples of our insistence on hitching our wagons to a star. It is one of the most difficult marriage forms that the human race has ever attempted, and the casualties are surprisingly few, considering the complexities of the task. (Margaret Mead, *Male and Female*)[20]

A society in which stable family relations prevail is of paramount importance to children. Yet it is impossible for the state to force people to live together and continue a marriage relationship, when they prefer, after responsible self-examination, to be divorced. Legislation forbidding dissolution of marriage bonds even when the interests of both partners and of any children are safeguarded, is unsound and immoral, as it deprives people of their freedom, encourages subterfuge and causes unhappiness. It is contrary to the ideal of marriage as a voluntary though legally protected association. On the other hand, this ideal is also violated by a succession of marriages and divorces, which may be part of the *dolce vita* of a small but much publicized irresponsible set of international "society."

Society can do a number of things to improve family life. Birth control is essential to the spacing of children and is absolutely necessary for the "control of sexual power" and of the population explosion. Society can also act positively. It is of the most urgent importance that it give its young members wholesome, enriching sex and family education, emphasizing frankness, responsibility and the ideal of a good life. Such education must be modern in its orientation, otherwise it will be derided by the students and lose all value. Education should also decrease the pollution of public taste, particularly evident in the obsessive interest in violence, pornography and prurience.

Finally, let me make some remarks about the ethics of sex relations.* This is a tremendously complex problem and not a subject in which I can claim special expertise. But perhaps this is not as necessary for the philosopher, whose task it is to offer broad ethical principles at a time when old ideas about sexual behavior are changing under the impact of new developments and new insights.†

What are some of the new developments and insights that are important to our consideration of the morality of sex relations, and what are their consequences?

(1) We have freed ourselves more and more from the shackles of the dichotomy of body and soul, that is, the distinc-

---

* I limit the discussion to heterosexual relations.

† The insights gained through the investigations of human sexuality by Freud, modern psychiatrists and physiologists have had the most profound effect on contemporary thinking. Furthermore, anthropologists have found that sexual behavior has been regulated—more or less satisfactorily—in many different ways by many different people. Our own sexual behavior is not the only feasible one. (See Margaret Mead, *Male and Female, op. cit.*)

tion between the carnal, sinful flesh of man and his pure higher
spirit. We appreciate that sex is part of the totality of life, and
that it constantly influences us. It is natural and can be beautiful.
It can also be the source of romantic love. At times it is a tremendously strong passion that may be either enhancing or destructive. It is of the greatest biological and cultural importance as the
means of procreation and consequently as the basis of family life.
Healthy sex relations are fun and enjoyable; they may even be
ecstatic. However, having established the importance of sex, we
have tended to overemphasize it and perhaps even make a cult of
it.

(2) The process of education has been extended so that
sexually mature teen-agers and most young adults remain in
school or college much longer than formerly. These young people have a powerful urge to gratify their sexual drives, and, as we
know, they often do. This is true not only of college students but
of high school boys and girls too, particularly those who feel restricted by present-day school life. Moreover, sexual pleasure is
free and temptingly at hand. Sexual self-restraint may seem quite
irrelevant to the adolescent where an orderly family life may be
nonexistent.

(3) Since we allow tremendous freedom to small children,
they naturally expect the same treatment when they become adolescents and young adults. The latter live outside the bounds of
the family circle, in a society of their contemporaries that is
isolated, in some degree, from the mature adult society. Temptations to gratify their sexual passions are numerous and opportunities to do so are easily available. "Emphasis on rigorous discipline and duty [have given] way to approval of enjoyment as an
end in itself." [21] There is, however, a difference between "rigorous discipline" and sound self-discipline. Have we, in our permissiveness and tolerance of *la dolce vita*, perhaps gone overboard
in the relaxation of certain restraints? Would some taboos be advisable? Would they be accepted? Fortunately, the large number
of quite successful marriages among our young people, presumably as satisfactory as marriages have previously been in Western
society, testifies to the soundness of our youth in general, even
though their sexual behavior has changed.

(4) We tend to recognize the moral equality, equal dignity
and equal freedom of men and women. This affects not only the

legal, economic and political position of women, but also their education, their sexual standards and their aspirations. At the same time most societies have generally recognized and to a large extent still recognize the so-called double standard of sexual morality. For men abstinence is regarded as unnatural. Chastity, however, was regarded as the only proper condition of unmarried females. Girls, therefore, are counseled to remain virgins until marriage.

> There is ample testimony in the outcries of moralists that even in the olden days these conventions were not perfectly administered. But they were sufficiently well administered . . . because of the way people lived.

> The woman lived a sheltered life. . . . She lived under the constant inspection of her family. She lived at home. She worked at home. (Walter Lippmann)

Traditionally there are two kinds of females, those who are "decent," i.e., virginal, and therefore "acceptable," and those—by no means a small group—who were regarded as bad, who offered their bodies for sexual gratification either freely or for money. Today we seem to have become ambivalent in our feelings about female sexual morality. We still have a strong distaste—at least a theoretical one—for prostitution, regarding it as sexual exploitation, destructive of the females involved and humiliating for both males and females. Yet, a considerable number of young women regard it as quite proper and natural to enjoy sexual pleasures before marriage just as their male friends do. It is precisely this aspect of the situation which has aroused such widespread feeling that sexual relations are chaotic today—"maximum freedom and minimum responsibility"—and have reduced society to a state of utter demoralization. This, however, seems rather far-fetched, considering that prostitution, involving the majority of men and a considerable number of women, has never evoked a comparable outcry from moral critics of society.

The rules for "good" girls were simple: Don't! *With freedom has come complexity and anxiety.* Should I or shouldn't I? The trouble is that there is a wide variance between what is officially acceptable and what people actually do, and this makes choices quite difficult for the young woman. Should all standards then be disregarded as just old-fashioned preachments, or can they make sense to our free young women?

What should emerge from this all too brief analysis? We must first recognize the fact of the goodness and joy of sex. This idea is not new; it is new only in relation to an ascetic Pauline, Puritan, or Victorian view. The majority of the people of the world, past and present, have understood the naturalness of sex and have appreciated its pleasures. The Biblical Song of Songs begins: "Let him kiss me with the kisses of his mouth—for thy love is better than wine." The young man later responds: "How fair and how pleasant art thou, O love, for delights!" (Please do read this marvelous poem.)

That a high percentage of modern unmarried young women are sampling the pleasures of sex is well-known.[22] However, we should not lose sight of another finding: "By the time [the American] college girl marries . . . the odds are possibly fifty-fifty she still remains technically a virgin." (Gael Greene)* Would it not be more natural and esthetically preferable to follow the Scandinavian girls, who are reported to pet less but to indulge in intimate relationships earlier? Extensive research shows that college girls who engage in pre-marital intercourse do so to a large extent with the men they later marry. They are, therefore, for the most part not promiscuous. Does this not then considerably reduce the potential element of immorality?

Abstinence and the control of sexual passion are generally not harmful. Although pre-marital and extra-marital sexual relations are common, female and even male abstinence is not at all exceptional among young men and women who feel free to say "no" without necessarily damaging their standing among their peers. They ought to say "no" also if they are uncertain about the propriety of sex relations for themselves in general or with a particular partner. Some young people want to "save" the ultimate intimacy for marriage. To say "no" is particularly advisable for adolescents of high-school age. They are immature and should neither act recklessly nor tie themselves up in relationships that may be a hindrance to their future development. This is sound and yet highly impractical advice for many groups of

* According to other studies the odds in favor of the virginity of *college girls* are quite high. One authority goes so far as to indicate that owing to "the control and discipline required to prepare academically for college, and to remain in college . . . it is likely that promiscuity occurs more frequently among high school girls than among college women." (Mervin B. Freedman)

teen-agers in our large cities, not only those who live in corrupting slums.

What additional ethical suggestions can the humanist philosopher make with respect to contemporary sex life? Today more than ever it seems quite unnatural and unrealistic to recommend complete male and female premarital or extramarital abstinence. We ought not to assume an *absolute duty* of premarital chastity, but perhaps we should recognize a prima facie *ideal* of chastity outside of marriage. Here a distinction ought to be made between fully mature adults, and adolescents and immature young people; mature adults may claim greater freedom. Promiscuity, however, violates the ideal of beauty in life and endangers the social order; society has a legitimate interest in the protection of the family institution.

For young people and particularly young teen-agers it may be better to hold to the ideal of chastity unless the young persons involved plan to marry each other or are bound together in a meaningful relationship. This may very well be the esthetic attitude of many young people themselves; it would explain, at least in part, the feelings of guilt or shame many experience in regard to uninhibited promiscuity. Yet I am not certain that this is the soundest and most humane position; I also have some sympathy with Walter R. Stokes' more broadminded view, which is, however, contrary to the opinion of many enlightened educators:

> In no event can I see anything unethical or anti-social in the simple joy of autoerotic pleasure or . . . in the enjoyment of sexual intercourse as an experience delighted in by two *affectionate* and *responsible* people and requiring no other justification, even though other purposes may sometimes be served. (My italics)

The ethical philosopher will point out that what holds true for family life is equally true for sexual relations between men and women, whether mature or immature: we should be guided by the principles of fairness, goodness and excellence. Toward this end, young people especially, must be helped to understand that heterosexual activity, which involves intimate physical and emotional relations with another person, is not on the same level as other forms of sensual pleasure and selfindulgence, such as eating a delicacy or drinking a good wine. It is particularly important to stress that each partner should show consideration and loving-kindness for the feelings and interests of the other. We must *give* if we want to *receive*. Here, as elsewhere in human relations, Kant's imperative holds: Never treat a person simply as a means, but always as an end.

While sexual passion may be good and enriching, it may also be personally destructive. As the poet writes: "We never would have loved had love not struck swifter than reason, and despite reason." (Robert Graves) It is incumbent upon us to act with responsibility, controlling our sexual drives sufficiently so that neither partner to the sexual act is hurt as a result. For the young girl Miss Greene has these words of caution:

> The abuse and misuse of sex creates genuine tragedy that we can no longer ignore. Pregnancy, illegitimacy, early marriage and forced marriage, abortion and venereal disease . . . are only the most readily identifiable symptoms of ignorance, pretence, anxiety, hostility and self-destruction.

This warning should also be pondered by the young man, who shares the responsibility for, but rarely the consequences of, a passionate moment. Sexual life can be beautiful only if tenderness and love inform it.

> Love is an intensive awareness of the other person, a feeling of respect for him or her as a human being and an instinctive attitude that the needs of the other person are as important to you as your own needs. (Maurice Zolotow)

The specific role of sexual activity in the realization of excellence lies in its contribution to fulfilled manhood and womanhood, to a fulfilled marriage relationship, and to fulfilled fatherhood and motherhood. In this area an essentially hedonistic attitude, whose goal is to make "conquests," prove "virility," or desirability, is somehow degrading and may be exploitative. A feeling for common decency, individual dignity and personal integrity ought to act as a restraint on purely physical promiscuity. The natural modesty and reserve of many young women—and of young men, too—deserve to be respected, and inhibitions and guilt feelings ought to be deferred to.

What answer is there, then, to young Moses Wapshot's question to his girl: "What harm can there be in something that would make us both feel so good?" [23] Ethics does not give general and uniform answers to the problem of what we can do with the freedom that is ours. Decisions must be based on the particular circumstances, on individual responsibility, on deep moral convictions and on the sense for ideal values. As one young student explained to Miss Greene: "You couldn't go wrong if you really tried never to hurt anyone, but the most important person not to hurt was yourself."

Does this solve the sexual problems of young people? It does not, because they are young, and often immature, passionate and often unwilling to consider the consequences of their attitudes and actions. They are in opposition to their parents and resentful of a hypocritical moral standard still regarded by many as ideal. Anxious to experiment, they are all the more easily aroused and influenced by the salacious books they read, motion pictures saturated with sexual activity and the public discussion of bedability. They have a particularly difficult time in a period of change and uncertainty. Yet, with all these difficulties, their education in sexual matters is grossly neglected or so old-fashioned as to be useless. Nor does it help puzzled young people to know, as all of us realize very well, that in the sexual sphere nearly every one of us all too frequently transgresses against his own ideals. Consequently, we ought to be careful in judging others and remember what Confucius had to say on the subject long ago: "The Master said, I have never yet seen anyone whose desire to build up his moral power was as strong as his sexual desire." (IX: 17) Basically, our primary duty in these matters is not to debase our own esthetic ideals. If a feeling of disgust comes over us when we contemplate an act of ours, this may very well be a warning that we have violated our own self-respect, though we may not have hurt anyone else.

We must also consider sex in marriage. Beyond the virtues we have emphasized several times, a truly happy marriage requires mutually satisfying sexual relations. General understanding, mutual care, companionship, common interests and fidelity —essential as they are—are not, by themselves, enough; in addition, a proper basis must be worked out for a good sexual life. Only then will a marriage be strong, stable and fulfilling.

To preserve the family "every society teaches that one cannot satiate his sexual desires with full freedom." (I. L. Reiss)

However, extramarital activity is, and always has been, wide-spread.* This is the stuff of gossip and scandal and grist for world literature (masterpieces as well as trash), movies and television. Kinsey observes somewhat cynically—but with a good deal of truth—that "even those males who disapprove of extramarital coitus for their own wives may be interested in securing . . . coitus with the wives of other males." Sexual dissatisfaction, general unhappiness, the fact that a marriage has become an "empty shell," the desire for new pleasurable experiences, and the temptations of alternate attractions are the most common causes of "extra-curricular" activities, whether of a fleeting and sporadic or of a more lasting nature. (In some contemporary cultures the more enduring relationships between married men and their mistresses or concubines are tolerated or permitted.) Philandering may deeply hurt and humiliate the other spouse. It may create emotional and other difficulties for the third party, and it may degrade both partners of the outside relationship. Extramarital relations must usually be regarded as violating our standards of morality and beauty of life; we will rarely go wrong if we heed the Seventh Commandment—"You shall not commit adultery"—and the Tenth—"You shall not covet your neighbor's wife."

Here at the conclusion of our treatment of ethical conduct —its norms and ideals—let me emphasize two themes that ought to dominate our decision-making. There is, first, the *equal* respect we owe to everyone as a person, even though one may deserve little or none for what he has done with his talents and his life, while another may deserve a great deal on the basis of his accomplishments. There are all kinds of men and women on this earth and they all have a prima facie right to enjoy life and to pursue their affairs in freedom and in accordance with their own choices and abilities.

A highly educated Westerner, a slight South Asian woman working tirelessly in a rice paddy, a Congolese hunter, an Arab nomad, a Buddhist monk, they are all part of humanity. And what diversity there is among the people with whom we come in daily contact! Let us constantly keep in mind what Martin Buber

* Kinsey's studies show that half of all married males in his sample and a quarter of all married females had engaged in extramarital sex relations.

has said so beautifully: "Everyone has in him something precious that is in no one else."

The second important theme is the constancy of our task. Since we are not perfect, we often *do* lose sight of rightness and our higher aspirations. However, we should not despair of ourselves or of society, nor *ought* we neglect to do the best we can. The goal for each individual and for humanity as a whole is a realistic one but at the same time a distant one. As Donne said: "When thou has done, thou hast not done, for I have more." Let me conclude with a quotation from the Talmud:

> It is not incumbent upon you to complete the work, but you are not free to desist from it altogether.

NOTE: To complete the outline of a modern world view would require us to elaborate on the application of ethical principles to the organization of political life and to education, and thus to deal with the philosophy of politics and of education. To do justice to these subjects would expand this introduction beyond a reasonable size and I have, therefore, limited myself to the few hints which I have given in the chapters on ethics.

Both Plato and Aristotle discussed education and politics extensively. Philosophers ever since have dealt with these subjects. In modern times both Bertrand Russell and John Dewey did so, and the latter, particularly, exerted a great influence on the philosophy and practice of education. A modern treatment of the two subjects with references to both older and modern literature can be found in:

O'Connor, D. J., *An Introduction to the Philosophy of Education* (New York: Philosophical Library, 1957).

Scheffler, Israel (ed.), *Philosophy and Education* (2nd ed., Boston: Allyn and Bacon, 1966).

Benn, S. I. and R. S. Peters, *Principles of Political Thought* (New York: Free Press, 1965).

Quinton, Anthony (ed.), *Political Philosophy* (London: Oxford University Press, 1967).

CHAPTER XI

The Justification of
Ethical Beliefs

"Imperatives of right, and the validity of them, have no other determinable and final ground than that character of human nature by which it is called rational."

—C. I. LEWIS[1]

"Adeimantes: No one has proved that a soul can harbor no worse evil than injustice, no greater good than justice."

—PLATO, *The Republic*

Objectivity of Ethical Values

"Do we really know whether anything is good?" Nearly everybody has strong opinions about many specific ethical issues, and we do not hesitate to pass such judgments as: slavery, genocide and murder are bad; I ought to be more charitable; A did a wonderful thing. Few would challenge the idea that there is a difference between right and wrong, even though in times of moral uncertainty it may be difficult to judge certain actions—an illegal demonstration, a case of promiscuity, a "white" lie—as being right or wrong. However, when we examine the ground of moral judgments, that is, the problems of *critical* ethics, we are perplexed. The basis of ethics has become more and more suspect as men have gradually lost faith in an ethics established by religion and found no substitute on which to predicate their particular moral judgments. Many people retire to a weak, "This is just my subjective opinion. Perhaps you won't agree with it." In most instances, this is an erroneous self-observation motivated by the speaker's fear that he may be thought to express some theory of ethical objectivity, absolutism, or intolerance that would undermine his own ideal of tolerance and open-mindedness. It is difficult to imagine, however, that one who says, "Slavery is wrong" or "Hitler and his cohorts were brutal tyrants," merely expresses a personal attitude. In truth, he is not talking about his state of mind at all, but is passing judgment—either true or false—on slavery and Hitler, asserting that they are bad.[2] We would regard anyone as morally obtuse, perverse and wrong who would not agree to the truth of these assertions.

Even when a less obvious moral problem is debated, as when two brothers discuss their obligations toward their old parents, the judgments expressed concern not so much their feelings as their sense of duty. It is, of course, understood that both brothers express their own opinions, but Brother A is interested not in whether Brother B reports a correct self-observation, but in B's opinion on what they ought to do. (The situation is no different in a scientific argument. When A claims that the study of method X will lead to a cancer cure and B casts doubts on A's proposal, it is truistic to say that A and B express their own "subjective" thoughts. The argument is not concerned with A's and B's states of mind, but with the content of A's and B's assertions about a cure for cancer.)

But this clarification does not help us to make any headway. Even the man who is firmly convinced that slavery and mass murder are bad, wonders whether these judgments and other ethical judgments can be proved. After all, other civilizations permitted slavery, and Aristotle defended it; the Nazis in our own day gloried in the killing of those whom they regarded as submen.

How then can there be an objective ground for ethics?

Before entering on a discussion of this most difficult and controversial subject, let us see how far we have progressed. We have found, I think, that it is possible to establish a consistent and coherent* theory of *practical* ethics, that is, a system of general

---

* Coherence also played a role in our treatment of the truth of everyday knowledge. See Chapter III.

directives for the conduct of our lives. Of all philosophic tasks, this is the most essential. The principles established and their consequences conform, I believe, to the opinions of enlightened men. They avoid the one-sidedness of the teachings of several of our great moral teachers without rejecting their insights. The duties and ideals set forth embrace justice, helpfulness, freedom and love; excellence and harmony; healthy sensuality and restraint.

In evaluating our survey of ethical ideas we must remember that it had to be concise. Furthermore, no system can perform the impossible task of dealing with all concrete moral dilemmas. The reason lies not merely with the necessary generality of the philosophic treatment but also in the fact that life is extremely complicated. (Even science cannot tell us which apple blossom will open first and which bee will fertilize it.)

That we have succeeded in developing an ethical system which is coherent and which appeals to common sense and reflective reason is a considerable triumph of philosophic endeavor. It is a persuasive, though not a sufficient, argument for the truth of the system, and should encourage us in our search for a foundation, which is the subject matter of critical or *metaethics*. Even if philosophers are in sharp disagreement about metaethics, we cannot help feeling that the problems of the justification of ethical beliefs will somehow find a solution. There must be some intellectual basis for ethical assertions. Even if certain controversies cannot be solved now, we ought not lose confidence in the correctness of moral evaluations. In mathematics some problems have known answers but the proof for these answers has not yet been discovered.

Bertrand Russell, in his *History of Western Philosophy*, asks the intriguing question: "If Buddha and Nietzsche were confronted, could either produce any argument that ought to appeal to the impartial listener? . . . What could either say?" After expressing his agreement with Buddha's ideas, Russell continues: "I do not know how to prove that he [Buddha] is right by any arguments such as can be used in a mathematical or a scientific question." Yet notwithstanding the lack of proofs of ethical judgments, Bertrand Russell not only has never hesitated to express his opinions on numerous moral problems but has had a sufficiently strong belief in his ideals to go to prison for them:

for his pacifism in the First World War and recently for his activities in opposing the nuclear arms race.

How do we know that good is good, that right is right, that we ought to love our neighbor and strive for excellence? Can we find this out in a way similar to the one we used when we established that "there are people here now"? We can see actions and we can see and hear expressions of joy or of pain. We cannot see or hear whether an action was right and whether expressions of joy or pain are caused by proper or improper behavior. We can find out what people like and dislike. We know what we desire, but this is often not what we ought to desire. Offhand, it seems that there is a definite difference between what is desired—a factual question—and what is desirable—an evaluative question; between *descriptive* and *prescriptive* judgments. Psychology and social science can tell us about people's observable wants, but social science cannot tell us what we ought to want to do. Assuming that the conquest of a small country and the killing of its people would bring about greater satisfaction of the wants of a larger nation, would that make the war right? Most of us are convinced it would be unjust. But how do we know this and how do we know that "a soul can harbor no worse evil than injustice"?

Common sense and the social sciences tell us what people do: they go to church, and they go on picnics; they organize a free enterprise system; they love, feed and spank their children; they demonstrate, take drugs, throw beer cans along highways; they are promiscuous, generous, angry and loving. But observation of certain ways of behavior does not constitute a judgment of their goodness or badness. We evaluate customs, those of our own people and those of other civilizations. On what basis do our approvals and criticisms rest?

We are convinced that there are moral or—sometimes—esthetic reasons for our critical evaluations. Our judgments are not wholly arbitrary. Nor are they merely judgments of taste, as whether to wear kimonos, sarongs, slacks, or dresses; or to use French or Russian dressing on our salad. These are discretionary choices of national habit or personal taste, and it makes no sense to argue about them. With regard to ethical judgments, however, it makes a good deal of sense to ask whether we have judged correctly or wrongly; whether our ethical assertions are true and justifiable or false and unjustifiable.

Can Ethical Judgments Be Proved?

Can ethical judgments be proved? The word "proved" has a double meaning. (1) By proof in the strict sense of the word we mean a logical deduction from more general statements which we know or assume to be true, or which we choose as basic statements. The best example of this use of the word "proved" is in mathematics, where theorems are proved, i.e., deduced, from a small number of general postulates or axioms. But we also constantly "prove" statements on everyday matters without giving much thought to the logic we automatically apply. If I hand a salesclerk a five dollar bill in payment for a $3.45 purchase, I expect to receive change of $1.55. If I am told that Mr. Y, whom I just met, is in mourning because his father-in-law died the day before, I realize that Y is or was married to the daughter of the deceased.

To prove any valid conclusions we must know some true premises. To prove ethical theories deductively we have to know ethical statements more basic than the ethical theories to be proved. And how do we find these? Perhaps by still more basic principles. Eventually we must reach ultimate principles, for which we cannot produce still more ultimate principles and which we cannot prove deductively—otherwise the chain would be endless. For ethical statements, and for inductive truths also, to have any foundation there must be a cognitive ground for the ultimate principles other than logical deduction.

(2) We thus come to a broader meaning of the word "proof." We think something is proved, if it can be justified (vindicated, supported, established) in an objective and convincing manner. The statement that "there are people here now" cannot be proved in the first sense, but was proved, i.e., justified, in the second sense.

Let us now apply this process to ethics. Let us assume the following dialogue between an older person, A, and an adolescent, B:

A: "You ought not to have taken the package of cigarettes without paying."

B: "Why not?"

A: "It's stealing!"

B: "So what?"

A. "You ought not to steal. By stealing you deprive the storekeeper of his property. You would not want to have your things stolen from you. What you do not want others to do to you, you should not do to them. This is in accordance with the general rule that we ought to act justly. And you ought to be just." This logical, step-by-step advance from the specific command to the general principle ends the *logical proof* of the original reprimand. If B now asks, "Why should we be just?" and adds, "I am much better off if I steal a little here and there as long as I don't get caught," what can A answer? Should he reply, "To be just is a moral command," B might laugh in his face. "To hell with morals! I look out for myself."

A: "But you oughtn't to."

B: "And why not?"

Suppose A now tries as a last resort the following pragmatic answer: "Because it is bad for the community if you act immorally," and B comes back with, "What do I care? I am not a do-gooder." "Indeed," A replies, "you are an immoral egoist! And you oughtn't to be." By this time B, not at all interested in philosophic palaver, has walked away. By logical steps A has gone back to the most general ethical postulate, and no other logical, deductive steps are possible. Any further proof would have to be proof in the second sense; i.e., justification, validation of the basic ethical principle, that we ought to act justly.

To prove or justify ethical principles is not a very meaningful undertaking in the argument between A and B, or in similar disputes. But other thoughtful people are interested. And, aside from the greater or lesser practicality of the search for validation, there is a deep intellectual, that is, philosophic, interest in the foundation of ethics.

Before tackling metaethics I ought to call your attention to the fact that a great many ethical arguments do not proceed in the manner of the discussion between A and B. Often the factual situation that gives rise to an ethical disagreement is complicated, and clarification of it will frequently be all that is necessary to bring about agreement on the proper way to proceed. Then there are cases in which an acting party faces a difficult dilemma, say, between telling the truth and thus hurting someone deeply and telling a protective "white lie." In such cases, both alternatives can be defended on the basis of identical principles, but the weighing of the imponderable pros and cons leads to different results. In ordinary life most ethical disagreements are of the kind just mentioned, but there are other kinds, too. Sometimes people dispute basic principles, as in Bertrand Russell's fantasy discussion between Buddha and Nietzsche. As for the ideal of human equality, there is no unanimity on its range. Even now there are people who regard it as perfectly right for men to "rule over" women, or for whites to dominate Negroes.

Assuming that there are two contradictory basic moral principles, how do we decide between them? What is the warrant for any basic ethical assertion? Or, to put it differently, what is the "ultimate ground of the right?" (C. I. Lewis) And what is the "ultimate ground" of our obligations and ideals? These seem to be meaningful questions, but "questions are pointless if decision is impossible." We must now ask, "Is a decision regarding the validity of our ethical ideas possible?"

More than a hundred years ago, John Stuart Mill, in the very first paragraph of his *Utilitarianism*, wrote:

> From the dawn of philosophy, the question . . . concerning the foundation of morality . . . has occupied the most gifted intellects, and divided them into sects and schools, carrying on a vigorous warfare against one another. And after more than two thousand years the same discussions continue . . . neither thinkers nor mankind at large seem nearer to being unanimous on the subject, than when the young Socrates listened to the old Protagoras.

The "warfare" Mill talks about continues undiminished today. Some new and interesting theories have been developed in this century born of the controversies over the objective and intuitionist viewpoint of G. E. Moore's *Principia Ethica*, which appeared in 1903. In fact, the main concern of contemporary ethical philosophers lies in metaethics, in an analysis of the moral judgment.*

---

* *The Moral Judgment* is the title of the previously mentioned recent paperback edited by Paul W. Taylor containing "Readings in Contemporary Meta-Ethics." The fact that most of these readings are taken from works written since 1950 and, aside from an excerpt from Moore's book, go no further back than 1930, shows how lively the discussion is at the present time. A systematic treatment of the several modern theories can be found in the treatises cited in the first reference of chapter IX.

Conscience and Religion as Basis of Ethics

The average person, not "sicklied o'er" with philosophic theories or skepticism, when asked about the ground of his ethical precepts, would probably refer to his conscience or to his religion. *Conscience* is the aggregate of our moral feelings and opinions as we have acquired them through early influences (superego), education and life experiences. It may contain genuine moral insight, but most often it "speaks with many voices." (Blanshard) The reference to conscience is no answer to our critical question because we must ask immediately for the justification of conscience itself. However, as conscience is merely the accidental totality of an individual's ethical notions, it varies from person to person (just as does people's everyday knowledge). Consequently, it makes no sense to justify it as such; what has to be justified or disproved are the particular notions making up our conscience. My conscience tells me that Negro children ought to go to integrated schools, while the conscience of a member of the Ku Klux Klan tells him that these children ought to go to separate schools. This particular disagreement has to be analyzed and decided, we cannot rely on mere conscience.

Does ethics then rest on *religion*, as a large number, perhaps the majority, of Western people believe? Let us consider this from the viewpoint of our Judeo-Christian tradition, which finds the revelation of God's commands in the Bible. But what is it that God commands? Is it "an eye for an eye"—"love thy neighbor"—"love your enemies"? It is men who make the choice and find the first of these commands barbaric and the last too visionary, other-worldly, and perhaps dangerous to our welfare and that of our family and country. If the Bible were the real basis of our ethics, we could not object to polygamy, slavery and capital punishment—institutions taken for granted there. Since Biblical days, it is not God's known revelation but thoughtful men who have brought about "some of the greatest improvements ever made in the moral sentiments of mankind." (Mill) The only excellences the Bible preaches are the love of God and of justice; the ideal of all-around excellence was first proclaimed by Greek thinkers. And, finally, God has not given identical precepts to the adherents of the various religions of the Judeo-Christian tradition. To cite only one example: God has commanded Catholics

to regard the marriage bond as a sacrament that cannot be severed, but Protestants and Jews are permitted to divorce their
spouses.

There are even greater quandaries. Western religious thinkers often argue and preach as if they were completely unaware
of the fact that those who base their religion and ethics on the
Bible and its subsequent tradition embrace, at the most, not more
than one-third of humanity. There are Oriental people, whose
religions do not accept the Biblical tradition and whose ethics
frequently do not rest on their religion at all. Many Eastern religions have little to say regarding personal ethics, being com-
prised largely of metaphysical beliefs and ceremonies. Furthermore, the many unbelievers and humanistic idealists of past
millennia and of the present, outside or within Judeo-Christian
civilization, have not grounded their ethics on any religion. The
number of people today who are convinced of the truth of a
secular world view has been growing constantly, though many
remain members of churches and synagogues. And there are the
two great atheistic, Communist commonwealths that account for
one-third of humanity. Even if one looks upon Communism as a
substitute or a pseudo-religion, there is no question that the
ethics of its followers, which in its everyday aspects is not very
different from ours, is not based on the revealed commands of a
transcendent God, but is this-worldly and "scientific." Paul
Ramsey's statement[3] (by no means exceptional among Western
religious thinkers) that "Without God, no moral obligation" is
an expression of a surprisingly parochial viewpoint and completely overlooks the all too plain fact that moral obligation is
possible independent of the realm of God.

The attempt to vindicate ethics by grounding it on religion
is confronted by a still more fundamental difficulty. This was
pointed out by Plato long ago in his brief dialogue *Euthyphro*[4],
where Euthyphro and Socrates discuss whether the gods would
approve of a son denouncing his own father as a murderer. Socrates wonders about the rightness of such behavior and then asks
the basic question: "Is what is holy holy because the gods approve it, or do they approve it because it is holy?" The question,
in revised and modernized terminology, is this: Is something
good and right because God approves it and commands us to act
accordingly, or have good and right a value independent of
God's approval? The mere fact that we can ask these questions

shows that the words "good" and "God" have different meanings.

If we consider the second alternative of the *Euthyphro* problem and take the position that we obey God's commands because we have evaluated God's commands and found them to be right, then we must have ethical knowledge with which to compare God's commands and the search for the basis of this knowledge must go on. "The concurrence of a deity then becomes superfluous." (A. J. Ayer)

But if we adopt the first alternative and assume that God's approval is sufficient ground of the right, we must be puzzled indeed by some of the behavior He condones. In all the wars that have been fought, many for religious reasons, did He approve one side and not the other, or does He approve both sides? Did He sanction the burning of practically all of Tokyo but not atom-bomb destruction of Hiroshima? It seems that today we are trying to clarify the problem of the ethics of nuclear bombing without giving much thought to the designs of the Almighty. Or to mention another current problem: Does God tell us whether non-violence or more militant religion will help the Negro most? Only experience in different situations and localities can decide this question.

In studying the Bible, we find that God committed, commanded, or tolerated some incredible acts. How can we not regard His killing of all the first-born children of the Egyptians as an unbelievably barbaric punishment? What about human sacrifice—not for the glory of the Aztec gods—but as part of the revelation of the Biblical God? The story of how God commanded Abraham to sacrifice his only son Isaac, as a test, and restrained him only at the last moment has provoked vast amounts of theological interpretation. But God's failure to prevent Jephthah from actually sacrificing his daughter, has escaped popular and theological attention (Judges 11). And can non-Christians help being astounded that the sacrifice and crucifixion of His own beloved Son should have been part of God's design? If we regard some of God's reported actions as primitive or as violating ethical ideals, we have given up the principle that God's approval is sufficient to stamp an action as good; there must then be another independent source of our moral standards, which enables us to evaluate God's commands and deeds and the happenings described in the Bible.

Still another problem confronts the religious believer. The non-believer may ask why we should obey God's commands. The believer's reply that the imperative "Obey God's commands!" is part and parcel of his religion cannot convince the questioner. The position of famous theologians that it is not up to man to question God's commands, arbitrary or unethical as they may seem, contravenes naive conscience as well as informed ethical thinking. "Without a prior conception of God being good or His commands being right God would have no . . . claim on our obedience." (Ewing) The fact that God is by definition the highest law-giver and thus the highest authority does not change the dilemma. Why should we unquestioningly obey any authority, even the highest? There cannot be a "higher" answer to this question for those who try to base ethics on God's approval.[5] The believer simply has to rely on his faith in order to live with the religious paradox of God's outrageous actions and commands.

Numerous thinkers, particularly in recent years, have tried to obviate some of the difficulties entailed in basing ethics on religion by defining "religion" as standing for the sum total of mankind's highest ideals, and "God" as another, more symbolic term for the same thing. They have chosen to continue to use these venerable and respected words, although they have abandoned belief in revelation and in the traditional notion of God as a supernatural entity. But this device only creates a new problem. The statement that ethics is based on religion, then, means that ethics is based on "the sum total of mankind's highest ideals." This is an empty truism: ethics is based on ethics. Mere change in terminology does not further our search for the justification of ethics.*

The Bible gives us very practical reasons—promises and threats—to obey God's commands.† The moral man thus becomes an opportunist to gain a seat in heaven: he shuns wrongdoing, not because it is wrong, but because he wants to escape the torment of hell. This attitude debases ethics, making it a matter of mere prudence. However, to secure the benefits of heaven and

---

* The relation of science and religion is obfuscated by a similar abuse of terms; see Chapter V.

† ". . . that thy days may be long upon the land . . ." (from the Fifth Commandment, Ex. 20:12) or as the New Testament indicates in many places: the wrongdoers "will go away into eternal punishment, but the righteous into eternal life." (Matt. 25:46)

avoid eternal damnation, we would have to know what God's commands are, and these, as we have seen, are by no means easy to discover. Moral behavior that entails sacrifices on our part here on earth would make utilitarian sense only if we had faith in the reality of the eternal bliss of heaven and in the eternal "unquenchable fire" of hell—matters that modern man has difficulty in accepting and which, of course, are totally unacceptable outside the Judeo-Christian sphere.[6]

Morality and Traditional Religion

Besides the metaethical philosophic question of the relation between religion and ethics, there is the very practical question of the utility of religion.[7] Are religious beliefs necessary to induce man to behave properly? Is the fact that religious conviction has declined and that many feel "God is dead" responsible for whatever moral decadence may exist in the world today? Is religious education a requisite for character education? If we define religion as the sum total of ethical ideals, or some similar formulation, then by mere definition moral behavior is based on religion. But this means no more than that moral feelings and insight are required for proper behavior, which is platitudinous. The real question is whether belief in the supernatural God and Biblical revelation is a precondition for the moral conduct of mankind. Is it true, as Paul Ramsey says, that there is "no morality without immortality" and that "without God, there is *nothing* a man is bound not do do"?*

Although the question raised here is not philosophic, but one of education and sociology, let us give it a little thought. As far as I know, no thoroughgoing, conclusive, factual studies have ever been made of the contribution of religious beliefs (in the conventional sense of the term) to moral behavior. It goes without saying that children who have a proper education show, in general, better behavior patterns than children who have been exposed to poor standards. It can therefore be easily concluded that children of so-called "good" Christian or Jewish homes have less tendency to delinquent, criminal, or promiscuous behavior than children from "bad" homes. But this merely proves the

---

* This is not the opinion of theologians, religious philosophers and educators alone. Lord Denning (high court judge) is reported to have said, in connection with the Profumo affair (1963), "Without religion there can be no morality and without morality there can be no law."

beneficial influence of a good home environment and does not establish, as religious educators claim, the decisive role of the religious element. "The moral influence of early religious training owes more to its being early than to its being religious." (Hospers)*

I do not mean to claim scientific validity for my personal observations, but I must say I cannot find any difference in the moral attitude and discipline of people brought up under the influence of traditional religion and those whose parents are non-believers. It may be argued that even non-believers are affected by the general atmosphere of a religious culture. This, however, is a fatuous objection in view of all the delinquency, crime and other unethical behavior in this sometimes-called "Christian nation." † Whatever causes may underlie such behavior, lack of a specifically religious education is not one of them. Such behavior shows how little value people place on their so-called eternal blessings and how little they fear the fires of Hell.

The practical irrelevance for personal behavior of the Western religious tradition (whatever its truth may be) may also be experienced by any visitor who observes individual morality in Oriental countries or in Russia. (Is there any country where traveling is made more pleasant than in Japan where the people are polite and helpful, and the general civic morality high?) Contrary to Ramsey, even without God there are certain things a man is bound not to do.

John Stuart Mill, in *Utility of Religion*, enumerates some of the factors that hold the fabric of ordered society together. He lists early education, authority, public opinion and "regard for the sentiments of our fellow creatures," and, not the rewards of "a problematical future existence but the approbation of those whom we respect." "Where the penalties of public opinion cease, the religious motive ceases also." Manners, customs, general attitudes and laws are more important than religious ideologies in the generally peaceful conduct of community life.

---

* Let me recall here my previous observation that the mere teaching of moral precepts is not a sufficient means of character education.

† No real distinction can be drawn between the moral viciousness of pagan and of religious people. Torture, the burning of so-called heretics, aggressive wars, slave-trade and gas chambers have been perpetrated by Christian people. The Old Testament describes the wartime cruelties of the Hebrews. Fanaticism, one of mankind's worst curses, has frequently been the outgrowth of religious fervor and intolerance.

There is considerable debate about the "utility of religion" in world history. But we can not speculate on the question of what mankind's fate would have been if culture had dispensed with religion, or whether the influence of religion has been good or bad for humanity. Suffice it to restate here that the moral quality of mankind does not depend on its religiosity, on belief in God and immortality. "The ethical behavior of man is better based on sympathy, education, and social relationships, and requires no support from religion. Man's plight would, indeed, be sad if he had to be kept in order through fear of punishment and hope of rewards after death." (Albert Einstein)

Empirical Basis of Ethics

I have gone into considerable detail with respect to the religious justification of ethics because of the high standing of religion in our society and the large claims made for it as the one and only appropriate basis for moral wisdom and moral conduct. But, since the days of antiquity, laymen and philosophers have also advanced secular bases for ethics. These can be classified (though somewhat arbitrarily) into three main groups:

1. *The naturalistic position:* The basis of ethics can be found in empirical knowledge.

2. *The emotivist position:* Ethical statements merely express personal emotions and attitudes. Consequently, it is not possible in ethics to speak of knowledge and truth.

3. *The rational position:* Ethical non-empirical knowledge does exist. Its basis lies in man's unique ability to evaluate things according to standards and to regard himself bound by obligations.

I will treat the first two groups relatively briefly, though this will not do them full justice,[8] and elaborate on the third position, as I am inclined to accept it as a proper justification of ethics.

1. The great success of the scientific method in giving us reliable knowledge of the world has been a strong inducement for laymen and philosophers alike to ground ethics on an empirical basis. Furthermore, the ideal of the unity of knowledge would remain unattainable unless ethical knowledge were either a mere

phantom or a special normative "science" to be developed by the inductive method. From this point of view the study of human nature and of social life forms the basis of ethics.

We know that men have drives, interests, feelings of pleasure and happiness; also feelings of discomfort, dissatisfaction and unhappiness; they have pro and con attitudes. What better indication could there be that something is desirable or undesirable than the fact that it is either "an object of favorable interest" (R. B. Perry) or that it is avoided by a great many people, perhaps the majority? A public opinion poll could thus establish the values held by members of a society and even the ranking of such values. A study of this kind would be empirical.

But there are problems. Assume a society in which there are more free people than slaves, and suppose that a poll shows slavery is preferred by the majority. Would that make slavery a morally acceptable institution? And if the proportion between free men and slaves changes and the poll now expresses a majority vote against slavery, does that change the ethical status of slavery? Undoubtedly, the values prevailing in a society tell us what *seems* good, not what *is* good. The chief criticism of the Kinsey reports was the impression they seem to convey that by establishing what was "natural" sexual behavior they also established what was proper behavior. The behavior of people in a society and their evaluations may be altruistic, but they frequently are selfish, cruel, warlike and degrading. If valid moral principles exist, they cannot be based on a study of actual human behavior. Public opinion cannot be a self-serving justification of the standards held in a society nor of its institutions. Ethical disputes cannot be settled by statistics or sociology.

Close examination of the motivations and actions of individuals may perhaps be more helpful in establishing ethics on a factual basis. The goal of most individuals seems to be to bring about a maximum of pleasant personal experiences and to prevent unpleasant experiences as much as possible. Everyone, it is said, tries to act in accordance with his own best interests. However, we also know that we sometimes hold goodness and loving-kindness above our own interests. What, in the theory of personal self-interest, can be the basis of goodness, of justice and excellence? We may think to find the motivation for ethical actions in the good feeling that a person may derive from being just or doing good. But this device is deceptive, as was previously discussed in Chapter X. As we saw then, the good feeling that comes from doing good is the result of the prior evaluation that justice and benevolence are worthy goals; only after we have discovered that we ought to be just and do good can we take satisfaction in living up to our "better nature." The very expression "better nature" points up the predicament inherent in basing ethics on an empirical study of human nature. The fact that we differentiate between our baser and our better nature presupposes an ability to make such a distinction and to "bring standards to the world." (P. Taylor)

All this is an endeavor which goes beyond science. Science cannot explain why we ought not to follow evil tendencies or succumb to a lazy peace of mind, but should strive for ideals. These standards of our better nature are the basis for the development of proper pro-and-con attitudes, for our capacity to praise, admonish and warn, and for forming and asserting particular and general moral commands. Not the totality of our natural qualities, but our moral cognition is the ground of our duties and ideals, of our obligations and commitments.[9] None of these things, particularly obligation and commitment, can be grounded on any wish, desire, or any other psychological state, or on any state of society, or on any other fact of nature. The idea that our actions are subject to "oughts" cannot be explained by any scientific, empirical, or naturalist theory.

The distinction between the naturalist and the ethical view is illuminated by Frankena's observation that when we make "factual assertions we are not thereby taking any pro or con attitude . . . we are not recommending, prescribing, or anything of the sort. But when we make an ethical or value judgment we are *not neutral* in this way." (My italics) There is quite a difference in attitude when we say of a person that he has blue eyes and when we say that he is charitable.

The gap between factual-scientific and ethical thinking has found its classical expression in the statement that from what *is*, we cannot conclude what *ought* to be. That good ought to be promoted can neither be confirmed by perceptual observations nor derived from descriptive, i.e., empirical judgments. To try to do so is to succumb to G. E. Moore's "naturalistic fallacy," a famous expression in modern metaethical philosophy. The normative realm of evaluating, praising, condemning and prescribing cannot be scientifically justified. This is so because of the simple, logical rule: "No imperative conclusion can be validly drawn from a set of premises which does not contain at least one imperative." [10] An ethical theory and an ethical argument require norms at their base.

I would now like to examine several theories of ethics which may be subsumed under the general category of naturalistic or empiricist theories.

a. According to the *genetic explanation*, it is the development of mankind and of each individual which lays the basis for ethics. This is true to the extent that if mankind and each one of us had not developed to the state we have reached, we would not harbor moral feelings or have a conscience or a superego, nor could we give thought to moral philosophy. As far as this obvious fact is concerned, ethics is on an equal footing with mathematics, science and all other intellectual and practical activities. We would have no feelings about or knowledge of anything whatsoever if these capacities had not been evolved by mankind and by each individual. Naturally, the genetic explanation also applies to the development of error, superstition, dishonesty, immorality and cruelty; whatever is, has developed at some time. Cultural development and individual education merely explain facts; they justify nothing. Only evaluative thinking and, in the last analysis, philosophy can make valid distinctions.

b. A related naturalistic explanation, popular among biologists, maintains that we can justify the good by basing it on "evolutionary direction." (Julian Huxley) But before we can say that the trend of evolution is good or upward and that we should follow it, we must know independently what good and upward are. Aside from this logical difficulty, we may also question whether human development has actually been beneficent. Consider the population explosion, the problems inherent in urbanization, and in man's growing technical capacity to kill an enormous number of people. Evolution is governed by biological laws, and we cannot know where it will lead—upward, downward, or even to extinction.[11]

I close this section with the last sentence of C.I. Lewis' important work, *An Analysis of Knowledge and Valuation*: "What is right and what is just, can never be determined by empirical facts alone." [12]

c. There is, finally, a naturalistic theory of a rather different character. It dispenses with the development of a structured ethical theory of values and commands, and is based on the nature of actual decision-making in the context of each individual's life experiences.* "Moral science is not something with a separate province," John Dewey has said. But even if ethics is an intrinsic component of life in general, this does not mean that we cannot study it as a separate discipline.

Whenever we come face to face with a "problematic situation" and wonder what we should do—punish a child, divorce a spouse, increase a charitable contribution, risk the family's living standards by leaving one's job—we mull the situation over before coming to a decision. We weigh the purpose or purposes we want to achieve, the advantages and disadvantages, the means we must take, the costs and dangers involved. And we also weigh whatever moral precepts we take for granted that bear on the total problem. The means we use and the goals we wish to attain are intertwined and have to be adjusted to each other; they often cannot be thought of as independent factors, and this is true likewise of morality.† Contextualists hold that general ethical principles have no status apart from actual concrete situations. As William James wrote about seventy years ago, we must approach "every dilemma" as "a unique situation." This view relates contextualists to today's existentialists, who also do not accept ethics as a systematic discipline and admonish us to solve our moral quandaries through "authentic decisions"—whatever that may mean.

Dewey's treatment of values and morality is, to a large extent, a detailed though often obscure description of how, through reflective thinking, we try to resolve problematic situations and come to "creative" and socially useful decisions. However, no convincing reason has been advanced as to why a systematic treatment of normative ethics is impossible and why we cannot go beyond our individual ethical notions to general, rationally established rules, despite the fact that all situations are somehow unique and actually held goals differ from individual to individual and depend on circumstances and culture.[13]

* Because of this, R. Brandt calls this theory "Contextualism."
† The impossibility of disentangling means and goals is a central point of Dewey's *instrumental philosophy*. Are good food, marriage, knowledge and kindness means to something else, or are they independent goals?

The Emotive Theory of Ethics

2. I now turn to another important theory, which also denies the possibility of establishing a set of ethical principles, but for the surprising reason that there are no ascertainable ethical truths. "Questions as to 'values' lie wholly outside the domain of knowledge." (Bertrand Russell) "The value statement, 'killing is evil' . . . is merely an expression of a certain wish. . . . [It] is nothing else than a command in a misleading grammatical form. . . . It is neither true nor false. It does not assert anything and can neither be proved nor disproved." (Rudolf Carnap)* In 1936, A. J. Ayer—at that time one of the outstanding younger English philosophers—published his *Language, Truth and Logic*, which, because of its brevity, clarity and sharpness of argument, has become a milestone of contemporary philosophy. In it Ayer wrote: "The sentence 'It is your duty to tell the truth' may be regarded both as an expression of a certain sort of ethical feeling about truthfulness and as an expression of the command 'Tell the truth'. . . . They [ethical judgments] have no validity whatsoever. . . . They are unverifiable for the same reason as a cry of pain or a command is unverifiable—because they do not express genuine propositions."

Charles L. Stevenson's *Ethics and Language*, published in 1944,[14] offers the most elaborate description and analysis of the emotive-imperative theory—a name given to the viewpoint expressed in the previous quotations—which is shared by other modern philosophers besides those cited. The quintessence of Stevenson's book may be found in the following quotations:

"This is good" means *I approve of this; do so as well.*

Ethical statements have a meaning that is approximately, and in part, imperative. This imperative meaning explains why ethical judgments are so intimately related to agreement and disagreement in attitude.

* *Philosophy and Logical Syntax.* Quoted in Abraham Kaplan, "Logical Empiricism and Value Judgments" in *The Philosophy of Rudolf Carnap* edited by Paul A. Schilpp (La Salle, Ill.: Open Court, 1963). It is significant for the role that philosophers as philosophers play in contemporary culture that the name of Carnap is unknown to the general, even the intellectual, public although among contemporary philosophers he is regarded as one of the most pre-eminent.

Stevenson's key word "attitude" stands for "purposes, aspirations, wants, preferences, desires."

Most people reading for the first time that ethical statements are "neither true nor false" and that they "have no validity whatsoever" will probably be taken aback. These rather extreme judgments are the outgrowth of a general philosophic perspective called logical positivism, which flourished in the 1920's and 1930's. Logical positivists maintained that meaningful sentences either must be propositions of a logical or mathematical character or they must be verifiable by sense-experience. All other sentences, including ethical ones, are meaningless; they do "not assert anything." Nevertheless, some place must be found for ethical utterances; we cannot simply drop them from human intercourse. We must regard them, says the theory under discussion, as expressions of feelings, attitudes, or imperatives. Stevenson pleads that the emotive theory does not want to sweep aside ethics, in which we "must [be] engaged . . . with absorbing seriousness," and he criticizes Carnap's "unguarded" formulations.*

According to the emotive theory the statements, "It is good to help our neighbors" or "It is wrong to steal," may have the grammatical form of assertions, but they really do not assert anything. They are either exclamations or imperatives. They are equivalent to such expressions as "Good!" "Bad!" "Dreadful!" "Oh God!" "Ouch!" "Hmm!" "Do that!" "Stop doing this!" Ethical sentences simply express, vent and display feelings, emotions and attitudes about something, and they may imply or express commands. They praise, encourage, condemn, warn, or command. Neither exclamations nor vocalizations of attitudes nor imperatives can be true or false. They do not *describe* an individual's state of mind, his feelings or approvals; such descriptions would be assertions that could be true or false. Rather, ethical utterances are expressive, evocative, persuasive and prescriptive. They do not themselves convey knowledge, and consequently the emotive theory is called non-cognitive whereas the naturalist and rational theories are both cognitive. (Of course, it is possible to draw factual conclusions—correct or incorrect—

---

* One reason for the development of the emotive theory was the difficulty philosophers had in finding a justification of ethics in either a naturalistic or a rational theory. The emotive theory makes this search unnecessary.

about a speaker from his emotive utterances.) As our moral feelings or attitudes are usually expressed directly to one or more people, they are intended to evoke feelings in others and motivate them to share our feelings or to do something or not to do something.

One of Stevenson's main accomplishments is a careful analysis of ethical disagreement. Divergent preferences among people may be the result of different attitudes or of different beliefs. Let us suppose that a young boy faces his parents after he has mischievously thrown a stone through a school window. The father says sternly, "You deserve a good spanking." The mother protests, "Spanking is immoral." The cognitivist would say that there is a disagreement in ethical judgment here; only one of the two judgments can be true. The emotivist would say there is no clash of *judgments* here but two divergent *attitudes:* let's spank, let's not spank. Persuasion may bring about an agreement in attitude, or it may not. But it is possible that different beliefs have caused the divergent attitudes. The father may think that spanking is the best means to cure the boy of his mischievousness, while the mother may believe that spanking is brutal, will hurt the boy's pride and interfere with his moral growth. If one parent can win the other parent over to his evaluation of the educational method (a factual, psychological question), they may also reach agreement in their moral attitude regarding spanking. It is Stevenson's general opinion that the cause of divergent attitudes frequently lies in opposing beliefs and that agreement on the factual question will often eliminate difference in attitude. But if agreement on the factual situation does not also resolve divergent preferences, then only persuasion remains. If A says: "Slavery, good!" and B says: "Slavery, dreadful!," they may try by persuasion to come to an agreement in attitudes, but according to the emotive theory it makes no sense to say that it is a valid truth that slavery is immoral.

Are we then fooling ourselves when we think that we can engage in rational thinking about the moral value or disvalue of slavery or the equality of women? Evaluative *thinking* is primary, and moral attitudes are the outcome of our deliberations. It is not the other way around. This is not to say that there are not certain situations where a spontaneous emotive reaction may occur. If we should see a man endangering himself to pull a child out of the way of an onrushing truck, we would be overcome with gratitude and admiration; the sight of a man beating a child or a dog would fill us with horror and disgust. But when we are confronted with a moral dilemma, we consider what we ought to do and ask ourselves questions; we do not confine ourselves to weighing emotions or attitudes. We try to find an objective moral viewpoint even though we cannot be certain, as for example, when dealing with the pregnant adolescent (see chapter VIII). After we have reached a definite value judgment, say that Hitler was a vicious murderer, we go a step further and claim that it is justified and valid and call on all men to accept what we have found to be true. The emotive theory, on the contrary, by its very nature, precludes a normative justification of ethical attitudes, holding that these are matters of personal inclination, not of an objective moral viewpoint and philosophy. Furthermore, on the basis of the emotive theory it is difficult, if not impossible, to explain how we can ascribe obligations and commitments to others. If someone is not inclined to obey traffic laws or take care of his children, we can suggest to him that he should do so, if that is our attitude. But how can we say that he has an obligation if he does not feel it?

I will forgo raising additional objections to the emotive theory.[15] "This theory . . . is at odds not only with traditional views but also with our common sense ideas and our ordinary ways of speaking." (Alexander Sesonske) At the same time it ought to be mentioned that the proponents of this theory have done some very stimulating work in the analysis of the multifunctional nature of ethical language. Ethical language is not limited solely to the statement of ethical evaluations. Under certain conditions, it is persuasive, commendatory, directive and prescriptive; it is performatory when we promise something. Even a factual sentence may serve several purposes. Suppose my wife and I are at a party and she comes to me and says, "I am feeling quite miserable." She does not intend merely to state a fact; she also wants to evoke my sympathy and lead me to ask, "Shouldn't we go home?" The analysis of the multiple purposes of language is one of the main subjects of modern philosophy.

Rational Basis of Ethics

3. Ever since Plato and until recently, most thinkers have found the "proof" of "ethics within the cognizance of the ra-

tional faculty" (Mill), that is, except for the religious justification of ethics. In modern times the rational position has appeared
in two versions. Most of the prominent ethical philosphers of the
recent past—Moore and Ross, for example, but not Mill—have
been ethical intuitionists, who thought that moral insights are self-
evident and that we apprehend them intuitively. They maintained that we have an immediate, clear and certain knowledge
of the idea of good (Moore), of prima facie duties (Ross), of the
ought (Ewing), and of the truth of ethical propositions in
general. Ewing went so far as to say that we "see" ethical principles intuitively.[16]

Now, while it is true that we frequently have "quick and
ready insight . . . without rational thought and inference" (a
dictionary[17] definition of intuition) into a particular ethical situation or problem, generally speaking ethical principles are not self-
evidently and intuitively perceived. Because of this Ewing revised his opinion in a later book[18] and quoted approvingly from
two other philosophers: "The intuitionist position rests on a serious over-simplification" (O. A. Johnson). "The word 'intuition'
carries the suggestion that we do not, or even cannot, deliberate
and calculate in deciding what we ought to do." (Stuart
Hampshire) A much better idea of the nature of the apprehen-
sion of ethical knowledge is conveyed if we call it *rational insight*. (Ewing uses the term "direct cognition.") In order to
evaluate the moral ramifications of a particular problem, we
often have to analyze, weigh, compare, think and use our critical
sense in the study of the aspects of a specific situation.

Nor is the truth of general moral principles intuitively certain, as is shown by the extensive arguments about them. But if
the final ground of these principles is "that character of human
nature by which it is called rational" (C. I. Lewis), then only an
investigation of the role of reason in ethics can establish the justification of ethics. Many attempts have been made along these
lines, renewing in a modern manner Kant's enterprise of a critique of practical reason, but no agreement has been reached
among present-day ethical philosophers. I will now try to describe to you in broad outlines one such theory, which seems to
me to offer a promising approach.[19]

The starting point of this justification of ethics is the idea of
a *way of life*. To the extent that we are free to choose at all, we

try to conduct our lives so that we accomplish certain goals in certain ways. While the several goals which people adopt may conflict with each other or with the means used to achieve them, we can theoretically construct certain ways of life. An *ethical point of view* is a phase of a rational way of life, that is, a way of life which can be *reasonably* justified. The expression "rational way of life" does not mean that there is only one rational way of life; the term envisages a broad spectrum of rational ways of life, as varied as individualities, talents, conditions and cultural stages and traditions require and as varied as the irrational ways mentioned later.

I must also warn against another misunderstanding, that calling a certain way of life rational indicates that we want to, or can, exclude emotional elements from life. By no means! The rational way of life does not banish pleasure and pain, sensual and esthetic feelings, ambitions, jealousies and passions. Rather, the rational way of life requires that most of the time we have sufficient insight and self-control to master disturbing and degrading drives and not let them master us and deflect us from rational goals.

Most people pursue a rational way of life, but of course there are exceptions. The wastrel, the tramp, the hippie, the derelict, the sadist, all live outside the ideals of a rational way of life. They are the anti-heroes, sometimes abnormal, with whom modern literature is so profoundly concerned. The rational (or irrational) way of life has a theoretical as well as a moral dimension. The "absurdist" who proclaimed in a letter to the *New York Times* that "reason and science per se are indeed an illness" is irrational. So is the fundamentalist who, in the face of obvious facts, sticks to his absolute belief in the Bible's creation story. To this group belong the fanatics, who sacrifice not only themselves, but their families as well, to some all-or-nothing idea, as Ibsen's Brand does. Zen adherents, insofar as they teach in paradoxes and contradictions, also follow and glorify the irrational.

Is there any way of convincing a tramp, a tyrant, a fanatic, or an absurdist of the wrongness of his way of life? Only if he is able and willing to listen to reason, that is, if he adopts to some extent the rational way of life. But one who rejects reasoning cannot be enlightened. If you tell him that without reasonable order human existence, probably including his own, will become "solitary, poor, nasty, brutish and short"—Hobbes' famous description of the state of nature—and his answer is "I don't care," then reasoning has come to an end and there is no point in carrying the matter any further. Nothing whatsoever can be "proved" to a cynic or skeptic who brushes arguments aside and insists that *de principiis non est disputandum*. To the extent that an individual's ultimate commitment to an irrational way of life cannot be overcome (because of his refusal to listen to logic and facts) we have a "disagreement in attitude" such as the emotive theory describes.

However, for one who wonders about the kind of world we want, there are many good reasons why he should choose the rational way of life. The rational way of life and its choice can be justified—"vindicated" is the term Taylor and Hospers use— to any reasonable person.

> Far from being arbitrary, such a decision would be the most well-founded of decisions, because it would be based upon a consideration of everything upon which it could possibly be founded. (R.M. Hare, quoted by both Hospers and Taylor)

The rational way of life alone "offers the conditions of a satisfactory human life for people living in groups." (Frankena) It alone is consonant with human dignity and ideals. The fact that we are studying philosophy and trying to find out how to make sense of our lives shows that we have adopted that way of life.

Only a free man can choose, and insofar as he is thoughtful, enlightened and unbiased, he chooses rationally. We are not talking here of an actual psychological event in a person's life but of a considered general preference for the rational way of life. But "the concept of a rational choice among ways of life is a concept of an ideal." (Taylor) If none of us lives up to the conditions of a fully rational choice, we may nevertheless try to follow the best among us when they try to examine rationally the best way to live.

One aspect of the rational way of life is moral thinking and conduct. We deny our reasonableness if we deny the truth of moral ideas. If we opt for rationality in our living, we thereby adopt the moral point of view, for we then ask ourselves how we ought to live, what kind of people we should be, what we ought to strive for.

How do we find out what the moral point of view within the framework of a rational way of life implies? By determining what value judgments and ethical commands will "stand up . . .

in the light of the most careful thinking and the best knowl-edge." (Frankena) And those will stand up which would be stip-ulated by an "ideal observer" (a term used in modern ethical theory), that is, someone who is impartial, fully informed, in good mental health, calm and reflective, and thus able to weigh evidence and willing to universalize; someone who is also imagi-native, sensitive, courageous and animated by kindness. A spe-cific or a general ethical judgment is true, valid, or justified if it stands up under our scrutiny when we try, as nearly as we can, to exercise the qualities of an ideal observer.

We do not form ethical judgments in isolation. We compare our ideas with the moral insights of all those in our society who instinctively or with full awareness have adopted the rational way of life. This is as close as we can come to objectivity in ethics. But, as I have pointed out before, ethical judgments usu-ally cannot be established with mathematical certainty or even with the definiteness of many inductive conclusions, for life is complicated and the weighing of interests and goals imponder-able. Nevertheless, there exists a certain consensus on the evalua-tion of the morality of behavior. It is the exceptional cases of disagreement that cause the greatest uncertainty and the most dis-cussion. We may try to find a justifiable resolution of our uncer-tainty by consulting with those whom we hold in highest respect —the observers who seem most ideal, men, living or dead, whose opinions and deeds mankind admires. I believe Hospers' observa-tion is correct that *"most ethical disputes would be resolved if people were truly impartial, knew all the relevant facts, had great imaginative sympathy with others."* Whether proper deeds will follow is, of course, a very different matter when we face the alternatives of being "practical" and adopting the attitudes of the majority—being "outer-directed"—or of being idealistic and following our conscience.

Any rational justification of ethics presupposes that human beings have the capacity to make valid determinations of the value of goals and of what they ought to do. I agree with Solo-mon E. Asch who observed in his *Social Psychology:*

> The sense that certain things should be done, that others should not be done, is universally known. It is part of the human mini-mum. . . .[20]

Much earlier, Thomas Jefferson had written:

The moral sense, or conscience, is as much a part of man as his leg or arm. It is given to all human beings in a stronger or weaker degree.

These observations are borne out by the general uniformity mankind is gradually reaching in the appreciation (though not necessarily the achievement) of ethical ideals: the ideal of peace, the abolition of slavery, the preference for monogamy, the love of knowledge, international helpfulness (limited though it may be) in the fight against poverty, starvation and disease. And finally, as far as philosophers are concerned, it should be noted that while they are not necessarily "ideal observers," there is wide agreement among them not only with regard to particular moral judgments, but also on the importance of ideals in general, though there are sharp differences and much uncertainty in metaethical theories.

Why Be Moral?

In concluding let us try to be as clear as possible about our answer to the skeptic's taunting challenge: "Why be moral? Anyone who acts morally is stupid." Leonard Nelson once Socratically conducted a discussion on this subject[21] in which I participated as a young student, when, I venture to say, I too was confused. As the discussion progressed, we made the rather obvious discovery that the question involves two quite dissimilar value scales. We judge actions according to the advantages that accrue to us or to others, and we judge them also on the basis of their morality and intrinsic value. These different evaluations do not necessarily lead to different results. Yet quite frequently we do find ourselves in circumstances where it may be advantageous to be immoral, to lie, cheat, seduce, cut corners, or do any number of other "forbidden" things or not do that which we ought to do. Why, then, forgo possible gains and pleasures and be moral?

In dealing with this question we must distinguish between motivation and justification. It is quite true that men often do good for the pure love of it and can be animated by ideals. While the religious person may act for the glory of God, duty for its own sake may be a motive for the humanist. Our ideal of character may be one of the driving forces in our life. On the other hand, most of the time we routinely give first consideration to our own welfare and that of our family as we go about our daily affairs.

Our concern in this discussion is not with the psychological and often conflicting motives of our action, but with philosophic justification. To the question, Why ought we to be moral? the only answer is because we ought to be. Virtue is its own reward. Within the framework of the moral point of view no further justification of ethics is necessary or even possible. Just as the defense of logic—if we were asked to defend it—would require logical arguments and thus presuppose logic, from the moral point of view a defense of morality is likewise circular. The question, therefore, ought I to do what I ought to do? is obviously meaningless.

I have previously given reasons why people should adopt the moral point of view as part of a reasonable way of life. Yet the moralist is in a much more precarious position answering the moral skeptic than answering a skeptical Barbusse who insists that nothing can be tested, nothing can be verified; why then believe in logic and common-sense truth? To the skeptical Barbusse we can at least point out what will happen if he tries to walk through a wall or in front of a speeding car, if he stops eating, if he neglects a high fever, if he builds a house without using some common sense. If he disregards ordinary logic and facts he will not live long. We do not have such forceful arguments for the moral skeptic. As far as the mere survival of individuals and of humanity on earth is concerned, a morally reasonable way of life between individuals, tribes and nations is not imperative, omitting here consideration of obliteration by nuclear destruction. Without it—difficult though it may be to imagine—human existence would be disastrous and in the long run perhaps destructive of large groups; nevertheless, it is theoretically possible. But if mankind's aspirations are to find fulfillment, life must be based on the rationality possible to human beings. In the rational framework morality is vindicated, as is the whole system of humanistic ethics we have developed.

None of the foregoing convincingly answers the individual who says that he agrees with everything we have said, that he accepts theoretically our vindication of the moral point of view and of the idealistic life, and that he knows he shares in all the benefits of an ordered society, but then asks why he personally should be moral, why he could not cleverly just look out for himself while wearing the mask of a moral conformist, perhaps even of a do-gooder. He is not satisfied with our answer, "You ought to be moral." Cynic that he is, he wants to know whether we can adduce any reasons that would demonstrate to him and people like him that it would be expedient for him to be moral. (A similar problem cannot be raised by one who in his decision-making does not want to respect the laws of logic and natural common sense. He will quickly starve or get killed.)

The cases I am talking about must be more specifically circumscribed. It is, of course, no use trying any kind of justification to a Hitler, a derelict, or certain kinds of psychopaths, people who are without insight into values or into their own future and the ways of their fellow man. Kai Nielsen, in an interesting essay, *Why Should I Be Moral?* [22] suggests that we also regard as irrelevant what he calls desert-island examples, that is, peculiar people or peculiar situations that hardly ever exist or happen and are cleverly thought out to embarrass the philosopher by proving that his theories do not work in improbable situations and under extreme complications. Here we should consider everyday men in everyday situations when they ask: Why should *I* be moral?

Nielsen finds the best reply to this question in Plato's and Aristotle's idea that "only the man with a well-ordered soul will be 'truly happy.'" ". . . if a man decides *repeatedly* to act non-morally where he can get away with it, he will not, as a very general rule, be happy." Most normal individuals, the kind of people we are and meet, will somehow be bothered if they engage in cleverly disguised and secret wrong-doing.

> It will cost you your peace of mind, you will pay in psychic suffering, happiness will be denied you. But as a rational egoist happiness is supposedly your goal.

> Surely we can and do get away with occasional selfish acts—though again note the usual burden of guilt—but given the world as it is, a deliberate, persistent though cunning policy of selfishness is very likely to bring on guilt feelings, punishment, estrangement, contempt, ostracism and the like. A clever man might avoid one or another of these consequences but it would be very unlikely that he could avoid them all or even most of them. And it is truistic to remark that we all want companion-ship, love, approval, comfort, security and recognition. It is very unlikely that the consistently selfish man can get those things he wants. . . . it may be objected: "But suppose someone doesn't want those things, then what are we to say?". . . .

THE JUSTIFICATION OF ETHICAL BELIEFS
313

The proper thing to reply is that people almost universally are not that way and that in reasoning about whether I should or should not be selfish, I quite naturally appeal to certain very pervasive facts (including facts about attitudes). . . .

We cannot discuss here Nielsen's graphic account of the reaction of a clever and successful adulterer, a kidnapper and a bank embezzler. Each one must ask himself whether a possible "pervasive sense of uneasiness" makes their respective deeds really worthwhile. To be sure, "the individual egoist can correctly argue that it is not always clear that he would be unhappier in such a situation if he did what was wrong." Presumably there are some successful criminals and wrongdoers who are not concerned about detection, who are not troubled by loss of self-respect or with remorse and qualms of conscience; who sin and yet are content. But such individuals are rather unusual specimens. For most people brought up in an orderly environment, that is, home and school, and for all those not alienated from society, it would be difficult, if not impossible, to act unethically without suffering significant damage to their equanimity and happiness. Man has both a sinful and a moral nature, but he finds it difficult to live with himself when he succumbs to a temptation that goes against his better nature. There is wisdom in St. Paul's remark: "What the law requires is written on their hearts." To the thoughtful man who asks, "Why should *I* be moral?" We can answer, so "that thy days may be long" and good.

Continuing in a Biblical vein, I close this argument with these words from Proverbs (3:13, 15):

Happy is the man that findeth wisdom. . . .
She is more precious than rubies,
And all the things thou canst desire
    are not to be compared unto her.

Whatever may be our theory about the character of ethical utterances and the justification of ethical beliefs, whether these utterances are based on religious beliefs or on "natural law"—a theory I have not discussed—or on human rationality, whether they express attitudes, commands, desires, or reasonable judgments, we must recognize that men hold certain acts to be preferable, justifiable, fitting and good, and others to be wrong, unjustifiable, unfitting and unworthy. We have an obligation to do the former and avoid the latter. Let us have confidence in our reason and the courage to believe in values.

CHAPTER XII

Religion and Truth

"Religion is essentially the act of holding fast to God."

—MARTIN BUBER

Of all philosophic questions, the one that is most important and at the same time most unclear is: "Does all our studying, all our work, our life, the universe as a whole, have any meaning?" For thousands of years most people in the Western world have looked to religion for an answer; the meaning of existence, the purpose of life have been found in obedience to God's will. The religious believer carries the conviction that not merely man's destiny but that of the whole universe stands under God's benevolent direction and derive their meaning from Him.

Although belief in God's existence and His goodness has waned, it is nevertheless essential to discuss the meaning and truthfulness of the religious view of the world. Religion is a subject of constant searching and unending debate, religious bodies exert a strong influence on our politics and education, and religious doctrines are among the bases, often the sole basis for the world view of a great many people. The percentage of people belonging to churches has been constantly increasing in the United States, and public opinion polls seem to show that a majority of the American people firmly believe in God.

What is Religion?

What is religion?* Although it has often been claimed that the word "religion" cannot be defined and its meaning has been endlessly disputed, it must have some understandable content as all of us use it and seem to connect some definite ideas with it. When we hear or use the word, we think mostly of one or all three of the following entities: we think of God and believe in or doubt of Him; we think of churches, temples, and similar religious edifices; we think of the great religious establishments, such as Catholicism, Protestantism, Judaism, Buddhism, the so-called world religions. Because there are three meanings, obviously closely related, but not identical, frequent misunderstandings and arguments about religion occur.

An additional difficulty arises from the fact that the word "religion" is often used, particularly in recent years, with a reference so broad that belief in God or in some other Higher Being is not essential. It is frequently not clear whether one who uses the word is speaking of personal beliefs or of social institutions; if we assume that someone is referring to beliefs, we sometimes cannot tell whether he means a kind of belief in the traditional God or belief in some broad, idealistic, godless world view.

Two renowned, lifelong students of religion have propounded definitions of it which are similar in meaning. Joachim Wach defines "religious experience [as] a response to what is experienced as *Ultimate Reality* . . . that which conditions and undergirds all." (My italics) "There is an Infinite Behind the Finite." †

In his essay, *Is Life Worth Living?* [1] William James writes:

* See Wilfred C. Smith, *The Meaning and End of Religion* (New York: New American Library, 1962, paperback) Chap. 2, for the origin of the word and its meaning. A great deal can be learned from this book, although I disagree with Smith's suggestion that we should discontinue using the word "religion" because of its confusing meanings. I believe with Nagel that, "linguistic habits are too deeply ingrained and too widespread to make such a ban possible."

† *The Comparative Study of Religions* (New York: Columbia University Press, 1958, paperback); see also excerpt from *Types of Religious Experience*, in *Philosophy of Religion*, edited by John E. Smith (New York: Macmillan, 1965, paperback). The first contains an extensive and the latter a brief biography of Wach. Wach mentions three additional qualities of religious experience: "its intensity," that it is "a total response," and "issue in action." However, the characteristic of religion mentioned in the text suffices to distinguish religions from other phenomena.

Religion has meant many things in human history; but when
. . . I use the word I mean to use it in the supernaturalist
sense, as declaring that the so-called order of nature, which constitutes this world's experience, is only a portion of the total
universe, and that there stretches beyond this visible world an
unseen world . . . in its relation to which the true significance
of our present mundane life consists. . . . Whatever else be
certain, this at least is certain—that the world of our present
natural knowledge *is* enveloped in a larger world of *some*
sort. . . .

Central in both definitions is the expression of a *dualistic
world view.** The religious believer distinguishes between an unseen, perfect, supernatural, infinite, ultimate realm and the dependent, visible order of nature. Clearly, the two great monothe-
istic world religions based on the Bible—Judaism and Christianity, which denominate as God the ultimate, supreme reality
behind the known universe—fall within these definitions. I shall
use the term "religion" in accordance with customary practice,
and will limit my treatment largely to Judaism and Christianity
because they are the religions significant for our present
endeavor.†[2] When I speak of God I mean the traditional God of
the Bible, of the synagogue and church. At a later stage I will
discuss modern interpretations of God.

Even though we accept the word "religion" in the sense we
have just discussed, we must still distinguish two other main

---

* Most contemporary religious thinkers, but not all, stress the dualistic view.
Peter L. Berger in *The Sacred Canopy* (New York: Doubleday, 1967) writes:
"Religion is the human enterprise by which a sacred cosmos is established. The
sacred cosmos is confronted by man as an immensely powerful reality other
than himself." Martin E. Marty in *The Search for a Usable Future* (New York:
Harper & Row, 1969) says of religiousness that it "would imply relating . . . to
ultimacy."

† Wach's and James's definitions apply also to most other entities which
are generally called religions. The pagan religions of both primitive and highly
developed civilizations, including the Greek and Roman, make the distinction
between the earthly, human sphere and a more or less clearly developed, ultimate magic world, or a reality of superhuman and usually immortal gods. Of
the Far Eastern religions, several of which are sometimes said to be godless,
Wach writes that "only a misunderstanding can make Buddhism and Con-
fucianism into such [godless religions]. Buddhism and Jainism may have started
as criticisms of the traditional or of any positive characterization of Ultimate
Reality, but they soon developed into genuine religions. Confucius strongly
affirmed a transcendental faith in his references to cosmic order (Tao) and to
the ordinances of heaven." Compare Wilfred C. Smith, *op. cit.*: "Christians
have regularly failed or refused to recognize that the faith of non-Christians
has that transcendence; that God does in fact encounter men in Buddhist, Moslem, and Hottentot forms."

meanings associated with the word. The term can be considered as referring to the religiousness of a person, that is, to the particular beliefs he holds about the Ultimate, or it can refer to specific institutions in society established in consequence of certain beliefs about the Ultimate. "I am a Christian (a Jew, etc.)" can mean "I believe in the teachings of Christianity (or of Judaism)." It can also mean that I am a member of a church (or of a synagogue). A religiously motivated individual may or may not be a member of a religious body. If he is a member, he may believe in the tenets of the organization, but it is also possible that his membership may not indicate anything about his beliefs.

The organized religious systems, above all the so-called world religions, embrace an unbelievably rich variety of changing elements: myths, beliefs, commands, theologies, holy books, prayers, rites,* holy places and buildings, priests, prophets, holy men, administrators. Religions have been a great inspiration in the development of architecture, pictorial art, sculpture and music. Not all religions are inspiring to the same degree in all areas, to be sure, for religions are prodigiously varied: magnificent in some respects, terrifying in others.

Religions are not immutable, permanent entities. In the first place the orientation of a believer will probably pass through many changes in the course of his lifetime. In the second place the beliefs, the rites and the organization of religious institutions have greatly altered in the course of their history. Such modifications and innovations are extensive even in the Bible itself, creating endless difficulties in the interpretation of this basic document. The present is again a time of many changes, seen in the work of the Ecumenical Council, the modern Protestant theologies and the God-is-dead movement.

A terminological question often raised is whether Communism, totalitarianism, nationalism and the democratic faith can be regarded as religions.† In my opinion, it is impractical to call these phenomena religions as this would disregard an essential distinction among world views. Some of these ideologies are opposed to what is usually meant by religion. Besides, it would not be in accord with ordinary traditional usage. It is better to follow

* Religions have developed special rites to celebrate and give meaning to important turning points in human life—birth, the coming of maturity, marriage —and particularly death.

† Attempts to equate science with religion were discussed in Chapter V.

Wach, who writes that "there can be no 'godless' religion." If "man relates himself not to ultimate but to some finite reality" (Wach), it is preferable not to use the term "religion" for these man-centered world views, but rather to regard them as pseudo- or in some cases, semi-religions.* Language, however, is flexible and there is no way to prevent people from using the word in a broader sense than we ascribe to it here, thereby giving up the dualist feature as the decisive characteristic of "religion."

Erich Fromm is one of those who uses the word in an extended sense. For him "religion [is] any system of thought and action shared by a group which gives the individual a frame of orientation and an object of devotion" (*Psychoanalysis and Religion*, paperback). William T. Blackstone writes in *The Problem of Religious Knowledge* (paperback): "Religious beliefs are to be viewed as those beliefs which play an all-pervasive role in the life of a man, a group, or culture, determining most of the attitudes and reactions of that man, that group, or that culture." Julian Huxley, in *Religion Without Revelation* (paperback), defines "religion" thus: "What, then, is religion? It is a way of life." But most people would not regard every way of life a religion, particularly if it is not institutionalized.

Some of these secularisms, however, do share many elements with genuine religion. For one thing, they give their adherents an ethics. They generate a group feeling among their followers, a unifying world view, a mystique, a sense of destiny. This is also true to some extent of the "new religious culture" of the young, hailed as a spiritual revival, and evidenced by such communal activities as mass demonstrations, rock festivals and the more intimate drug trips. Some young people emphasize "love," others proclaim a radical idealism and activism, still others probe Eastern mysticism. All these activities are dissociated from the traditional religious establishment and its theologies.

Secular, if not atheistic, ideologies may become "religions" by replacing the ultimate, infinite God with a secular, non-transcendent "substitute God." But this only creates "verbal theists," to borrow a phrase from the Harvard philosopher, Harry A. Wolfson, who wrote with some irony:

> Nowadays, lovers of wisdom are still busily engaged in the gentle art of devising deities. Some of them offer as God a thing called man's idealized consciousness, others offer a thing

---

* Pseudo-religion is the term used by Wach.

called man's aspiration for ideal values . . . still others offer a thing called the cosmic consciousness . . . or a thing called the ground of being. I wonder, however, how many of the things offered as God . . . are not again only polite but empty phrases for the downright denial of God by him who is called fool in the Scripture lesson . . . ! [3]

Philosophers, writers and many theologians, who have given up belief in the traditional God, like to call some of the "things" mentioned by Wolfson or similar ones "God" because the word carries such highly virtuous connotations. But to seek to enhance ideologies through mere redefinition does not make matters clearer and only confuses categories. "Man's aspirations for ideal values" (from Wolfson's list), the "active relation between ideal and actual," [4] "the totality of all the good in the world" (a description favored by a rabbi I know) are self-sufficient expressions; it is unnecessary to define them in terms of "God." And they certainly have nothing to do with the personal God of the Bible, which is what most people mean when they use the word.

Some thinkers identify nature with God and interpret happenings in nature as aspects of the Divinity. Nature in all its beauty and its terribleness is God, and man, too, is an aspect of God. Creator and creation are thus equated, and the transcendence of God disappears. The result is Pantheism, which is a monistic world view. But this identification of nature and God or the mere renaming of nature cannot give it an aura of sanctification or establish a unity out of the infinity of separate things in the universe.

Pantheistic tendencies, the deification of nature, have a universal appeal and can be found in philosophic, religious and poetic writings. Mystics want to dissolve the world in God; all things are then united in God. But the greatest appeal of pantheism—seeing nature as God—has been to the poets of the romantic period, who blended esthetic and religious feelings. It is no accident that Spinoza, interpreted as a pantheist, was held in high favor by many poets.

Besides the main philosophic problem of this chapter dealing with Western man's belief in God, religion presents us with a great many historical, sociological, psychological and educational questions of considerable interest and importance.

One puzzling cultural problem is whether organized religions have contributed to enlightenment and scientific progress or to the psychological enslavement of mankind. We may wonder about the hold religion has on man, the influence of religion on moral behavior, peace of mind, inner balance, and the value or disvalue of religious education. And there is the study and enjoyment of religious architecture, art, poetry, music and literature. However, interesting as these matters are for the religiously inclined person and for the humanist, we cannot deal with them here.

We cannot properly evaluate "the emotional weight of religion" (David Riesman) in modern Western societies and its influence as an institution unless we appreciate how different its role is in other, particularly older, cultures. With us, religious faith, ethics, ceremonies and organizations are only one ideological and institutional aspect of private and public life competing for importance with other ideologies and institutions. In many societies, including those of the West until the Reformation, one religion was, and in some cases still is, strongly interwoven into the daily life of people; for them religion represents the major intellectual and spiritual way of life. In our secular age, however, this is no longer true for most Western countries. American cultural synthesis* blends a belief in the value of adherence to a religion with a belief in the value of America as a nation, and in democracy, in a practical, nonreligious but idealistic ethics, and in the findings and accomplishments of science.

Our cultural situation is distinguished by the fact that we are living in a society of several (at least in theory) ideologically intolerant and exclusive religions. "The God of the 'other religion' is always an idol." (Emil Brunner) † It was easy to have strong religious convictions when everyone had the same religion. But in an environment in which our neighbors cling to their religion as we do to ours, an element of uncertainty is added to religious faith in general.‡

* I am obviously speaking of the culture of the overwhelming majority of the people, not of numerous left and right wing opponents, radical students, or Black Power advocates.

Martin E. Marty, *Varieties of Unbelief* (Garden City: Doubleday Anchor, 1964, paperback), speaks of "American culture religion"; see him for greater elaboration and also for condemnation of the reduced role of religion. See also the searching study by Harvey Cox, *The Secular City* (New York: Macmillan, 1965, paperback).

† The Occidental observer notes with surprise the peacefulness with which Shinto and Buddhism live together in Japan. Indeed, Japanese families celebrate weddings with Shinto, and funerals with Buddhist rites.

‡ Our situation bears a certain resemblance to that described by Edward

Moreover the character of religious faith has strikingly weakened. This becomes manifest if we compare whatever is held to be religious faith today with the deep confidence which our grandparents still had. The Psalmist sang: "The Lord is the strength of my life in this will I be confident." (Psalm 27) Bach glorified God in his magnificent Cantatas with these words, for example: "God alone shall have my heart, In Him I find the highest good." (Cantata 169) He expressed his firm belief in Jesus, the Savior, over and over again and his longing for death as a stepping stone to union with God:

> With joy I see the gate of death;/ For when the drear journey is ended,/ There I'll find no woe or grief/ But joy and peace forever blended (Cantata 82).

Such belief now would be quite exceptional.

God

My main task in this Chapter is a philosophic analysis of what it means to encounter Ultimate Reality, or, in everyday language, an analysis of the truth of contemporary Western religion insofar as it consists in belief in God.* How can this belief be justified?[5] (Since the validity of belief in the divinity of Jesus as God's Son depends on our belief in God the Father, we can forego a separate discussion of Christ, except where belief in Him is central to certain modern theologies.)

In dealing with God, we will start with the vague, old-fashioned, conventional religious faith as held, sometimes only outwardly, by most regular "believers." These believers feel that there has to be a "something" that created and rules the universe and takes care of man. From this derives belief in God. What God is and what we know about Him is found in the Bible,

---

Gibbon in a well-known quotation from his *The Decline and Fall of the Roman Empire:* "The various modes of worship, which prevailed in the Roman world, were all considered by the people as equally true, by the philosopher as equally false, and by the magistrate as equally useful." It does not necessarily follow from this resemblance, however, that we need a saving great new world religion or a religious revival, as has been frequently concluded and as Toynbee has proclaimed.

* We are not concerned in this chapter with deeds and obedience to God's commands that spring or ought to spring from our experience and love of God, matters that are forcefully stressed by all Western religions. We have discussed the foundation of ethics on religion in the previous chapter.

which our faith traditionally rests on.* According to the Bible God is the *personal* Supreme Being, not some metaphysical or theological abstraction.† He is the majestic Creator of the universe, and as such He is radically different from His creatures. He is the eternal, infinite, omnipotent, all-knowing Lord. He is ultimate, independent of any other entity. He is perfect, righteous, just, merciful, and all-loving. He is our sanctuary and our savior, who made "man in His image, in the image of God He created him." He is beyond, or above, or outside the created universe, and therefore supernatural, i.e., transcendent, yet judges us and is somehow deeply involved with the world and exerts an influence on our lives. Though invisible to the eye, He reveals Himself. He is incomprehensible, yet we know of Him. John Hick sums up the traditional Judeo-Christian concept of God as follows:

> God is conceived as an infinite, eternal, uncreated, personal reality, who has created all that exists other than himself, and who has revealed himself to his human creatures as holy and loving.[6]

Traditional Basis of Belief in God

How do religious people know that God exists and has the attributes assigned to Him? What, in other words, is the ground for the truth of their God-belief? Obviously, religious belief cannot be justified in the same way that we justified the truth of the statement, "There are people here now," for God cannot be perceived with any of our senses because He is transcendent.

1. The faith of the believer rests fundamentally on the authority of the Bible and of the Jewish or Christian tradition and is reinforced by his religious insights and feelings, which I will take up later. The revelation of God in the Bible, whether directly or indirectly through prophets or through His Son, is the infallible authority for the truth of religious beliefs. The faith of the believer is his assent to a message communicated by God.

---

* It is significant that the Bible, though frequently and justifiably called "the unknown book," still is the most popular, most discussed, most preached about, and in parts the most widely read book.

† Just as the ethical ideas of the Bible gradually develop, so also the idea of God. His character as it appears there changes from a tribal deity to the universal God.

"The books of the Bible . . . 'have God for their author.'"
(Hick quoting the First Vatican Council of 1870.)

Believers are persuaded to accept the authority of the Bible
as God's word in the same manner that we all accept various
authorities in many practical matters and particularly in scientific, technological, medical, or economic questions about which
we may be uninformed. However, we know that claims of truth
in matters of fact rest on experiments, and thus on perceptual
observations, that are infinitely repeatable. No experiments or
perceptual observations seem possible when we deal with Ultimate Reality. Yet the Bible tells us that Adam and Eve, Abraham, Moses, some of the prophets and others heard the voice of
God. They are "bearers of religious authority." So is Christ, of
whom the Gospel of St. John (1:18) says: "No one has ever seen
God; the only Son, who is in the bosom of the Father, he has
made him known."

How can we accept as true the unverifiable statements and
accounts of happenings of thousands of years back? Why not
also believe the stories of Zeus and the other gods reported by
Homer? Jews and Christians accept the authority of the Bible
but not the authority of the Koran, the Upanishads and the
teachings of Buddha. Why do we in the Western world believe
that our Scripture is revealed by the true God? This is part of
our religious faith and not provable in any other manner.*

However, we do face serious difficulties. With the exception of some strict fundamentalists, few serious persons today believe that God created the world in six days as related in the
Bible. It is notable that the early rabbis and church fathers—long
before modern science—recognized that the creation story and
much else in the Bible had to be understood as allegory and metaphor and that these myths must be "demythologized," to use a
new term. The Alexandrian Jewish philosopher, Philo (about 20
B.C.—40 A.D.), was the first to develop a systematic allegorical
interpretation of the Hebrew Bible. "It is quite foolish," he
wrote, "to think that the world was created in six days or in a
space of time at all." Influenced by Philo, Origen (185[?]–253
A.D.), an early Church Father, queried:

> For who that has understanding will suppose that the first, and
> the second, and third day, and the evening and the mornings,

---

* The so-called proofs of the existence of God will be dealt with subse-
quently.

existed without a sun, and moon, and stars? and that the first day was, as it were, also without a sky? *

The earnest search for the deeper meaning of the Biblical story has been a constant endeavor of theologians and clergymen for two thousand years, culminating in the influential treatment of the New Testament as myth by the contemporary theologian Rudolf Bultmann.† Through demythologizing the Bible, theologians as well as laymen hope to discover its inner spiritual meaning and "truth." For them Biblical stories are not merely poetic inventions; they reveal the nature and workings of God. We thus face very difficult problems of interpretation when we read the Bible and try to go beyond its literal meaning. This search, however, does not apply equally to all parts of the Bible, not to more or less correct reports of historical events, the poetry and the commands and laws. Our questioning concentrates on such matters as the deeper meaning of the religious myths and allegories and how they can be properly approached by ordinary churchgoers.‡

If we accept the allegorical interpretation of the creation story,§ for example, God not only created the kind of world known to our ancestors—the sun, moon, earth, the plants, living creatures and man—but He presumably created the universe as we know it today, consisting of billions of galaxies each with

---

* See the longer quotation in Hick, *op. cit.*

† Published with other essays under the title *Kerygma and Myth* edited by H. W. Bartsch (New York: Harper & Row, 1961, paperback). The terms allegory, analogy, metaphor, myth, symbol, differ in meaning, but in a religious context they can be used almost interchangeably to indicate that words, sentences, and stories have "higher" meanings differing from their ordinary meanings and describe, hint at, or stand for religious "facts" and "truths" difficult, if not impossible, to express and make intelligible otherwise. The problems of analogy and symbolism are dealt with systematically in Chapter 5 of *The Problems of Religious Knowledge* by William T. Blackstone (Englewood Cliffs: Prentice-Hall, 1963, paperback). This is an excellent, concise, and comprehensive philosophic description and analysis of modern treatments of religious knowledge, and contains extensive references to other literature.

‡ Orthodox, Evangelical, Catholic and general believers are inclined to accept a more literal interpretation of the Bible unacceptable to followers of liberal theologians and to metropolitan intellectuals. In consequence of the uncertainty of Bible interpretation and demythologizing, we face the difficulty that everyone has to make his own religious edifice, discarding some old "truths," holding onto others.

§ The creation stories of Genesis 1 and 2 leave open the question whether God created the world out of nothing or out of "a formless waste" (*Anchor Bible* [Garden City: Doubleday, 1964]). On the Biblical creation story and present theories of the origin of the universe, see chapter VI.

billions of stars and probably planets, some perhaps inhabited by manlike creatures. However we interpret the creation by God, it remains a *mysterious* happening. It can be accepted only as a religious belief because it transcends ordinary as well as scientific probing. The same is true of all the other stories in the Hebrew Bible involving God: God meeting the first man and his wife in Paradise, the Flood, the gruesome plagues visited by God upon the Egyptians. Mysterious, too, are the Virgin Birth, the Incarnation, the Crucifixion and Resurrection, and beliefs developed later, such as that of transubstantiation.

God is supposed to have revealed ethical commands. What kind of mysterious process is revelation? Did God really appear to Moses on Mount Sinai and give him the Ten Commandments? If not, how did God reveal His ethics to Moses and the Hebrews? Did He speak to the prophets? Are accounts that He did so to be understood as allegories indicating that the prophets were inspired by the invisible God? How do we know that they really were? How can a transcendent spiritual entity act at all in relation to the world and man? "It is not enough to say, with St. John of the Cross, that 'God without the sounds of words . . . teaches the soul . . . in a most secret and hidden way.' " [7]

The interpretations of Jews and Christians differ considerably. Thus, revealed truth is truth for some but not for others—a peculiar and indeed contradictory conception of truth. For example, the story of Adam and Eve's violation of God's command in Paradise gave rise to the Christian belief in original sin, a concept which has no place in Judaism. The most extreme divergencies exist, of course, in the acceptance of the New Testament as revealed truth by Christians, and its rejection by Jews. They may concede that a great ethical prophet, Jesus, taught in Judea during the reign of the Emperor Augustus, but they regard as blasphemous the idea that God sent His incarnate Son to earth to die on the Cross and be resurrected.

Finally, and most mysteriously, how can one picture or comprehend a personal Supreme Being or the idea of a something in some way beyond, above, or outside time and the universe? We are taught, that when we speak of a personal God, we do not mean a person in the ordinary sense. God is not a dignified, wise ruler, and bears no resemblance to any earthly creature whatsoever. He is, rather, the one and only spiritual person (the term

"person" in this connection is to be understood metaphorically).
But how can we imagine or think about a spiritual person?
When we say of God—the spiritual person—that He creates,
loves us, judges, is wrathful, "sent His Son," what are we really
saying? "Thou simply art outside all time." (St. Anselm) What
do these expressions mean? Do they tell us something truthful
about a Being?* Or are they perhaps, expressions of our personal
hopes and desires, and do we then adopt "verbal theism," a widespread attitude today?

Unlike the mysteries of the visible world, which are the subject of scientific investigations unraveling what is now incomprehensible, religious mysteries are sublime mysteries. The believer
is exhorted to accept humbly the verities of religion and to suppress his uneasiness, if any, trusting that the priest, rabbi, or theologian will somehow explain. But they, too, are helpless before
the "eternally hidden." The height of mystification is reached
when it is said of a religious "fact" that it is "too big for human
language and even human thought." If we cannot clarify the
central ideas of religion, then religious understanding becomes
impossible, and without religious understanding religion is in desperate straits.

The Bible neither explains nor reasons about God's existence. The existence and sovereignty of God are incontrovertible
realities, requiring no further proof.† Rabbinical and other theological apologetics have not made traditional beliefs easier to
understand and to accept.

The religious man possesses knowledge of two different
kinds. There are, on the one hand, everyday and scientific truths,
which are justifiable through observation and which are really
identical for people of any culture. On the other hand, there are
religious "truths," which not only vary between Jews and various kinds of Christians, but also for Muslems, Hindus, Buddhists,

* A reference to God the Son as incarnate in Jesus is not helpful here. "The
love and compassion displayed by Jesus were love and compassion manifesting
themselves in certain actions of a human being *with* a body. . . . [As God
does not have a body], the problem is not removed by pointing to a human
being, however distinguished or remarkable, who possesses a body." (Paul Edwards in "Some Notes on Anthropomorphic Theology," in *Religious Experience
and Truth*, edited by Sidney Hook [New York: New York University Press,
1961].)

† However, there seem to have been non-believers even in Biblical days
who claimed that "there is no God." The Bible calls them "wicked" or "fool"
(Psalms 10 and 14). In addition, the Hebrews often backslid into pagan idolatry,
"belied the Lord," and were duly castigated by Moses and the prophets.

and adherents of other great religions in which hundreds of millions staunchly believe.*

The notion held by some people that all religions proclaim one truth and one God is unfounded. As we have noted, the religions based on the Bible differ in their essential teachings, and among the many Christian denominations there is considerable variation and even conflicting beliefs.

Religious Experiences

2. Belief in tradition and revelation is confirmed by certain experiences that seem to testify to the existence of God. Belief is fortified by the apparent visibility of the workings of God in nature and by the experience of the divine in our religious feelings. "It is one thing merely to believe in a reality beyond the senses and another to have experience of it also. . . . Beside the inner revelation from the Spirit there is an outward revelation of the divine nature." †

> The heavens declare the glory of God
> And the firmament showeth His handiwork.
>
> (Psalm 19)

* A very informative discussion, sympathetically imagined by the English philosopher Ninian Smart—*World Religions: A Dialogue* (Baltimore: Penguin Books, 1966, paperback)—between a Christian, a Hindu, and two representatives of different strands of Buddhism seems to me convincing testimony to the uncertain character of religious truth. (The participating Muslim and Jew, believers in an unqualified monotheism, play only a minor role.) The dialogue does not (and is not supposed to) give a conclusive answer to the fundamental questions raised by Smart in the Introduction: "If revelations are many, how can we choose between them?" and "Why be a Christian rather than a Buddhist?"

Particularly significant for us in the Western world is the Hindu's objections to the "notion that God has a Chosen people," to "the scandalous particularity involved in Christian belief," and to the "unattractive" idea "that we have to look to a particular time and place for our salvation. . . . It does seem absurd that salvation should come through a particular person. For don't we all have some sort of access?"

The humanist finds the truth claims of the several discussants equally extravagant and unconvincing.

† Rudolf Otto, *The Idea of the Holy* (New York: Oxford University Press, paperback). This study of religious "intuitions and feelings" has been a most influential theological work since its original appearance in 1917. It was Otto who introduced the term "numinous," now widely used in the analysis of religious phenomena. The emotion of the numinous is the religious feeling of the presence of the divinity, of the spiritual, of the holy. See also excerpts from A. E. Taylor's essay, "The Vindication of Religion," in John Hick, *The Existence of God* (New York: Macmillan, 1961, paperback), and, in the same collection, the arguments raised by Bertrand Russell in "The Debate on the Existence of God" (in the paragraphs on "Religious Experience").

The world is so tremendous and superb, so full of beauty, so awe-inspiring, its varieties so overwhelming and arranged with such extraordinary organization, that we seem to be witnessing the creative purpose. The loveliness and liveliness of a small child, an apple tree in blossom on a spring morning, the starry sky at night, the greatness of the human mind—these are "god-manifesting facts." How can it not be true that there is a benevolent "hidden universal power" at work "sustaining an infinity of created beings or forces in existence, and exercising on their natural emotions a widely spread and infinitely patient creative influence or persuasion"?[8] Our astonishment that such a magnificent world exists—the cosmological astonishment—seems to impel us to believe in God as the great Creator, whose shaping hands are evident in the upward pull of evolution.

However, in stressing the beauty and benevolence of the world and regarding them as God-manifesting, we reveal blindness to the destructiveness of nature and to the evil in man—a blindness not shared by Hindus and Buddhists. The world is so dreadful, so bloodstained and full of misery that it might just as well have been planned and created by Satan instead of by God.

The evilness of nature and of man presents Western religion with two closely related problems. The first is the contradiction between the imagined visibility of the wonderful workings of God in the world and the actual facts of nature. The second is the flagrant, indeed infinite, discrepancy between God's assumed protective love and justice, wisdom and omnipotence, and the suffering of every individual afflicted with mortal disease, killed by lightning, raped or murdered, or the hundreds of millions who spend their lives in grinding, soul-destroying poverty, or die in famines, plagues, wars (Crusades in the name of religion) or gas chambers.* If God really loved this world, not one single feeble-minded or deformed child would be born. But if the so-called God-manifesting facts in nature are illusory, we are then thrown back on revelation and on an unquestioning trust in God, accepting Job's famous affirmation: "Though He slay me, yet will I trust in Him" (Job 13:15).

* In ancient times people prayed to their tribal or national god or gods for victory, but for the past two thousand years the churches of combatant nations have called upon the one universal God to bless their murdering arms. Each power uses the universal God of love as an instrument of its own national policy. What a mockery of the wonderful idea that there exists an all-loving force in the universe.

The problem of the wickedness of man, supposedly created by God in His image, has been endlessly debated since the prophet Habakkuk, more than 2,500 years ago, asked:

> Thou that art of eyes too pure to behold evil,
> And that canst not look on mischief,
> Wherefore lookest Thou, when they deal treacherously,
> And holdest Thy peace, when the wicked swalloweth up
> The man that is more righteous than he . . . ?
>
> (Habakkuk 1:13)

I do not think that any answer has been or can be given which would satisfy a thoughtful believer except the meaningless answer that we face a mystery, if not a paradox.[9] Why not accept, then, as naturalists do, the brute fact that nature and man are as they are? It is a fact—calling for no religious speculation—that we see nature as beautiful and well ordered and also as ugly, destructive and disorganized, that men love but they also hate, that some men are good-for-nothings and others great artists, scientists and inspiring moral leaders.

When we stand in awed admiration before unimaginably complicated events in nature, whether it be the behavior of nuclear particles, the infinitely more complicated happenings in the chemistry of cellular processes, or the workings of the human mind, and wonder at the magnificent organizations supposedly worked out by the Creator, we might ask ourselves whether a really wise Creator could not have planned mechanisms and processes equally effective but much simpler and less subject to malfunction.

A much more fundamental point is raised by the scientific interpretation of nature. Science has explained an enormously extensive and constantly growing range of natural processes without ever having to face the necessity of assuming the existence of a supernatural organizer. And there is no reason whatsoever to assume that there is a limit to the possibility of rational scientific explanations of processes in nature. The religionist's claim that the universe cannot be understood without postulating the existence of a mysterious Ultimate Reality is unsubstantiated. The assumption of God as an omniscient planner is supererogatory, and the God hypothesis is an arbitrary complication.

The experience of our "religious," numinous feelings, particularly the feeling of awe, seems to put us in touch with the holy, the divine. An impressionable person may be overcome by emotions of dread and personal nothingness before the majesty of God. (A naturalist would say before the majesty of the universe.) We experience feelings of solemnity and calm, which we may interpret as the peace of God, feelings of reverence on entering a great cathedral or an old Buddhist temple, on visiting the Parthenon or the Lincoln Memorial, or on hearing Handel's *Messiah*. There are "surmises or inklings of a Reality fraught with mystery and momentousness." (Otto) We feel impulses of gratitude when we are thankful for good health, for the benefits and pleasures of an ordered family life, for the bounties of success, for escape from a dangerous situation. Whom can we thank but God?* But if there should be no God, whom can we be grateful to? Fate? Luck?

It cannot be doubted that many, perhaps all, people experience certain "religious feelings" at times. We should not try to explain them away. Misunderstanding would be avoided if we called the numinous feelings "spiritual." However, subjective feelings cannot establish the existence of an entity, not even of an entity that cannot be perceived, of a transcendent reality which is "wholly other." Knowledge of the reality of nature is based on our sensual perceptions and not on our enjoyment of it. Because of our intuitions of beauty, or, in some cases, of fright or abhorrence, we do not assume an additional existence of a realm of God or of beauty or of fearfulness.[10]

That spiritual emotions do not compel us to assume the existence of religious entities can be deduced also from the fact that non-believers can and do entertain these same emotions. Natural outlets for our spiritual emotions and apprehensions are poetry, myths, drama, art and music, but it is quite another matter to try to intellectualize and systematize profound experiences of the "God-manifesting facts" and of our numinous feelings and transform them into knowledge of a personal God or an impersonal Ultimate Reality.

* On the other hand, can we blame God for misfortune? Religion tells us we should not, and we are thrown back to Job's affirmation. But how can we praise God for the good things that come our way and not reproach Him for the evils we suffer?

"Proofs" of God's Existence

3. Theologians and philosophers of religion have sought other persuasive proof to strengthen the basis for the belief in the existence of God. So-called "natural theology" is an attempt to validate the existence of God by the use of natural reason unaided by revelation. Such attempts were made by the scholastic theologians of the Middle Ages who tried to develop logical and metaphysical *proofs* for the existence of God. The high point of this development was reached by Maimonides (1135–1204) and Thomas Aquinas (1225–1274). Thomism is still the basic philosophy of the Roman Catholic Church. The natural theology of the seventeenth and eighteenth centuries went even further. It dispensed with revelation altogether in an attempt to validate the existence of God entirely through logical means and through the observation of the orderliness and beauty of nature.

The most distinguished achievement of natural theology is the formulation of the three famous *proofs* of the existence of God bearing the technical labels ontological proof, cosmological proof, and teleological proof.[11] These proofs are generally regarded as faulty, and thus have failed to establish God's existence. The modern attitude is that no *rational* argument can convince a thoughtful non-believer of the truth of religion and the existence of God. Only those who are already convinced will find intellectual arguments plausible. Today reliance is placed on faith as a believer's inner experience and on personal decision. The Living God in our hearts makes natural theology superfluous. As the Bible says, "Trust in the Lord with all thy heart, and lean not upon thine own understanding." (Prov. 3:5)

However, the classical proofs are so important in the history of Western religion and in Catholic theology that they cannot be ignored, and I shall describe them here, starting with the cosmological and teleological proofs, which are based on God's working in nature and have considerable appeal to the layman. The ideas underlying them have come up previously.

Aristotle tried to demonstrate the necessity of an unmoved mover as the first cause of all changes in the cosmos. He argued that natural events cannot be thought of as an infinite sequence without beginning. There had to be a necessary first cause which itself is not part of nature. The *cosmological proof* is the result of the identification of the unmoved mover and first cause with the creating and loving God of the Bible. It relies on two questionable assumptions, that the cosmos itself cannot be thought of as existing without a beginning and that there must be a Being who is a first cause.

But if we are disinclined to accept a self-caused eternal cosmos, we should be equally disinclined to accept an eternal creator, for the same question arises again, how can we explain *His* existence? The answer that He has been from eternity to eternity is no less mysterious than the eternity of the universe. It is certainly no better an answer than Bertrand Russell's remark: "The universe is just there and that's all."

The *teleological proof*, also called proof from design, is really not proof at all but a frequently used, impressive argument for the existence of a divine organizer. It was plausibly stated by Isaac Newton as follows:

> This most beautiful system of the sun, planets, and comets could only proceed from the counsel and dominion of an intelligent and powerful Being.

The English philosopher William Paley (1743–1805), in his *Natural Theology; or Evidences of the Existence and Attitudes of the Deity Collected from the Appearances of Nature* (the full title is worth considering) used the analogy of the watchmaker to prove his point, an analogy that has often been cited. It goes like this. If during a walk, "I found a watch upon the ground," I would not think that, unlike a stone, "the watch might have always been there." Because of the artfulness of its machinery "the watch must have had a maker." Similarly, Paley argues, "the works of nature" require a maker and designer. But it is a poor analogy to argue from a man-made piece of machinery, using existing materials, not merely to a great designer, but to a "universe-maker"; from a particular object to the totality of all objects (which itself is not an object but an abstraction of our thinking); from something within our experience to something completely outside experience. Moreover, the argument for the existence of a supernatural, loving designer-creator loses all plausibility when we consider, as we have already done, all the evil in nature and in human activity. "We must frankly admit," Paton writes, "that we can detect no purpose or meaning in the vast distances and wild eruptions of the universe—and certainly no purpose centered on the welfare of man."

It goes without saying, of course, that there is a system of order and regularity in nature which Newton helped to establish, to which all the scientists before and after him contributed, and which, in fact, we observe in our daily lives. That is the way the world is. However, we cannot deduce from the orderliness of nature the necessity and existence of a divine Designer.

There are common elements in the idea of "God-manifesting facts" and in the two proofs discussed, the cosmological and the teleological, that we can discern the existence of a creative and benevolent God in nature. The ideas of the benevolence of nature and of God's goodness are widespread, for when the goodness of our own life is not a fact, we have at least the hope of God's benevolence. But these are questionable romantic Western notions. Nature is neutral and does not bother about human strivings. Moreover, it is impossible to establish and prove supernatural facts from natural ones. If there is a realm that is transcendent, beyond nature, we cannot learn about it through empirical observation.

We come finally to the *ontological proof*.* It is the most abstract of the three proofs and will strike the layman as a peculiar way to approach God as it tries to establish the existence of God by purely logical means. Stripped down to the barest outline, the argument runs as follows: The idea of God is the idea of a Being *perfect*, i.e., complete in every respect. A concept of a Being that has all the perfections we ascribe to God (omniscience, all-loving, etc.) but lacks existence is not a concept of a perfect Being. Consequently, the idea of a perfect Being must include existence as one of its attributes. Since we think of God as an absolutely perfect being and as perfection implies existence, we must necessarily conclude that God exists.

But mere thinking cannot establish the existence of anything, including the existence of God. There is no road leading

---

* Ontology is that branch of metaphysics which deals with the nature of being. The ontological proof was originally developed by St. Anselm (about 1033–1109), Archbishop of Canterbury. Refuted during St. Anselm's lifetime, it was nevertheless kept alive and later restated by Descartes in the seventeenth century. In the opinion of most but by no means all philosophers, Kant definitely refuted all three proofs. Some contemporary logicians are still intrigued by the ontological proof and spend logical ingenuity on developing or defending ontological proofs and others on developing counterproofs. Original sources in John Hick, *The Existence of God, op. cit.*

from definitions and logical abstractions to the existence of objects. St. Anselm prayed, "Thou so truly art, then, O Lord my God, that Thou canst not even be thought of as not existing." But skeptics and atheists from the late Greco-Roman civilization to our day, and early Buddhists as well, demonstrate that there is no problem at all in thinking of God as not existing. There is no logical contradiction in the denial of God.

A salient philosophic argument against the ontological proof, stated by Kant, runs as follows: We can define the nature of, say, a cow, a unicorn, a hundred dollar note, and also of God. A definition does not include the existence or non-existence of the defined object. It does not follow from the characterization of an entity that it exists. Therefore, the definition of God leaves it open whether such an entity exists or does not exist. A definition of the perfect being does not establish the truth of the sentence, "Such a being exists." Let me conclude with John Hick's remark:

> In spite of immense intellectual investment which has gone and is still going into the various attempts to demonstrate the existence of God, the conclusion . . . that this is indemonstrable is in agreement both with the contemporary philosophical understanding of the nature and limits of logical proof and with the biblical understanding of man's knowledge of God. (*Philosophy of Religion*)

In a frequently quoted aphorism Pascal made this distinction: "God of Abraham, God of Isaac, God of Jacob, not of the philosophers and scholars." It is the Biblical God whom believers worship and praise.

Faith

4. In spite of the breakdown of natural theology and the inadequacy of all rational arguments for the existence of God, the vast majority of today's religious-minded people and clergymen continue to take positions which *seem* to be in accord with or similar to "old-time religion." Many liberal theologians and philosophers of religion stress another of Pascal's ideas: "It is the heart which experiences God, and not the reason. This, then, is faith: God felt by the heart, not by the reason." *

* *Pensée*, 278. The better known "The heart has its reason, which reason

"God is One who is directly known in His approach to the human soul." (John Baillie) He reveals Himself as a given presence and reality for all who are open to Him when they stand before Him in awe, in prayer, in obedience. The individual believer experiences the majesty and love of God as a matter of his inner life. "Seek ye the Lord while He may be found; call ye upon Him while He is near." (Isa. 55:6) The modern view is well expressed by W. C. Smith:

> Faith . . . is deeply personal, dynamic, ultimate, is a direct encounter relating one in anguish or in ecstasy or in intellectual integrity or simply in humdrum household duties to the God of the whole universe, and to one's . . . neighbor. . . . God does not reveal religions; He reveals Himself. (The Meaning and End of Religion)

The reliance on personal faith in God—not faith in traditional Biblical revelation—is by no means an entirely new trend, though it has become more prevalent in twentieth-century thinking. Its roots go back to the Bible itself and to the founders of the Reformation. Yet we may very well question whether this analysis of religious experience reports a living reality that goes much beyond purely intellectual effort and its presentation in sermons and religious literature. How many people today have searched for and encountered the presence of God and thus achieved a living faith? It is possible that there is a gap between "pulpit and pew," between the magnitude and intensity of the professional occupation with modern theology and its problems and the religious emptiness of the passive "faithful".* But this is a factual, not a philosophic question about which we lack reliable and unbiased information.

What role, then, can the Bible and religious tradition play

---

does not know" is part of the preceding Pensée. Another basis for belief is embodied in Pascal's famous "Wager" (Pensée 233).

> Let us weigh the gain and the loss in wagering that God is. Let us estimate these two chances. If you gain, you gain all; if you lose, you lose nothing. Wager, then, without hesitation that He is.

But this is a totally unsatisfactory approach and can hardly be taken seriously, although William James presented a similar argument in his essay, "The Will to Believe." (This matter is fully treated by John Hick.)

    * ". . . the frame of reference within which modern man defines the essential human dilemma has lost its transcendental reference." (Father John Thomas, S.J.)

for the religious person if his faith rests more on God's direct revelation of Himself and a personal encounter with Him than on the authority of the Bible? The Bible can still be his teacher. One need not believe that the Bible was written by God Himself or presents the infallible Word.* Rather, the modern religionist will regard "the books of the Bible . . . [as] confessions of individual questioning. . . ." (Leo Baeck) "The inspiration of the Biblical writers is their receptive and creative response to potentially revelatory facts." (Paul Tillich) The non-fundamentalist has no difficulty in accepting the idea that the "Scriptures . . . are . . . conditioned by the language, thought forms, and literary fashions of the places and times at which they were written." (from the 1967 Confession of the United Presbyterian Church)

Does encounter with God, i.e., faith as understood by modern theology, give us religious knowledge? We would know that God exists should we really encounter Him. But do we know any more than that when awareness of God is an "illumination from within" and not a matter of thought, thus a non-cognitive event? When "God is present to the soul itself," how, except through tradition, can we interpret His holy presence? Faith as an experience is sometimes compared to the experience of worldly love. Detailed knowledge of the beloved is not a result of love, though it is colored by it; it is the result of an endless number of sensual impressions of a living being. Can religionists say anything about God except that "one feels grasped, possessed, overwhelmed," that they sense His love, and similar statements, which are not about God but about their own inner state? Biblical religion, however, has a great story to tell about God: He created the world; He gives us moral precepts; He will judge and punish or save; He is—or is not—triune. How can one learn these religious facts from a living encounter with God? The relation of the personal God-experience to theology is a rather nebulous one as theology is the ever changing rational systematization of the cumulative tradition of each religion, varying in accordance with the *Zeitgeist* of the particular age in which it is formulated. It has small connection, if any, with the experience of the Living God. Hick's explanation that "reason is at work in the

---

* "The Word"—a central term in Christian theology—refers to the first verse of the Gospel of St. John: "In the beginning was the Word [*logos*] and the Word was . . . God."

systematic formulation of what is believed on the basis of faith," does not solve the mystery of the transition from encounter to detailed knowledge of God.

The basic difficulty lies in the confusion of "belief in" with "belief that." There is no problem in relating belief in God to encounter with God. If we should actually experience an encounter with God and know that we have encountered Him, we will believe in His existence and we will supposedly love Him. However, by "believing" we mean chiefly not "belief in" but "belief that," a more or less firmly held conviction *that* a certain state-of-affairs exists, for example, that the weather will be cold, that God is loving-kindness. It is said that faith results in belief. Hick writes that "theological propositions, as such, are not revealed, but represent human attempts to understand revelatory events." But the non-believer finds it impossible to understand how we can go from the revelatory event, i.e., from a non-perceptual, purely spiritual encounter, to belief *that* God has the qualities ascribed to Him. What actually occurs is that the personal encounter with God is transformed into the totality of the traditional beliefs about the Biblical God demythologized in conformity with twentieth-century ideas.

An encounter with God is a personal experience which is unverifiable by any objective standards. Let us assume that I have had such an experience. I know I have had it, just as I know that I have had a certain dream and that it was about a wild animal attacking me. But should my experience of God convince me that God exists? How do I know that what seems to me a "colloquy with the divine" is not merely "a soliloquy"? It is not strange that the Jew encounters Jehovah, the Christian encounters God the Father, the Son, and the Holy Ghost, and the Muslim Allah? The doubting plain man or the skeptical philosopher will argue that the God-encounter should be regarded as an interesting psychological event that authenticates its truth as little as any dream story does.

When I read about the Biblical "fear of God" or about revelation and the encounter with the "eternal Thou" in Martin Buber, or a philosopher's suggestive description of "the establishment of the personal relationship or faith *in* God" (H. H. Price) —just to take a few examples—it occurs to me that there seem to be some people who have perceptive powers, possibly an "inner sense," totally lacking in me and perhaps in most people whom I know. Though I am sensitive to the cosmological astonishment—the grandeur and terribleness of the world and of experiences in it—I am conscious of neither the fear nor the presence and love of God. His "spiritual fire" has not visited me. I thus have the choice of either regarding my acquaintances and myself as "blind and deaf" or assuming that those who have experienced God have seen a vision, heard a voice, or had some other mystical experience or are erroneously interpreting their spiritual feelings.

I am not inclined, however, to deny that others—saints, mystics, theologians, ordinary people—may have had the religious experiences on which their faith in God is based. It would be presumptuous to doubt the seriousness and sincerity of religious believers and to regard their reports of religious experiences as fabrications. The Bible, Cardinal Newman, Tolstoy and innumerable other people, famous and plain, serve as illustrations. It has been claimed that it is possible to give psychological explanations for religious experiences; one of the best known is that attempted by Freud in *The Future of an Illusion*. Whatever the correctness or value of *causal* explanations may be, they cannot decide the truth or untruth of these beliefs.[12] The unacceptability of religious beliefs is not based on their origin but on philosophic arguments.

The difficulties underlying trust in faith have led religious thinkers to elaborate a dualistic theory of the sources of knowledge.* There are supposedly two different kinds of knowledge: ordinary experiential knowledge and the higher order of revelation and faith, through which we apprehend the "facts of faith." Notwithstanding his suffering, his faith gave Job the confidence to exclaim: "I know that my Redeemer liveth." Faith is the rock on which Jewish and Christian believers stand.†

One of the earliest and most significant expressions of the idea of a special source of religious knowledge is to be found in the famous and still often quoted "paradox" (as it is called) of

* The term "dualism" is used in three different connections: metaphysical dualism (nature and a higher realm beyond nature) discussed in Chapter III, p. 58 ff; the dualism of body and soul, see Chapter VII, pp. 153–159; and, finally, the dualism in the sources of knowledge (reason and faith) discussed here. There is a close connection between these three dualisms, which are accepted by religious believers.

† The difference between the scientist's pragmatic faith and the religious believer's absolute faith has been discussed in Chapter V, p. 117.

Tertullian: Credo quia absurdum.* This may be freely translated as saying that I accept on faith matters which seem absurd (to reason). The particular absurd matters to which Tertullian was referring were the principal dogmas of Christianity regarding the birth, Crucifixion and Resurrection of God's Incarnate Son.†

It is impossible to relate here the history of the long struggle between reason and faith, and in particular the frequent passionate condemnations of "the sinful pride" of reason by ardent churchmen.‡ Today, reason has fewer attackers; in the contemporary world it is faith that is on the defensive. We cannot have faith in God unless there is divine revelation, the entry of the divine into the human sphere, or the "leap into faith" (Kierkegaard), the daring decision to rely on faith against reason in matters of religious truth. Yet, "before I can believe, I must in some sense understand *what* I am to believe." (Kai Nielsen) If a "belief is incomprehensible and necessarily so, one cannot see what is being accepted, on faith or otherwise." (B. Williams)

If we hold that religious beliefs may be, or perhaps must be, paradoxical—God is all-loving yet permits sickness and war, Christ is man and God—then anything may be true. By what principle can we distinguish between true and false or heretical beliefs? Where do we stop if we break with the "principle of intellectual rectitude"? (Blanshard)[13]

Strenuous attempts have been made to get around the paradoxical nature of religious statements. We seem to avoid it when we emphasize the certainty of our belief in God, but at the same time, concede that we cannot use clear terms to describe Him and rely on mystifying expressions. But then what we mean when we talk about God remains in the realm of the unknowable, and we must abandon the anchor that Biblical interpretation seems to give.

We could also drop description of God altogether and simply accept the fact that we believe in Him, a something, and in so

---

* Tertullian was one of the first Fathers of the Church (about 145–220). The above words are not the exact ones used by Tertullian; see Bernard Williams, "Tertullian's Paradox," in *New Essays in Philosophic Theology*, ed. A. Flew and A. MacIntyre, (New York: Doubleday Anchor, 1955, paperback).

† "Christianity's idea is the paradox," Kierkegaard wrote in his Journals. He emphasized the "absurd" and paradoxical nature of Christian beliefs. See also Unamuno's affirmation of "inner contradiction," above, Chapter II, p. 34.

‡ Martin Luther wrote that "[faith] grips reason by the throat and strangles the beast."

doing admit that because religious insight deals with the *ineffa-ble* in the human heart it is too deep for words. But if our ideas about God are ineffable, how can we utter them, argue about them, defend them and delimit one complex of religious convictions from others? God-belief may be inexpressible, but has in fact given birth to an immense literature, and its fertility seems inexhaustible. Indeed, compliance with the sometimes suggested "retreat into silence" and reliance on religious emotion alone would put an end to all oral and written religious tradition and make it impossible for each individual to formulate and consider his particular religious faith. He would not know what God he is adoring or praying to, if he could not somehow find expressions for his faith. Silence would, of course, end all divisive religious squabbling.*

To get around Tertullian's difficulty, some contemporary writers, influenced by certain Wittgensteinian ideas, claim that religious tenets cannot be fairly criticized by a non-believer because religious language is an autonomous "language-game" which cannot be attacked by an outsider with the tools of ordinary non-religious language. It is indeed true that there are different language-games—everyday talk, science, mathematics, ethics, esthetics, theology—and consequently we have to deal with the meanings of terms and statements in accordance with the rules of each sphere. But it is also true that the unity of reason and discourse cannot be severed so that statements which plain reason finds paradoxical or false can be held to be true in another language-game, that of science† for example. As Kierkegaard and others readily agree, the fact that religious language

* I must forego treatment of mysticism, an interesting phenomenon by no means limited to Western religious tradition. Beliefs, creeds, religious propositions disappear in mystical ecstasy. Union with God is an intuitive and wondrous wordless encounter. However, we would not know anything about these experiences if mystics did not give up their silence and speak within the framework of their particular religious tradition. The inner compelling assurance of the mystic does not overcome any of the difficulties of the truth of religious experience. The autobiographical reports of mystical vision may be true as reports of psychological happenings but cannot vouch for the existence of God. "God is not an inner state" (Nakhnikian). (Regarding mysticism, see Evelyn Underhill, *Mysticism* (New York: Dutton, 1930, paperback), and the several works of W. T. Stace dealing with mysticism; see also Paton, *op. cit.*)

† The apparently paradoxical language used by physicists in describing light and other electromagnetic phenomena as waves and also as streams of particles, discussed in chapter V, pp. 104 ff., cannot be resorted to for the purpose of defending the legitimacy of religious paradoxes. The seeming scientific paradox disappears when "the mathematical language of quantum mechanics" is used.

sounds satisfactory to believers, does not make it any the less absurd. Their obvious pride in the absurdity of religious beliefs, in paradox and mystery,* and their certitude does not make religion more convincing to adherents of other religions or to non-believers. Indeed, their attitude may very well be taken as a sign of their "storm in the soul," to use Norman Malcolm's expression.

Rudolf Bultmann's confession states the difficulty of religious belief very well:

> The man who wishes to believe in God as his God must realize that he has nothing in his hand on which to base his faith. He is suspended in mid-air, and cannot demand a proof of the Word which addresses him.

But, as I have said previously, an individual's experience of the Word does not establish objective truth. It does not discharge the burden of proof which, as Sidney Hook writes,

> rests entirely upon those who assert that there exists another kind of knowledge over and above technological, common sense, empirical knowledge, and the scientific knowledge which is an outgrowth and development of it. (*Quest of Being*)[14]

We call *absurd* that which is unreasonable; a statement is *paradoxical* when it contains a contradiction—"a contradiction cancels itself and leaves nothing." (P. F. Strawson) To attempt to explain something by calling it a *mystery* is to dodge the fact that we cannot give the explanation needed. The satisfaction many religious thinkers derive from irrationalism, from a willing acceptance of double-think and double-talk, violates what to me is one of the cardinal principles of human conduct: the ideal of truth.

There is another basic paradox in the fact that God is believed to exist utterly beyond the world of human experience and knowledge; yet the believer claims to have knowledge of Him, that He is near to us and has spoken to us. But if God's realm is a transcendent one of Ultimate Reality, then He is by

---

* "The hall-mark of logical inconsistency clings to all genuine pronouncements of faith." Religious claims "are mysteries in which God reveals Himself as the Incomprehensible." (both quotations from Emil Brunner, found in Blackstone, *op. cit.*) "The paradoxes are not fatal to religion. Religion has to deal in apparent contradiction, for words are not adequate to describe the ultimate Mystery" (Ninian Smart). See also the defense of the "obvious unreasonableness of Christian belief" by Richard Taylor in *Religious Experience and Truth*, Sidney Hook (ed.), *op. cit.*

His very nature beyond our reach and "cannot be fathomed, comprehended, or reasoned out." (Wach) Anything we say about Ultimate Reality must, therefore, be unverifiable and arbitrary. In fact, how does a believer know that there is an Ultimate Reality at all, when so many of us have never encountered it?

Oddly enough, this argument, which ought to be convincing to any reasonable person, is accepted only by empiricists, naturalists and skeptics, who consider the truism, what is *in principle* beyond our knowledge is and remains beyond knowledge, as a basic rule for our understanding of the world.* The religious believer, however, finds that "Ultimate Reality does open itself, manifest, or reveal itself. . . . Underhill has put it very aptly: 'That which we really know about God is not what we have been clever enough to find out, but what the Divine Charity has secretly revealed.' " (Wach) But this idea does not solve the enigma of the Ultimate Reality changing its ultimacy and, in fact, according to Christian belief, appearing bodily among men.

Verifiability

The most basic argument about the truth of religious assertions raised by contemporary philosophers, and not merely by the logical positivists, concerns the cognitive significance of *key* religious statements which purport to give us information about God and His relation to the world.[15] We are not concerned here with statements of "religious" feelings (gratefulness, concern, worry, remorse, awe), with ethical and ritualistic prescriptions or language indicating a general attitude toward nature and life, with the language of prayers and blessings. We are also not concerned with certain empirical assertions that appear in religious discourses.

The statements philosophers have called into question constitute the most basic claims about the existence and nature of God: God exists, God loves us; "God seeketh that which is pursued" (Eccl. 4:15); God sent His Incarnate Son to redeem man-

---

* This should not be confused with matters which were or seem to be beyond our knowledge for *technical reasons*, such as the other side of the moon (until recently), galaxies billions of light years away, or the physiological processes correlated with thinking.

kind. Now, what do these statements assert? Some philosophers have claimed that such statements are meaningless. Along with others, I should like to make a more limited claim, namely, that they lack factual significance. Statements about God are not factual in the narrow sense of the word, although they are regarded as factual in a broader sense in that they supposedly deal with certain mysterious conditions of the universe. However, these basic claims of religion are bereft of any cognitive or factual content because it is in principle impossible to discover whether they are true or not and how they can be verified or proved false.

Let us examine the underlying problem by studying the cognitive character of two sentences not concerned with God: John was a lion in a previous existence; John will become an angel after his death. Any attempt to verify or refute these "factual" assertions is futile and must be given up. They can neither be proved nor disproved. They are therefore outside the sphere of empirical investigation, though they may still be meaningful in fantasies or fairy tales.

The same is true of assertions about God. They cannot be proved through natural theology (the three proofs), religious experience, or in any other way. They may be stated as paradoxes, but then for that very reason they are not merely unverifiable but meaningless. There is no conceivable evidence to support accepting or denying them. They are "not at any point anchored to reality." (Hepburn) Nothing in the world either points conclusively to the existence and love of God or is incompatible with it. Religious "assertions" therefore only appear to assert something. Actually, they do not give us any information and have no descriptive significance. The question, "Does God exist and love us?" is a useless one for it cannot be answered.

The assertion of the factual emptiness of fundamental religious assertions is in such outrageous contradiction to general religious opinion that I would like to analyze the specific analysis of the statement, "God loves His world." The Occidental believer who expresses praise to God permits no counterclaim against it, but what can "God's love" mean when we observe actual conditions in life? "All is misery," the Buddhist says. Antony Flew is right when he says that the "seeming assertions [of religious people] are really vacuous." [16] And Blackstone asks regarding claims of God's goodness, power, and love:

What clear meaning can a hypothesis have which is compatible
with any empirical state of affairs and incompatible with
none? *

The empirical emptiness of religious statements is demonstrated by the fact that most religious adherents make their
everyday family, professional and political decisions without giving much if any thought to the existence and workings of God.
There is little if any noticeable difference between their way of
life and that of non-believers, except that they spend some time
in religious activities, while the others do not. Generally speaking, confidence that God exerts His influence on our daily doings
has become attenuated. Fundamentalists, of course, take it for
granted that God will hear their prayers and perhaps change the
course of events, for most other believers prayer serves largely to
relieve personal tensions; it contributes to their "peace of mind."
    Moreover, religious-minded people use the myths and
imaginative language of religion ("God is with us under the
stars") as an expression of certain attitudes toward and feelings
about the world as a whole and about particular happenings in it.
Much of religious language and many religious myths are really a
form of romantic poetry or "a kind of cosmic esthetic which
simply cannot be argued." (Chaim Potok) Furthermore, for
many non-traditional "believers" the idea and the term "religion" stand for moral commitment and for meaning in life, based
on the commandments and love of a God who is not looked
upon as a separate active entity in the universe. God is instead
man's ideal commitment or the forces in the universe that make
the development of man possible—nature's most God-like creature. These "verbal theists" † have none of the difficulties which
I have discussed, because their religion has become a humanism,
though adumbrated by Jewish or Christian traditions and rites.

    * I will omit here the claim made by past, and even some modern theo-
logians and philosophers of religion, that immortality may bear out the goodness of God (eschatological verification). I can hardly imagine a less convincing argument. There are not only the extreme difficulties of the whole idea
of personal immortality as a factual heavenly possibility, but also the logical
difficulty that nothing that happens to the immortal soul can wipe out the actual
suffering on earth. Whatever happens to a child in heaven who starved to
death on earth, nothing can erase the fact that he did die of hunger. On
eschatological verification see the books by Hick cited previously, and for criticism see Blackstone, *op. cit.* Several other modern defenses of traditional and
liberal theology have not been treated here. They can be found in Hick's and
Blackstone's books.
    † See above p. 318.

Contemporary Trends in Theology

It is obvious that traditional and liberal faiths, with which I have dealt so far, find themselves in considerable difficulty today, although this is due not so much to doubting their arguments as it is to the impact of science and technology. Many people have accepted, openly or covertly,* secular, mostly agnostic, naturalism in the place of a religious world view. However, religious motivation and tradition are so strong and persuasive that during the last thirty or forty years several eminent theologians have sought to develop new combinations of secularism and Christianity, or Judaism.† These new radical theologies play a rather striking role at the present time. This makes a brief treatment of their various positions advisable although it is quite uncertain how deeply the laity is influenced by these theologies. While radical theologians employ religious stories, symbolism and terminology, and usually also the term "God," they border on or actually represent a peculiar form of atheism. The idea of a transcendent realm of God has been abandoned, and we can therefore speak of the disappearance, absence, or, with Buber, of "the eclipse of God" or join in the lively revival of the Nietzschean slogan: "God is dead." [17]

Of the three famous theologians, Karl Barth, Rudolf Bultmann and Paul Tillich, who exerted a deep influence on theology after the First World War, Tillich (1886–1965), who taught and preached in the United States since 1933, where he became the leading spokesman of radical theology, is probably the foremost, "one of the great minds of the twentieth century." (John Macquarrie) He taught most of the young non-fundamentalist theologians. His new theology combined and transformed Lutheranism, early nineteenth-century German idealist philosophy and existentialism. But I will limit the discussion to a few elements of Tillich's theology and not discuss his existentialist psychology (predicament, concern, guilt, estrangement, finitude). In Tillich's

* Flannery O'Connor's comment about "a good Christian" is true of many Christians and Jews: "She was a good Christian woman with a large respect for religion, though she did not, of course, believe any of it was true."

† I will not deal with Zen Buddhism, cherished by many small groups because of its mystic and contemplative elements. It does not value knowledge, religious theories, or metaphysics, but rather lays stress on a non-conceptual illumination requiring considerable spiritual training.

theology, set forth in comprehensive detail in the three volumes of his *Systematic Theology*, we enter a strange, new world. While this difficult work is unknown to the laity, his shorter writings (fifteen have been published as paperbacks), such as *The Courage to Be, The Shaking of the Foundations*, have found a wide readership.

I will concentrate my discussion on the central doctrine of any theology, the nature of God.[18] "The being of God is being-itself." Tillich also calls God "the ground of being." "The being of God cannot be understood as the existence of a being alongside others or above others." "God is . . . not *a* being," not even the "highest being." Instead, "he is the power of being in everything and above everything, the infinite power of being." "God participates in everything that is; he has community with it; he shares in its destiny."

These definitions and explanations demonstrate that Tillich did not believe in *an entity separate and beyond the world*. Tillich seems to present a monistic view. However, he does speak of transcendence: "As the power of being, God transcends every being and also the totality of beings—the world."

According to Tillich, these statements are to be understood symbolically as "nothing . . . can be said about God as God which is not symbolic," except that "the statement that God is being-itself is a nonsymbolic statement."

It may seem unfair to put these highly baffling quotations together, but it is the best way to demonstrate how far removed Tillich's writing is from the traditional style of discussing God. These quotations also point up the difficulty of comprehending Tillich's theology. And if we read what Tillich has to say about the several terms he uses in his explanation of God (being-itself, the ground of being, the power of being, the cause, the substance, the structure), we discover new difficulties.[19] Tillich seems to envisage an ideal realm of "being-itself," * which we cannot explain by reliance on ordinary word-meanings, nor by traditional ideas about God. I quite agree with David Jenkins that "the traditional theistic talk about a personal God is no more (although admittedly no less) *logically* difficult than is the talk

* In the chapter under discussion Tillich also writes: "*God does not exist* [my italics]. He is being itself beyond essence and existence. Therefore, to argue that God exists is to deny him." If, disregarding Tillich's special terminology, we accept the ordinary sense of the assertions "God does not exist" and "God is not a being," we find that we are approaching a God-is-dead view.

about 'ultimate reality' and 'ultimate concern' which is urged
upon us." [20]

There are other serious puzzles; for example, Tillich's discussion of Eternal Life. It is not immortality in the usual sense of
the term because the supernatural realm where our spirit may be
with God has vanished.

Tillich's expression "being-itself" has become quite prominent in contemporary discussions of God. This is also true of
Tillich's term "ultimate concern." [21] " 'God' . . . is a name for
that which concerns man ultimately. . . . Whatever concerns
man ultimately becomes God for him." In a similar vein, Tillich
writes in *The Shaking of the Foundations:*

> If that word [God] has not much meaning for you, translate
> it, and speak of the depth of your life, of the source of your
> being, of your ultimate concern, of what you take seriously
> without any reservation. . . . If you know that God means
> depth, you know much about Him. You cannot then call your-
> self an atheist or unbeliever. . . . He who knows about depth
> knows about God.*

What is "ultimate concern"? There is a dangerous ambiguity in this term. According to John Hick, it "may refer either to
an *attitude* of concern or to the (real or imagined) *object* of that
attitude." We may wonder whether our psychological experience of concern establishes God or whether God as being-itself
becomes our ultimate concern. Such alternatives are blurred and
straddled in Tillich's complicated terminology, attractive for
some, appallingly obscure for others. There is a further serious
difficulty in the "ultimate concern" theology. If God is identified
as the object of man's ultimate concern, "it means that there are
as many Gods as there are objects of ultimate concern." (S.
Hook)†

Tillich's account of God has come under the crossfire of
theological and philosophic criticism. The former asks whether

---

* I quote this passage because it is one of the key quotations in *Honest to
God* (Philadelphia: Westminster Press, 1963, paperback) by John A. T. Robinson, Bishop of Woolwich, which, written with an apparent simplicity, was a
great sensation in England in 1963 and to a lesser extent here. *Honest to God*
tries to merge the radical theologies of Tillich, Bultmann, and Bonhoeffer. The
stir created by this book is an indication of the prevailing religious ferment
and interest in new religious thinking. The man-centered view of God adopted
in *Honest to God* is severely criticized in *The Honest to God Debate, op. cit.*
See also Ved Mehta, *The New Theologians* (New York: Harper & Row, 1965).

† On science as the scientist's ultimate concern and religion, see chapter V.

Tillich's theology is still Christian.* Besides the objections previously mentioned, philosophers have raised basic questions about Tillich's emphasis on the symbolic nature of *all* statements about God and have wondered whether this thorough symbolism might not deprive his theology of meaningfulness.[22]

There is a fundamental difference between the nature of symbolism in traditional religion, which I have discussed before (above, pp. 323–325), and in Tillich's theology. The symbolism of traditional religion rests on a firm belief in the transcendent personal God and, in traditional Christianity, also on a belief in God's Incarnate Son. Therefore, as Alston says, "in practice religious symbols function against the background of a complex system of beliefs about supernatural beings." For Tillich, however, God is not a supernatural person but being-itself, and apart from this statement "nothing else can be said about God as God which is not symbolic." As all of Tillich's theology therefore is symbolic, we must go from symbol to symbol. Our search for symbols and their interpretation takes place in a cognitive void. How then can we choose between symbols and find the proper ones? Why should power, king of the world and churches be symbols of God, if we know nothing about God except other symbols? Why not weakness, hatred, injustice, slave, or slums? Without some frame of reference our evaluation of symbols is wholly arbitrary and consequently useless for the purpose of opening a way of understanding God.

Tillich's actual procedure, however, strays from his general theory, for he has tied the choice and interpretation of his symbols to his *prior* acceptance of the God of a non-symbolic Christianity and to his concern with the ambiguities and difficulties of human existence. The old Christian content is poured into new, obscure, metaphysical bottles.

The symbolic character of all descriptions of God, of being-itself, in Tillich's "metaphysical theology" [23] gives rise to an-

* Guyton B. Hammond, *The Power of Self-Transcendence*, (St. Louis: Bethany Press, 1966, paperback), points out several theological criticisms and refers to other critical literature, quoting Kenneth Hamilton's remark that Tillich's system is "incompatible with the Christian gospel."

Tillich, notwithstanding his liberal, humane spirit, gives a definite preference to Christianity, and thus invites confrontation with the Hindu's criticism in Ninian Smart's discussion (cited above, p. 327). In the third volume of *Systematic Theology* Tillich mentions that the "criterion" of the "New Being in Jesus the Christ" "elevates the churches above any other religious group." See also the last section of *The Courage to Be* (New Haven: Yale University Press, 1952, paperback).

other, even more crucial difficulty. What do Tillich's symbols mean? * The meaning of metaphors employed in ordinary usage is normally quite intelligible, that is, they can be translated into or reduced to realistic terms. If I say of an angry man that he roars like a lion, I am not tied to the metaphor as I can describe this occurrence in literal language without using metaphors. Similar metaphors are also intelligible because they are reducible. But can this be done to Tillich's symbol of God as being-itself? According to Tillich, being-itself neither exists nor does not exist, and it lacks the personal character and the relatedness to man of the traditional God. In addition, it is not accessible to observation. There is therefore no possibility whatsoever of reducing or translating it. Such terms as "divine life and its eternal glory and blessedness" (the last words of the third volume), "ground of all abundance," "ground of life," "structure," although they use everyday words (life, glory, ground, structure, abundance), likewise have no reducible meaning as used by Tillich. Since all explanations given for these expressions are, according to Tillich, also symbolic, "literal significance is never achieved." (Edwards) Thus Tillich's theology remains within a symbolic, non-literal, closed circle without achieving intelligibility.

Tillich's theology is an esoteric, intellectual mysticism of being-itself. Standing at the brink of atheism, it is an unfulfilled effort to talk meaningfully to modern man about God. His work demonstrates that radical theology faces insurmountable difficulties in speaking to modern skeptical ears about God within the framework of Biblical revelation. Non-traditional theologians today have these alternatives: they can lose themselves in obscure definitions of God and Ultimate Reality, combining these with a completely demythologized story of God and Christ, or they can view God as a human category, an ultimate concern, or they can proclaim that God is dead and that ethics, religious rites or a belief in Christ has taken His place.

An intense confusion therefore reigns in theology at the present time. Ferment has even emerged in the Catholic Church, catalyzed by Vatican II (1962–1965), and the authority of the

---

* Tillich raises this question in his first essay in the Hook volume, but his answer employs the very metaphysical terms whose meaning is to be clarified.

Some of the following remarks apply generally to symbolism in religious thinking.

Pope has been somewhat eroded. Nevertheless, a great many religious adherents still acquiesce in traditional religious and moral beliefs. But these suffer under the impact of our freer and more hedonistic behavior patterns, and under the spread of our vastly increased scientific knowledge of the universe. It is not surprising that religious uncertainty and indifference has increased and that many people have lost their belief in God.* But what is paradoxical is that the idea of God's death could find champions even among theologians.

This innovation in theology was greatly influenced by the personality and writings of the young anti-Nazi German theologian, Dietrich Bonhoeffer,† who was killed in a concentration camp in 1945. Bonhoeffer lost his life while still struggling with the clarification of his ideas and, at the time of his death, was in some sense a believing Christian. As far as I know he did not use the God-is-dead slogan, but he did speak of "religionless Christianity," which has become a new theological catch phrase and seems to mean a Christianity that does not rely on theology and the apparatus of the church.

The following are a few significant and often quoted passages from his *Letters and Papers from Prison*[24] which are eloquent testimony to the unrest in current religious thinking.

> How do we speak of God without religion, i.e., without the temporally-influenced presuppositions of metaphysics, inwardness, and so on? How do we speak . . . in secular fashion of God? In what way are we in a religionless and secular sense Christians . . . as wholly belonging to the world?

> Man has learned to cope with all questions of importance without recourse to God as a working hypothesis. . . . Everything gets along without "God," and just as well as before.

> God is teaching us that we must live as men who can get along very well without him. . . . Before God and with him we live without God.

* "But it seems that something has happened that has never
    happened before; though we know not just when, or
    why, or how, or where.
Men have left God not for other gods, they say, but for no
    god. . . ." (T. S. Eliot, "Choruses from 'The Rock.' ")
† The largest part of Ved Mehta's book, *The New Theologians, op. cit.,* deals with Bonhoeffer, of whom Mehta writes that "he has probably affected more Christian theologians and, through them, more Christians of every sort than any other one theologian of our time."

Another important element in the development of atheistic theology has been the substitution of ethics for conventional beliefs concerning God. This innovation has been succinctly stated in John Hick's heading to the reprint of an important essay by R. B. Braithwaite: "Religious Language is Ethically but Not Factually Significant." * Braithwaite agrees with modern secularists and with radical theologians in holding that religious propositions are not to be taken as a "fundamental truth about the universe." However, influenced by Wittgenstein's idea that "The meaning of a word is its use in the language," Braithwaite examines the use of religious propositions and finds "that the religious assertion is used as a moral assertion." Religious assertions "specify the *form of behavior* which is in accordance with what one takes to be the fundamental principles of the religion in question." (My italics) † The ideological assertions of various religions, even if they indicate the same moral principles, "are associated with the thinking of different stories." It is not necessary that the stories be accepted as truth as long as they are "entertained in thought." Religious propositions are "profitable to [a] man helping him to persevere in the way of life he has decided upon." Braithwaite refers to Matthew Arnold's well-known "description of Religion as morality touched by emotion." A Christian is a man who "proposes to live according to Christian moral principles and associates his intention with thinking of Christian stories."

But how can the Biblical myths exert the expected influence if they are merely poetic fables without relation to eternal truth about God? The Bible is then like a lifebelt thrown to a drowning man, which, because it is porous has no buoyancy though it looks like a saving support. Furthermore, why should we single out the particular moral value of the New Testament story? Why go beyond the Hebrew Bible? Why not live with Bud-

---

* See John Hick, *The Existence of God, op. cit.* Braithwaite's essay, "An Empiricist's View of the Nature of Religious Belief," originally a lecture, published in 1955, created quite a stir among contemporary philosophers and theologians because in it an analytic philosopher, interested mostly in the philosophy of science, came to the defense of religion.

† Kai Nielsen calls such sentences "ideological." "An ideological sentence . . . is a sentence which *appears* to be used to make an empirical hypothesis but in actuality functions as a value-judgment. . . . They increase the psychological effectiveness of a certain value-judgment for some people by making them seem to be crucial but mysterious laws of nature."

dha's stories, or with Homer's, Shakespeare's, Dostoevsky's, or
Camus'? Braithwaite, in consequence of his argument, could
hardly care less except to say that *he* prefers the Christian story.
The generalized content of Braithwaite's argument constitutes a
psychological-historical theory, that for him and millions of
other people a particular set of religious stories has a moral value.

Braithwaite and the God-is-dead theologians, while sharing
the basic view of secular thinkers, differ from naturalistic and
humanistic thinkers in holding that certain elements of importance in traditional religions ought to and can in some form or
other survive, such as myths, ritual, religious ethics and "the centrality of Jesus."

What interest can the humanist have in the new trends in
theology? His ethical idealism does not need religious ideologies,
rites and organizations as support for proper behavior. Consequently, his interest is merely that of a spectator of these peculiar
contemporary cultural developments. It would be impractical
for us to deal at length with God-is-dead theology which was a
rather brief but sensational episode in the nineteen-sixties.[25] It
was instigated by a small number of gifted theologians, mostly
Protestant. They openly proclaim that theology itself should
embrace atheism, thus calling for an atheistic Christianity and Judaism. (As theology is the study of God, the phrase "God-is-
dead theology" is strange and paradoxical, but by now established. Moreover, if God never existed, the idea of his death is
meaningless, except insofar as it may indicate that some people
who at one time believed in God have abandoned that notion.)
The denial of the existence of gods or God—atheism—is by no
means a new philosophy. Atheism and secularism never formed
cohesive organizations—probably an impossible enterprise—and
therefore never matched the educational and political influence
of organized religion. But what is new is theology without God.

Let me quote a few significant expressions of the theologians
of the "godless religion." I begin with Rabbi Richard A. Rubinstein:

> The divine-human encounter in our times . . . is totally non-
> existent.

> [Religion] is the way in which we share and celebrate, both
> consciously unconsciously, through the inherited myths, rituals,
> and traditions of our communities, the dilemmas and the crises
> of life and death, good and evil. . . .

The significance of the religious community, both Jewish and Christian, [is] to me—the absurd, pathetic attempt, for which there can be no substitute, to make a meaningless life meaningful.

Paul M. van Buren asks: "How can the Christian who is himself a secular man understand his faith in a secular way?" He relates his theology to Braithwaite, but he analyzes in much more specific detail than Braithwaite the importance of the history of "the man Jesus of Nazareth" to modern man—"a considerably reinterpreted figure" of Christ.* To be "grasped and held" by this story will lead to a new "perspective of faith." "Holding to the humanity of Christ, to the man of Nazareth," we will "'catch' something of the contagious freedom of Jesus." The fruit of faith is "love . . . the exercise of this freedom in serving one's neighbor." While van Buren repudiates the expression "God is dead," he finds that "the word 'God' is dead." "Questions about 'God' will receive their only useful answer in the form of the history of that man [Jesus]."

Van Buren accepts the possibility that the history of Socrates "might conceivably have a liberating effect on the person. . . . He would be 'in Socrates,' let us say, not 'in Christ'" He also points out that "Christians have never been able to *prove* the 'superiority' of their historical perspective." In his more recent writings he seems to have gone further in the acceptance of "a variety of viewpoints." What van Buren basically represents is a secular humanism employing the symbolism of an idealized Jesus of Nazareth.

With respect to William Hamilton, one is not always sure whether in referring to God's death he is making an observation about modern culture—that God has disappeared for us so that we are experiencing His eclipse—or whether he is reporting a theological and cosmic discovery—God's non-existence. He is probably the best-known and most publicized of the God-is-dead theologians; however, he has not yet worked out a systematic treatment of his views. Hamilton has been greatly influenced by Bonhoeffer's idea that man must solve his personal and social

---

* This reinterpretation produces a circular result. The Jesus described in the Gospel appears as a first-century apocalyptic Jewish prophet, compassionate but also extremist and angry. Modern liberal and radical Christian theologians have replaced Him with a modern, wholly good, Tolstoyan, self-sacrificing, radical idealist. Then they turn about and are "grasped" by the saintly figure which is the product of their own reinterpretation.

problems without God. He agrees with Nietzsche, who said of God, "We have killed Him." Consequently, we must now, according to Hamilton, "turn from the problems of faith to the reality of love." "We move to our neighbor . . . out of a sense of the loss of God." "Our worldly work . . . is mapped out . . . by Jesus Christ and his way to his neighbor."

But how can the central role of Christ whose religious significance rests on the Father who sent him and an ultimate commitment to Him be reconciled with a denial of God's existence?

The currently acclaimed theology-of-hope is a return to more historical Christian doctrines. It is concerned with God's promise for the future, and maintains that hope for a better world ought to be the primary experience of the religious person. The symbol for this is Christ's Resurrection.*

It is impossible to evaluate the influence of contemporary theological shifts on future religious belief and church life. These are factual, not philosophic, questions and they must remain speculative. Two results are fairly probable. First, modern theology, with its emphasis on ethics, Christlike behavior and secularity, is strengthening the humanistic tendencies and the activities of organized religion in the social and political sphere. Second, the God-is-dead debate—popularized in many paperback books and by mass media—may have further weakened the hold of conventional religious world views and thus may make secular atheism more acceptable.

However, it is highly doubtful that synagogues and churches will soon become empty. Social changes make their way very slowly. Traditional church services, religious observations and celebrations will, in all probability, continue for a long time. For millions of people participation in worship services and church membership rests not so much on religious belief as on a combination of other—psychological and sociological—factors: ancestral bonds and tradition; psychological needs; neighborliness; spiritual, esthetic and idealistic feelings; the pleasure and beauty of religious rites; the opportunities for celebrating life's beginning and its high points and for marking its end; and, last but not least, ethnic identification, community standing and social pressure.† With the spread of Jewish, Christian, and secular

---

* For Jews, the messianic idea has always been central to their beliefs.
† The last three factors are particularly important in the United States,

atheism many houses of worship may assume more and more the
nature of community centers. But the organized traditional religions with their thousands of clergymen still play such an active
role in the cultural life of the Western world that, in all probability, the day is far off when, as Voltaire phrased it more than two
hundred years ago, "the last priest . . . (will lie) buried under
the wreckage of the last church."

In conclusion I want to state the secular viewpoint against a
number of general arguments often used in support of religion.
There is a widely held impression, similar to Kierkegaard's idea,
that "the postulate (of God's existence) is . . . a life-necessity."
This may have been a correct self-observation and equally true
for some other persons, but it is totally untrue for mankind as a
whole. Men have led and can lead successful and meaningful
lives, even though they did not and do not believe in the existence of gods or God. In fact, there is a constructive force in
religious unbelief. Man's selfhood and self-confidence and resolution may be fortified by the realization that he is not dependent
on the unfathomable whim of God and that he is not "a miserable sinner" needing salvation through God. We are not debased
if we regard ourselves, not as the children of God, but as children and part of nature.

Tillich states another argument very well, that "a secular
world . . . excluded those deep things for which religion
stands: the feeling for the inexhaustible mystery of life, the grip
of an ultimate meaning of existence, and the invicible power of
an unconditional devotion." However, the "deep things" can
equally enter the life of the humanistic secularist. He, too, may
be a man of feeling and high ideals, who can express in an appropriate manner his sense of the mystery of life, its meaningfulness,
and his humane devotion.

The fear has sometimes been voiced that atheism will cause
psychological and moral chaos. Though this is frequently presented as if it were an incontrovertible fact, it is actually a propa-
gandistic argument and usually no attempt whatsoever is made to
offer factual data. It is a truism that personal and civic morality is
necessary to avoid personal and civic chaos. But personal and
civic morality—and "the implicit American creed"—is not dependent on any kind of belief in God.

---

where, of all the predominantly Protestant countries, religious life is most
active.

Finally, modern times are not infrequently described and criticized as a "faithless age." But disbelief in God obviously does not imply complete unbelief. Belief in truth, love, goodness and beauty does not require religious faith.

Traditional Western religions have made their peace with science by accepting scientific discoveries and theories which were long regarded as heresies. Perhaps the day will come when Western civilization will also make its peace with the "heresy" of a godless world view, freeing itself from the remnants of myths and dogmas that originated long ago in the Near East. "In the future all supernaturalism conceivably might come to seem as archaic as animism now does." (H. J. Muller) On that day the costly, and frequently beautiful, houses of worship will serve general community purposes and the energy and resources now spent on theological interpretation and argumentation, on religious propaganda and organizational activities, will be freed for the betterment of our lives on earth.

CHAPTER XIII

Existentialism

What Is Existentialism?

An exposition of existentialist philosophy actually does not belong in a discussion of modern naturalism; however, even though interest in it seems to be declining, existentialism is still of sufficient importance, particularly to nonphilosophers, to justify some historical, descriptive and critical remarks about it.[1]

"Existentialism" is a fashionable word today though its meaning puzzles most people, who believe that only specialists know exactly what it refers to. It is not merely that it seems difficult to define "existentialism"; we use many abstract words in ordinary discourse—"philosophy," "truth," "morality," "religion"—whose meaning we know though we would find it difficult to define them. The feeling of perplexity about the word goes deeper than that, for existentialism seems to be something enigmatic. But people are unnecessarily diffident. While the writings on existentialism may be difficult to understand, the word itself indicates its meaning. It is an oversimplification, but for our purposes it may be said that existentialism is a philosophy that is primarily interested in what is supposedly closest to man—his own existence and its meaning.

In its narrowest sense the term "existentialism" is customarily applied to the disparate philosophies of four twentieth-century Continental philosophers and several religious thinkers who, in the nineteen-forties and fifties, created quite a stir by their opposition to the then prevailing philosophies and traditional theologies. They were concerned mainly with the nature, meaning and problems of the "human condition" and with the manner in which man experiences himself, his freedom and the fatefulness of his existence.

The most widely known and esteemed nonreligious existentialists are Karl Jaspers (1883–1969) and Martin Heidegger (born 1889)—both German—and Jean-Paul Sartre (born 1905) and Albert Camus (1913–1960)—both French. (Camus was born and spent his youth in Algiers. Unlike the others, he was not a professional philosopher.) Although these four men are called existentialists and are often discussed together, they by no means represent a homogeneous school and—except for Sartre— have repudiated this designation. Heidegger's *Being and Time*, which appeared in 1927 (English translation 1962),[2] may be regarded as the first major formulation of modern existentialist philosophy. It greatly influenced Sartre's *Being and Nothingness*, published in 1943 (English translation, 1956).[3] * The leading religious existentialists are Franz Rosenzweig and Martin Buber, both German-born Jews, Étienne Gilson and Gabriel Marcel, French Catholics, and Martin Bultmann and Paul Tillich, German Protestants.†

There are, then, numerous and different existentialist philosophies, but nevertheless they share certain characteristic features and a distinctive mood of philosophizing. They differ from each other in content, and each uses a different complicated terminology. There are atheistic as well as religious existentialists, and existentialists also stand in opposing political camps. Heidegger was an active National Socialist during some years of the Hitler

* A most decisive influence on existentialist philosophers, particularly on the technical aspects of Heidegger's and Sartre's systems was exerted by the "phenomenology" of the German philosopher Edmund Husserl (1859–1938). Heidegger's *Being and Time* is dedicated to Husserl, whose assistant he had been at Freiburg. Sartre called his *Being and Nothingness*, "An Essay on Phenomenological Ontology." But both Heidegger's and Sartre's philosophies differed greatly from Husserl's. Any brief explication of phenomenology must be unsatisfactory, but broadly speaking it is a systematic, objective, non-psychologic analysis of the phenomena experienced in pure consciousness. The reader is referred to special studies, for example, Quentin Lauer, *Phenomenology: Its Genesis and Prospect* (New York: Harper & Row, 1965, paperback). Several of the general studies of existentialism contain a chapter on Husserl.

† After 1933 Buber lived in Israel and Tillich, as previously mentioned, in the United States.

period.[4] Jaspers, who believes in democracy, was relieved of his position as professor at Heidelberg in 1937, but was reinstated in 1945. He later taught in Basle, Switzerland. Sartre has Communist sympathies. The diversity is made even greater by the fact that several of the existentialists have experienced a decisive change in their thinking. The mysticism of the later Heidegger is quite different from the spirit of his *Being and Time*. Sartre's emphasis used to be on his existentialism, but his interest in Marxism and Communism has now become dominant. And between the time when he wrote *The Stranger*, an early work, and the time when he wrote *The Plague*, Camus' thinking had undergone considerable change.

A number of men, considered existentialists in a broader sense, are the forerunners of today's existentialism, in particular the Danish theologian Sören Kierkegaard (1813–1855), "the father of contemporary existentialism," Pascal and Nietzsche. In an even more general way we can say of existentialism, as William James said of pragmatism, that it is "a new name for some old ways of thinking." We regard as existentialist certain works of religious and secular literature that emphasize the uniqueness and precariousness of human existence and wonder about its fate and meaning, foremost among them the tragedies of Shakespeare, the Book of Job, the tragic plays of the three great Greek tragedians and others. Mention should also be made of the works of such important nineteenth- and twentieth-century novelists as Dostoevsky, Tolstoy (whose story, *The Death of Ivan Ilyitch*, is often referred to by existentialists), Melville (*Moby Dick*), Kafka and others. And, of course, both Sartre and Camus use the play and the novel to expound their philosophy. Though every drama and novel deals with human affairs and conflicts, only those are regarded as existentialist which go beyond the telling of an interesting story to a consideration of the problematic in man's existence. A similar existentialist mood may also pervade certain paintings and sculptures of old as well as new masters.

Finally, there has come into use an extended, nonphilosophic application of the term "existentialism" which characterizes the general feeling and consciousness of certain phases of modern art and literature in which "all's cheerless, dark, and deadly." (Shakespeare) Terms used by certain existentialists— anxiety, despair, alienation, nothingness, absurdity—echo in this literature, of which Archibald MacLeish has this to say:

It would be impossible to find in the literature of any epoch a more nearly unanimous repudiation than in the plays, fictions, commentaries, poems which regard themselves as most expressive of our time. It is commonly said . . . that the hero has been replaced with us by the antihero. . . . Ordinary, unheroic man has dwindled until nothing but his morbid fears, his exceptional vices, his "extreme situations" are significant, and common human life itself has lost its literary interest; only its "absurdity" inspires a novel or a play.

"Existentialist" is also applied occasionally to the unconventional thinking—or lack of clear thinking—and behavior of rebellious groups composed mostly of young people who affirm or act out the absurdity of their own and contemporary society's existence.

Existentialism in the English-Speaking World

In the English-speaking world existentialist philosophy has been of interest mainly to men of letters, though it has also aroused curiosity in a wider, educated public. It is the basis of existentialist psychiatry. Existentialist religious thinkers, like Buber and Tillich—the latter considerably influenced by Heidegger—have given theology a new direction. But there are only a small number of philosophers in the United States and England who are actually followers of existentialist philosophy.* The philosophic treatises of Jaspers, Heidegger and Sartre have had hardly any influence on most philosophers here or, in fact, on non-philosophers. Paradoxically, though the existentialists enjoy a far-flung reputation, their main philosophic work has received little attention. The only exception is Sartre's widely read lecture, *Existentialism Is a Humanism*,† delivered in 1946. The concern with existentialism as a philosophy has been strongly influ-

* English-speaking philosophers are, of course, acquainted with the theories of existentialism. Heidegger's *Sein und Zeit* received a noteworthy review by Gilbert Ryle, one of the most outstanding English philosophers, shortly after its publication. When the translation appeared in 1962, Sidney Hook reviewed it at length for the *New York Times*.

The best known exponents of existentialism in America are William Barrett and John Wild. Some of the many writers on existentialism are merely interested students of this philosophy.

† Reprinted in Walter Kaufmann's selection. Sartre later regretted the publication of the somewhat informal lecture as a "mistake." Its ethical ideas are "incompatible with the rest of Sartre's philosophy." (Mary Warnock, *Existentialist Ethics*, New York: St. Martin's Press, 1967, paperback.)

enced by the high esteem in which the fine novels, dramas and essays of Sartre and Camus are held.[5] And this was enhanced by the singularly prominent role writers play in France. The anti-Nazi activities of Sartre and Camus also contributed to the prestige of existentialism, and the existentialist meetings and discussions in the left-bank coffeehouses of Paris helped keep interest in it alive. It should be noted, however, that interest in existentialism has been declining here—and in Europe as well—under the impact of exciting political events and new activities of young people.

One of the most decisive reasons why English-speaking philosophers have been little affected by existentialism is the fact that existentialists seem to work in a different sphere from most English and American philosophers. They do not deal with most of the matters that particularly concern empiricists, such as logic and epistemology, the philosophy of language, mathematics, and science, ethics and its foundation. Non-existentialist philosophers try to establish the nature and criteria of general, objective knowledge in all fields of intellectual endeavor. They share the rationality of the scientific method and outlook. Existentialists, on the other hand, are more interested in what Kierkegaard calls "subjective truth, inwardness," meaning the attitudes and beliefs of the individual person, those by which he lives. Because they concentrate almost exclusively on *subjective* consciousness, existentialists not only show little or no interest in science, but often feel a disdain for it, that is, for the *objective*, systematized truth about nature and man.

Origin of Existentialism

Existentialism can best be understood as both an ideological protest and a reaction to contemporary events. The protest started with Kierkegaard's deeply felt opposition to Hegel's system-building, rationalistic "philosophy of pure thought." Although contemporary philosophy shows less interest in system-building, it is accused as well of having abandoned the real concerns of man. Twentieth-century philosophy seems to concentrate on the minute problems of formalistic analysis which are of interest only to other philosophers. Its technical aspects reinforce the impression that it lacks interest in issues that are alive, in things that matter. It has thus become as incomprehensible to

laymen as the scientific specialties. It is charged with being divorced from everyday life, with remaining silent when we ask:
What is happening to man? Why do we exist? Why does the
world exist? Has the philosopher, in his ivory tower, nothing to
say about the forlornness of the individual, his strivings, failures
and atomized existence? He seems to adhere all too faithfully to
Wittgenstein's dicta: "The solution of the problem of life is seen
in the vanishing of this problem," and "Whereof one cannot
speak, thereof one must be silent." The existentialist disapproves
of this silence and intellectualized narrowness, which seems to
leave man bereft in the face of the urgency of his problems. Actually, almost all thoughtful people everywhere are asking ultimate questions and have feelings of *Weltschmerz* and anxiety, the
empiricist philosopher as well as the existentialist. However, the
way the empiricist deals with these problems differs greatly from
the existentialist's, and he in his turn wonders whether the pon-
derous philosophic tomes of the existentialists are any less cerebral, and whether they really offer balm to man's suffering soul.

Another protest against academic philosophy, and against
theology as well, came from Nietzsche. One of the problems he
raised was that of the meaning of human existence in a world
that had suffered the death of God. With the death of God "the
tables of the good" are broken, and we face "the great sickness,
the great nausea." In opposition to the traditional morality of
objective rules he proclaimed the heroic morality of the sovereign individual. These Nietzschean ideas, though they leave us in
moral uncertainty, are central in existentialism.

Contemporary existentialism also developed as a reaction to
the holocaust of the two World Wars and the political and economic problems that beset Europe as an aftermath of these wars.
It is a philosophy of crisis. Heidegger's magnum opus, *Being and
Time*, appeared in 1927, after Germany's defeat in the First
World War and the postwar inflation which impoverished the
German middle class. Sartre's first existentialist work, *Nausea*, a
philosophic novel dealing with its hero's boredom, melancholy,
absurdity, nothingness, appeared in 1938, at a time when the
shadow of Hitler's bloody dictatorship, power drive and anti-
Semitism darkened the skies over Europe and, only two years
before the defeat and occupation of France. Sartre and Camus
fought together in the French underground, trying to undermine Hitler's hold on France. Camus' first novel, *The Stranger*,

dealing with a totally alienated individual, appeared in 1942. The world has not been at rest since 1914. It has been a long period of turmoil, of political catastrophes and economic uncertainties, and the end is not yet in sight.

Finally, existentialism is a reaction to and revolt against the "dehumanization and objectivation" (Tillich) of man in our modern technical society, which frustrates and demoralizes him. Modern mass society isolates the individual in the very midst of the rootless crowds of the big cities.

> [Existentialism is the] protest of the free individual against all that threatens or seems to threaten his unique position as . . . a free subject who, though a being in the world and so a part of nature, at the same time stands out from the background of nature. (Frederick Copleston, S.J.)

Our existence has become a riddle to us, so the argument goes, as it has lost all meaning. After the death of God we are alone, without bearings, and our life is a brief, "absurd" event in a limitless, unfeeling universe. "The man who has seen the death of God . . . cries out: 'Do we not now wander through an endless Nothingness?' " (William Barrett quoting Nietzsche) The individual is helpless and meaningless. Despairing, he is overwhelmed by the maelstrom of history, for, with the collapse of all political utopias, social and political activity seems to be futile. Yet existentialists have failed to offer any new, valid goals; though some have gone beyond the limits of their existential thinking and turned to Marxism or humanism.

Existentialism, Naturalism and Psychology

Notwithstanding the great difference in language, method, content and spirit between existentialism and contemporary naturalism, as twentieth-century philosophies they share certain very basic characteristics. Neither naturalism nor existentialism is interested in great rational systems describing the metaphysical order of the universe, such as philosophers in the past worked out. The main reason for this is the fact that numerous problems which used to be the subject of speculative metaphysics are now dealt with by scientific investigation. In this development the idea of a transcendent ultimate real—of God or of things-in-themselves—beyond the material world has gradually been given up by most philosophers, except religious thinkers, whether existential or not.*

The world view, not only of naturalistic philosophy, but also of nonreligious existentialism, is colored with secularism. French existentialists acknowledge this ("God is dead") and German existentialists imply it. There is only this world, here, into which we are born ("thrown") and from which we must depart without hope of immortality.

Existentialists have another reason for not being interested in systems that embrace the totality of the universe: their attention is focused on the problems of human existence. Existentialism deals with the concerns of the individual. As each individual is a unique being, possessing both rational and irrational traits, existentialists claim that he ought not to be and cannot be forced into the strait jacket of a structured, orderly system.† They adhere tenaciously to Kierkegaard's assertion: "An existential system is impossible. [It] cannot be formulated." It is almost as if the world of nature and of science, medicine, technology and exploration does not exist for existentialism. It is, therefore, even in its aims only a partial, incomplete philosophy.

Existentialism is mainly concerned with two questions. First, there is the matter of the individual's ethical problems: it enjoins man to strive for authenticity. Second, the existentialists offer an analysis of man's being-in-the-world (Heidegger's expression). To describe "the different modes of state-of-mind" (Heidegger), "certain basic human moods" (Barrett), "to embrace from the inside the total human condition" (Sartre), we must of necessity examine ourselves and other men. However, this study cannot be conducted speculatively or philosophically; it can only be carried out empirically, even though existentialists may call their analyses and their particular treatment phenomenological or ontological. To point out the factual character of studies of man may seem a trivial observation, but it is basic for understanding the principal preoccupation of existentialists. Some of the same empirical matters are treated by clinical psychologists, others by social psychologists, anthropologists and

* Heidegger, Jaspers and Sartre continue to use the ambiguous term "transcendent," but its meaning has changed because it refers to a dimension in human awareness.

† The orderliness of natural science and of naturalistic philosophy does not deprive the individual of his uniqueness or of his humanity.

EXISTENTIALISM   365

sociologists—by people like Freud, Fromm, Riesman—whose
writings are of interest to general readers and, of course, by
innumerable others. Is existentialism, then, in so far as it deals
with nonethical problems, not philosophy at all, but rather a
branch of or a special kind of psychology or anthropology?

Whether we should regard the nonethical writings of the
existentialists as philosophy at all is a semantic question and depends on how far we wish to extend the realm of philosophy. If
we identify philosophy with world view, then anything that
serves as a building block for a modern world view may be regarded as a part of philosophy. This would also apply to scientific findings of astronomy and biology, of psychology and
anthropology, which are components of our world view. However, if we define philosophy more narrowly, then psychology
and anthropology must be classified as natural or social sciences.
Therefore, existentialism, since it examines the existence and condition of man, belongs among the sciences, surprising as this may
seem.

Certain key terms of existentialism bear out the psychological character of this "philosophy." The titles of several of
Kierkegaard's books contain some of them: *The Sickness unto
Death* ("despair is the sickness unto death"), *Fear and Trem-
bling, The Concept of Dread*. Other key terms are alienation,
anguish, anxiety, bad faith, boredom, care, forebodings, nausea
(as the feeling of absurdity, boredom, forlornness). All of these
express psychological concepts. One of Heidegger's main themes
is our anxiety in the knowledge that our *Dasein* [personal ex-
istence] is "Being-towards-death." Jaspers coined the term
"boundary situations" for dread, conflict, guilt, suffering and
awareness of death. Sartre emphasizes nausea and the sense of
nothingness.* Most of Camus' *The Myth of Sisyphus* deals with
man's feelings of absurdity.

Because it stresses somber and desperate moods and feelings
and the inner turmoil which men may experience, existentialism
has been regarded as a philosophy of weariness, as "an anatomy
of melancholy." "We are by nature unhappy consciousnesses
without any possibility of escaping from our unhappy state."
(Sartre, quoted by Anthony Manser)[6] This is probably one reason for existentialism's appeal in a turbulent and destructive

* The table of contents of Sartre's *Being and Nothingness* shows his preoccupation with psychology.

world. Affirmative concepts—love, idealism, beauty and happiness—are absent,* but satisfaction, beauty, enjoyment and pleasure have by no means been eliminated from human life. Existentialism is reflected in Picasso's *Guernica*, not in a sunny landscape by Cézanne, yet both are symbolic of our existence. Abraham Kaplan rightly criticizes existentialism for asserting "as fundamental for the human being not joy, but sorrow; not passion, but boredom; not understanding, but self-consciousness." [7] Both despair and contentment have their roots in individual inclinations and momentary experiences, influenced by the temper of the prevailing culture; they cannot be ascribed to the ontology of human existence.

Kaplan further points out that the existentialist "at bottom really [is] a kind of amateur literary psychologist." While the existentialist makes assertions, he submits no tests, he offers no clinical data, he does not investigate whether his personal impressions apply widely to his contemporaries as well as to men of other ages and cultures. Nevertheless, his often acute and fascinating psychological insights mark him as a rather sensitive and perceptive, although perhaps alienated, observer.

The assumption that anxiety, alienation, guilt ("*Dasein* as such is guilty" [Heidegger]) are inevitable features of all human existence deprives these terms of their specific meaning. The allegation that men as such are guilty does not erase the distinction between the guilt of Hitler, of President Kennedy's assassin, or of a bank robber, and the "existential guilt" of most men, who are not criminals. Our language must be able to express the distinction between guilt and innocence. If anxiety is a quality of the existence of all men, how are we to describe the special condition of the pathologically disturbed person? New terms would have to be invented to clarify the muddled moral and psychological vocabulary. Though all men may be guilty and anxious in some metaphysical sense, we must not lose sight of the fact that there are innocent people, as well as guilty ones, emotionally well-balanced people as well as neurotics.† These distinctions are important for ordinary discourse, as well as for psychologists and

---

* This is not true of some of Camus' works, for example, *Summer in Algiers* and also *The Plague*.

† We encountered a similar misuse of language in Chapter III, in the discussion of the statements "Maybe everything is an illusion," etc.

moralists. Because existentialist usage does not recognize them, it is difficult to say exactly what existentialists mean.

Existentialists tend to condemn traditional philosophers for overlooking the uniqueness of the individual and his loneliness. That each individual stands alone is in a sense a truism and presents no problem: an individual is an individual. However, the feeling of loneliness which we may at times experience is a matter for psychology, not for philosophy. It is doubtful whether existentialist philosophy has done anything to overcome man's loneliness or any of his other existential difficulties.

The uniqueness of each individual is self-evident, but it can be exaggerated; after all, people do share many traits. Existentialists do not and cannot bring to life the individuality of the concretely existing individual, as theoretical discussion, whether scientific or philosophic—existential as well as traditional—requires generalization. Existentialist "philosophy" examines man, not individual men. Only novels,* plays, biographies, diaries, or case studies can deal with particular people. While criticizing the abstractions of academic philosophy as lifeless, the existentialists have developed schemes which are different, but certainly no less abstract and general and, in addition, they are often exceedingly complex and murky.

Some existentialist writing is pervaded by the romantic disappointment that it is impossible for philosophy to encompass human existence. Existentialism comes close to life only to the extent that it becomes psychology. But thinking is thinking; it never can become life.

> To exist is simply *to be there*.

> The world of explanation and reason is not the world of existence. (Sartre, *Nausea*)

Existentialist Ethics

Freedom and authenticity† are the basic ideas of existentialist ethics. "I choose, therefore I am," writes Jaspers, existentially transforming Descartes' famous "Cogito, ergo sum" (I think,

---

* "The novel is the one bright book of life. Books are not life. . . . But the novel . . . can make the whole man alive tremble" (D. H. Lawrence).

† Authenticity is the quality of being true to the beliefs and goals that emanate from the core of each individual's personality.

therefore I am). "I *am* my freedom," Orestes proclaims in
Sartre's *The Flies*. Man is a nothing, according to Sartre, till he
forges his life through his own free choices. "Be what you
choose to be!" Sophocles' Antigone proclaimed more than two
thousand years ago. Modern stress on creative freedom through
which we transcend our everydayness originated with Nietzsche: "The child is innocence and forgetting, a new beginning.
. . . For the game of creation . . . a sacred 'yes' is needed:
the spirit now wills his own will. . . ."

Existentialists lay great stress on personal moral posture and
on the task of conducting life in accordance with one's own free
decisions. Our fate depends on us. It is a truism that we make our
own decisions; no one else can do it for us. Most people are more
or less clearly aware of the importance of their choices as they
affect—for good or ill—their everyday life, as well as the decisive points of their careers. This gift of freedom is the basis of
much soul-searching and anxiety (Heidegger's "care"). But it is
not true that each life begins with a clean, empty slate on which
we can write with complete freedom. Everyone is dependent on
"the 'material' of one's life, one's dispositions, station in life, intellectual and emotional resources as they are at any moment
'given'." (R. Hepburn) Each life has a past and an outer and
inner environment. We are therefore not as unlimited in our potential or as absolutely free as some of the existentialists would
have us believe. Encouraged as well as restricted by these given
conditions, we acquire certain characteristics which make it possible to predict our actions to some extent. While we have the
freedom to choose the path we will follow and to change to another, actually only the exceptional man has the capability and
courage to give a new turn to his life. Moreover, in making decisions we cannot overlook the consequences which our acting or
failure to act will have on our own future life and on that of our
family and others whom our action touches. We live in a society
and we should adhere to the basic standards set by that society;
otherwise society will end our freedom and creativity by imprisoning or killing us.

The goal of our existential freedom ought to be authenticity. We ought to strive to live in accordance with our own real
being. We ought to have "the courage to be as oneself" (Tillich)
—but should it be the courage of a gangster or that of a self-
sacrificing idealist? We must be honest with ourselves and not lie

to ourselves in "bad faith" (Sartre) about our true nature and our motives.* But how can we distinguish our authentic, genuine selves from the unauthentic though deeply felt deception? There is no shortcut to "Know thyself!" and we are left without counsel in the midst of the complications and contradictions of our uncertainties and neuroses.

In a way, we are thrown back to old Polonius' admonition: "To thine own self be true." Our individual integrity should be our foremost aim. Our decisions ought not to be superficial and thoughtless. ". . . it is not so much a question of choosing the right as of the energy, the earnestness, the pathos with which one chooses." (Kierkegaard)

We must have the "resoluteness" (Heidegger) to live up to the full potentialities of our being. Therefore, we ought not unauthentically to follow the crowd or our peers or lazily adopt the conventional—"nauseating"—life of the society into which we have been born. It shall not be said of us: "One comes along, one finds a life, ready-made, one only has to put it on." (Rainer Maria Rilke) Existentialists try to prod us to a realization of the urgency of our choices: In his "being-toward-death" (Heidegger) man is granted only this one life, which he must endeavor to use solely for his own *essential* purposes. All existentialists agree wholeheartedly with the fashionable, and to a considerable extent justified, deprecation of modern technological, mass society, its conventionality, its leveling effect. They urge us to rebel † against this society, but they leave us in the dark as to the meaning and goal of our protest, although they are too serious to proclaim mere rebelliousness. This double-pronged appeal to authentic, unconventional self-realization, and to absolute freedom and rebellion has made existentialism very attractive to young people. But other ethical thinkers have made similar appeals to which the above quotations from Sophocles, Socrates and Shakespeare bear witness.

It is a remarkable feature of existentialism that while it seeks to kindle moral ardor, it fails to give ethical guidance for authentic living. Authenticity as such is an empty notion unless it is supported by an ethical doctrine or an analysis of worthwhile ideals. In the first place, existentialists question whether the valid-

---

* The psychology of "bad faith"—"self-deception" is W. Kaufmann's translation—is one of the chief subjects of Sartre's *Being and Nothingness*.
† "I rebel—therefore we exist." (Camus in *The Rebel*)

ity of any ethics can be established at all unless we assume God as law-giver. Thus they share the theological prejudice that only God can justify ethical norms. Secondly, existentialists deny the relevance of general objective ethical rules and universal ideals because of their desire to protect individual integrity and their fear of curtailing individual freedom. Referring to *Being and Time*, a sympathetic student of Heidegger, Lazzlo Versényi, writes: "The work provides no method whereby man can be helped—let alone help himself—to grow to the full stature of authentic existence." This is also true of the other existentialists. What they fail to see is that this lack fosters moral uncertainty, if not skepticism.

From the passionate individualistic appeals of Kierkegaard and Nietzsche it is impossible to gain any idea of what human society ought to be like and what man in society ought to do in order to achieve the goal of individual development. A similar detachment from social reality is apparent in Heidegger. But Sartre and Camus have been politically active, fighting for justice and for antifascist, democratic, or communist goals. And Jaspers has searchingly examined Germany's guilt and the political developments there. While a humanitarian and humanistic atmosphere pervades most of the writings of these men, ideals are never treated in depth philosophically.* The high point of ethical development in existentialism is Dr. Rieux in Camus' novel, *The Plague*, which glorifies sacrifice and love. Indeed, Camus has been called—with considerable exaggeration—"the conscience of our time."

Religious Existentialism

In their call for authenticity, religious existentialists emphasize the challenge of authentic belief—belief "as oneself." They do not represent a unified school: they have proclaimed various ideologies, depending on their religious affiliation, their philosophy and their theology.[8] Their distinguishing characteristic is stress on the inwardness of religious experience, which cannot be found in the mechanical, depersonalized religion of the institutionalized churches. Religion can arise only out of the divine encounter with the living God, out of personal experience of and

* At the end of *Being and Nothingness* Sartre indicated that he planned to "devote . . . a future work" to ethics. But it has remained unwritten.

dialogue with the Thou. Religion requires involvement of each individual in God's work.

But what happens to belief in the events reported in the Old and New Testament, to theology, to religious tradition? Even if we tone down the creedal element of religion or transmute it through radical demythologizing, certain central beliefs ought to remain—God as creator, ruler and law-giver—otherwise existentialist religion becomes atheistic existentialism, or humanism. Thus, religious existentialism shares the difficulties of religious belief which we have discussed and, in addition, suffers from the weaknesses of existentialism, particularly its subjectivity and obscurity.

Difficulties of Existentialism

At the present time, when many thoughtful people cannot find meaning in religion and regard a humanistic ethics not merely as old-fashioned but as a failure, existentialism has been eagerly probed in the hope that it may offer a modern personal philosophy of life. But, not one definite attitude toward life can be found among the several existentialists. Moreover, no conclusions about the value of man's life can be drawn from the existentialist emphasis on the contingency of man's existence and from an analysis of his psychological condition and extreme experiences. The contingency of our existence makes life neither meaningless nor absurd.

The question of the meaning of man's life cannot be solved without a full recognition of values and disvalues. True, authenticity—deeply felt sincerity and searching honesty—is an important value, but it does not provide us with a guide for the problems of life and give meaning to it. Nor is it sufficient to stress that it is the task of each individual to give fulfillment to his life. Existentialism, therefore, fails us in our search for the solution of personal dilemmas and for life's meaning, which is considered by many to be one of the most pressing philosophic and spiritual problems.

The student of the philosophic—not the literary—works of the existentialists is further disappointed by their obscurity. Precision of thought, sharp outlines and the avoidance of vagueness, which distinguish the works of the classical as well as most modern English-speaking philosophers are disregarded in the wordy and oracular expositions of "the rival high-priests of existentialism." (Henri Peyre) Existentialism prides itself on being able to address modern man, but its philosophy is couched in an abstruse language, for which a decoding key is difficult, if not impossible, to find. Forty years ago Gilbert Ryle said of *Being and Time*: ". . . Many of his [Heidegger's] conclusions for lack of comprehension I must abandon unexpounded." It is ironic that more recently the same American philosopher, James K. Feibleman, who described Heidegger's *Being and Time* as "the most important philosophical work to come out of Europe in this century," characterized it as "in a sense almost unintelligible."

"Being" or "Nothingness," concepts which play no role in empiricist philosophy, are key terms for existentialist philosophers. The "question of Being" is the central problem of Heidegger's work, but what "Being" is remains an enigma. "Being is something which 'there is' only in so far as truth is. And truth *is* only in so far and as long as *Dasein* is." The second sentence is merely a truism. It is the first sentence that raises troublesome questions: Does it mean that the being of the universe is dependent upon our truthful knowledge of it? Or that "there is no other universe than the human universe, the universe of human subjectivity," as Sartre has written? Is the universe, then, our creation? Perhaps not, for Heidegger also makes the strange assertion "Man is the shepherd of Being."

Nothing and nothingness are equally puzzling. They are negations and indicate the absence of whatever entities are under discussion. For existentialists, however, "nothing" and "nothingness" also stand for psychological concern with this absence; they stand for death and fear of death, and, finally, they seem to be a kind of active force. "Nothing is that which makes the revelation of things as such possible for our human existence. . . ." And this statement of Heidegger's is followed by the much derided: "It is in the Being (*Sein*) of the things-that-are that the nihilation of Nothing (*das Nichten des Nichts*) occurs." [9]

Being and nothing are not special entities or realms, whose characteristics we can investigate and about which we can make descriptive statements. There is no basic ground ("Being") which all existing entities have in common and of which we can ask: What is Being?

It is a common error to assume that when we cannot under-stand a difficult argument, it is because of our lack of intelligence or the esoteric nature of the subject matter. However, the reason could lie in the fallaciousness or the sheer incomprehensibility of the reasoning. Clear writing is a moral matter. It prevents decep-tion of the writer and of the reader and the expenditure of time and effort in the interpretation of obscurities. Heidegger's "ab-stractitis" * is one of the main reasons why the study of his enor-mous philosophic output has developed into a special cult among certain devotees and why his, as well as Jaspers' and Sartre's ar-guments have found so little echo in philosophic circles in Eng-land and the United States.

There is another important reason why naturalistic philoso-phers pay scant attention to existentialist philosophy. They doubt whether existentialists have clarified any philosophic problems or contributed anything significantly new in the way of insights beyond their sometimes stimulating, though one-sided and subjective, psychological observations.

One of Sartre's best known philosophic ideas—"existence precedes essence"—is a typical example of a "discovery" which hides trivial notions. Sartre claims that

> [Man is the] one being whose existence comes before its es-sence, a being which exists before it can be defined by any conception of it. . . . We mean that man first of all exists, en-counters himself, surges up in the world—and defines himself afterwards. (*Existentialism Is a Humanism*)

Expressed in less abstract language, what Sartre has in mind is that the individual person must exist in his actual uniqueness *before* we can think about him in general abstract terms (es-sences). However, if we know that a certain being is a man, we already know a great deal about him, namely, those essences which he shares with all other men. Although we do not know the particulars of his existence, we know that he has two legs and two arms, that he can think, feel, act and so on. We do not know what his special qualities are or what he has made of himself un-

* "A writer uses abstract words because his thoughts are cloudy; the habit of using them clouds his thoughts still further; he may end by concealing his meaning not only from his readers but also from himself." H. W. Fowler, *A Dictionary of Modern English Usage* (2nd rev. ed.; New York: Oxford Uni-versity Press, 1965).

less we are acquainted with the actually existing individual. This is not only obvious, it is also a fact that applies to all other objects, such as dogs, houses, or pictures, where there are individual differences between members of the same class. In other words, we know the essences of a thing if we know what class it belongs to. We can know the particular specifications of the individual object only when it appears before us.*

Existentialists have surrounded the ordinary, though important, facts of life with a philosophic aura of complexity and mystery. We need no philosopher to tell us that our whole being (except for our own free choices) is contingent. We are "thrown" into this world without any desire or effort on our part, we do not control the time and nature of our death except when we commit suicide, and we come into a preexisting and ongoing world that is not arranged for our particular benefit. Nor do we need a philosopher to tell us that we deal with tools ("ready-to-hand equipment") and with other persons ("being-with-one-another") and that their relation to us affects us deeply, nor that we anxiously look "ahead" of ourselves into the unpredictable future and to our own death.[10] Our experience with these immutable facts creates many epistemological, emotional, ethical and spiritual problems with which philosophers have dealt. This is also the material that has inspired poets, artists and musicians, as well as religious thinkers and mystics. It is questionable whether contemporary existentialists have made any contribution in the presentation and clarifications of the problems with which life and death present us that surpasses, or even equals that of the Bible, Shakespeare, Pascal's Pensées, or the writings of Kierkegaard and Nietzsche, or the works of many great novelists. Existentialist philosophy has the reputation of being "of much value for opening the eyes of materialists to inward things" (Austin Farrer), which seem to be neglected by science and by naturalistic or rational philosophy. It is supposed also to deepen our encounter with the ultimate questions, which mystify many men because they wonder how to go about finding answers. Every human being experiences the joys and agonies of

* The problem of existence and essence has a long tradition in the history of philosophy. See Alasdair MacIntyre's chapter on existentialism in *A Critical History of Western Philosophy*, edited by D. J. O'Connor (New York: Free Press, 1964). This problem is not regarded as meaningful by contemporary empiricists.

"inward things" and the puzzling ultimate questions, although the intensity with which he does depends on his sensitivity and thoughtfulness. Whose eyes are opened by the stilted prose of the existentialists? Here art and literature speak louder than any philosophy can.

CHAPTER XIV

On Ultimate Questions and the Meaning of Life

> To everything there is a season . . .
> A time to weep, and a time to laugh,
> A time to mourn, and a time to dance. . . .
> —ECCL. 3:1–4

In this final chapter I want to consider the ultimate questions,* those basic and fundamental questions regarding the meaning of the universe and of life. What is it all about? What does it all mean? Do our lives make sense? Is it worth all the struggle? As neither science nor religion are of help, we wonder how we can find answers to the things that trouble us, particularly to such a nebulous query as what is it all about? In fact, are these real questions at all, or are they expressions of puzzlement and disquiet? Whatever these questions may mean, they are as old as literature and philosophy, and are asked at some time by most thinking persons.

The Meaningfulness of Nature as Such

While sitting at my desk and mulling over these problems, I looked out the window. It was a cool, unfriendly November day. The flowers were gone; the grass had lost its green luster; the trees were bare and presented a chaos of intertwining

* Prologue, p. 12, chapter I, p. 17.

branches. The lively children who played ball in the yard had disappeared.

I connected what I saw with the questions I had been thinking about. What did this sad landscape signify? Sadness—mortality—emptiness. Where are the men and women who hopefully planted the trees near my house? What happened to the settlers who first looked at the large old oak at the end of the garden? And, still further back in time, I thought of the Indians who roamed over this land when it was still primeval forest.

The wintry, bare environment was meaningful for me. But does it have other, perhaps universal, significance? And what of all the people who lived here before me? They are forgotten, as are the Indians; no one remembers their names. I realized that I, too, will be forgotten in another three generations, just as my great-grandparents have become mere names in family documents and on gravestones. One must ask again, what is it all about? Vanity? Nothingness?

Would my mood have been different on a pleasant day in May, with the fruit trees in full bloom under a blue sky and the yard full of happy children? Would my thoughts have turned to death, oblivion and nothingness? Death is an inescapable finality, terminating everything. But must it mean nothingness? Can anything or anyone who has existed or exists now really be considered a nothing?

We must take a hard look at these ultimate questions. First, let us take a specific case, and apply our questions to the oak tree. What does it mean, what does it signify *as such?* What is its purpose? The qualifying words "as such" are important; they indicate that I consider the oak tree merely as a physical entity apart from its relation to me and to others.

The oak tree is a natural phenomenon and as such it seems to have no meaning and to signify nothing more than that it is there. It began a long time ago, but some day it will disappear, dissolving into the chemical elements from which it grew. It is useful to squirrels, birds, insects, as well as mosses, lichens and germs which live on it and in it. Its wood may be useful to us. But *as such* it has no purpose. I repeat, it is just there.

If we believed in the presence of a Divinity in the cosmos, of a God who cared about every single part of His world and planned its role, or if we assumed that all natural events were parts of a universal, meaningful order—links of a "great chain of being"—the oak tree would be part of an ultimate realm of values. But from the point of view of naturalist philosophy these are idle assumptions: the oak tree simply *is*, one aspect of an unending sequence in accordance with natural laws.

Looking at the beautiful and venerable oak tree, we may hesitate to say that it lacks meaning and significance. However, we are less reluctant to accept the meaninglessness of stones at the foot of the oak tree or of the rocks nearby. And if we contemplate the millions or billions of jellyfish bobbing up and down in the oceans, or the legions of crawling, burrowing, flying insects, the uncountable grains of sand covering the beaches and bottoms of the oceans, or the trillions upon trillions of distant stars, we find it easier to accept their mere being, their meaninglessness, their lack of significance and purpose.

What is true of the creatures and material objects in the universe is equally true of the universe as a whole. The universe as such is meaningless and without significance. Does it have a purpose? Can we ask: For what reason is there a universe? "Why is there any being at all and not rather nothing?"—Heidegger's well-known question.*[1] Like the oak tree, the universe as such and being as such have no purpose at all. No reason, either good or bad, can be given for its existence; it just is. The nature of nature is to be. Consequently, when contemporary would-be metaphysicians raise the question of the ground of being (often written Ground of Being) and try to solve "the riddle of existence" the answer must be silence.†

The ultimate meaninglessness and purposelessness of the universe follows from the meaning of the words "meaning," "significance," "purpose." The nature of these words will become clearer after a brief digression to consider a simple challenge that laymen often regard as a difficult "philosophic" puzzle: "Is there a crash when a tree falls in a forest and there is neither man nor animal to hear it?" If by "crash" we mean a certain loud *noise* and not the mere physical event of a tree falling down and causing special airwaves, then by definition a crash is impossible when there is no one to hear it. A noise is a sensory experience and can occur only when there is a human or animal perceiver. Without

---

* Similar questions have been raised by earlier philosophers. An obvious answer to Heidegger's question would be to ask: Why shouldn't a universe exist?

† I repeat the well-known last sentence of Wittgenstein's *Tractatus:* "Whereof one cannot speak, thereof one must be silent."

a perceiver there can be no noise. Similarly, the application of the three terms, "meaning," "significance," "purpose," presupposes a mind that appreciates meaning and significance and can set itself purposes, a mind that interprets, evaluates, sets goals. Without a consciousness which directs its thoughts, feelings and intentions toward the universe and its parts, there is no meaning, no significance, no purpose.

"Purpose" is occasionally used instead of "function." The function of a dam, a traffic sign, or an airplane is equivalent to the purpose for which human beings made it. Men have a purpose. But we also use "purpose" when it does not involve intent. We speak of the purpose (i.e., function) of biological processes and organs which are necessary for the health and survival of living things. They function as though they were purposeful. However, they have developed in the course of evolution without any deliberate design. In this respect, these processes and organs are no different from geological or astronomical developments. It is not the purpose of the moon to inspire poets and lovers, nor of the oceans to offer a congenial habitat to certain plants and animals, nor of trout to tantalize and delight fishermen. It is not the intended aim of eyes to see, of wings to make flight possible, and of hearts, lungs and kidneys to function as they do. Neither animals, including man, nor plants have been cast in the role of purposeful engineers or builders in natural growing processes.

If relation to a mind is a prerequisite for the possibility of raising meaningful meaning-questions, then according to most modern philosophers it makes no sense to think of the meaning of the oak tree or of the universe as such. Instead of saying the universe has no meaning, we might say the problem of the meaning of the universe has no meaning. The terms "meaning," "significance," "purpose" cannot be applied to things as such. Statements about the meaning of objects as such, even if they are syntactically correct and therefore seem meaningful, actually have no meaning. Let me make this clear through an analogy. The non-philosophic question, "Is our oak tree making progress in learning French?" is a grammatically correct question, but it does not make sense. To answer "no" to this question is silly because the question itself is silly: "learning French" cannot be applied to oak trees. It is an open question among contemporary philosophers whether the kind of ultimate questions we are discussing should be answered by saying that things as such and the universe as such have no meaning and no purpose—they just are—or whether we should brush the questions themselves aside as being meaningless. For the layman this theoretical difference is rather unimportant.*

Perhaps the misguided "ardor for answering the unanswerable" is a characteristically Western trait. "The Chinese were content to leave the unknowable alone." (Herbert J. Muller) Western man, however, finds it difficult to accustom himself to intellectual modesty and stop asking "improper questions." He cannot "restrain that instinct which urges man to wish to know." (Unamuno)† "It may be that Tolstoy was right in saying that certain great questions are put to mankind not that men should answer them but that they should go on forever trying." (Alexander Cowie) ‡ ²

It would be pleasant to be able to think that we inhabit a purposeful, good universe, which can provide a home and anchor for human ideals. We would like "to feel at home in the world as something more than a chance product of a chance system." (John Canaday) Many manifestations of the universe strike us as beautiful and inspire in us feelings of admiration, awe, mysteriousness. How can it be that my majestic oak tree, a lovely sunset, a busy anthill, the starry sky are accidental and have no meaning? However, we must not let our "emotional sensibilities"

* The meaninglessness or unanswerability of these meaning-questions is the reason that naturalistic philosophers have paid little attention to "ultimate questions." This field has been left to existentialists, theologians, psychiatrists and essayists. However, the questions presented here are thoroughly discussed in two articles by Paul Edwards: "Life, Meaning and Value of" and "Why" in *The Encyclopedia of Philosophy*, ed. Paul Edwards (New York: Macmillan, Free Press, 1967). Reference is made also to two other contemporary philosophic treatments: Kurt Baier's lecture, "The Meaning of Life," the larger part of which is reprinted in *20th-Century Philosophy: The Analytic Tradition*, edit. by Morris Weitz (New York: Free Press, 1966, paperback), and Kai Nielsen's essay, "Linguistic Philosophy and 'The Meaning of Life,'" *Cross Currents* (summer 1964).

† These "ultimate questions" may very well be distressing challenges expressing "a personal predicament, . . . anxiety, fear . . . hope, despair." (Nielsen)

‡ The English philosopher Stuart Hampshire expressed a similar thought in his book *Spinoza, op. cit.*: "However cautious and empirical we may become, we will naturally sometimes pause to ask extravagantly general and all-embracing questions about the design of the world and about our place within it, if only because we cannot know what is, and is not, answerable until we have proposed the question."

bewitch us into making intellectual claims which, in reality, are visions and dreams if not merely empty words.

Any idealizing view can, of course, be contradicted by considering the ugly, destructive features of the universe. Nature in the raw is not beneficent; it does not purposefully concern itself with the welfare of its children, be they stars that explode or forests that are destroyed by lightning. Nor should we overlook the fact that looking at the world through rose-tinted spectacles is not a universal human characteristic. There are melancholics, and the slum-dwelling and famine-ridden peoples of the world may not appreciate the beauty and inspiration of nature.

Our modern anti-romantic disposition to look at the "shape of things through a glass clouded by anguish and fear" pervades Matthew Arnold's well-known lines from "Dover Beach":

> . . . the world, which seems
> To lie before us like a land of dreams,
> So various, so beautiful, so new,
> Hath really neither joy, nor love nor light,
> Nor certitude, nor peace, nor help for pain.

Thus, it has come about that the words "meaningless," "purposeless," "without significance," when applied to the world, have acquired peculiar, deplorable, hostile overtones. While the naturalist philosopher ascribes no meaning, i.e., *zero* meaning, to the universe, the feeling is widespread that this absence of meaning has a large negative dimension, or disvalue: we talk as if the universe owes us special consideration but fails to live up to its obligations. It is quite the thing to say that the world is "absurd," "a nothingness," but this observation is itself absurd. It is completely unreasonable to find fault with the universe for just being there, as it is, and for not paying any attention to our values. The fact that neither common sense nor science and philosophy can assure us that the universe is purposeful and "mindful of human aspirations," [3] does not make the universe or our activities in it absurd and our life futile, nor does it make philosophy useless.

When we wonder about the meaning of the universe, we should keep in mind what I pointed out in the very first chapter; that we cannot venture "beyond space and time" and should not waste our efforts trying to find truth "about something strangely beyond the ken of man . . ."

Man as a Creature of Nature

What are we finally to say about man as such—man as a creature of nature? Let us begin with Unamuno's urgent questions:

> Whence do I come and whence comes the world in which and by which I live? Whither do I go and whither goes everything that environs me? What does it all mean? (*Tragic Sense of Life*)[4]

Modern man tries to answer the first four of these questions through scientific investigation. We cannot easily overstate the extent to which science has displaced religious and metaphysical speculation about man's fate and thus fundamentally changed modern man's perspective on the ultimate questions. Nevertheless, large groups still remain untouched by this intellectual transformation, although it has been slowly at work since the days of Galileo.

What does it all mean as far as man is concerned? Man *as such*, as a creature of the universe shares its meaninglessness, if we disregard for the moment any meaning, significance and purpose that he may give to entities, including himself. He is there, purposeless as other parts of nature. Each man *as such* is just one of the many objects in the cosmos, an "it," to whom we can apply the same pronoun we use for all other objects. As Dylan Thomas wrote, man is "earth of the earth, his body earth, his hair a wild shrub growing out of the land."

This seeming dethronement of man has been a strong stimulus for modern writers to apply the senseless verbiage of "absurdity" and "nothingness," not just to the universe, but also to man. Man is called an absurd being in an absurd universe. It is, of course, quite in order to oppose the characterization of man as an "it," a mere creature, for he is indeed a meaning-giving, purposeful, acting "I." * We will deal with this aspect of our existence presently.

Man's natural fate was described in rather stark though poetic language by the young Bertrand Russell in a frequently cited passage:

* The "I"-quality of man does not put him outside the realm of nature. Our mental capacities, which are the reason for our self-identification as an I and which enable us to act purposefully, are an evolutionary development, unique but within nature.

> That Man is the product of causes which had no prevision of
> the end they were achieving; that his origin, his growth, his
> hopes and fears, his loves and his beliefs, are but the outcome
> of accidental collocations of atoms; that no fire, no heroism,
> no intensity of thought and feeling, can preserve an individual
> life beyond the grave; that all the labours of the ages, all the
> devotion, all the inspiration, all the noonday brightness of
> human genius, are destined to extinction in the vast death of
> the solar system, and that the whole temple of Man's achieve-
> ment must inevitably be buried beneath the débris of a universe
> in ruins—all these things, if not quite beyond dispute, are yet
> so nearly certain, that no philosophy which rejects them can
> hope to stand. Only within the scaffolding of these truths, only
> on the firm foundation of unyielding despair, can the soul's
> habitation henceforth be safely built.*

It is one feature of the *condition of man* to live a brief time
(astronomically and geologically speaking) on a minor planet,
which eventually will become uninhabitable and which still later
will probably cease to exist. However, humanity *may* continue
to exist for millions of years, much longer than it has existed thus
far. In astronomical terms, every one of us is a brief passing
event, and what we have done and accomplished individually
and collectively will eventually totally disappear. These are
facts. How we look at them and feel about them is an entirely
different matter, but one of central importance in the consideration of the meaning of life. Measured on a human scale, we live a
long time; there are 25,500 days and nights in the proverbial
threescore and ten years, during which, even in the most hum-
drum life, a great deal happens and which necessitates innumerable decisions.

Like many plants and animals, man propagates through sexual intercourse. According to some saints, sex is the greatest mistake in creation, but nature obviously does not agree, for it has
surrounded our reproductive life with the pleasures of love and

* From the essay, "A Free Man's Worship," reprinted in *Mysticism and
Logic* (Garden City: Doubleday Anchor, 1957, paperback), which Russell
wrote in 1903 when he was thirty-one years old. Russell steps beyond value-
neutral description when he speaks of "the firm foundation of unyielding despair," thereby anticipating a very modern characterization. In later years
Russell changed his pessimistic tone and became more interested in happiness, as
the title of one of his later books, *The Conquest of Happiness*, indicates. Although I am running ahead of myself, I want to add here that Russell on another occasion wrote: "When intellectuals question if life be worth living while
gardeners feel no doubt of it, it looks as if intellectuals had still something to
learn from gardeners, for *so long as life seems worth living, worth living it is*."
(My italics)

love-making. It is a momentous consequence of the life-preserving force of our biological nature that even when birth control can prevent pregnancy and when abortion is permitted, most people prefer to have several children. Of course, environment, economic factors and community pressure also play a role. The spontaneous pleasure most of us feel when engagements, weddings, pregnancies and births are announced in the circle of our acquaintances can be understood as an effect of what Bernard Shaw called the "life force," our animal nature. Intellectually considered, family formation may seem "absurd"—who knows what misery one's children may bring into one's life? Should not the wise man stay away from women and children, as some philosophers have actually suggested? This is, I submit, an inadequate goal, like those already discussed in chapter X. "To deny that one is an animal is to reduce oneself to half a man," Cicero says in Thornton Wilder's *The Ides of March*.

We are not asked whether we want to be born, "thrown" into this world. Men have often complained that "not to be born is good." (Eccl. 4:3)* A contemporary French author recently wrote:

> If you really want to know, I'd rather not have been born at all. I find life very tiring. The thing is done now, of course, and I can't alter it. But there will always be this regret at the back of my mind.[5]

And in *The Condemned of Altona*, Sartre has Johanna say poignantly: "The only truth is the horror of living."

And yet these writers do not kill themselves. Suicide, in fact, is a rather unusual event.[6] In the United States about 20,000 people kill themselves each year. While this is only one-hundredth of 1% of the total population, nevertheless 20,000 suicides is a disquietingly large figure. And yet it is, I think, an astonishingly small figure, considering the troubles that beset so many people —poverty, mental and physical sickness, hunger, loneliness, old age, business reverses and imprisonment. The most remarkable aspect of suicide, however, is that suicide rates are lower among the poor, even among the hundreds of millions of starving Indian peasants and the wretched slum-dwellers who endure constant misery in and around the large cities of Asia and South America.

* Similarly, the sixth-century Greek poet Theogenis: "Not to be born at all is the happiest lot for mortal."

There are several explanations for this somewhat paradoxical behavior. The human creature has a natural will to survive— an animal drive—as well as an instinctive fear of the unknown and an abhorrence of death. "Simply the thing I am shall make me live." (Shakespeare) Lofty religious and philosophic arguments and condemnations, a call for the "courage to be," probably play no more than a secondary role. Another reason for the abhorrence of suicide is the fact that practically all civilizations disapprove of it.* There is also the harm the self-killer may inflict on his family, if any, or on associates, neighbors, and even strangers. For all these reasons those whose life is miserable and seems unbearable, go on bearing it, and those who regard life as meaningless and themselves as absurd carry on, impelled by biological life-preserving forces and embarrassment in the face of the general condemnation of suicide. Dostoevsky's belief that, "following on the loss of the idea of immortality suicide appears a complete and ineluctable necessity for every man" is quite erroneous.

The Meaning of Nature to Man

The fact of the matter is that we are *not* mere creatures. Each human being is a thinking and an evaluating person, capable of making choices. Nature and its objects have meaning for us, and each one of us is significant to himself and to others. Nature may have no purposes and goals, but we do. We cannot escape the question, "What does it all mean to us?" Although, despairing of a sensible reply, we may answer our own challenge with a shrug of the shoulders.

We view the world from various perspectives. We have considered science—the theoretical examination and explanation of what is going on and of what may happen. Here, we shall concern ourselves with the philosophic significance and value of things and persons, with our esthetic and emotional sensibility.

What does the universe mean to us when we contemplate and evaluate it? "The infinite immensity of spaces" frightened Pascal, but it does not humble others. Freud speaks of "the

* Two well-known exceptions are the ethics of the Stoics, which permitted a free choice of death, and the traditional Japanese glorification of suicide because of loss of face (hari-kiri).

awareness of our perplexity in the mysteriousness that reigns everywhere. These questions are always there." * The universe is awe-inspiring and beautiful; the universe is dreadful and cruel. How we view it depends on what we choose to see and what our personal feelings are. We admire a rainbow, high mountains, a redwood tree, a lovely butterfly. Floods, tornadoes and earthquakes throw us into a panic. What could be more cruel than the devastating plagues nature has caused? We shrink in terror from the sight of a tiger tearing apart an antelope, or a shark tearing a swimmer to pieces. There is nothing more loathsome than a dead animal crawling with maggots and insects. But this is nature. The same event or the same creature may have entirely different meanings for different people. A thunderstorm may inspire anxiety in some and humility in others.

The snake is a curious example of widely varied evaluations. It is a symbol of Satan, of wiliness and treachery; but it has also become a symbol of wisdom and healing. Some religions have looked upon the snake as an animal of good fortune and prosperity.

When we try to *understand* natural events, we look for objective truth. But when we *evaluate* nature intellectually, emotionally, or esthetically, when we look for meaning in that sense, we are outside the realm of truth.† "The great world of joy and pain" (Wordsworth) has not just one single truthful meaning, but entirely different ones at different times and for different individuals and different cultures. It is the beholder's eye that determines and shapes appreciation. Men used to regard the high passes and snow-covered mountains of the Alps merely as obstacles. That they were beautiful and majestic was "discovered" by Petrarch in the fourteenth century. Did the Dutch landscape painters of the sixteenth and seventeenth centuries see the same shiny green fields that the Impressionists painted, and are these the same as Van Gogh's turbulent fields?

---

* Man's wonder about the universe is magnificently expressed in the famous questions addressed by God to Job (Job 38–41), and the Psalmist acknowledges the twofold aspect of man's view in the well-known lines of Psalm 8:

When I behold Thy heavens . . .
The moon and the stars. . . .
What is man, that Thou art mindful of him? . . .
Yet Thou hast made him but little lower
    than the angels,
And hast crowned him with glory and honor.

† We are dealing here with what is unfortunately frequently called "subjective truth."

When the Reverend Francis Kilvert, one hundred years ago, wandered through the countryside of western England on a "beautiful autumn morning," this is what he saw:

> The luxuriant meadow grass shone green and silver with the hoary webs and sheets of dew. The hills and woods and distances were richly bloomed with azure misty veils, the sweet sudden solitary song of the robin from the hornbeam broke the morning calm, and here and there a yellow leaf, the herald of autumn, floated silently from the limes.

But no doubt there were men then who saw nothing of this and thought nothing of what they did see, like the modern motorist who drives through the countryside at top speed.

Is nature our friend or our foe? God made us "rule over the fish of the sea, the birds of the sky, and all the living things that creep on earth," and He gave us every "seed-bearing plant . . . and every tree that has seed-bearing fruit . . . for food." (Gen. 1) Most of the time man has found or raised ample food by the sweat of his brow. His habitat ranges from the freezing Arctic to steaming jungles, and he has accustomed himself to an enormous variety of conditions. Nature has also provided us with numerous and ample raw materials, which we have used to build houses for ourselves and our gods, and on which our whole technical civilization depends. We face a desperate question, however: Will nature's bounty last indefinitely or will we face the ultimate exhaustion of our water and mineral resources as a result of the population explosion and reckless waste.

But nature also injures and even destroys us. Frequently, fields are flooded or parched and crops are destroyed by swarms of locusts or other insects. Nature has created famine in many different ways. In previous millennia, large inhabited parts of the globe were covered with glaciers and other parts were deserts. The earth has been shaken by destructive earthquakes and volcanic outbursts. We have suffered hurricanes and floods that have been described in stories much older than the Bible.[7] These catastrophes are not to be understood as punishment for our sins, nor are bountiful harvests, lovely springs, magnificent scenery rewards for our excellence. "The universe is not aware that we are there." (Thornton Wilder)

Man's greatest enemy, other than death, is sickness. We have done a great deal to overcome disease, but so far we have not been able to conquer some of its worst forms. Why this terrible suffering? Why does leukemia kill a brilliant adolescent? Why does a blood clot at childbirth deprive a family of their young mother? Why did Raphael, Mozart, and Schubert die in their thirties, depriving the world of further products of their genius? These are lamentable natural happenings that befall man the creature, and it is fruitless to search for philosophic meaning where there is none. As Tolstoy has said, why try for an answer where none is forthcoming. There is only a biological explanation of a creature's fate; but though the philosopher will recommend Stoic self-control, we cannot suppress our emotional reactions, and while time is a healer, the wound, the bitter regrets, still remain. No one escapes these afflictions. "The heart of man has long been sore, and long 'tis like to be." (A. E. Housman)

The Problem of the Meaning of Man's Life

When we raise the question of the meaning of man's life, we are really thinking of several quite different problems; we have dealt with two so far, (1) the meaningless or unanswerable question of ultimate meaning, i.e., meaning apart from human evaluations, and (2) the ethical question of what the meaning of our lives ought to be, a question that permits detailed philosophic treatment.

Another set of questions concerns our actual evaluation of the meaning of the human condition. This evaluation proceeds along three different lines; we ask the meaning of human life in general, and we ask the meaning of a particular man's life. This question has two aspects: what does a man's life mean to him and finally what does it mean to others. The answers to these questions depend on our factual knowledge of what mankind and a particular period, group, or individual are like, what they have achieved or are achieving. The answers also depend on the ideological and psychological attitude of the questioners.

The objective values of humanistic ethics are one of the scales by which we measure the meaning of man's life, the significance of societies, and the significance of individual men and women. Other scales are timebound; they are the result of subjective emotional and esthetic evaluations and the changing perspective from which we view the existence of mankind as a whole and of an individual. This is beyond the realm of truthful assertions. Interpretations and an appreciation of a culture, a historical period, or a particular group and an individual life change like artistic and literary taste, fashions and ideas of feminine beauty.* Nor are they necessarily uniform through all strata of society, at any one moment in time. "We create the world we live in by our expectations and attitudes, our ideas and ideals, and the ways in which we interpret and manage our experience." [8]

A basic difficulty in assessing the significance of man is the paradox of his existence, so well stated by Shakespeare:

> What a piece of work is a man! how noble in reason! . . . in action how like an angel! . . . the beauty of the world! the paragon of animals! And yet, to me, what is the quintessence of dust?

We may share Hamlet's admiration for man, and we may wonder that a being as creative as man could come into existence through the progress of mere natural forces. Like Hamlet we are disturbed by the contradiction between man's possible nobility and the fact that he is made of mere dust, the minerals of the universe. Yet this does not necessarily diminish us.

Apart from biological factors, there is only one feature that all men share. Ethics requires that we treat each other with equal respect under equal conditions. Beyond this, it is impossible to say that there is any other single and universal significance that men have for one another. Man is a complex creature, in a constant state of tension between reason and unreason, love and hate, dedication and cowardice. Sometimes he is driven by his passions, another time he is self-controlled. He builds and he destroys. He is confident and serene, anxious and alienated. Not all men are "noble in reason," nor do they all behave nobly. The meaning people have for other people depends on propinquity; on their personalities, style of living and activities; on their economic and social relations; on the manner in which they treat each other and their fellow men. These factors determine our feelings towards other men, as well as their feelings towards us. Esthetic evaluation of physical appearance also plays an important role, particularly between the sexes. All men, individually and in groups, have meanings for themselves and for others; they are

* Johann Sebastian Bach's *Passion According to St. Matthew* was forgotten for one hundred years. During his lifetime Van Gogh's pictures found no purchasers, but now, seventy-five years later, some are worth hundreds of thousands of dollars. On the other hand, who today reads yesterday's best sellers?

not mere nothings, they are not absurd. "A simple life is its own
reward, and continually realizes its function." (Santayana) Few
people are great and important—makers of history. Most have
significance only for themselves and for a small circle who themselves are also without great significance. But no living person is
totally without meaning, even if it is only negative.

Although it is impossible to formulate general evaluations of
man, writers and thinkers have never ceased trying to do so.
They range from the Biblical glorification of man as created in
God's likeness* and Sophocles' exclamation, "Numberless are the
world's wonders, but none more wonderful than man," to T. S.
Eliot's "Men and bits of paper whirled by the cold wind." Poets
used to compare the life and nature of man to that of leaves and
flowers, but it is characteristic of our age to equate us—"the hol-
low men"—with bits of paper and to call us degraded, "bloody,
ignorant apes" and "a foul brood" (Samuel Beckett), whose lives
are lived in a "wasteland." Some ages have seen humanity mir-
rored by its heroes; today literature and art depict man as the anti-
hero. Pascal combined both extremes in a phrase of his *Pensée*,
434: Man is the "glory and refuse of the universe." We dero-
gate the stature of man, emphasize his worthlessness and his inhu-
manity to man and beast. His cruelty has never been expressed
with more bitterness than by de Maistre (1754–1821), long before the Atomic Age:

> [Man's] destructive hand spares nothing that lives: he kills to
> nourish himself, he kills to clothe himself, he kills to adorn
> himself, he kills to attack, he kills to defend himself, he kills to
> instruct himself, he kills to amuse himself, he kills to kill: proud
> and terrible thing, he has need of everything, and nothing can
> resist him.† (*Soirées de Saint-Petersbourg*)

In contrast to Shakespeare's optimistic:

> There is some soul of goodness in things evil,
> Would men observingly distill it out. . . .

the current intellectual mood is rather that there is some soul of
badness even in things good. What worthy deed is not done presumably for intentional or unconscious self-glorification or for

* "In the faces of men and women I see God" (Walt Whitman), and, to
cite another romantic poet: "The majesty that from man's soul looks through
his eager eyes." (William Morris)
† Compare Sigmund Freud, *Civilization and Its Discontents, op. cit.*, part V.

good public relations? "Human nature is not black and white, but black and gray." (Marjorie Bowen) In the Middle Ages men were also strongly convinced of their depravity and sinfulness, but during the eighteenth and nineteenth centuries, the Age of Reason, Romanticism and Queen Victoria, man had confidence in the possibility of his own goodness.

Though condemnation of man is frequently expressed, there is today no agreement that he deserves it; indeed, many thoughtful people disagree. They wonder whether the character of man has really become more demoralized or whether contemporary events have made us more despairing. Just as in other periods, millions of decent, though not perfect, people—many quite distinguished—seem glad to be alive. They enjoy their families, go confidently about their work and appreciate the benefits of our era. A deep gulf separates them from the "absurdists," represented largely by groups of young people and certain writers and artists. According to these only the "lowbrow" can have a confident view of the human condition, which is actually hopeless and nightmarish. The Theater of the Absurd and the Theater of Cruelty are manifestations of this point of view.

If we go from the general to the particular and ask what is the meaning of an individual life, we must ever be alert to stifle the deep-rooted and burning urge to wonder about some eternal, ultimate, metaphysical meaning. We should realize that the only answerable question is, What does a man's life mean *to himself* and *to others*? Unfortunately, many people, when asked what life means, answer, off-hand, that it means nothing. But they are deceiving themselves with an easy slogan. It is impossible for any life not to have some content; except in extreme circumstances, it has meaning for the person who lives it and for those among whom it is lived.

The conditions of life vary. Some hours or days may be empty and without meaning, others may be bleak or even dreadful and still others may be good or even great. To a great many, "life is a state in which much is to be endured, and little to be enjoyed." (H. J. Blackham) But there are also those who feel that their life contains much that can be enjoyed. For the masses of men life is governed by the grinding poverty in which they find themselves. But even then life is rarely all gray and may contain some meaningful aspects. Primitive, tribal and village life, though poor, may offer many satisfactions to people who have never known anything different.

Writers from Biblical days to those of modern times have indulged their resentment by finding that, as F. Scott Fitzgerald puts it, "life is essentially a cheat and its conditions those of defeat." * No one has expressed himself with a deeper pessimism than Macbeth:

> Life's but a walking shadow, a poor player
> That struts and frets his hour upon the stage
> And then is heard no more; it is a tale
> Told by an idiot, full of sound and fury,
> Signifying nothing.†

Life today is often seen in extreme terms: full of abnormalities, lust, sadism, crime, drug addiction, poverty and concentration camps. The all-destroying Bomb is its symbol. To us it may therefore seem unbelievable that a poet in the last century could have written:

> How good is man's life, the mere living! How fit to employ
> All the heart and the soul and the senses for ever in joy.

Robert Browning and all the other romantic poets tried to turn their eyes away from the social evils in their world; we concentrate on them. They glorified the beauty and sadness of youth, love, life and nature, but who today would sing:

> There's joy in the mountains
> There's life in the fountains.
>   (Wordsworth)

Yet play, love, life and nature may still be joyous.‡

Our literary and artistic culture is bewitched by "the monstrousness of life, [its] wicked dream." (Saul Bellow) At the same time, the constant flowering of human culture, the accomplishments of great humanistic and scientific endeavors could never be without gifted men who devote their energies to activities which to them and to their contemporaries have a worthwhile meaning. Even pronouncements on the nothingness of life

---

* Compare T.S. Eliot's "Man's life is a cheat and a disappointment; all things are unreal, unreal and disappointing."

† Compare Hamlet: "How weary, stale, flat and unprofitable seem to me all the uses of this world."

‡ "O world you are too beautiful by far." (Edna St. Vincent Millay)

testify that something in life is significant to those who make them. "To create is to affirm." (Charles I. Glicksberg)

Existence cannot be meaningless to people who as parents enjoy children and as children enjoy play. Almost everybody enjoys sports, as participant or as spectator. We listen to symphonies, operas, jazz; we watch television and look at the great paintings, sculptures and buildings wrought by human hands. More and more people travel to see the beautiful scenery and unusual sights of our own and of foreign countries. Scientists pursue their investigations. Physicians minister to our health. Industrialists build great factories, and businessmen make our economic life possible. Teachers educate the young. Government officials and politicians keep group life going somehow. How can all these activities be without significance? In *Our Town*, Thornton Wilder points out: "Choose the least important day in your life. It will be important enough." Similarly, we can say: Take the least important person in your life. He will be important enough. "A simple life is its own reward, and continually realizes its function." (George Santayana)

We seem to have transformed Browning's, "God's in His heaven: All's right with the world" into God's not in His heaven, all's wrong with the world. But the joyless mood of our intellectual culture is not peculiar to this age. It pervaded the late Middle Ages, even though people were God-fearing then. This is how J. Huizinga describes that time:

> At the close of the Middle Ages, a sombre melancholy weighs on people's souls. Whether we read a chronicle, a poem, a sermon . . . the same impression of immense sadness is produced by them all. It would sometimes seem as if this period had been particularly unhappy, as if it had left behind only the memory of violence, of covetousness and mortal hatred. . . . It was, so to say, bad form to praise the world and life openly. It was fashionable to see only its *suffering* and *misery*, to discover everywhere *signs of decadence* and of the near end—in short, to *condemn the times or to despise them.* (My italics.)

> We look in vain . . . for the vigorous optimism which will spring up at the Renaissance . . . [expressed in] the exultant exclamation of Ulrich von Hutten, "O world, O letters, it is a delight to live!" (*The Waning of the Middle Ages*)[9]

A pessimistic view of life was taken by early Buddhism. Buddha taught that everything is impermanent and transitory, a source of universal suffering and misery. Real happiness can be found only in a Nirvana beyond this earthly life.* However, in the course of a development of 2,500 years which extended over many nations and cultures, Buddha's "truth" has found infinitely varied interpretations. But not only has it not prevented many Buddhist communities from leading cheerful lives, it has actually contributed to their serenity.

Man is an acting being, and life is a challenge—often a difficult one—for everyone who is free and mentally able to choose what he will do. Our own reason ought to direct us to be just and good and to strive for excellence and the harmonious beauty of our lives, at the same time, of course, attending to our physical needs. We ought to be a "productive personality." What our life means depends on what we do with it. The world as such does not and cannot know values, we ourselves carve out realms in which values—good and bad, beautiful and ugly—prevail. *It is we who create the meaning of our lives.*[10] It is a mistake to "conclude that there can be no purpose *in* life because there is no purpose *of* life." (Baier) Similarly, we cannot think of mankind as having a function. We are not like tools or medicines or buildings; we are as such without function. But we can and ought to give our lives purpose and function, and in doing so our lives take on meaning and significance for ourselves and for others.

We cannot live according to a blueprint that antedates our existence. We must choose and act according to purposes, a task which even the most primitive people must undertake. President Franklin D. Roosevelt was right in his belief "that you only live once and you ought to live each day as happily, fully and meaningfully as you can." It is a good thing to enjoy living, but it is impossible to do so in isolation. "The wonderful and awful possibilities of being a human being" (H. J. Muller) open up for us only when we start a family, engage in work, enter common enterprises, or go beyond these into public life.

Some existentialists hold, all too one-sidedly, that man lives only in his actions. "It's what one does, and nothing else, that shows the stuff one's made of." (Sartre, *No Exit*) † Goethe had already expressed a similar idea when he wrote: "If you want to rejoice in your own value, you must bestow a value upon the

---

* It was a long held Christian belief that "this world" is misery and evil and that blessedness is attainable only in heaven with God.

† "A man is the sum of his actions, of what he has done, of what he can do." (Malraux, *Man's Fate*) See chapter VII, p. 168 and chapter XIII, p. 367 f.

world." However, in considering the meaning of a man's life, we cannot overlook his thoughts, emotions and standards, his good and bad qualities, his creative and destructive gifts.

Of all men, one is most important to me: myself. Each person is of infinitesimal magnitude in the totality of the universe, but each is unique to himself. Walt Whitman opens his "Song of Myself" with the line, "I celebrate myself, and sing myself," and later he affirms: "Nothing, not God, is greater to one than one's self is." Whether we celebrate and sing or bemoan ourselves, whether we look upon ourselves as great or as unimportant or worthless, nothing is more meaningful and significant to us than we are ourselves. It is sheer nonsense to talk of our meaninglessness. It is I who enjoy myself or suffer physically or mentally. "The pleasures of heaven are with me and the pains of hell are with me." (Walt Whitman) Whatever of the universe I experience, it is I who do the experiencing. It is I who ought to believe in my own worth. "The image which people carry of themselves within their own hearts is one of the greatest of all motive forces in human thought and behavior." (Isaiah Berlin) While inner and outer forces may buffet me, it is I who am spurred on by my ambitions, who apply my strengths to accomplish my purposes. Also it is I who may be too tired or sick to strive for anything. Since everything comes to me through my own consciousness, only I can think my thoughts, dream my dreams, feel my loves, my moods, my happiness, my sorrows. Thus in a sense we are alone. No other human being can really partake of our experiences, not even the deepest friendship and the most ardent love we feel. Nor is anyone else shaken with our passionate hatred. Our tears burn only our eyes. When we are busy, we are often oblivious of our essential cut-offness, but at other times, and particularly when we are young, we sometimes have a shattering sense of aloneness, of alienation from those close to us. These are psychologically important experiences, but we are not dealing with psychology here. Philosophically, my remarks are in a sense truistic: the I is the I.

The meaning each one of us finds in his own life depends not only on his fate and his own acts, but also on his education, interests and opinions. Our reasonableness, our instinctual drives, our strengths, our fears, our self-conceits vary. To an affirmative person his neighbors and indeed the whole world appear in a different light than they do to a depressed man, different to a poor and to a rich man, to a revolutionary, an artist and a comfortable suburbanite. All of us do not react in the same manner to changing political and economic realities or to the gradually altering conditions of family life. We age: the world, other people, have a different meaning for an adolescent, a student, a bride, a mother, a harassed business, professional, or working man; for an aged person. All of us perceive ourselves differently at various stages of our lives.

It has been said countless times that life is *futile*.* In relation to the universe, life is neither futile nor useful, it just is. For man, on the other hand, life has not been futile, rather, it has been remarkably productive. It is quite a different matter when we consider whether certain individual lives can be regarded as futile. This, naturally, would depend on the particular circumstances of the individual. A life may be totally wasted. Misfortunes may be so numerous or so overwhelming that they exhaust a person's strength. Painful and long-lasting illness may defeat a man's courage and hope. The life of a criminal, a drug addict or a sadistic dictator may seem destructive to us, and if we can use the word "meaning" at all in connection with it, we might say that such a life has negative meaning.

An intellectual attitude and conviction that life is futile must be distinguished from the *feelings* of emptiness and meaninglessness or a *mood* of weariness and uselessness, which may come over us at times, but which may pass in an hour or a day. These moods may develop into an aggravated state of depression and despair; at that point rationality has ended.

The Tragic View and Other Aspects of Life

In any discussion of the meaning of life the most frequent reference is to its *tragic* nature.[11] The idea that the lot of man is tragic is as old as Western literature. The stories of the Homeric heroes, of Achilles and Hector slain in battle, of the murdered Agamemnon, of Ajax becoming insane, and of others, were old

* That most bourgeois lives are futile, "a terrible, monstrous lie," seems to be the message of Tolstoy's moving story, *The Death of Ivan Ilyitch*. When he wrote this story, he had found the meaning of life in "that portion of the doctrine of Christ which inculcates love, humility, self-denial, and the duty of returning good for evil."

folk tales later used by the three great tragic poets of ancient Greece. In the Old Testament, the Book of Job tells a tragic tale, if we disregard the last verses (42:7–17), which are generally considered to be later additions.

What does it mean to say that life is tragic? The dictionary[12] definition of "tragic" refers first to the dramatic form of tragedy, which deals with "a conflict between the protagonist and a superior force (as destiny) and having a sorrowful or disastrous conclusion that excites pity or terror." It then goes on: "deplorable, lamentable." * "Tragedy" is defined as a "disastrous event, calamity, misfortune." But it is not true that everything that is disastrous or lamentable is tragic. Earthquakes and hurricanes are disasters; the destruction of a tree, the death of a pet dog are misfortunes, but none of these are tragic. The tragic concerns the human sphere. We can find tragedy only where there is a moral element, where someone strives for values and goals which for some reason he cannot attain. As a result, his aspirations may be unfulfilled or they may even be betrayed. While the death of a dog may be merely sad to an adult, to the child who owns it it may be a tragedy. The child's love for the dog, his striving for a mutuality of experience, the unconscious satisfaction he derives from his dominance over the "dumb beast" have received a brutal blow.

The exalted nature of classical tragedy has made the term "tragic" seem unapplicable to men and women in ordinary circumstances. But the "universal plight of the Little Man" (H. J. Muller) is not merely pathetic, it is also tragic. Critical debate has centered around Willy Loman, the futile hero, or rather non-hero, of Arthur Miller's *Death of a Salesman*.[13] Discussing this play, Brooks Atkinson makes the following observations:

> It would be either arrogant or pedantic to deny the dignity of tragedy to the millions of obscure people who have died for causes in which they believed or in circumstances they could not control.
>
> That this divine substance of creativity in the human spirit should go to waste or be unfulfilled is black tragedy.

Chekhov can be regarded as the master of "the tragedy of low life," "the tragedy of attrition, the gradual frustration, the grow-

---

* The definition in the *Oxford Dictionary* also includes "calamitous, disastrous, terrible, fatal." The meaning of the tragic sense of life in Miguel de Unamuno's book of that title is different, he refers to the religious paradoxes, which he believes are implicit in man's necessary belief in immortality.

ing weariness, the final hopelessness," ending in Uncle Vanya's outcry, "What shall I do with my life and my love?" [14]

I would say that all human lives contain tragic elements, yet we can be cheerful, happy and serene. We must all die, and it is our nature as a thinking and striving "I" that makes death and our consciousness of its certitude tragic. We live with the constant knowledge that all our plans, ambitions and relationships must come to an end, as well as all our satisfactions and pleasures. But it is also true, that to many death comes as liberation from sickness, despair, and misfortune.

The tragic aspect of our lives derives even more from the limitations that we experience during our lifetime. The fulfillment of our goals depends at least in part on the benevolence of nature and of our social environment, but one or the other or both may fail to cooperate. Most of us must leave our high hopes hopelessly behind us. "Our ripest fruit we never reach." (Oliver W. Holmes) We are not always as strong and healthy as we would like to be for the kind of life we would like to lead, and our intelligence and mental stamina may not be sufficient to attain what we strive for. Ambition is a virtue in our society, and people may suffer tragic conflicts and misfortunes because of it. Time and energy are severely limiting factors. The pursuit of one goal may interfere with others. Earning our daily bread or carving out a niche in the competitive struggle may leave some time for recreation, but may not permit serious efforts in science or art or in the study of philosophy. A young woman may find her career as a chemist or physician cut off—at least for some years—when her children are born. "The selves we might have been are eloquent witnesses of values we failed to enjoy." (S. Hook) Social and financial circumstances constrain us, as well as the educational, cultural and political environments in which we grow up and live.

In our civic life we suffer from the tragic conflict of ethical goals. Many people in the South have found themselves faced with the tragic dilemma of leading the kind of lives they were brought up in and like, or living up to new ethical ideals. If they stay where they are, are they not the beneficiaries of an immoral system and thus tragically guilty? * The average German during the Nazi regime could not escape choosing between silence in the face of barbarism and concentration camps, or death. Most of us,

* This is similar to the situation of many whites in South Africa.

sitting comfortably in our living rooms and never having had to face such fatal choices, rarely hesitate to proclaim the guilt of others. However, do we not all share the guilt for the sins of a society in which poverty, preventable misfortune and injustice prevail? I discussed this puzzling question previously in the chapter on ethical norms and conduct without coming to a definite conclusion. It is a question frequently dealt with in contemporary drama. It is thrown at us by our young people. All men far too frequently bear the much less dramatic guilt of violating their own ideals of goodness and neighborliness by unpunished and unpunishable acts of selfishness, disloyalty, deplorable impatience and frequent lovelessness.

Although life *is* tragic, the tragic element of man's eternal dissatisfaction is not the dominant note in most people's lives. Thoreau's observation that "Most men lead lives of quiet desperation" is an exaggerated view, though there is a good deal of truth in it.

There is a great difference not only in the magnitude of the tragic element in individual lives, but also in the intensity with which it is felt. A confident young person may hardly be conscious of the limitations he encounters, while a serene person may overlook them most of the time. The masses of mankind have limited goals. They may be downtrodden and conditioned to the hard life for generations, so that, while their situation seems tragic to us, it may seem natural to them. A hard-working executive, an architect full of plans, a scientist pursuing interesting leads or a busy mother, may be so absorbed in their activities that they have neither the time nor the inclination to worry about their own or mankind's tragic fate. Yet they too may experience the tragic sense in a bitter personal disappointment or the misfortune of a friend, or it may be something heard or seen that makes them aware of the undeniable tragic elements of life. Even the most fortunate suburbanite in our affluent society does not entirely escape frustration in his work or in his relation to children, and many a prosperous façade hides tragedy.

It would be a grievous mistake to consider the tragic meaning of life as the one and only one or as the basic and essential one (whatever basic and essential may mean). Perhaps I have given it a disproportionate amount of space; but I have done so because it is this meaning that is stressed by so many who feel that we are

living in a tragic, absurd age. Life is much richer. Moreover, it is
full of contrasts. We might draw a lesson from the different images artists have given of the world. The Virgin Mary is por-
trayed in deep mourning standing under the cross on which her
Son has been nailed, and also as a lovely Italian Madonna in a
flowery spring landscape playing with a plump *bambino*. We
look at Rembrandt's thoughtful and somber face in a museum,
but when we turn around, we are in the company of lively
Dutch families, carousing adults and children running about,
playing with dolls, dogs and cats. Scenes of martyred saints,
fallen soldiers and burned villages, display man's cruelty to man.
Flowers and bright landscapes depict a better, peaceful, more
beautiful world, and so do lovely nudes.

Let us be realistic. If life is often tragic, it is also often comi-
cal. Just as there is unquestionably truth in the great tragedies, so
there is truth in the comedies. There are frequent and good reasons to be amused and to laugh. Life can be a joy, a quiet pleasure and a triumph over difficulties.* This then will be its meaning. Life is learning, travelling, playing with children, singing
and listening to song. Life is meaningful because of the good
works someone does or the lovable character he has. Life may be
glorious because of heaven-storming enthusiasms or because of
loving and consummating love. We can become absorbed in a
tragic drama without feeling tragic ourselves. We can also enjoy
comedy, the ballet, music and competitive sports. There is an
endless variety of interesting hobbies. Fortunately, even work
may be gratifying. Let us not underestimate the satisfaction life
offers, the humorous moments, the ebullience of young people.

The view that man's life is "a tale told by an idiot . . . sig-
nifying nothing" ought to be called the *sordid* view. It claims

---

* As a contrast to the overly stressed crime, war and corruption of and in
today's world, I quote from Walt Whitman's *Specimen Days* (New York: New
American Library, Signet, 1961, paperback).

Sunday, August 27 [1877]—Another day quite free from marked prostra-
tion and pain. It seems indeed as if peace and nutriment from heaven subtly
filter into me as I slowly hobble down these country lanes and across fields,
in the good air—as I sit here in solitude with Nature—open, voiceless,
mystic, far removed, yet palpable, eloquent Nature. I merge myself in the
scene, in the perfect day. Hovering over the clear brook water, I am
soothed by its soft gurgle in one place, and the hoarser murmurs of its
three-foot fall in another. Come, ye disconsolate, in whom any latent
eligibility is left—come get the sure virtues of creek shore, and wood and
field.

Although Whitman's particular paradise is no more, he who searches can still
find quiet retreats even near our largest cities.

that man's existence is wretched, absurd, meaningless; that he is dominated by low instincts and passions. Instead of priding himself on his greatness, this view holds that man ought to realize that he is no more than a miserable creature crawling over the earth, like the insect of Kafka's *Metamorphosis*. To be sure, even a good man may commit a contemptible act or be pitiful, as he is in Kafka's story. But the generalization that all human beings are completely degraded is devoid of truth.

The opposite extreme from the sordid view may be called the *romantic* view. Sometimes in moments of particular happiness—in youthful idealism, in love, in the glow of a great success—we may feel as though we are in paradise and that this is the best of all possible worlds. This is a cheerful illusion, belied by man's general condition on earth. The various beliefs held by visionaries in the possibility of forming a Utopia have been shattered by the experiences of all reformers and revolutionary movements. Perfection can only be dreamt of in an existence beyond this world: in heaven with God or in a desireless Nirvana.

Speculation about the meaning of life seems so pervasive, so bound up with our precarious existence, that we cannot imagine an intelligent culture in which the problems of ultimate meaning would not be raised. But this does not always appear to be the case. H. J. Muller writes of the Chinese of the Empire that they "were a cheerful, pragmatic people who were never given to brooding over the first and last questions. Thus their philosophy was almost entirely ethical and political; they produced little or no metaphysics and theology." Furthermore, in traditional, quiescent, and thus non-progressive societies, aims are limited, and consequently, the tragic dissatisfactions of a changing, turbulent society are lacking. For us, however, every personal or public goal reached is but a stepping stone to further goals. Our constant striving to improve our individual lives and our society represents a distinctive, admirable, but tragically unfulfillable drive of our civilization. Our lives would no doubt be easier if we speculated less and asked fewer unanswerable questions, but life would be more apathetic and less fascinating. I wonder whether in the self-confident age of the Renaissance, known as the Age of Discovery, and in the Age of Enlightenment men brooded as much about the meaning of life as we do now.

I end this section with a quotation from Eugene O'Neill suggesting life's many meanings:

I see life as a gorgeously-ironical, beautifully-indifferent, splendidly-suffering bit of chaos, the tragedy of which gives Man a tremendous significance, while without his losing fight with fate he would be a tepid, silly animal. I say "losing fight" only symbolically, for the brave individual always wins. Fate can never conquer his—or her—spirit.

The Art of Living

The meaning that we ascribe to our own lives depends, as I have indicated, on our outlook, on how we face the manifold experiences and "crises" of each day, and on how we face our total fate which often seems malevolent and destructive of our purposes. The way in which we come to terms with life, our art of living, ought to be subject to the ideal of humanism and pre-eminently that phase of it which I have called the esthetic ideal of harmony. In chapter X, I mentioned Aristotle's ideal of "the great-souled man" and Spinoza's "nobility," DeWitt Parker's "conception of tragic harmony" and Blanshard's "rational temper." All these expressions hint at the attitudes we need to cultivate in order to feel that our own lives are meaningful. The humanist does not find salvation and redemption in eternal life but in the worthiness of his earthly life span. We ought to appreciate the blessings life has given us and affirm with pride our individuality and the merit of our work. The hope and the joy we spread will be reflected back to us and in turn enrich our lives. "Every man that is glad doeth the things that are good, and thinketh good thoughts, despising grief." (*Shepherd of Hermas*).[15] This is the best "pursuit of happiness."

There is no life that does not suffer disappointment. Even the man who is successful beyond his wildest dreams usually is not as satisfied as he expected to be and he tries, restlessly, for ever higher goals. Herein lies the greatness of man. But there are always limits. While we must make every effort to overcome difficulties and protest against them, when effort and protest make sense, "[there] is no use quarrelling with fate"—according to Ernest Jones "a favorite expression" of Freud's when he was suffering from a very painful, incurable cancer. When the wheel of fortune turns against us, we must adopt the Stoic acceptance of the unavoidable and arm ourselves with patience and resignation. David Riesman calls on us to have "the nerve of failure," that is, "the courage to accept the possibility of defeat, of failure, without being morally crushed." [16] "Life is harsh, but it has always been harsh. . . . [It would be unworthy of us to] agonize and attitudinize about circumstances that hundreds of generations have lived through without comparable self-pity." (John Gardner)

Moral man feels a particular dissatisfaction with himself because he knows—unless he fools himself—that he does not live up to his own ethical standards. He suffers the "anxiety of guilt," as Tillich puts it. Nevertheless, in spite of his moral failures, he ought to "be strong and of good courage." *

People have always been deeply disturbed that their fate bears little relation to their goodness or badness. A righteous man like Job or a hard-working, charitable neighbor of ours may sustain grievous misfortune; a Gandhi or a John Kennedy is assassinated; but a cruel conqueror, a wicked tyrant, a robber baron, a successful thief, may prosper. In stories and plays evildoers get their comeuppance, but in real life they often keep their winnings. Vain demagogues may govern, and the wise may have to drink the hemlock cup. We have to accept the fact that life is like this, that fate does not operate on principles of justice. A sense of irony is a big help in maintaining a balanced outlook.

But if fate is blind, and evil can befall a good man, how can O'Neill claim that "the brave individual always wins"? In a practical, worldly sense this is obviously not true. However, O'Neill continues: "Fate can never conquer his—or her—spirit." That is the same spirit that made Socrates, condemned to death, say: "No evil can happen to a good man, either in life or after death." The good man has a certain "attitude to life's afflictions." [17] He has "that courage which voluntarily accepts unavoidable suffering." In short, the good man can be harmed, he cannot escape death, but he will remain "strong and of good courage" and true to the meaning that he has chosen to give his life. This is the spirit that has animated mankind's true idealists; it is an idealism that is by no means dead today, as witness the men and women of the underground, who fought against Fascism and died or, more recently, those whites and blacks who fight against racial intolerance. Most men in the Armed Forces are drafted. Yet the innu-

* It was in these words that Moses exhorted the Israelites and Joshua when he knew that his death was approaching. (Deut. 3:6, 7, 23.)

merable heroic deeds they perform beyond the call of duty are testimony to the worthiness they have chosen for their lives or for their death.

The Life of Evildoers

What is the meaning of the life of evildoers? In answering this question, we must distinguish their work and deeds from their personal characteristics. In labeling certain people evildoers, we characterize their personal lives as having a negative value and significance. What meaning may such a person assign to his own life? A scoundrel may rationalize what he does and deceive himself into believing that it is all right. Or he may be stupid and not realize the disvalue of his deeds. There are cynics who just don't care and blasé sophisticates who act as if they don't care. Their own lives may seem meaningless to them, and indeed also to us.

There are nihilists, not necessarily evil, who deny the existence of values and thus, in fact, the meaning of their own existence. But, as I have said, the activities of their own lives belie this nihilistic evaluation. To them their lives are worth the effort they must make to stay alive. People have rarely committed suicide in weary protest against the meaninglessness of their lives. Even despair concerning his usefulness and the emptiness of his existence hardly ever leads a man to kill himself, as we have discussed previously. The source of such despair may lie in the impotence of one's creative faculties or in miserable living conditions, sickness and old age. Despair may also overcome a man whose intellectual and moral freedom is suppressed, or who has been reduced against his will to a Grand Inquisitor's "sheep." He may be filled with self-contempt, with a sense of his own absurdity, devoid of all hope and yet hanging on to life. Here the meaningless "I" is resisted by the creature's instinctive "animal faith."

Man's Attitude Toward Death

Eventually we must all die. "How must the wise man die even as the fool!" (Eccl. 2:16) In death we are all alike; this fate we share with all complex organisms. Death is important, as I have pointed out, because death makes room for new growth.

What does our death mean to us? Death as such has no

meaning; it is just a natural happening. It has meaning only in so far as it terminates valuable relationships or ends work that is esteemed highly. In these cases, death makes life sorrowful and emptier.

What does the knowledge of the constantly increasing nearness of death mean to me? It does not frighten me, as it did Martin Luther, who felt that "the fear of death is the one misery that makes us more miserable than all creatures." Nor would I say that "the uncomfortable and unpredictable dark void of death . . . drowns me in mortal fear and mortal grief." (Rose Macaulay) The thought of my eventual death is one with which I have learned to live quite comfortably. I know I am part of the great universe in which everything constantly changes—a notion romantically expressed in an appealing saying ascribed to Confucius: "Death makes a man a clod of earth from which a blade of grass may grow." [18] With death always in the background, or possibly lurking close at hand, does not then life become a richer gift? ("A living dog is better than a dead lion." [Eccl. 9:4])

I must say, however, that I find Epicurus' equanimity— "death is nothing to us"—rather unbelievable. And it is difficult to live up to Spinoza's famous precept: "A free man thinks of nothing less than of death and his wisdom is a meditation not of death but of life." Though life is often unpleasant and disappointing, and death would end it all, life is often pleasant and interesting, and there is so much still to do, to learn and to see— why does it have to stop? In addition, most people are interested in public and cultural matters, and in scientific developments; they wonder how the world will look in the year 2000. Parents are curious about how their children and grandchildren will fare.

It is obvious that death means different things to different people in different ages and in different cultures. As for man's personal attitude toward his own death, Shakespeare describes both extremes magnificently:

Ay, but to die, and go we know not where;
To lie in cold obstruction and to rot;
This sensible warm motion to become
A kneaded clod; . . .
. . . 'tis too horrible!
The weariest and most loathed worldly life
That age, ache, penury, and imprisonment
Can lay on nature is a paradise
To what we fear of death. (*Measure for Measure*)

Cowards die many times before their deaths;
The valiant never taste of death but once.
Of all the wonders that I yet have heard,
It seems to me most strange that men should fear;
Seeing that death, a necessary end,
Will come when it will come. (*Julius Caesar*)

If we are to live up to the ideal of humanistic harmony, courage to be must be paired with courage to die, that is, resignation to our inevitable fate. "A man dies nobly when, awaiting his own extinction, he is interested to the last in what will continue to be the interests and joys of others. . . ." (Santayana)[19] We can answer Tolstoy's question: "Is there any meaning in my life, which will not be destroyed by the inevitable death awaiting me?" The answer is a clear-cut yes. The meaning Tolstoy's life had while he lived cannot ever be extinguished and the meaning of his work continues to this day and will continue far into the future. Similarly, the utterly malevolent meaning of Hitler's life and work cannot ever be destroyed. The meaning of the "little man's" life is no different: the values his or any other life has are actualities which nothing can destroy. Although this remark merely expresses the triviality that, what was, was, it is a thought we ought not to disparage.

Humanistic resignation and courage are only two of the possible attitudes that man has taken with respect to death. A belief in immortality, that is, in some form of eternal life, gives death an entirely different significance.* That man's soul or some shadowy, immaterial substance somehow survives man's death has been the dominant conviction throughout history. In the Christian world, men trusted St. Paul, who wrote, "Death is swallowed up in victory." This expresses a spirit that breathes, for example, through many of Bach's Cantatas and Hymns: "Come, sweet Death, come, blessed Peace." Our being in heaven with God and the angels, it was held, also would reunite us with our loved ones. On the other hand, death has been feared as the grim Reaper bringing "all earthly glory" to an end and threatening man with the coming of the Last Judgment and the eternal punishment of the fires and tortures of Hell.† From the early

---

* I have criticized the belief in immortality in chapter VII, p. 159.
† See J. Huizinga, *op. cit.*, chap. "The Vision of Death." Walter Kaufmann, in the chapter entitled "Death" of his *The Faith of a Heretic*, *op. cit.*, provides a convincing retort to the dread of death (nothingness) of certain modern writers and philosophers.

days of Greek philosophy, some thinkers have expressed skepticism about the possibility of survival; in the ensuing centuries the pendulum has swung back and forth.[20] Today, the widespread naturalistic outlook has eroded belief in immortality. In the infinity of the universe there is neither a place for a heavenly meeting with our dear ones nor a place for souls to be tortured. Who now fears hell except the hell that is here on earth? Biology has shown us the natural origin of life and is explaining the fact that organic and minding processes do not require the assumption of an eternal soul. Death is final extinction. When the deterioration of age or illness, or an accident terminates the biological processes of the creature Man, the personal "I," with its striving, enjoyment and misery, ceases too.

It bears emphasis: The humanist does not search for salvation beyond the grave through redemption nor need he be saved from nothingness. He finds the meaning of life in Shakespeare's famous counsel:

> Men must endure
> Their going hence,
> Even as their coming hither:
> Ripeness is all. (*King Lear*)

And what is ripeness but to do one's best in striving for the humanistic ideal of the love of truth, goodness and beauty, for tragic harmony, animated by "a spirit of compassion and a spirit of reverence" (H. J. Muller) for all the good and the beautiful that there is in the world.

RECOMMENDATIONS

W. T. Jones, *A History of Western Philosophy* (2nd ed.; 4 Vols., New York: Harcourt, Brace & World, 1969, paperback). Jones presents an objective description of the work of the important philosophers, supplemented by some critical comments. The extensive excerpts from the major writings of many philosophers give the reader an idea of each philosopher's manner of philosophizing. Jones also adds brief comments on the different cultural backgrounds in which the several successive schools of philosophy developed.

The philosophic problems treated in the present volume are examined in great detail and with unusual clarity and relative simplicity in the two Introductions by John Hospers: *An Introduction to Philosophical Analysis* (2nd ed.; Englewood Cliffs: Prentice-Hall, 1967), and *Human Conduct: An Introduction to the Problems of Ethics* (New York: Harcourt, Brace & World, 1962).

Two shorter Introductions are: Joseph G. Brennan, *The Meaning of Philosophy* (2nd ed.; New York: Harper & Row, 1967), and Hunter Mead, *Types and Problems of Philosophy* (3rd ed.; New York: Holt, Rinehart & Winston, 1959).

All four Introductions contain bibliographies.

Two encyclopedias of philosophy are available: J. O. Urmson (ed.), *The Concise Encyclopaedia of Western Philosophy and Philosophers* (London: Hutchinson, 1960), a useful one-volume work; and Paul Edwards (ed.), *The Encyclopedia of Philosophy* (New York: Macmillan & Free Press, 1967), the eight volumes of which contain detailed articles on the major philosophic problems and the life and work of philosophers who have played a role in the history of discipline.

In recent years a plethora of *popular science* books has appeared, many in paperbacks. I esteem highly the small comprehensive book: Victor F. Weisskopf, *Knowledge and Wonder* (Garden City: Doubleday Anchor, 1962).

For an authoritative listing of popular paperback books in the several branches of the sciences see: Hilary J. Deason (ed.), *A Guide to Science Reading* (New York: New American Library Signet, 1968 [kept up-to-date], paperback).

Numerous other recommendations have been made in the footnotes and in the references that follow.

Chapter I: What Is Philosophy? Its Role in Life

1. Ernest Nagel, "Naturalism Reconsidered," reprinted in *Logic Without Metaphysics* (New York: Free Press, 1956). A well-known essay which I recommend.

2. *The Nicomachean Ethics*, quoted in Robert F. Davidson, *Philosophies Men Live By* (New York: Dial Press, 1952).

3. *The True Believer* (New York: Harper & Row, 1951, paperback).

4. *Uses of the Past* (New York: Oxford Univ. Press, 1952, paperback). This is a provocative study of the meaning of history.

Chapter II: Truth

1. John Hospers, *An Introduction to Philosophical Analysis* (2nd ed.; Englewood Cliffs: Prentice-Hall, 1967).

2. *Tragic Sense of Life*, trans. J. E. Crawford Flitch (New York: Dover, 1954, paperback).

3. *Irrational Man. A Study in Existential Philosophy* (Garden City: Doubleday Anchor, 1954, paperback).

4. W. T. Jones, *A History of Western Philosophy* (2nd ed.; 4 vols.; New York: Harcourt, Brace & World, 1969, paperback).

Chapter III: Everyday Knowledge

1. Quoted in Nagel, *Logic Without Metaphysics*.

2. *Perception*, quoted in Hospers, *op. cit.*

3. Hospers, *op. cit.* These problems are exhaustively treated by Hospers, chap. 8.

4. *Mind and the World Order* (New York: Dover, paperback; originally published in 1929).

5. *The Three Dialogues*, quoted in Joseph P. Brennan, *The Meaning of Philosophy* (2nd ed.; New York: Harper & Row, 1967).

6. Nagel, *op. cit.*

Chapter IV: Error and Skepticism

1. Charles Frankel, *The Case for Modern Man* (Boston: Beacon Press, 1955, paperback).

2. Ashley Montagu, *Man: His First Million Years* (New York: New American Library, 1958).

3. Quoted in Bertrand Russell, *History of Western Philosophy* (New York: Simon & Schuster, 1959, paperback).

4. Quoted in W. T. Jones, *op. cit.*

Chapter V: The Nature and Role of Science

1. See Ernest Nagel, *The Structure of Science* (New York: Harcourt, Brace & World, 1961), particularly chap. 14; also Hans Meyerhoff (ed.), *The Philosophy of History in Our Time* (Garden City: Doubleday Anchor, 1959, paperback), Part II: "Clio—Science or Muse."

2. From Ernest Nagel's Preface to *Philosophy of Science*, eds. Arthur Danto and Sidney Morgenbesser (New York: Meridian Books, 1960, paperback).

3. Quoted in Catherine D. Bowen, *Francis Bacon* (Boston: Little, Brown, 1963, paperback).

4. See Norman Campbell, *What Is Science?* (New York: Dover, 1952, paperback; originally published in 1921), chaps. VI and VII. These chapters deal with the relationship of mathematics to science.

5. See Nagel, *The Structure of Science*, chaps. 11 and 12.

6. See Selig Hecht, *Explaining the Atom*, revised by Eugene Rabinowitch (New York: Viking, 1954, paperback). This is a clearly written popular book.

7. See Nagel, *op. cit.*, chap. 5. See also G. Holton, *Introduction to Concepts and Theories in Physical Science* (Cambridge, Mass.: Addison-Wesley, 1952), chap. 8.

8. See L. Susan Stebbing, *Philosophy and the Physicists* (New York: Dover, 1958, paperback; originally published in 1937).

9. See Nagel, *op. cit.*, chap. 6, "The Instrumentalist View of Theories" and "The Realist View of Theories."

10. Herbert Feigl, in *Dimensions of Mind*, ed. Sidney Hook (New York: Collier, 1961, paperback).

11. Quoted in Holton, *op. cit.*

12. *The Laws of Nature* (New York: Scribner's, 1956).

13. *Ibid.*

14. For details, see Holton, *op. cit.*, chaps. 12–14.

15. *Science and Method*, quoted in Holton, *op. cit.*

16. Ernest Nagel, "The Place of Science in a Liberal Education," in *Education in the Age of Science*, ed. Brand Blanshard, *Daedalus* (Winter, 1959). See also Charles Frankel, *The Case for Modern Man, op. cit.*, chap. VII, "The Progress of the Human Mind."

17. Campbell, *op. cit.*

18. *The Atoms Within Us* (New York: Columbia Univ. Press, 1961, paperback).

Chapter VI: "Man's Place in Nature"

1. A. C. B. Lovell, *The Individual and the Universe* (London: Oxford Univ. Press, 1959).

2. See Lovell, *op. cit.*

There are several good popular books on cosmogeny and the nature of the universe by Isaac Asimov, George Gamow, Fred Hoyle and Robert Jastrow.

3. *Some Things Worth Knowing* (New York: Harper & Row, 1958).

4. See G. G. Simpson, *This View of Life: The World of an Evolutionist* (New York: Harcourt, Brace & World, 1964, paperback), chap. 13. This is a well-reasoned skeptical opinion about the possibility of the development of extraterrestrial humanlike creatures.

5. Ernest Borek, *The Atom Within Us, op. cit.*

6. See George and Muriel Beadle, *The Language Of Life* (Garden City: Doubleday, 1966, paperback).

7. See Victor F. Weisskopf, *Knowledge and Wonder* (Garden City: Doubleday Anchor, 1962, paperback), chap. titled "The Development of Life."

8. Hospers, *op. cit.*, chap. 19 and Nagel, *op. cit.*, chaps. 11 and 12 are comprehensive treatments of the philosophic problems of emergence and reduction.

9. See G. G. Simpson, *The Meaning of Evolution* (Rev. ed.; New Haven: Yale Univ. Press, 1967, paperback), chap. titled "Man's Place in Nature."

10. A fuller exposition can be found in the popular works by George and Muriel Beadle, Julian Huxley, G. G. Simpson and others.

11. *Evolution in Action* (New York: Harper & Row, 1953).

12. Jacquetta Hawkes and Sir Leonard Woolley, *History of Mankind: Prehistory and the Beginning of Civilization* (New York: Harper & Row, 1963).

13. *Ibid.*

14. Montagu, *op. cit.*

15. See Kenneth Macgowan and Joseph A. Hester, Jr., *Early Man in the New World* (Garden City: Doubleday Anchor, 1962, paperback). See also Hawkes and Woolley, *op. cit.;* Montagu, *op. cit.*

16. See D. Diringer, *The Story of Aleph Beth* (London: Lincolns-Prager, 1958, paperback).

17. See Herbert J. Muller, *Uses of the Past, op. cit.*

Chapter VII: Man's Mind and Freedom

1. Herbert J. Muller, *Issues of Freedom* (New York: Harper & Row, 1960).

2. Dean E. Wooldridge, *The Machinery of the Brain* (New York: McGraw-Hill, 1963, paperback).

3. *The Mind and its Place in Nature* (New York: Humanities Press, 1925).

4. *The Concept of Mind* (New York: Barnes & Noble, 1949, paperback).

5. Reprinted in Nagel, *Logic Without Metaphysics, op. cit.*

6. See the essays by Herbert Feigl and Stephen C. Pepper, and the critique by Richard B. Brandt in *Dimensions of Mind*, ed. Sidney Hook (New York: Collier, 1961, paperback); also essays by U. T. Place and J. J. C. Smart in *The Philosophy of Mind*, ed. V. C. Chappell (Englewood Cliffs: Prentice-Hall, 1962, paperback); also Richard B. Brandt and Jaegwon Kim, "The Logic of the Identity Theory," *The Journal of Philosophy*, Vol. LXIV #17 (September, 1967).

7. U. T. Place, "Is Consciousness a Brain Process?" in *The Philosophy of Mind, op. cit.*

8. Nathan Brody and Paul Oppenheim, "Application of Bohr's Principle of Complementarity to the Mind-Body Problem," *The Journal of Philosophy*, Vol. LXVI, #4 (February, 1969).

9. Wooldridge, *op. cit.*

10. Alan Ross Anderson (ed.), *Minds and Machines* (Englewood Cliffs: Prentice-Hall, 1964, paperback) contains some of the important technical philosophic essays on this problem, beginning with A. M. Turing's much debated essay of 1959, "Computing Machines and Intelligence."

11. Jones, *History of Western Philosophy*, *op. cit.* See also Brand Blanshard, "Current Strictures on Reason," *Philosophic Review*, LIV (July, 1945), a well-known article which raises a similar argument.

12. "The Freedom of the Will," from *Knowledge and Society* by the University of California Associates (1938), reprinted in *Readings in Philosophical Analysis*, eds. Herbert Feigl and Wilfred Sellars (New York: Appleton-Century-Crofts, 1949). This is a frequently referred to, though not very recent, exposition of the contemporary theory, which has roots that go back to Hume.

13. Sidney Hook (ed.), *Determinism and Freedom in the Age of Modern Science* (New York: Collier, 1958, paperback).

14. Quoted in Hook (ed.), *op. cit.*

15. Truman Capote, *In Cold Blood* (New York: New American Library, 1966, paperback). John B. Martin, *Why Did They Kill* (New York: Ballantine Books, 1953, paperback). These two books vividly describe senseless murders and the background of the young men who committed them. See also Curtis Bok, *Star Wormwood* (New York: Knopf, 1959). This book is a fictionalized life study by a former Pennsylvania Judge. The narrative is interspersed with pertinent legal and philosophic essays.

16. See H. D. Lewis, "Moral Freedom in Recent Ethics," reprinted in *Readings in Ethical Theory*, eds. Wilfred Sellars and John Hospers (New York: Appleton-Century-Crofts, 1952), and C. A. Campbell, "Is 'Free Will' a Pseudo-Problem?" reprinted in *A Modern Introduction to Philosophy*, eds. Paul Edwards and Arthur Pap (Rev. ed.; New York: Free Press, 1965). See also C. D. Broad, "Determinism, Indeterminism and Libertarianism," reprinted in *Free Will*, eds. Sidney Morgenbesser and James Walsh (Englewood Cliffs: Prentice-Hall, 1963, paperback; originally published in 1934).

17. See "The Freedom of the Will," in *Readings in Philosophical Analysis*, *op. cit.*

Most introductions to ethics include a chapter on free will. For example see John Hospers, *Human Conduct* (New York: Harcourt, Brace & World, 1961), chap. 24. See also Richard Taylor, *Metaphysics* (Englewood Cliffs: Prentice-Hall, 1963, paperback). Taylor argues against the so-called "soft determinism," which I discuss.

18. I owe this reference to an article by Norman Podhoretz, "The Literary Adventures of Huck Finn," *New York Times Book Review*, December 6, 1959.

19. *The Structure of Science, op. cit.*

20. *Elements of Analytic Philosophy* (New York: Macmillan, 1949).

21. "Free Will and Responsibility," reprinted in *Readings in Ethical Theory, op. cit.* Originally published in 1936.

22. See the complete translation in Walter Kaufmann, *Existentialism from Dostoevsky to Sartre* (New York: Meridian Books, 1956). See the reference regarding this lecture in chapter XIII, p. 360.

Chapter VIII: Are There Ethical Norms?

1. C. I. Lewis, *The Ground and Nature of the Right* (New York: Columbia Univ. Press, 1955). This is the first sentence of Lewis' fine book.

2. *Civilization and Its Discontents* (New York: Norton, 1962, paperback).

3. On the problem of cultural relativism, see p. 202, especially the reference listed there.

4. "Personal Ethics," in *Preface to Philosophy*, by W. E. Hocking, *et al.* (New York: Macmillan, 1946).

5. "Wanton Reason," in *Philosophical Studies*, Vol. XII (1963).

6. *System of Ethics*, trans. Norbert Guterman (New Haven: Yale Univ. Press, 1956).

7. Reinhold Niebuhr, "Rational Resources," in *Moral Man and Immoral Society* (New York: Scribner's, 1932). This chapter describes the assistance morality receives from rationality.

8. *Five Types of Ethical Theory* (Paterson, N. J.: Littlefield, Adams & Co., 1959, paperback: originally published in 1930).

9. See Arthur Koestler, *Reflections on Hanging* (New York: Macmillan, 1957); also Hugo A. Bedau (ed.), *The Death*

Penalty in America (Garden City: Doubleday Anchor, 1964, paperback).

10. *Death of a Man* (New York: Random House, 1957).

11. See James Flint (ed.), *A Conflict of Loyalties: The Case for Selective Conscientious Objection* (New York: Pegasus, 1969, paperback).

12. See Solomon E. Asch, *Social Psychology*, reprinted in *Value and Obligation*, ed. Richard B. Brandt (New York: Harcourt, Brace & World, 1961) for a fascinating critique of relativism.

13. *The Concept of Law* (New York: Oxford Univ. Press, 1961).

Chapter IX: Ethical Norms and Conduct

1. See Hospers, *op. cit.;* William K. Frankena, *Ethics* (Englewood Cliffs: Prentice-Hall, 1963, paperback); and P. H. Nowell-Smith, *Ethics* (Baltimore: Penguin Books, 1954).

Hospers treats ethics in considerable detail, and Frankena deals with most of the important questions in a concise manner. Nowell-Smith's approach represents contemporary Oxford philosophy.

2. See Roderick M. Chisholm, "Supererogation and Offence: A Conceptual Scheme for Ethics," in *Ethics*, eds. Judith J. Thomson and Gerald Dworkin (New York: Harper & Row, 1968, paperback). This essay was originally published in *Ratio* (June, 1963). See also J. O. Urmson, "Saints and Heroes," in *Essays in Moral Philosophy*, ed. A. I. Melden (Seattle: Univ. of Washington Press, 1958). This is a particularly important essay.

3. Quoted in Brand Blanshard, *Reason and Goodness* (London: Allen & Unwin, 1961).

4. *Nietzsche* (New York: Meridian Books, 1956, paperback). A fascinating study.

5. Quoted in *The Portable Nietzsche*, ed. Walter Kaufmann (New York: Viking, 1954).

6. Quoted in Kaufmann, *Nietzsche*, *op. cit.*

7. Many editions are available.

8. *Ethics* (London: Oxford Univ. Press, 1912).

9. "In Search of a Credible Form of Rule-Utilitarianism," in *Morality and the Language of Conduct*, eds. G. Nakhnikian and H. Castaneda (Detroit: Wayne Univ. Press, 1961).

10. Blanshard, *Reason and Goodness*, *op. cit.*

11. See Walter Kaufmann, *Faith of a Heretic* (Garden City: Doubleday Anchor, 1961, paperback).

12. See Hospers, *op. cit.*, chap. 1D.

13. Nelson, *System of Ethics, op. cit.*

14. *The Moral Point of View* (Ithaca: Cornell Univ. Press, 1958).

15. Blanshard, *Preface to Philosophy, op. cit.*

16. *Ethics* (London: English Univ. Press, 1953). An easily readable survey.

17. See in Brandt, *Value and Obligation, op. cit.*, particularly Jerome Michael and Herbert Wechsler's article, "The Basic Problems of Criminal Law: Ends and Means," from which the Plato and Bentham quotations were taken. This volume also contains a chapter from Kant's *The Philosophy of Law*, from which the Kant quotations were taken.

Brandt's, Ewing's, Frankena's and Hospers' introductions each contain a section on punishment.

18. The first quotation is from Hart, "Negligence, *Mens Rea*, and Criminal Responsibility," in *Free Will*, eds. Sidney Morgenbesser and James Walsh, *op. cit.* The second quotation is from Hart, "Legal Responsibility and Excuses," in *Determinism and Freedom*, ed. Sidney Hook, *op. cit.*

19. Ewing, *op. cit.*

20. *The Right and the Good* (London: Oxford Univ. Press, 1930).

Chapter X: Ideals to Live By

1. See Ursula M. von Eckhardt, *The Pursuit of Happiness in the Democratic Creed* (New York: Praeger, 1959).

2. Quoted in W. T. Jones, *The History of Western Philosophy, op. cit.*

3. Quoted in Robert F. Davidson, *Philosophies Men Live By, op. cit.*

4. *Science and Criticism: The Humanistic Tradition in Contemporary Thought* (New Haven: Yale Univ. Press, 1943).

5. See Hume's and Schopenhauer's pertinent remarks in Hospers, *op. cit.*

6. See Wittgenstein, *Tractatus* 6.43 (London: Routledge & Kegan Paul, 1922).

7. See Hospers, *op. cit.*, for a fuller treatment of the problems of ethical and psychological egoism and hedonism.

8. *Issues of Freedom* (New York: Harper & Row, 1960).

9. *Science and Criticism, op. cit.*

10. See Aristotle, *Nicomachean Ethics*, quoted in Davidson, *op. cit.*

11. See John W. Gardner, *Excellence* (New York: Harper & Row, 1961, paperback) and *Self-Renewal* (New York: Harper & Row, 1964, paperback). These are two enlightening popular books.

12. Nelson, *System of Ethics, op. cit.* The theory of ideals has been elaborated by Leonard Nelson.

13. The first, third and fourth quotations are quoted in Blanshard, *Reason and Goodness, op. cit.*

14. Richard Robinson, *An Atheist's Values* (New York: Oxford Univ. Press, 1964).

15. R. M. Hare, *Freedom and Reason* (New York: Oxford Univ. Press, 1963, paperback).

16. See Spinoza's eloquent remarks about the ideal of the wise man quoted in Stuart Hampshire, *Spinoza* (Baltimore: Penguin Books, 1961, paperback).

17. See DeWitt H. Parker, *Human Values* (Ann Arbor: George Wahr, 1944; originally published in 1931), chap. XIV titled "The Value of Play," for a more extended discussion.

18. See Brandt, *op. cit.*; Frankena, *op. cit.*; Hospers, *op. cit.* See also Richard B. Brandt (ed.), *Social Justice* (Englewood Cliffs: Prentice-Hall, 1962, paperback).

19. *A Preface to Morals* (Boston: Beacon Press, paperback; originally published in 1929).

20. *Male and Female* (New York: Dell, paperback).

21. Lester A. Kirkendall, with Elizabeth Ogg, *Sex and Our Society* (New York: Public Affairs Committee, 1964, paperback). This is an excellent little pamphlet which mentions other important literature. See also Evelyn Millis Duval, *Love and the Facts of Life* (New York: Association Press, 1963, paperback); "Sex Education of Adolescents," *Marriage and Family Living* (November, 1960); and "The Control of Adolescent Premarital Coitus," *Marriage and Family Living* (August, 1962). The two articles in *Marriage and Family Living* present a challenging exchange of views on how best to promote sexual morality among young people.

22. See Gael Greene, *Sex and the College Girl* (New York: Dell, 1964, paperback), a serious though impressionistic and

sensationalized description of the sexual ideas and behavior of college girls on many campuses. She offers some sensible educational and ethical suggestions, and includes an extensive bibliography. See also Carl Binger, "The Pressures on College Girls Today," *Atlantic Monthly* (February, 1961), an essay which I recommend highly; and Ira L. Reiss, *Pre-Marital Sexual Standards in America* (New York: Free Press, 1964, paperback).

23. John Cheever, *The Wapshot Chronicle* (New York: Bantam, 1957, paperback).

Chapter XI: The Justification of Ethical Beliefs

1. *The Ground and the Nature of the Right, op. cit.*

2. See Paul Edwards, "The Case Against Naive Subjectivism" in Paul Taylor (ed.), *The Moral Judgment, Reading in Contemporary Meta-Ethics* (Englewood Cliffs: Prentice-Hall, 1963, paperback). I discussed the general problem of "subjective truth" in chapter II.

3. *Nine Modern Moralists* (Englewood Cliffs: Prentice-Hall, 1962, paperback).

4. Reprinted in Brandt, *Value and Obligation, op. cit.*

5. See Brandt, *Ethical Theory, op. cit.,* chap. 4. See also Ronald W. Hepburn, *Christianity and Paradox* (London: C. A. Watts, 1958), chap. VIII, "Secular Ethics and Moral Seriousness."

6. Walter Kaufmann, *Critique of Religion and Philosophy* (Garden City: Doubleday Anchor, 1959, paperback), paragraphs 55 and 68.

7. John Stuart Mill, "Utility of Religion," in *Essential Works of John Stuart Mill,* ed. Max Lerner (New York: Bantam, 1961, paperback).

8. Details may be found in the works of Brandt, Ewing, Frankena, Hospers and Taylor.

9. Mill, "Nature," quoted in Hospers, *op. cit.*

10. See R. M. Hare, *The Language of Morals* (London: Oxford Univ. Press, 1952) for an extended discussion.

11. Theodosius Dobzhansky, *Mankind Evolving* (New Haven: Yale Univ. Press, 1962, paperback), chap. 12.

12. *An Analysis of Knowledge and Valuation* (LaSalle, Ill.: Open Court, 1946).

13. See Brandt, *Ethical Theory, op. cit.,* and Blanshard,

Reason and Goodness, op. cit. These two works offer detailed criticism of contextualism and instrumentalism.

14. Excerpts from Ayer and Stevenson are reprinted in Taylor, *The Moral Judgment, op. cit.*

15. The literature on ethics cited previously, note 8, deals extensively with emotive theory.

16. Ewing, *Ethics, op. cit.*

17. *Webster's Seventh New Collegiate Dictionary* (Springfield: C. & G. Merriam, 1963).

18. *Second Thoughts in Moral Philosophy* (London: Routledge & Kegan Paul, 1959).

19. See Hospers, *Human Conduct, op. cit.*, last chap., "Final Considerations," which is "greatly indebted" to Paul W. Taylor's *Normative Discourse* (Englewood Cliffs: Prentice-Hall, 1961), as is my own outline. See also Frankena, *op cit.*

20. Excerpt in Brandt, *Value and Obligation, op. cit.*

21. See Leonard Nelson, *Socratic Method and Critical Philosophy* (New York: Dover, 1965, paperback). Originally published in 1949.

22. *Estratto Rivista Methodos*, Vol. XV, #59–60 (1963).

Chapter XII: Religion and Truth

1. *The Will to Believe and Other Essays in Popular Philosophy* (New York: Dover, paperback, originally published in 1897).

2. Comprehensive works on the various religions are John P. Noss, *Man's Religions* (3rd ed.; New York: Macmillan, 1963); Ninian Smart, *The Religious Experience of Mankind* (New York: Scribner's, 1968).

Smaller works dealing with the subject are David G. Bradley, *A Guide to the World Religions* (Englewood Cliffs: Prentice-Hall, 1963, paperback); Wilfred C. Smith, *The Faith of Other Men* (New York: New American Library, 1965, paperback); Johnson E. Fairchild (ed.), *Basic Beliefs* (New York: Hart, 1959, paperback).

3. "Sermonette: The Professed Atheist and the Verbal Theist," in *Religious Philosophy* (New York: Atheneum, 1965, paperback). The scripture lesson to which Wolfson refers is Psalm 14, "The fool hath said in his heart, 'There is no God.'"

4. John Dewey, *A Common Faith* (New Haven: Yale Univ. Press, 1934, paperback).

5. See Hospers, *Introduction to Philosophical Analysis, op. cit.*, and Anthony Flew, *God and Philosophy* (London: Hutchinson, 1966, paperback) for a thorough examination of the many arguments for the existence of God.

6. *Philosophy of Religion* (Englewood Cliffs: Prentice-Hall, 1963, paperback). This book deals with the Judeo-Christian tradition, not with the general philosophy of religion.

7. H. J. Paton, *The Modern Predicament* (New York: Collier, 1955, paperback).

8. Austin Farrer, *God Is Not Dead* (New York: Morehouse-Barlow, 1966). This is a beautifully written modern defense of God-belief by a theologian who is familiar with science. The title of the American edition is misleading, as Farrer does not deal with the God-is-dead theologies.

9. The literature on this subject is enormous. See the comprehensive treatment in John Hick, *Philosophy of Religion, op. cit.* (additional literature is mentioned there); two short essays by Anthony Flew in *New Essays in Philosophical Theology*, Part 6 (quoted in part in Hick's book); John Stuart Mills, "Nature and Utility of Religion," reprinted in part in John Hick (ed.), *The Existence of God* (New York: Macmillan, 1964); George Santayana, *Reason in Religion* (New York: Collier, 1962, paperback; originally published in 1906).

10. See George Nakhnikian, "On the Cognitive Import of Certain Conscious States" in Sidney Hook (ed.), *Religious Experience and Truth, op. cit.* See also Kai Nielsen in the same volume.

11. These and other proofs are dealt with in detail in the books cited in note 5, and in the books by Paton, Kaufmann, Hick and Blackstone previously mentioned. See also Nagel, "Philosophical Concepts of Atheism," in Fairchild (ed.), *Basic Beliefs, op. cit.*

John Hick, *The Existence of God, op. cit.*, contains some of the original sources and criticisms.

The general ideological background of scholastic theology is presented in Jones, *A History of Western Philosophy, op cit.*, chap. 14, and in Muller, *The Uses of the Past, op. cit.*, chap. 8, "The Medieval Legacy."

12. William Alston, "Psychoanalytic Theory and Theistic Belief" in *Faith and the Philosophers*, ed. John Hick (New York: St. Martin's Press, 1964).

13. Blackstone deals thoroughly with the religious paradox. See also Ronald Hepburn, *Christianity and Paradox*, *op. cit.*; Brand Blanshard, "Critical Reflections on Barth," in John Hick (ed.), *Faith and the Philosophers*, *op. cit.*; Arthur Danto in Sidney Hook (ed.), *Religious Experience and Truth*, *op. cit.*; W. T. Stace, *Religion and the Modern Mind* (Philadelphia: Lippincott, 1952, paperback), a sympathetic treatment of the theory of the two realms of knowledge (two universes of discourse).

14. *Quest of Being* (New York: Dell, 1961, paperback).

15. It is not necessary to review here the debate of philosophers of the last forty years concerning meaning and the verifiability principle. It is extensively discussed by Blackstone and by Hospers, *Introduction to Philosophical Analysis*, *op. cit.* A. J. Ayer's *Language, Truth, and Logic*, one of the basic studies on this question, contains a part dealing with theology which is reprinted in Hick, *The Existence of God*, *op. cit.* See also Walter Kaufmann on "God and Ambiguity" in his *Critique of Philosophy and Religion*, *op. cit.* I am indebted to Kai Nielsen's many recent essays for suggestions and for clarification of my argument.

16. See Anthony Flew, in *New Essays in Philosophical Theology*, *op. cit.*, part VI. Reprinted in Hick (ed.), *The Existence of God*, *op. cit.*

17. See Nietzsche's ironic symbolic fable "The Madman" in *Gay Science*, and *Thus Spoke Zarathustra*, both reprinted in *The Portable Nietzsche*, *op. cit.* "The Madman" is an important part of William Hamilton's essay in J. J. Altizer and William Hamilton (eds.), *Radical Theology and the Death of God* (Indianapolis: Bobbs-Merrill, 1966, paperback).

18. The following quotations are from *Systematic Theology* (3 vols.; Chicago: Univ. of Chicago Press, 1951–1963) I, Part II, "Being and God."

19. See Sidney Hook, "The Quest for 'Being,'" in *The Quest for Being*, *op. cit.* This essay discusses the terms "being" and "being-itself."

20. David L. Edwards (ed.), *The Honest to God Debate* (Philadelphia: Westminster Press, 1963, paperback); particularly Alisdair MacIntyre's essay.

21. See Kai Nielsen in *Religious Experience and Truth, op. cit.*, for convincing criticism of Tillich's "ultimate concern" theology.

22. Hook (ed.), *Religious Experience and Truth, op. cit.* This collection contains two essays by Tillich which deal with "The Religious Symbol," and searching criticism of several authors. See also Paul Edwards, "Professor Tillich's Confusions," *Mind*, LXXIV (April, 1965). Walter Kaufmann discusses Tillich's use of symbols and many other facets of his theology in *Critique of Religion and Philosophy, op. cit.*

23. I am indebted to Paul Edwards' essay, "Professor Tillich's Confusions," cited in note 22, for this term and the substance of my subsequent argument.

24. *Letters from Prison* (New York: Macmillan, 1962, paperback; originally published in 1953).

John A. T. Robinson, *Honest To God* (Philadelphia: Westminster Press, 1963, paperback), contains more quotations from Bonhoeffer than from any other theologian.

25. Gabriel Vahanian, *The Death of God* (New York: Braziller, 1961, paperback), is, I believe, the first book to use the "God-is-dead" verbiage in its title. But Vahanian is not a God-is-dead theologian, rather he analyzes "The Culture of Our Post-Christian Era."

Some of the most significant publications of the God-is-dead theologians are: Paul M. van Buren, *The Secular Meaning of the Gospel* (New York: Macmillan, 1963); Thomas J. J. Altizer, *The Gospel of Christian Atheism* (Philadelphia: Westminster Press, 1966, paperback); Thomas J. J. Altizer and William Hamilton, *Radical Theology and the Death of God, op. cit.*; Richard L. Rubinstein, *After Auschwitz* (Indianapolis: Bobbs-Merrill, 1966). Two brief critical surveys are Kenneth Hamilton, *God is Dead: The Anatomy of a Slogan* (Grand Rapids: William B. Eerdmans, 1966, paperback), and Thomas W. Ogletree, *The Death of God Controversy* (Nashville: Abingdon Press, 1966, paperback).

Chapter XIII: Existentialism

1. There are many surveys and interpretations of existentialism by William Barrett, H. J. Blackham, Ernst Breisach, James Collins, F. H. Heinemann, and many other works on individual existentialists.

There are two paperback collections of nineteenth and twentieth century existentialist writings: H. J. Blackham (ed.), *Reality, Man and Existence* (New York: Bantam, 1965, paperback); Walter Kaufmann (ed.), *Existentialism from Dostoevsky to Sartre, op. cit.* The most extensive anthology is Maurice Friedman (ed.), *The World of Existentialism: A Critical Reader* (New York: Random House, 1964).

Existentialism still awaits detailed analysis from an empiricist point of view.

2. Trans. J. Macquarie and E. S. Robinson (New York: Harper & Row, 1962).

3. Trans. Hazel E. Barnes (New York: Philosophical Library, 1956).

4. Maurice Friedman's anthology reprints some of the documents pertaining to Heideggers' National Socialist activities.

5. The literary importance of Sartre and Camus is perceptively discussed in Henri Peyre, *French Novelists of Today* (New York: Oxford Univ. Press, 1967, paperback).

6. *Sartre, a Philosophic Study* (London: Athlone Press, 1966).

7. See his very readable lecture on existentialism in *The New World of Philosophy* (New York: Random House, 1961, paperback).

8. See Eugene B. Borowitz, *A Layman's Introduction to Religious Existentialism* (New York; Dell, 1966, paperback), a brief survey of religious existentialism.

9. *Existence and Being* (Chicago: Regnery, 1950, paperback).

10. See *The Faith of a Heretic, op. cit.* The chapter on death critically discusses the existentialist treatment of death.

Chapter XIV: On Ultimate Questions and the Meaning of Life

1. From Heidegger's 1949 introduction to *What is Metaphysics?* quoted in Kaufmann (ed.), *Existentialism from Dostoevsky to Sartre, op. cit.*

See also Walter Kaufmann's excellent criticism of Heidegger's question in "Heidegger's Castle" in *From Shakespeare to Existentialism* (Garden City: Doubleday Anchor, 1959, paperback).

2. Tolstoy expressed this idea in an early short story, "Lucerne."

3. See Ernest Nagel, "The Perspectives of Science and the Prospects of Man," in *Sovereign Reason* (New York: Free Press, 1954).

4. *Tragic Sense of Life, op. cit.*

5. J. M. G. LeClezio in *Encounter* (November, 1965).

6. See Erwin Stengel, *Suicide and Attempted Suicide* (Baltimore: Penguin Books, 1964, paperback). This is a brief introduction to the subject and contains a bibliography of important recent writings.

7. See *Genesis, The Anchor Bible* (Garden City: Doubleday, 1964), comments to chaps. 5–8.

8. H. J. Blackham (ed.), *Objections to Humanism* (London: Constable, 1963).

9. *The Waning of the Middle Ages* (Garden City: Doubleday Anchor, 1956, paperback).

10. See Hepburn, *Christianity and Paradox, op cit.*, chap. 8.

11. See Sidney Hook, "Pragmatism and the Tragic Sense of Life." *Commentary* (August, 1960). This was originally an address delivered to the American Philosophic Association. See also Herbert J. Muller, *The Spirit of Tragedy* (New York: Washington Square Press, 1956, paperback), and *The Uses of the Past, op. cit.*

12. *Webster's Seventh Collegiate Dictionary, op. cit.*

13. See Brooks Atkinson in *New York Times*, December 12, 1961; also Muller, *The Spirit of Tragedy, op. cit.*

14. See *The Spirit of Tragedy, op. cit.* Muller makes some excellent remarks about Chekhov.

15. A second century work by one of the Apostolic Fathers, quoted in Muller, *The Uses of the Past, op. cit.*

16. See David Riesman, "The Ethics of We Happy Few," reprinted in *Individualism Reconsidered* (New York: Free Press, 1954, paperback).

Riesman derives his term from Sidney Hook's reference to the expression "failure of nerve," which Hook applies to contemporary intellectuals.

17. See Peter Winch, "Can a Good Man be Harmed?" *Proceedings of the Aristotelian Society* (1966).

18. In a similar vein, see Walt Whiman's "Song of Myself," No. 52.

19. See *Death of a Man, op. cit.* Mrs. Wertenbaker describes the last months of her life with her husband, who was suffering from terminal cancer, and testifies to his stoic courage to die.

20. See Jacques Choron, *Death and Western Thought* (New York: Collier, 1963, paperback).

Abraham, 223, 268, 293, 323
Absolute, 60, 189; *see also* Ultimate
Abstraction, 373
Absurdity, 307, 365, 381, 382, 391
Accident, 134
Action(s): commendable, 212–13; as sum of man's life, 394; voluntary and involuntary, 176–77; *see also* Duties; Ethics
Adams, John, 263
Age of Discovery, 71*n*, 401
Age of Enlightenment, 26, 247, 401
Age of Reason, 81, 247, 391
Age of Romanticism, 391
Agnosticism, 116, 345
Aiken, Henry, 222, 230
Alienation, 365, 366
Allah, 179, 337
Altizer, J. J., 423, 424
Alston, William, 348, 423, 424
Altruism, 216, 218, 230
Analogy, 152, 165
Analysis, formalistic, 361–62
Anderson, Alan R., 415
Anguish, 365
Animism, 356
Anthropology, 364, 365
Antigone, 135
Antihero, 360
Anxiety, 362, 365, 366; of guilt, 403
Apology (Plato), 19, 203*n*
Appearances, subjective, 51–52
Aquinas, St. Thomas, 16, 71, 88, 331
Aristocracy, ideal of, 262
Aristotle, 19–20, 24, 26, 30, 32, 41, 84, 113*n*, 158, 171, 177, 197, 210, 234*n*, 262, 265, 271, 283, 285, 312, 327, 331, 402, 419
Arnold, Matthew, 351, 381
Art, 120, 270; of living, 402–4; primitive, 138–39
Asceticism, 249
Asch, Solomon E., 309, 417
Asimov, Isaac, 413
Astronomy, *see* Universe
Atheism, 116, 318, 334, 349, 354, 355, 358, 371; religious, 345–56 *passim*
Atkinson, Brooks, 397
Atomism, 167; *see also* Particles

Attitude, 302, 303, 304, 308, 313
Aurelius, Marcus, 269
Authenticity, existential, 364, 367, 368–370, 371
Authority, 71, 116, 296; Biblical, 322–323, 336; highest, 294; papal, 349–50; relinquishing freedom to, 249–51, 254
Autonomy, moral, 235
Awareness, *see* Mind
Axioms, 40, 41, 42, 288
Ayer, A. J., 152*n*, 293, 302, 421, 423

Bach, Johann Sebastian, 321, 389*n*, 406
Bacon, Francis, 51, 70–71, 88
Bacon, Roger, 70, 71
Bad faith, *see* Faith
Baeck, Leo, 336
Baier, Kurt, 231, 380*n*, 394
Balance, aesthetic, 271
Barbusse, Henri, 28, 30, 31, 43, 61, 65, 192, 311
Barnes, Hazel E., 425
Barrett, William, 35, 36, 360*n*, 363, 424
Barth, Karl, 345
Beadle, George and Muriel, 413, 414
Beauty, 27, 119, 256, 261, 272, 356, 366, 407; intellectual, 112; love of, 235, 265, 269–70; natural, 112, 113; as personal harmony, 270–71
Beck, Lewis, 156
Beckett, Samuel, 390
Becquerel, Henri, 89
Bedau, Hugo A., 416
Beethoven, Ludwig van, 163, 256, 269
Behavior: causal, 108; Christlike, 354
  human: ethical principles and, 289–99; social sciences and, 86, 87; immoral, 237–46
  moral: 196–97; distinction between pagan and Christian, 296; evaluation of, 309; religion and, 295–97; sexual, *see* sex relations; *see also* Ethics
Being, 378; existential, 372; of God according to Tillich, 346; great chain of, 377–78; ground of, 319, 346, 378; in-the-world, 364; itself, 59, 346, 347, 348, 349; nature of, 333*n*; perfect, 333; power of, 346; towards-death,

Being (*continued*)
365, 369; with-one-another, 374; *see also* Existence
Belief(s), truth and, 31, 32–34; *see also* Faith; God
Bell, Daniel, 186
Bellow, Saul, 240, 392
Beneficence, 234
Benevolence, 210, 217, 227
Bentham, Jeremy, 210, 243, 247, 248, 418
Berger, Peter L., 316*n*
Berkeley, George, 54–55; *see also* Idealism, Berkeleyan
Berlin, Isaiah, 395
Bible, 31, 73, 88, 115, 121–22, 153, 158, 186–87, 189, 197, 198*n*, 234*n*, 248, 278, 296*n*, 307, 313, 316, 317, 321, 327, 331, 332, 349, 371, 374, 384, 386*n*, 387, 390, 397, 403*n*, 404, 405, 407; allegorical interpretation of, 323–25; demythologization of, 323–25; on freedom of will, 170–71; God's commands in, 291–95; *see also* Faith; God; Myths; Religion
Bill of Rights, 26
Binger, Carl, 420
Biochemistry, 94
Biology, 86, 92–93; molecular, 128–29, 144, 148
Biophysics, 178
Blackham, H. J., 391, 424, 425, 426
Blackstone, William T., 318, 341*n*, 343–44, 422, 423
Blanshard, Brand, 16, 193, 197, 204, 219, 226, 236–37, 261, 271, 291, 339, 413, 415, 417, 418, 419, 420, 423
Bohr, Niels, 107, 109
Bok, Curtis, 415
Bonhoeffer, Dietrich, 347*n*, 350, 353–354, 424
Boredom, 365, 366
Borek, Ernest, 115, 128, 413, 414
Borowitz, Eugene B., 425
Boundary situations, 365
Bowen, Catherine D., 412
Bradley, David G., 421
Bradley, F. H., 17
Brain, *see* Mind
Brain-washing, 173, 191
Braithwaite, R. B., 351–52, 353
Brandt, Richard, 22, 163, 211*n*, 219, 221, 272, 301*n*, 414, 417, 418, 419, 420, 421
Brennan, Joseph, 409, 411
Briggs, Asa, 146
Broad, C. D., 154–55, 162, 165, 415
Brody, Nathan, 414
Bronowski, J., 228

Bronze Age, 139
Browning, Robert, 24, 37, 62, 392
Brunner, Emil, 320, 341*n*
Buber, Martin, 282–83, 337, 345, 358, 360
Buddha/Buddhism, 251*n*, 252, 260, 286, 290, 315, 316*n*, 320*n*, 323, 326, 327*n*, 334, 343, 351–52, 393–94
Bultmann, Rudolf, 323, 341, 345, 347, 358
Buren, Paul M. van, 353, 424
Burke, Edmund, 268–69
Business, ethics and, 226–28

Campbell, C. A., 415
Campbell, Norman, 114, 174, 412, 413
Camus, Albert, 80–81, 352, 358, 359, 361, 362–63, 365, 366*n*, 369*n*, 370, 425
Canaday, John, 380
Capitalism, 143
Capote, Truman, 415
Cardozo, Benjamin, 77
Care, 365, 368
Carnap, Rudolf, 302, 303
Carroll, Lewis, 14–15
Castaneda, H., 417
Categorical imperative, 211, 217, 220, 258
Categorical optative, 264
Cather, Willa, 254, 259, 270
Catholicism, 20, 23, 88, 89, 122*n*, 250, 252, 266, 315, 331, 349–50; *see also* Religion
Causality, 95–101 *passim*, 108, 179, 338
Cause, *see* First Cause
Chappell, V. C., 414
Character, 180, 310; imperative of, 235; moral, 234–37
Chase, Stuart, 124, 127, 137
Chekhov, Anton, 257, 397–98, 426
Chisholm, Roderick M., 417
Choice, 176–77, 178–80, 208, 385, 394; in daily life, 67; existential, 367–68, 369; freedom from and mental peace, 249–53, 254; making moral decisions, 221–28; non-causal free, 174–75; pursuit of happiness and, 257–60; rational, 308; *see also* Ethics; Will, freedom of
Choron, Jacques, 427
Christ, 30–31, 68, 90, 131, 140, 203*n*, 213, 216, 228, 231, 238, 250, 260, 321, 322, 323, 326, 349, 396*n*; centrality of, 352, 354; crucifixion of, 293, 325, 339, 354; as God incarnate, 325, 326*n*, 342–43, 348; humanity of, 353; reinterpreted figure of, 353; resurrection of, 325, 339, 354; role of in godless theology, 353, 354

Christianity, 18, 26, 68, 121, 153, 167, 187, 197, 216, 261, 316, 317, 327*n*, 345, 348; principal dogmas of, 339; religionless, 350; *see also* Religion
Christian Science, 157
Churchill, Winston, 229
Civilizations: ancient, 140–41, 142–43; cycle theory of, 142–43; *see also* Culture
Cognition, 303, 304, 306
Coherence, 47–48, 51, 53, 65
Collins, James, 424
Commands, *see* Bible; Duties; God
Common sense, 11, 18, 30, 39, 54, 63, 66, 82–83, 105, 157, 159, 169, 194, 217, 237, 245, 286, 287, 305, 311, 312
Communism, 26, 72, 185, 292, 317, 359
Compromise, moral, 228–29, 230
Comte, Auguste, 60*n*
Concern, ultimate, 347, 348
Confucius, 90, 213, 281, 316*n*, 405
Conscience, 149, 193, 269, 291, 300, 309, 310; *see also* Ethics; Religion
Consciousness, 46, 185; cosmic, 319; of death, 365, 398; distinction between performance and, 166–67; idealized, 318; meaning, purpose, significance and, 378–79; mind and, 153, 156; physical reality and, 165; subjective, 361; unhappy, 365
Constitution, U.S., 26
Contextualism, 300–1
Contradiction, 34, 36, 38, 39, 49, 50, 339, 341
Copleston, Frederick, 363
Cosmogony, *see* Universe
Cosmos, 316*n*, 331–32, 377, 382
Courage, 406
Courant, Richard, 40
Couzzens, James, 236
Cowie, Alexander, 380
Cox, Harvey, 320*n*
Creation, The, 121
Creation story, 73, 87–88, 121–22, 129, 307, 324–25; *see also* Myths
Criminality, 23, 172–73, 241–46, 263; capital punishment question, 199–200
Crito, 19, 197, 201, 203, 224, 225, 228
Crucifixion, *see* Christ
Culture(s), 135, 136, 137; dichotomy of in Western society, 267–68; evolution of, 138–41; primitive American, 139–40
cummings, e. e., 63
Curie, Marie and Pierre, 89
Cynicism, *see* Skepticism

Damnation, eternal, 295
Danto, Arthur, 412, 423

Darwin, Charles, 120*n*, 132
Dasein, 365, 366, 372
David and Bathsheba, 189–90, 205
Davidson, Robert F., 251, 411, 418, 419
Day, Clarence, 185
Deason, Hilary J., 410
Death, 118, 372, 377, 385, 387; consciousness of, 365, 398; Epicurean view of, 251–52; fear of, 405; of God, *see* God, question of existence of; inevitability of, 69, 70; man's attitude toward, 404–7; organic development and, 134
Decision, *see* Choice
Declaration of Independence, 26, 182, 247, 260
Deduction, 39, 288
Democracy, 143, 263
Denning, Lord, 295*n*
Descartes, René, 41, 153, 174, 333*n*, 367–68
Determinism, 26, 171–81 *passim*
Dewey, John, 25, 109, 158, 244, 289, 301, 422
Dialogues (Plato), 23, 68, 215; *see also* individual dialogues
Dictionary of Modern English Usage, 373*n*
Dignity, equal personal, 214
Dirac, P. A. M., 97
Diringer, D., 414
Disorder, 117–18
Dixon, W. Macneile, 26
Dobzhansky, Theodosius, 90, 135*n*, 136, 137, 143, 144, 420
Dolce Vita, La, 263
Donne, John, 268, 283
Dostoevsky, Fyodor, 66, 120, 180, 207*n*, 208, 239, 249, 352, 359, 385
Dream(s), 29, 47, 56, 62, 97
Dualism: metaphysical, 58–60, 315–16, 318, 338*n*; of mind and body, 153, 156, 157–61, 174, 338*n*; in sources of knowledge (faith and reason), 338–342
Duncker, Karl, 255, 258
Duty(ies), 210–13, 217, 219, 230–31, 235, 249, 258, 268, 285, 286, 299, 310; actual, 211, 212; prima facie, 204, 205, 211–12, 214, 217, 220–21, 226, 306; of self-sacrifice, 216; social, 264–265; *see also* Ethics
Duval, Evelyn Millis, 419
Dworkin, Gerald, 417

Eckhardt, Ursula M. von, 418
Economics, 70, 86, 89, 91, 100, 114, 184, 273; *see also* Science
Eddy, Mary Baker, 157

Education, 69, 80, 145, 146, 185, 186, 267, 273, 275, 283; religious, 295, 320; sexual, 275, 276, 281; Western, controversies concerning, 267–68
Edwards, David L., 423
Edwards, Paul, 326n, 349, 380n, 409, 415, 424
Einstein, Albert, 33, 102n, 105, 109, 297
Egoism, 214–15, 216, 312, 313
Eliot, T. S., 26, 62, 350n, 390, 392n
Elitism, 262
Emerson, Ralph Waldo, 252–53
Emotion, 147, 256, 380–81
Emotive theory, 297, 302–5, 308
Empiricism, 60, 333, 342, 361, 372, 374n; freedom of will and, 174; mind and, 156, 158; religion and, 344; study of man and, 364–65; ultimate questions and, 362; see also Naturalism; Science
Ends, see Means and ends
Enlightenment, 197, 238
Environment: cultural, 136, 137; social, effect on individual morality, 239–40
Equality, 214, 216, 290; sexual, 276–77
Epicurus/Epicureanism, 197, 248, 251–253, 254, 261, 405
Epiphenomenalism, 160
Epistemology, 44, 361; see also Knowledge
Error(s), 65, 80; Baconian idols and, 70–71; due to historical period, 72–73; prejudice as, 72; scientific, 109–111
Essence, 369; existence and, 373–74
Esthetics, see Beauty
Ethics/Ethical, 18, 20, 31, 32, 33, 35–36, 41, 60, 79, 113, 119, 265, 318, 371; action, see Choice; business, politics and, 226–28, 239; categorical imperative, 211, 217; changing customs and, 191–92, 206–8; character and action, 234–37, 239–40
    choice and action: 193–94, 239; existentialism and, 223–24; making moral decisions, 221–28
    in civic life: civic obedience question, 200–1, 203, 225–26; conflict of goals, 398–99; common sense, 194; compromise, 228–29, 230–31; criminality and, 241–46; critical, 284–315; cultural differences and, 191, 192; deception, question of, 224, 226; decisions, see Choice; defined, 192–93; duty, 210–13, 226, 230–32; evaluation, 192–97, 304–5, 310; existentialist, 364, 367–70; in family life, 273–75; freedom of will and, 169n; general rules and exceptions, 203–5, 224; higher,

228; history of, 197–98; ideal observer, 309, 310; judgment, 236–37, 310; justice, 213–16, 227; killing, ethical problems involved, 198–202, 206; means and ends, question of, 211, 213, 228–32; medical 226n
    morality: defense of, 310–13; higher flights of, 269; sentimentality and, 201–2
    moral urge, 264; motivation, 196–197, 310–12; personal, 238; philosophic, practicality of, 194–97; point of view, 209–10, 227, 307, 308–309, 311; practical, 285–86; punishment and immoral behavior, 237–46 passim; religious, 247, 284–85, 306, 320; rightness, subjective and objective, 233–37; role of, 193–94; separation from religion, 197–98; sexual, 184, 208, 275–82; social environment and individual morality, 239–40, 244; substitution of for religious beliefs, 351–52, 354; theory, 196–97, 222, 224, 288, 309; truth, 190–92, 206, 207; utilitarian, 217–21, 225, 226, 228, 229, 230, 231, 241, 242–43, 245
    values: modern skepticism and, 182–86, 205, 207–8; question of existence of, 182–83, 185, 186–91, 198, 207; sociological problems affecting, 183–86, 207–8; see also Happiness; Ideals; Law(s); Meaning; Metaethics; Religion
Euthyphro, 292, 293
Evaluation, 192–97, 304–5, 310, 386, 388
Evil, 149, 172, 240, 394n, 396n, 403, 404; choice between two or more, 222; in man and nature, 328–29; 332–33, see also Ethics; Punishment
Evolution, theory of, 120n, 125, 127–128, 131–35, 138, 141, 165, 266, 328, 379, 382n; as ethical basis, 300; religion and, 121–22
Ewing, A. C., 149, 153, 212, 237, 245, 265, 294, 306, 418, 420, 421
Excellence, 210, 213, 217, 247, 260–65, 272, 273, 279, 280, 286, 298, 394; love of, 235; religious concept of, 265, 291
Existence, 15, 19, 54, 116, 230, 355; contingency of, 371, 374; essence of, 373–74; personal, 365; religious view of, 314; riddle of, 378; of objects, 333–34; see also Existentialism; God; Life; Meaning
Existentialism, 21, 34, 35, 126, 345, 380n, 394; absence of system in, 364; in art and literature, 359–60; defined, 357–60

difficulties of: essence and existence, 373–74; meaning of existence and, 371; philosophical obscurity, 371–73, 374–75

in English-speaking world, 360–361; ethics of, 364, 367–70; forerunners of, 359; individual and, 364, 367, 370, 371; modern technical society and, 363, 364, 368, 369, 370; moral choice and, 223–24; naturalism and, 359, 362–63; negative character of, 365–66; origin of, 361–63; philosophers, 358–59; as philosophy of crisis, 362–63; psychology and, 363, 364, 367; religious, 358, 359, 370–71; science and, 361
Expediency, 229
Experience, 18, 19, 36, 51, 52, 53, 62, 65, 66, 119, 131, 332; brain process and, 162–64; direct, 45–46; existentialism and, 370; inner, 44, 45; natural, 316; painful, 249; religious, 315, 327–30, 335, 338, 340n, 343; transcendence of, 117; see also Idealism, Berkeleyan; Knowledge
Experiments, 69, 323; scientific, 91, 98, 99, 108–9, 117

Fact(s), 48, 49, 74, 323; god-manifesting, 333; natural, 96; religious, 326; scientific, 89, 99, 111; supernatural, 333; truth and, 31; see also Reality
Faddism, medical, 70
Failure, nerve of, 402–3
Fairchild, Johnson E., 421, 422
Faith, 60, 116, 320–22, 323; animal, 404; bad, 365, 369; definition, 117; leap into, 339; pragmatic, 338n
    religious, 34, 42, 117, 118, 331; Biblical revelation and, 335–38, 339; dualistic theory of sources of knowledge, 338–42; personal revelation and, 335–38, 339–40, 341; reason and, 334, 336–42; secular idealism and, 355–56; scientific, 116; see also Religion
Family/Family relations, 272, 273–75, 276, 384; modern American, 185; society and, 275
Fanaticism, 296n
Farrer, Austin, 372, 422
Fatalism, 179
Fate, 172, 402, 403; freedom of will and, 179; natural, of man, 382–83
Faulkner, William, 239
Feeling, 44–45; religious, 329–30, see also Emotions
Feibleman, James K., 372
Feigl, Herbert, 162, 412, 414, 415

First Cause, 331–32
Fitzgerald, F. Scott, 392
Fleming, Sir Alexander, 89
Flew, A., 339, 343, 422, 423
Flint, James, 417
Formalism, 210, 231, 361–62
Forms, Platonic, 59
Founding Fathers, 26, 203, 263
Fowler, H. W., 373n
Frank, Anne, 258
Frank, Phillipp, 69, 76
Frankel, Charles, 72, 208, 225–26, 412, 413
Frankena, William K., 235, 299, 308–9, 417, 418, 420
Freedman, Mervin B., 278n
Freedom, 243, 260, 280; creative, 368; cost of, 261; existential, 367–70; relinquishing of to authority, 249–51, 254; sexual, see Sex relations; society and, 368; see also Will
Frege, Gottlob, 39
Freud, Sigmund, 16, 25, 66, 70, 97, 183, 239n, 249n, 256, 275n, 338, 365, 385–386, 390n, 402
Friedman, Maurice, 425
Friendship, 268
Fromm, Erich, 180, 235n, 271, 318, 365
Fuchs, Klaus, 225
Function, 379, 394
Fundamentalism, 307, 323, 344
Future, 92; establishing truth concerning, 67–68, 69; of man, 141–46; moral decisions and, 222

Galileo, 83–84, 88–89, 94, 266, 332
Gamow, George, 413
Gandhi, Mahatma, 203, 225, 258, 403
Gardner, John W., 80, 239, 403, 419
Garvin, Lucius, 202n
Genetic(s), 52, 94, 129; as ethical basis, 300; fallacy, 165; theories concerning man's future, 142, 143–44
Geometry, 38, 40
Gibbon, Edward, 320–21n
Gilbert, William, 88
Gilson, Étienne, 358
Glicksberg, Charles I., 393
Glueck, Nelson, 140
God, 11, 15, 22, 41, 42, 77, 99, 112, 131, 157, 159, 179, 187, 188, 195, 204, 247, 253, 310, 315, 316, 319, 321–22, 377, 386n, 390, 393, 394n, 401; belief in, see question of existence of; Berkeleyan idealism and, 55; Biblical commands of, 291–95, 321n, 344; concept of good and, 292–93; as creator, 121–22, 124, 387; is dead, see question of existence of; definition of, 334;

God (*continued*)
  encounter with, 335, 336–38; as first
  cause, 331–32; Kantian dualism and,
  59, 60; man's kinship with, 121, 122;
  moral conduct and belief in, 295,
  296, 297; nature as, *see* Pantheism;
  omnipotence of and freedom of will
  question, 170–71
    question of existence of, 314, 317,
  345, 346*n*, 350, 352, 355, 356, 362,
  363, 364; the Bible and revelation,
  321–27, 334, 351–52; cosmological
  proof, 331–32; faith and, 334–42;
  natural theology and, 331–34; ontological proof, 331, 333–34; orderliness of nature and, 117–18; religious
  experiences and, 327–30; teleological proof, 331, 333–34; verifiability
  of statements concerning, 342–44
    secular, 318–19; Son of, *see* Christ;
  substitution of ethics for belief in,
  351; transcendence of, 322, 363–64;
  as ultimate reality, 314, 315, 316, 317,
  318, 321, 329, 341–42, 349; as unmoved mover, 331–32; without religion, 350; *see also* Bible; Religion;
  Theology
Goethe, Johann W. von, 255, 256, 394–
  395
Golden Rule, 205, 213–14, 216
Good/Goodness, 15, 18, 149, 172, 249,
  252, 256, 261, 264, 273, 279, 286, 306,
  319, 356, 362, 396*n*, 407; concept of
  God and, 292–93, 333; greatest, for
  the greatest number, 210, 217, 219–
  220, 226, 230, 231, 241, 247, 265; love
  of, 265, 268–69, 270; self-interest and,
  298–99; *see also* Ethics; Utilitarianism
Gorgias, 22, 215, 271*n*
Grand Inquisitor, 208, 249–50
Graves, Robert, 280
Greeks, ancient, 14, 16, 32–33, 49, 74,
  81, 88, 90, 111, 140, 153, 167, 171,
  191, 197, 225, 234, 238, 248, 316*n*, 334,
  396–97, 407
Greene, Gäel, 278, 280, 281, 319
Ground of Being, *see* Being
Guilt, 236–37, 244, 366, 399, 403
Guterman, Norbert, 416

Habakkuk, 329
Hallucination, 46, 47, 48, 50
Hamilton, Kenneth, 424
Hamilton, William, 353–54, 423, 424
Hamlet, 161, 392
Hammurabi, Code of, 140
Hampshire, Stuart, 306, 380*n*, 419
Handel, George, 330

Happiness, 15, 366; civic responsibilities and, 251, 252, 253; Epicureanism
  and, 251–53, 254; flaws in ethical doctrines concerning, 256–60; through
  fulfillment, 254–56; hedonistic paradox and, 256; greatest, of the greatest number, 247; maintaining mental
  and moral equilibrium, 253–54; Mill's
  ethics concerning, 256
    peace of mind as: 245, 271, 312;
  Epicureanism and, 251–53, 254; freedom of choice and, 249–51, 252;
  pursuit of, 257–60; sensual pleasure
  as (Hedonism), 248–49; *see also*
  Ethics; Pleasure
Hare, R. M., 272, 308, 419, 420
Harmony, 286; order as, 117; per-
  sonal, 270–73, 394, 402–4, 406; tragic,
  402; *see also* Ethics
Hart, H. L. A., 203, 206, 209, 225, 240,
  244, 418
Harvey, William, 89
Hawkes, Jacquetta, 133, 137, 138, 414
Heaven, 122, 294–95, 401, 407; *see also*
  Immortality
Hebrews, 14, 48, 68, 121*n*, 140, 187,
  191, 205, 296*n*, 327*n*; *see also* Judaism
Hecht, Selig, 412
Hector, 396
Hedonism, 217, 248–49, 256, 263, 280
Hegel, Georg, 26, 361
Heidegger, Martin, 358–59, 360, 362,
  364, 365, 368, 369, 370, 372, 378, 425
Heineman, F. H., 424
Hell, 112, 294, 295, 296, 406, 407
Hemingway, Ernest, 248, 268
Hepburn, R. W., 343, 368, 420, 423,
  426
Heracleites, 14
Herodotus, 73–74
Herschel, Sir William, 96
Hester, Jr., Joseph A., 414
Hick, John, 322, 323, 327*n*, 333*n*, 334,
  335*n*, 336–37, 344*n*, 351, 422, 423
Higher Realm, 60
Hillel, Rabbi, 213
Hindus, 31, 191, 326, 327*n*
History, 17, 20, 101, 363; cycle theory
  of, 142–43; historical process, 18–19;
  as science, 86–87
Hitler, Adolf, 201, 237, 285, 305, 312,
  358–59, 362, 366, 406
Hobbes, Thomas, 174, 307–10
Hocking, W. E., 416
Hoffer, Eric, 26, 42
Holmes, Oliver Wendell, 398
Holton, G., 412, 413
Homer, 257, 352, 396–97
Homo sapiens, *see* Man

Homunculi, 166

Hook, Sidney, 158, 164, 326*n*, 341, 349*n*, 360*n*, 398, 414, 415, 423, 424, 426

Hospers, John, 32, 202, 225, 226*n*, 296, 308, 309, 409, 411, 413, 415, 416, 417, 418, 420, 422, 423

Housman, H. E., 388

Hoyle, Fred, 413

Huckleberry Finn, 177

Huizinga, J., 406*n*

Human condition, 358, 364, 388

Humani generis (Encyclical), 122*n*

Humanism, 122, 310, 311, 344, 352, 363, 370, 371; art of living and, 402–4; critical, 27; defined, 265; new theological trends and, 352–56; *see also* Ethics; Ideals; Love

Human moods, 364

Hume, David, 249, 415, 418; *see also* Induction

Humility, 236, 260, 261, 262, 396*n*

Husserl, Edmund, 358*n*

Huxley, Aldous, 120*n*, 142, 266

Huxley, Julian, 120*n*, 128, 132, 134, 164, 300, 318, 414

Huxley, Thomas, 120*n*, 132

Huygens, Christian, 104

Hypocrisy, 240

Hypotheses, 39, 69, 101; *see also* Theories

Ibsen, Henrik, 212*n*, 257, 307

Idealism, 119, 146, 161, 228, 238–39, 352, 366
    Berkeleyan: 54–55, 156, 160; refutation of, 55–58; defined, 55*n*

Ideal observer, 309, 310

Ideals, 183, 230–32, 286, 294, 295, 310, 319, 320, 350; active, 260–65; active relation between actual and, 319; aristocratic, 262–63; beauty, love of, 265, 269–70; benevolence, 210, 217, 227; cultural, 212–13; excellence, 260–65; of family life, 273–75; goodness, love of, 265, 268–69, 270; happiness, 247–60; human equality, 290; immoral, 263–64; moral urge and, 264; passive, 260–61; personal harmony, 270–73; political, 269; in sex relations, 275–82; truth, love of, 265–268, 270; *see also* Ethics; Values

Idea(s): perfect, 59; transcendent, 131

Identity: inner, 224; psycho-neural, 161–64; *see also* Self

Idols, Baconian, 70–71

Ignorance, four causes of, 71

Illusions, 48, 49, 62–63

Immortality, 158–59, 344*n*, 347, 385, 397*n*, 406–7

Implication, 39

Induction, 95–101 *passim*, 152*n*, 165, 288, 298

Industrial Age, 139

Inferences, 39

Infinite, 315, 316

Insight, rational, 306

Inspiration, Divine, 131

Intellectual rectitude, 339

Intuitionism, 40, 152, 290, 306; religious, 327*n*, 329–30

Ionesco, Eugene, 239

Irregularities, 47

Isaac, 293

Isaiah, 205, 335

James, William, 7, 60, 301, 315–16, 335*n*, 359

Jaspers, Karl, 358, 359, 360, 364*n*, 367, 370, 373

Janism, 316*n*

Jastrow, Robert, 413

Jefferson, Thomas, 23, 228, 309–10

Jehovah, 337; *see also* God

Jenkins, David, 346

Jepthah, 293

Jesus, *see* Christ

Jews, *see* Hebrews

Job, 117, 328, 330*n*, 359, 386*n*, 397, 403

Johnson, O. A., 206

Jones, Ernest, 402

Jones, W. T., 167, 170, 409, 411, 412, 415, 418, 422

Judaism, 315, 316, 317, 345; *see also* Hebrews; Religion

Judgment(s), 31, 33; descriptive, 287, 299; Last, 406
    moral: 236–37, 310; justification of, 288–90; prescriptive, 287; *see also* Ethics

Julius Caesar, 179

Justice, 15, 19, 195, 205, 210, 211, 213–216, 217, 218, 221, 227, 230–31, 234, 242, 268, 269, 286, 287, 289, 291, 298; criminal, 241, 244; distributive, 272; divine, 328; fate and, 403; social, 240; *see also* Ethics

Justification, 310, 311

Justinian, 20

Kafka, Franz, 359, 401

Kant, Immanuel, 11, 21, 22, 27, 95, 120, 126, 174, 192, 194, 198, 210, 211, 213, 217, 220, 223, 234, 235, 242, 243, 244, 259, 264, 280, 306, 333*n*, 334, 418; *see also* Causality

Kaplan, Abraham, 302*n*, 366

Kaufmann, Walter, 216, 255, 360*n*, 369*n*, 406*n*, 416, 417, 418, 420, 422, 424, 425
Kennedy, John F., 68, 366, 403
Kepler, Johann, 89
Kierkegaard, Sören, 339, 355, 359, 361, 364, 365, 369, 370, 374
Kilvert, Francis, 387
Kim, Jaegwon, 414
King, Martin Luther, 203, 258
King Lear, 166, 407
Kinsey, Alfred, 282, 298
Kirkendall, Lester A., 419
Knowledge, theory of, 20, 24–26, 31, 146, 194, 224, 285*n*; dualism in sources of, 338–42
  empirical: 33, 83, 84–85, 341; Berkeleyan idealism and, 54–58; coherence and, 47–48, 51, 53; the doubter and, 52–53; dreams and, 47–48, 49, 51–52, 62–63; of external world, 44–47; fallibility of perception, 44, 47, 49–51; hallucinations and, 47, 48–49; of inner experiences, 44–45; introspective awareness as source of, 45; Kantian dualism and, 58–60; mind and sensual impressions, 51; possibility of truth in, 61–62, 64; reality and the poetic outlook, 62–64; reality of physical objects, 56–58; senses as source of, 44–46; sensual impressions and observational statements, 46–52, 53, 54; subjective appearances and objective reality, 51–52, 54, 58–60
  love of, 235; man's drive for, 252–253; perceptual, 35–36; purpose in acquiring, 266–68; sociology of, 73–74; unity of, 297–98; *see also* Language
Koestler, Arthur, 416
Koran, 323

Labor, drudgery of, 272–73
Language, 49, 51, 137, 140, 149, 157, 160, 361; ethical, 302–5; evolution of, 136; Indo-European, 140; observation statements, 29–30; religious, 340–41, 351; *see* Words
Lauer, Quentin, 358*n*
Law(s), 20, 74, 236, 295*n*, 296
  civic: 200–1, 203, 212, 225; moral right against, 225–26; criminal, 241, 242, 243–44; cyclical historical, 142–143; eternal, 225; of logic, 312; moral, 11, 100, 118, 190; Mosaic, 187, 242; natural, 98–101, 102, 112, 134, 148, 170, 171–81 *passim*, 378
  scientific: 39, 51, 83, 84, 87, 91, 92–95, 96, 98–101, 111, 117, 148, 206;

discovery of, 108–9; universal, *see* natural; violation of, 225; *see also* Theories
Lawrence, E. O., 180
LeClezio, J. M. G., 426
Lenin, Nikolai, 26, 230
Lewis, C. I., 18, 51, 59, 177, 233, 290, 306, 416
Lewis, H. D., 415
Libertarianism, 174–76
Liberty, 15, 269
Life: art of living, 402–4; defined, 158; eternal, 347, 406; of evildoers, 404; force, 384; futility of, 396; meaning of, 371, 388–96
  organic: as mystery, 130–31; early stages of, 129–30; explanation of, 127–30, 131; problem of, 362; rational way of, 306–10; simple, 390, 393; *see also* Evolution; Existence; Man; Meaning
Life With Father, 185
Lincoln, Abraham, 16, 75
Lin Yutang, 248
Lippmann, Walter, 274, 277
Locke, John, 24–25, 26, 36
Logic, 20, 35, 300, 361; defined, 39; ethics and, 289, 311, 312; of everyday usage, 39; existence of God and, 331, 333–34; mathematics and, 40, 41; relativism and, 66; skepticism and, 66; truth and, 38–39, 53
Logical positivism, 60*n*, 303, 342
Loneliness, 367
Love, 15, 119, 157, 273, 286, 336, 356, 366, 396*n*, 407; of beauty, 265, 269–270; of God, 328, 337, 338, 343–44; of goodness, 265, 268–69, 270; in sexual relations, 280, 383–84; of truth, 265–68, 270; *see also* Ethics; Golden Rule
Lovell, A. C. B., 123, 413
Luther, Martin, 34, 48, 237, 339*n*, 345, 405

Macaulay, Rose, 405
Macbeth, 161, 392
Macgowan, Kenneth, 140, 414
MacIntyre, A., 223, 339, 374*n*, 423
MacLeish, Archibald, 359–60
Macquarrie, John, 345, 425
Maimonides, 331
Maistre, Joseph Marie de, 390
Malamud, Bernard, 239
Malraux, André, 394*n*
Man: active and passive, 260; age of species, 13; animal nature of, 383–84, 385; biological characteristics of, 135–37; condition of, 383; conscious-

ness of self, 382, 398, 404, 407; cultural traits and development, 135, 136, 137, 138–41; dehumanization and objectivation of, 363; empirical study of, 364–65; evolution of, 84

future of: classical utopias and, 141–42; cycle theory of history and, 142–43; genetic trends and, 142, 143–144; population explosion and, 144–146

great-souled, 402; human condition and, 358, 364, 388; idealistic view of, 238–39; inner life of and scientific formulas, 93, 94; meaning of nature to, 385–88; nature of, 120

place of in nature, 120; creation story and, 121–22, 124, 129; cultural traits and development, 135, 136, 137, 138–41; evolutionary theory and, 121–22, 125, 131–35, 138; the future, 141–46; nature of organic life and, 127–31; special traits of *Homo Sapiens*, 135–37; universe and, 122, 123–27; primitive, 13, 73, 138–140; race differentiation, 137; as such, meaning of in nature, 382–85; suicide, will to survive and, 384–85; wickedness of, 328–29; *see also* Meaning, of man's life; Nature

Manser, Anthony, 365
Martin, John B., 415
Marcel, Gabriel, 358
Marriage, 274–75, 276, 279, 280; sexual relations in, 281–82
Marriage of Figaro, 190
Marty, Martin E., 316*n*, 320*n*
Marxism, 26–27, 266, 359, 363; *see also* Communism
Mass media, 71, 74–77
Materialism, 60*n*, 161, 374; mind and, 156–57, 159, 160
Mathematics, 17, 35, 288, 361; defined, 39–40; historical development of, 40–41; logic and, 40; in science, 91; truth and, 38; *see also* Science
Matter, 18, 36
Mead, Hunter, 409
Mead, Margaret, 274, 275*n*
Meaning/Meaningfulness: consciousness and, 378–79; factual, 35–36; of human condition, *see* of man's life; of man as such in nature, 382–85

of man's life: actions as sum of, 371, 394–95; complexity of his nature, 389; consciousness of self and, 382, 398, 404, 407; death and, 404–7; evildoers and, 404; general praise and condemnation of, 390–94; to himself and others, 388, 389–90, 391,

395–96, 402; humanistic ethics and, 388–89; ideal of harmony and, 402–4, 406; the individual, 391–93; paradox of his existence, 389; positive aspects, 400, 401–2; the romantic view, 401; self created purpose and function, 394, 395–96; the sordid view, 400–1; the tragic view, 396–400; of nature as such, 375–81

of nature to man, 385–88; understanding *v.* evaluation, 386; purpose, significance and, 378–80, 381, 382; questions, 379–80; study of, 35–37; ultimate, 388; of the universe, *see* of nature; of words, *see* Language; *see also* Ethics; Truth

Means and ends, 228–32, 280
Measure for Measure, 405
Meekness, *see* Humility
Mehta, Ved, 350*n*
Melden, A. I., 417
Melville, Herman, 359
Messiah, 330
Metaethics: intuitionism, 306

justification of ethics, problem of: 284–85, 286, 289, 290; conscience and, 291; emotive theory and, 297, 302–5; empirical approach, naturalism, 297–301; moral judgments, validity of, 302–3, 304, 309; naturalistic fallacy, 299–300; rationalism and, 297, 305–310, 311; religion and, 291–97

objectivity of ethical values: moral judgments, validity of, 284–85, 286–290; practical ethics and, 285–86; proving ethical judgments, 288–90; rational way of life theory, 306–10; religion and moral behavior, 295–97

Metaphysics, 17–18, 20, 41, 119, 156, 333*n*, 382, 391, 401; speculative, 363
Method, experimental, 83–84, 90, 109, 117, 297, 361
Meyerhoff, Hans, 412
Micah, 90, 205
Michael, Jerome, 245–46, 418
Michelangelo, 121, 256
Middle Ages, 16, 41, 48, 71, 88, 331, 391, 393
Midsummer Night's Dream, A, 47
Mill, John Stuart, 210, 211, 217, 218, 243, 247, 252, 256, 260, 290, 291, 296, 305–6, 397
Millay, Edna St. Vincent, 392*n*
Miller, Arthur, 214, 397
Milton, John, 25–26
Mind, 15, 18, 25, 95, 130, 169*n*, 195; abilities of and freedom of will, 147–148, 149–50; defined, 149; dualistic

Mind (*continued*)
    theories concerning, 153, 156–57,
    159, 160, 161, 174, 338*n;* electronic
    brains, mindedness of, 166–67; Epi-
    curianism and, 252; evolution of
    mindedness, 165–66; identity theory
    concerning, 161–64; knowing the
    mind of others, 148, 150–52
        monistic theories concerning, 156;
    idealist, 157, 160; materialist, 156–57,
    160; naturalist, 158–60; pan-psychism
    and, 165–66; perfect, theory of, 93;
    philosophic problems concerning,
    148; place of in nature, 148, 153, 156
        relation between body and, 148,
    153–56; epiphenomenalism, 160; psy-
    choneural theory, 161–64; psycho-
    physical parallelism, 160–61
        religious doctrines concerning,
    153, 158–59; sensual impressions and,
    51; states of, 49; existentialism and,
    364; *see also* Will, freedom of
Miracles, 98, 107
Mises, Richard von, 86
Moby Dick, 359
Modernism, 252
Modo geometrico, 42
Monism, 272, 274, 319, 346; mind and,
    156–57, 158–59, 160; naturalistic, 158–
    160
Montagu, Ashley, 66, 137, 412, 414
Montaigne, Michel de, 238
Montesquieu, 26
Moore, G. E., 210*n,* 247, 290, 299, 306
Morality, *see* Ethics
Morgan, Jr., Charles, 232*n*
Morgenbesser, Sidney, 412, 415, 418
Morris, William, 300*n*
Mosaic Law, 187, 242
Moses, 323, 325, 326, 403*n*
Motivation, 310, 311
Mozart, Wolfgang A., 120, 190, 388
Muller, Herbert J., 26, 177, 238*n,* 253,
    260, 261, 262, 356, 380, 394, 397, 401,
    407, 414, 422, 426
Muslims, 326, 327*n*
Mysteries, religious, 326, 341
Mysticism, 340*n;* Eastern, 318; *see also*
    Theology
Myths, 14, 48–49, 70, 72–73, 88, 115,
    171, 344, 356; ancient Greek, 121,
    238, 323
        Biblical, 77, 187, 323–25, 351;
    Adam and Eve, 323, 325; Cain and
    Abel, 170–71, 186, 187–89, 205;
    creation story, 73, 87–88, 121–22, 129,
    307, 324–25; *see also* individual
    mythological characters

Nagel, Ernest, 19, 27, 32, 86*n,* 119, 158,
    178, 315*n,* 411, 412, 413, 414, 422, 426
Nakhnikian, G., 340*n,* 417, 422
Nationalism, 317
Natural and unnatural, 263–64
Naturalism, 19, 21, 60, 122, 128, 134,
    303, 329, 330, 342, 345, 352, 364*n,* 373,
    407; critical humanistic, 27
        as ethical basis, 297–301; Contex-
    tualist theory, 300–1; evolutionary
    direction theory, 300; genetic ex-
    planation, 300; naturalistic fallacy,
    299–300; existentialism and, 357, 363–
    364; monistic, 158–60; ultimate ques-
    tions and, 380*n;* view of nature, 378,
    381; *see also* Ethics
Naturalistic fallacy, 299–300
Nature, 15, 22, 82, 88, 120, 330, 364;
    animal, 384; beauty of, 269–70, 272;
    benevolence of, 333; evil in, 328–29,
    332; God revealed through, 327–29,
    331–33; human, as ethical basis 298–
    299; question of natural and un-
    natural, 263–64; idealized view of,
    380–81; irregularities in, 95, 96–98;
    man as a creature of, 382–85
        meaningfulness of, 376–81; to man,
    385–88; mind and, 148, 153, 158;
    order and uniformity of, 25, 95–96,
    117–18, 128, 148, 316, 331, 333, 377–
    378; prediction of events in, 93–94;
    and question of causality and induc-
    tion, 95–101; scientific interpretation
    of, 329; *see also* Laws; Pantheism;
    Science
Nausea, 362, 365, 368
Necessity, natural, 246
Nelson, Leonard, 62, 194, 203, 214, 228,
    231, 242, 264, 273, 310, 418, 419, 421
Neolithic Age, *see* Stone Age
Neo-Platonism, 19
Nerve of failure, 402–3
Neurophysiology, 162
Newman, James R., 97
Newman, John, 338
Newton, Isaac, 16–17, 89, 94, 101, 104,
    332
Niebuhr, Reinhold, 17, 195, 269, 416
Nielsen, Kai, 194, 312–13, 339, 380*n,*
    422, 423, 424
Nietzsche, Friedrich, 210, 215–16, 249,
    262, 264, 271, 286, 290, 354, 359, 362,
    363, 368, 370, 374, 423
Nihilism, 223, 404
Nirvana, 201, 394
Nobility, 402
Noss, John P., 421
Nothingness, 363, 365, 371, 372, 377,
    378, 382, 392–93, 406*n*

Numinous, 327n, 329-30

Objectivism, 60, 290
Objects: as such, 379; existence of, 333-34; physical reality of, 102-3; totality of all, 332; truth and, 31; ultimate reality of, 30, 31
Obligation, 212-13, 292, 299
O'Connor, D. J., 374n
O'Connor, Flannery, 345n
Ogg, Elizabeth, 419
Ogletree, Thomas W., 424
O'Neill, Eugene, 401, 403
Ontology, 333n, 364, 366
Opinion, 71, 78-79
Oppenheim, Paul, 414
Order, cosmic, 316n
Origen, 323-24
Orwell, George, 142, 250
Otto, Rudolf, 327n, 330

Pacifism, 201
Pain: mental, 249-53; physical, 249, 251
Paleolithic Era, see Stone Age
Paley, William, 332
Pan-psychism, 165-66
Pantheism, 42, 319; see also Nature
Pap, Arthur, 36, 179, 415
Paradox(es), 39, 104; of existence, 389; hedonistic, 256; of religious belief, 338-42, 343, 397n; Tertullian's, 338-339, 340
Parker, DeWitt, 271, 402, 419
Parallelism, psycho-physical, 160-61
Particles: reality of, 102-7; subatomic, 164
Pascal, Blaise, 119, 126, 266, 334, 359, 374, 385, 390
Passion According to St. Matthew, 389n
Paterson, Alexander, 246
Paton, H. J., 332-33, 422
Peace, universal, 238
Pedagogy, 70
Peierls, R. E., 104, 106
Peirce, Benjamin, 39
Peirce, Charles, 39, 46
Pepper, Stephen C., 414
Perceptions, see Knowledge
Perry, R. B., 298
Petrarch, 386
Peyre, Henri, 119, 372, 425
Phaedo, 19
Phenomena, mental, 150; microphysical, 105; natural, 50, 97, 99, 101, 103, 189, 377
Phenomenology, 358n, 364
Philo, 323

Philosophy, 149; academic, existentialist attitude toward, 361-62; American society, 23-24, 26; clarification of language through, 157; computer theory and, 166-67; defined, 15-22 passim, 25, 29; of education, 283; ethical, modern skepticism and, 182-183; German idealist, 345; Greek, 14, 60; history, 14, 19-21, 156; instrumental, 301n; irrational, 34-35; language and, 14-15; man's concern with, 22-27
 modern, 21; attitude of, 59-60; formalistic analysis, 361-62; function of, 18-19; political, 26-27, 200, 203, 283; practical, 194, 211; of pure thought, 361; rational, origin of, 41-43; rationality and emotion, 16, 25; relevance and role, 11-27 passim
 of science: 194; causality and induction, 95-101; modern physics and, 102-8; sciences and, 16-17, 20, 21-22; task of, 81; theology and, 16; Thomistic, see Thomism; ultimate reality and, 17-19; see also individual schools and philosophers
Physics, 16-17, 20, 52, 83, 92, 93; laws of, 106; modern, problems presented by, 102-8; objects of, 102-3; particle, 102-7; quantum theory, 92, 101, 104, 105, 148; uncertainty principle, 105-108; see also Science
Picasso, Pablo, 161, 366
Pilate, Pontius, 30-31
Pius XII, 122n
Place, U. T., 414
Plato, 14, 15, 16, 18, 19, 21, 22, 23, 24, 26, 30, 41, 44, 49, 59, 68, 88, 158, 166, 197, 203n, 210, 215, 242-43, 248, 250, 251n, 262, 263, 265, 266, 270-71, 283, 292, 305, 312, 418
Pleasure: attainment of, 217-18, 256; Epicureanism and, 251; sensual, 248-249, 251, 263, 276; see also Happiness
Plotinus, 167
Podhoretz, Norman, 416
Poetry, 36, 37
Poincaré, Henri, 111-12, 116
Politics, 26, 42, 70, 239; ethics and, 226-28; modern, 183, 184-85, 186; philosophy of, 283
Population explosion, 144-46, 184, 275, 300
Positivism, 60n; logical, 60n, 303, 342
Potok, Chaim, 344
Pound, Ezra, 248
Pragmatism, 359
Predestination, 179

Prediction, freedom of will and, 180; historical, 142–43; scientific, 93–94, 95, 99–101, 117

Prejudice, 71, 72

Price, H. H., 46, 56, 337

Pride, 261, 262

Principles, 21; ultimate, 388; *see also* Ethics

Problem(s): of life, 362; factual, 108

Propaganda, mass-media and, 74–77

Prophets, Biblical, 210, 238, 325, 326*n*; *see also* individual prophets

Propositions, 31, 39, 42; truth and, 31–32

Proof(s), 39, 56; cosmological, 331–32; defined, 288–89; of God's existence, 331–34; ontological, 331, 333–34; teleological, 331, 332–33

Property, phenomenal, 163; physical, 163

Protagoras, 290

Protestantism, 315, 352; *see also* Religion

Prudence, 251

Psychiatry, 17, 89, 110; existentialist, 360; *see also* Psychology

Psychology, 16, 17, 21, 25, 66–67, 91, 93, 97, 100, 110, 155–56, 239, 275*n*, 287, 380*n*, 395; animal, 164; dynamic, 172; existentialism and, 345, 364–67; psychological warfare, 77; religious faith and, 338; *see also* Science

Public opinion, 296

Punishment: capital, 199–200, 241, 291; ethical, 199–200, 210; moral, 233; as retribution, 241–43, 244, 245; *see also* Ethics

Puritanism, 195, 240, 249, 278; *see also* Religion

Purpose, 377, 394; defined, 378–79; ultimate, 116–17; *see also* Meaning

Qualities, natural, 50, 299

Quantum theory, *see* Physics

Questions: basic, 12; evaluative, 287; factual, 287; moral, *see* Ethics; ultimate, 12, 17–19, 79, 99, 117, 124, 362, 374, 376, 380*n*; *see also* Meaning

Rabinowitch, Eugene, 412

Ramsay, Frank, 125–26

Ramsey, Paul, 290, 292, 295

Raphael, D. D., 178

Rationalism: 41–43, 303, 313, 374, 396, 402; as ethical basis: 297, 305–6, 311, 313; intuitionist position, 306; way of life, 306–10

Rationalization, 194–95

Realism, 18, relational or perspective, 60; *see also* Empiricism; Naturalism

Real/Reality, 15, 18, 46–47, 165, 266, 343; absolute, 59; appearance and, 48; atomic, 102–7; common sense view of, 11; factual, 249; finite, 318; God as ultimate, 314, 315, 316, 318, 321, 329, 341–42; monistic view of, 60; objective, 51; observed, 30; poetic outlook and, 62–64; of physical objects, 102–3; scientific view of, 11; sensual impressions and, 49–51, 52, 55–56, 58–60; substitution of images for, 71; of things-in-themselves, 58–60; three opposites of, 47; ultimate, 17, 29, 347

Reason, 25, 70, 81, 149, 286, 289, 394; faith and, 334, 336–37, 339; practical, 306; self-confidence of, 62; truth and, 34, 36; *see also* Dualism; Mind; Rationalism

Reductionism, 119, 131, 161

Reformation, 320, 335

Reification, 128, 158

Reiss, I. L., 281

Relativism, 65–66, 78, 79, 189; in ethics, 206–8

Relativity, theory of, 33, 102*n*

Religion, 12, 15, 20, 31, 33, 35–36, 79, 102, 157, 228, 247, 285, 382, 386; in American society, 314, 320*n*; as answer to purpose and meaning of existence, 314; as basis of ethics, 291–95, 306; concept of excellence and, 265, 291,; in contemporary world, 185; cultural problems concerning, 319–21

definitions of, 116, 344, 351; pantheism, 319; personal religiousness, 316–17; political ideologies as, 317–318; secular, 315–19; supernatural dualism, 315–16, 318

divergence of beliefs in, 77–79; Eastern, 292, 316*n*, 320*n*, 323; ethics and, 197–98, 291–95, 306; existential, 370–71; freedom of will and, 170–71; higher, 249; Judeo-Christian commands and tradition, 291–95; Man's nature and, 120; obscure statements in, 37

organized, 317, 352, 370; future of in modern world, 354–55; pagan, 316*n*; primitive, 13, 138; science and, 110, 112, 115–19, 294*n*, 317*n*, 345, 356; secularization of, 345–56 *passim; as* the sum total of ethical ideals, 294, 295; symbolism, in 348; theory of evolution and, 121–22; traditional,

moral behavior and, 295–97; utility of, 295–97; *see also* Bible; Faith; God; Myths; Theology; individual religions
Rembrandt, 120, 269, 400
Renaissance, 74, 81, 238, 393, 401
Republic, The, 19, 166, 197, 215
Requiem (Verdi), 166
Research, scientific, 84, 93
Resignation, humanistic, 406
Resurrection, *see* Christ
Retribution, 241–43, 244*n*, 245, *see also* Punishment
Revelation, 116, 294, 295, 322, 325, 327, 328, 331, 335, 336, 337, 339, 349
Riesman, David, 254, 261, 320, 365, 402, 426
Rights: inalienable, 212; reasonable, 212; ultimate ground of the, 290, 293
Righteousness, 228, 242
Rightness, subjective and objective, 233–37
Rilke, Rainer Maria, 369
Robbins, Herbert, 40*n*
Robinson, E. S., 425
Robinson, John A. I., 347*n*, 424
Robinson, Richard, 419
Rodin, Auguste, 120
Roman Catholic Church, *see* Catholicism
Romans, Ancient, 88, 197, 316*n*, 334
Romanticism, 392, 401
Roosevelt, Franklin D., 394
Rosenzweig, Franz, 236, 358
Ross, David, 177, 211–12, 220, 244, 245, 306
Rubinstein, Richard A., 352, 424
Rules, utility of, 220–21, 226, *see also* Ethics
Russell, Bertrand, 36, 266, 286–87, 290, 302, 372*n*, 332, 382–83, 412
Ruth, 238
Ryle, Gilbert, 149*n*, 157, 360*n*, 372

St. Anselm, 326, 333*n*, 334
St. Augustine, 88, 170
St. John, Gospel of, 30–31, 37, 42, 323, 336*n*
St. John of the Cross, 325
St. Matthew, Gospel of, 214, 228, 236, 294*n*
St. Paul, 117, 172, 196, 197, 313, 406
Salinger, J. D., 224
Salk, Jonas, 109
Salvation, 119
Santayana, George, 263, 390, 393, 406, 422

Sartre, Jean-Paul, 168, 180, 223, 232, 358, 359, 360, 361, 362, 365, 367, 368, 369, 370, 372, 373, 384, 394, 425
Schmeck, Jr., Harold M., 130
Schmitt, Gladys, 182
Scholasticism, 41, 331
Schopenhauer, Arthur, 55, 177, 318
Schubert, Franz, 252, 388
Schurz, Carl, 264
Science(s), 16–17, 18, 19, 20, 21–22, 33, 42, 62, 63, 74, 80, 142, 149, 158–59, 184, 186, 192, 224, 286, 329, 340, 364, 385; affirmative and negative values of, 114–15; applied; 84, 111; basic, 84–85; biological, 85, 91; controversies in, 109–10; defined, 87–95; decription and prediction, 83; discovery of scientific laws, 108–9; empirical, 87, 88–90; errors made in, 109–111; exact, 85, 91; existentialism and, 361; experimental method, 83–84, 90, 109, 117, 297, 361; factual knowledge and, 83, 84–85; generalizations in, 87, 94–95; history as, 86–87; humanistic idealism and, 146; man's nature and, 120; mathematics and, 39, 41, 91; medical, 45; modern, 267; moral, 301; natural, 66, 85; objective, 87, 90
philosophy of: 194; causality and induction, 95–101; popularization of, 92, 105, 113; precision in, 87, 91–92; prediction in, 93–94, 95, 99–101, 117; pure, aims of, 111–14; religion and, 110, 112, 115–19, 294*n*, 317*n*, 345, 356; rise of and free will question, 171, 175–76; scientific theory, question of, 101; social, 66, 85–86, 87, 93, 114, 193, 267, 287, 364–65; society and, 113–14; specialization, 91–92; speculation and authority as basis for, 87–88, 89; systematic order, 83, 92–94; transcendence of everyday knowledge by, 82–83, 84; truth and, 38; types of, 85–87; uncertainties of, 68–69; *see also* Empiricism; Evolution, theory of; Life; Man, place of in nature; Philosophy; Universe; individual sciences
Science Ponders Religion, 116*n*
Scientists, 114
Schilpp, Paul A., 302*n*
Scott, Robert F., 202*n*
Secularism, 316–91, 320, 345–56 *passim*; existentialism and, 364
Self, 18; deception, *see* Faith, bad; denial, 396*n*; fulfillment, 273; good, 264; identification, 382, interest, 298; knowledge, 260; modern confusion concerning, 66–67; pity, 403; realiza-

Self (*continued*)
 tion, 260, 271; respect, 261; sacrifice, 216, 218; sufficiency, 251; *see also* Consciousness; Man
Sellars, Wilfred, 415
Semantics, *see* Language
Senses, 44–45, 152, 164; mind and, 153, 154; *see also* Dualism; Idealism; Knowledge
Sentimentality, 202
Sermon on the Mount, 182, 196, 205
Sesonske, Alexander, 305
Sex relations, 272, 298; double standard, 277; ethics of, 275–82; love and, 383–84; in marriage, 281–82; modern revolution in, 184, 185, 208
Shakespeare, William, 28, 62, 65, 120, 193, 257, 352, 359, 369, 374, 385, 389, 390, 405–6, 407
Shapley, Harlow, 116*n*
Shaw, George Bernard, 384
Shepherd of Hermas, 402
Shinto, 320*n*
Sickness: existential, 362; physical, 387–88
Sidgwick, Henry, 214, 236–37
Significance, 134–35; defined, 378; *see also* Meaning
Silence, 362
Simons, Hans, 79
Simpson, George G., 89, 133, 135, 413, 414
Sin, 170, 188, 196, 240, 241, 252; original, 238, 239
Sinnott, E. W., 129
Skepticism, 28, 42, 52–53, 62, 182, 189, 205, 208, 239, 291, 308, 310, 311, 312, 334, 342; danger of, 81; defined, 66; healthy, 79–80; mass-media, propaganda and, 74–77; origin of, 65–66; refutation of, 79; self-confusion and, 66–67; *see also* Truth, quest
Smart, J. J. C., 162, 414
Smart, Ninian, 372*n*, 421
Smith, John E., 315*n*
Smith, Wilfred C., 315*n*, 316*n*, 335, 421
Snow, C. P., 119, 267
Socialism, 185
Society, *see* Ethics, Family, Politics
Sociology, 86, 298, 365; of knowledge, 73–74; problems of contemporary world, 183–86
Socrates, 15, 16, 19, 23, 24, 73, 201, 215, 218, 223, 224, 225, 228, 238, 265, 266, 290, 292, 353, 369, 403
Song of Songs, 278
Sophists/Sophistry, 18, 194–95

Sophocles, 135, 225, 368, 369, 396
Soul, 118, 127, 149, 335, 336, 383, 407; defined, 153; dichotomy of body and, 275–76; immortal, 158–59; *see also* Consciousness; Mind
Space and Time, 60, 381, *see also* Dualism
Specialization, 85, 267
Speculation, scientific, 88–89
Spinoza, Baruch, 21, 25, 41–42, 271, 319, 402, 419
Spirit, 149, *see also* Soul
Spitz, David, 263
Stace, W. T., 423
Stalin, Joseph, 240
State-of-mind, different modes of, 364
States-of-affairs, 31, 33, 57; empirical, 344
Statistics, 39, 76, 298
Stebbing, Susan L., 192, 233, 256, 412
Stein, Gertrude, 18
Steinberg, Milton, 205*n*
Stengel, Erwin, 426
Stevenson, Charles L., 302–3, 304, 421
Stoics/Stoicism, 197, 254, 385*n*, 402
Stokes, Walter R., 279
Stone Age, 136, 138–39
Stout, A. K., 180
Strawson, P. F., 272, 341
Strindberg, August, 239
Substance, 56, 346
Suffering: acceptance of, 403; human existentialism and, 362; natural, 387–388, *see also* Pain
Suicide, 384–85, 404
Sullivan, Walter, 132
Summum bonum, *see* Good, greatest
Supernaturalism, 98, 356
Superstition, 70, 71, 73
Symbolism: religious, 348, 349*n*; Tillichian, 346, 348–49
Synthesis, 92

Talmud, 205*n*, 232, 283
Taoism, 316*n*
Taylor, A. E., 327*n*
Taylor, Paul, 290*n*, 299, 308, 420, 421
Taylor, Richard, 341, 416
Technology, 39, 83, 84–85, 91, 111, 113, 115, 125, 143, 184, 202, 267, 345, 364; computers, 166–67
Ten Commandments, 182, 187, 196, 198*n*, 201, 204–5, 273, 282, 294*n*, 325
Tertullian, 338–39
Theatetus, 44, 49
Theism, 188
Theists, verbal, 344
Theogenis, 384*n*

Theology, 16, 41, 59, 153, 167, 188, 197, 238, 262, 380n, 401; atheistic, 345–56 passim
contemporary trends in: confusion found in, 349–50; God-is-dead theology, 352–54; religionless Christianity, 350; substitution of ethics for religious belief, 351–52, 354; Tillich's mystical theology, 345–49
existentialist, 360; modern, personal God experience and, 336–37; natural, see contemporary trends in, 345; see also Faith; God; Religion
Theorems: mathematical, 40, 288; philosophic, 41
Theory (ies), 21, 25; emotive, 297, 302–305, 308; ethical, 196–97, 222, 224, 228, 309; naturalistic, 167; scientific, 89–90, 91, 94, 97, 98, 99, 101, 109, 110–11; teleological, 217; see also Laws
Thinking, as social act, 72
Things: as such, 379, 380; inward, 375
Thomas, Dylan, 166, 382
Thomas, John, 335n
Thomism, 20, 21, 41, 331; see also Aquinas, St. Thomas
Thomson, Judith J., 417
Thoreau, Henry David, 203, 399
Tillich, Paul, 336, 345–49, 355, 358, 360, 363, 368, 403, 424
Timaeus, 88
Time and space, 18, 381; see also Dualism; Future
Titus, Harold, 126, 135
Tolstoy, 35n, 338, 359, 380, 388, 392n, 396n, 406, 426
Torah, 187; see also Bible
Totalitarianism, 250–51, 272, 317
Toynbee, Arnold, 87
Tradition, Judeo-Christian, 291–95; see also Religion
Tragic harmony, 402
Tragic view, of life, 396–400
Transcendence: divine, 346, 348, 363–364; existentialist, 364n
Transubstantiation, 325
Triad, Platonic, 265–70
Trinity, 336, 337
Trojan War, 48
Truth, 15, 17, 20, 21, 147, 256, 285n, 289–90, 341, 356, 381, 407; blind faith and, 42; cautious approach to, 79–81; contingent, 38, 43; correspondence theory of, 46; ethical, see Ethics; factual, 69, 79, 80–81, 113, 326; inductive, 288; irrational thinkers on, 34–35; knowledge and, 61, 62, 64, 74–77; logic and, 53; love of, 265–68,

270; man's drive for, 252–53; meaningfulness and, 35–37
nature of: definition of term, 30–34; observation statements and, 29–30, 44, 51; opposite attitudes toward, 28, 31; necessary, 38; objective, 386
quest for: Baconian idols and, 70–71; divergent religions and, 77–78; environment and, 67; future and, 67, 69–70; historical periods and, 72–73; mass-media, propaganda and, 74–77; opinion and, 78–79; past and, 67–68; prejudice and, 72; present and, 67–68; reason and, 34, 36; relative, see Relativism; self and, 66–67; substitutes for, 70, 76; technical difficulties involved in, 68–69
religious: obscurity of, 37; relativity of, 325, 326–27
scientific, see factual; subjective, 361, 386; testing and verification of, 42–43, 70; ultimate, 30, 79, 118; see also Ethics; Relativism; Religion; Skepticism
Turing, A. M., 415
Tuve, Merle A., 84–85, 112

Ultimate, 317; concern, 347, 348; ground of the right, 290, 293; sense of 17; see also God; Meaning; Questions; Reality
Unamuno, Miguel de, 34, 36, 339n, 380, 382, 397n
Underhill, Evelyn, 340n, 342
Unity, 217; philosophic craving for, 156
Universe, 364, 396; astronomical distances, 123; being of the, 372; decentered view of, 122; early theories concerning, 122; elements comprising, 126–27; eternity of, 332; meaningfulness of, 378–81; origin of, 123–125; the solar systems, 124–25; vastness of, 125–26; see also Nature
Unnatural, question of natural and, 263–64
Upanishads, 323
Urmson, J. O., 231, 232, 269, 409, 417
Utilitarianism, 210, 216, 217–21, 228, 230, 231, 241, 242–43, 245, 249, 256, 290, 295; act, 229; rule, 220–21, 225, 226, 229; ideal, 247; pluralistic and ideal, 218–19; see also Good; Happiness
Utopias, 269, 363, 401; classical, 141–42; undemocratic, 263

Vahanian, Gabriel, 424

Value(s): ethical, 182–83, 259, 398–99; greatest intrinsic, 219–20, 247, 256; social, 298; *see also* Ethics; Ideals
Van Gogh, Vincent, 61, 386, 389*n*
Vanity, 377
Vatican II, 349
Verdi, Giuseppe, 120, 166
Verification: eschatological, 344*n;* of religious statements, 342–44
Versényi, Lazzlo, 370
Victoria, Queen, 391
Victorian Age/Victorianism, 238, 240, 278, 391
Vietnam war, 185, 201, 225*n*, 240
Vinci, Leonardo da, 88
Virgin Birth, 325
Virtue, 235, 311
Visions, 48, 52
Voltaire, 171–72, 355

Wald, George, 125
Walsh, James, 415, 418
War, 200–1, 293
Warnock, Mary, 360*n*
Washington, George, 75, 119
Watts, C. A., 420
Way of life: rational, 306–10; religious, 318
Wechsler, Herbert, 245–46, 418
Weisskopf, Victor, 99, 102*n*, 104, 410, 413
Weltschmerz, see Anxiety
Wertenbaker, Lael Tucker, 200
West, Morris, 172
Whitehead, Alfred North, 128, 253
Whitman, Walt, 63, 390*n*, 395, 400*n*, 426
Wiener, Norbert, 166
Wild, John, 360*n*
Wilder, Thornton, 384, 387, 393
Will: categorical optative and, 264; of God, 314; moral, 234; to survive, 385

Will, freedom of, 182, 188, 244*n;* children and, 169, 170, 172–73; criminality and, 168, 172–73; debates concerning, 168–69; dualistic view and, 174; escape from, 180–81; ethical aspects of, 169*n;* fate and, 179; general determinism and, 171–81 *passim;* libertarian view and, 174–76; mental abilities and, 147–48, 149–50; mentally unbalanced and, 168, 169–70, 172–73; moral choice and, 167–68, 174–75, 176–77, 178–80, 208, 223–24; philosophic problems concerning, 148; prediction and, 179–80; quantum theory and, 108; religious question, 170–71; restrictions on, 168, 176, 179; Sartre on, 168; voluntary and involuntary actions, 176–78; *see also* Choice
Wilson, Colin, 28
Williams, B., 339
Williams, Tennessee, 219
Winch, Peter, 426
Wisdom, 313; apparent, 71; divine, 328; *see also* Knowledge
Wittgenstein, Ludwig, 18*n*, 60, 340, 351, 362, 378
Wolfson, Harry A., 318–19
Wooldridge, Dean E., 154, 155–56, 414, 415
Woolley, Sir Leonard, 414
Words: as tools, 14–15, 29, 31
Wordsworth, William, 63, 386, 392
World view, 17–19, 66, 102*n*, 316, 317, 365; *see also* Philosophy; Religion; Science

Yeats, William Butler, 78

Zen Buddhism, 251*n*, 307
Zolotow, Maurice, 280

Φ   E92FD

GRUNebaum ⸺